TOWNSHIP OF UNION
FREE PUBLIC LIBRARY

THE FLAVORS OF SOUTHERN ITALY

THE FLAVORS OF SOUTHERN ITALY

ERICA DE MANE

WILEY

JOHN WILEY & SONS, INC.

TOWNSHIP OF UNION
FREE PUBLIC LIBRARY

This book is printed on acid-free paper. ∞

Copyright © 2004 by Erica De Mane. All rights reserved

Published by John Wiley & Sons, Inc., Hoboken, New Jersey
Published simultaneously in Canada

No part of this publication may be reproduced, stored in a retrieval system, or transmitted in any form or by any means, electronic, mechanical, photocopying, recording, scanning, or otherwise, except as permitted under Section 107 or 108 of the 1976 United States Copyright Act, without either the prior written permission of the Publisher, or authorization through payment of the appropriate per-copy fee to the Copyright Clearance Center, Inc., 222 Rosewood Drive, Danvers, MA 01923, (978) 750-8400, fax (978) 750-4470, or on the web at www.copyright.com. Requests to the Publisher for permission should be addressed to the Permissions Department, John Wiley & Sons, Inc., 111 River Street, Hoboken, NJ 07030, (201) 748-6011, fax (201) 748-6008, e-mail: permcoordinator@wiley.com.

Limit of Liability/Disclaimer of Warranty: While the publisher and author have used their best efforts in preparing this book, they make no representations or warranties with respect to the accuracy or completeness of the contents of this book and specifically disclaim any implied warranties of merchantability or fitness for a particular purpose. No warranty may be created or extended by sales representatives or written sales materials. The advice and strategies contained herein may not be suitable for your situation. You should consult with a professional where appropriate. Neither the publisher nor author shall be liable for any loss of profit or any other commercial damages, including but not limited to special, incidental, consequential, or other damages.

For general information on our other products and services or for technical support, please contact our Customer Care Department within the United States at 800-762-2974, outside the United States at (317) 572-3993 or fax (317) 572-4002.

Wiley also publishes its books in a variety of electronic formats. Some content that appears in print may not be available in electronic books. For more information about Wiley products, visit our web site at www.wiley.com.

LIBRARY OF CONGRESS CATALOGING-IN-PUBLICATION DATA
DeMane, Erica.
The flavors of southern Italy / Erica De Mane.
p. cm.
Includes bibliographical references and index.
ISBN 0-471-27251-5 (Cloth)
1. Cookery, Italian--Southern style. I. Title.
TX723.2.S65 D45 2004
641.5945'7--dc22
2003021219

Printed in the United States of America

10 9 8 7 6 5 4 3 2 1

DEDICATED TO

FREDERICK ALLEN, MY PARTNER

IN ITALIAN AND AMERICAN ADVENTURES

CONTENTS

RECIPES: COOKING SOUTHERN ITALIAN STYLE 67

INTRODUCTION

I'M CONVINCED THAT THE FOODS A PERSON COOKS BEST embrace the flavors he or she grew up with. All the recipes in this book reflect my childhood. This is a very personal collection of recipes and thoughts on cooking, all anchored by the flavors of southern Italy, from which my family emigrated in the early 1900s along with millions of other poor, eager people. Southern Italy for me means the deep south: the Mezzogiorno regions of Campania, Puglia, and Sicily, where my family comes from, and to a lesser extent Basilicata and Calabria, whose bolder cooking I have grown to know and admire. These places are where I find my flavor palate.

What keeps southern Italian cooking fresh and alive for me is my desire to improvise with its flavors. I appreciate and love traditional regional dishes, but I almost never cook them the same way twice. The food from my grandparents' table changed very little. Eggplant parmigiano was always made with basil, meatballs always included parsley, and meat sauce was always flavored with oregano. It was all dependable and comforting, but preparing it seemed more a chore than a pleasure for my grandmother. My travels to the different parts of southern Italy have expanded my world of Italian cooking immensely. The flavors remain constant, but my creative use of them changes and grows. I'm also deeply influenced by New York City and its suburbs, where I've lived my entire life so far. Eating out in Manhattan's Italian restaurants has always had its highs and lows, but lately there have been more highs. Many excellent Italian chefs, imported and home-grown, have set up shop here, and I've learned a lot from them.

My family was not demonstratively Italian. All our last names had been changed, Di Menna becoming the European-sounding De Mane (one vaguely lecherous schoolteacher of mine singsonged "Erica De Mane, with the showgirl name" whenever he saw me in the hall). My father's mother changed her name from Inglese to the almost-Scottish-sounding Inglis (appropriately, I suppose, for what became a family of golf pros). It is not uncommon for upwardly mobile immigrants to have a streak of group self-hatred, or at least embarrassment, and this was certainly true of both my father's and mother's families. My father's mother always told people, even our own relatives, that she had been born in Darien, Connecticut, a traditional upper-class WASP stronghold. When I was a child, one of my cousins suggested that the family might actually be German, considering our blue eyes (which are not uncommon in southern Italy) and my grandfather's love of pig's knuckles, a passion he developed at his weekly lunches at the legendary Luchow's on Fourteenth Street in Manhattan.

It took quite a bit of digging to learn about Castelfranco in Miscano, my grandmother's birthplace, finally coaxing it out of my father's aunt. Of course, I was immediately itching to go there. When I finally did visit this ancient and dry little town on the border of Campania and northern Puglia and my grandmother got wind of it, she was mortified, and I felt guilty for months. My intention hadn't been to humiliate her or blow her cover, of course; I just needed to know what the place was like. And my mother doesn't even know where in Sicily her father, Errico Russo, was from (he went by Eric Ross, and his father, who had the gorgeous first name of Achille, was always called Charlie). Evidently, they were so happy living in Westchester that nobody ever brought it up.

Despite all this reticence about our background, the food on our table was classic and boldly southern Italian, if without some of the unusual dishes our more Italian neighbors offered, such as octopus or eels. The tastes were there: fresh basil from my father's garden; little jars of vinegar peppers (made by Progresso, but still pretty good); eggplant frying in olive oil; tomato sauce with anchovies; black olives scattered over fish; the bitter notes of escarole, chicory, and arugula; pasta with clams, flavored with parsley and garlic; the slightly medicinal aroma of raw fennel; lemon-and-white-wine-scented chicken; peaches steeped in sharp red wine; and more that I've preserved in my culinary memory bank. Many of these have their roots in the cooking of Campania, but the early death of my grandfather and namesake Errico led me strongly in the direction of Sicilian cooking, searching to fill in the gaps in my heritage.

You'll find many Sicilian-inspired recipes in this book. Some are my mother's family's recipes, but most were inspired by my travels to that complex island, where I've learned about blending sweet and sour flavors, adding spices like cinnamon and saffron to stews and pastas, making *sorbetti* flavored with jasmine flowers and salads laced with oranges and black olives— and where I've been intrigued by the many uses for mint. I've even imagined a ancestral town for myself. Sicily has many beautiful, elegant cities and towns, but I decided on unpretentious Randazzo, mainly because the one time I went there it seemed just the kind of dreary place one would want to get out of. I did have a very good lunch there of pasta with zucchini and pecorino, and a baked pork chop flavored with fennel, in a bare-bones truck-stop hotel restaurant with no lights in the bathroom. Like my family, they obviously took real pride in their food.

The craft of cooking lies somewhere between fantasy and reality, which I find a good place to be most of the time, especially in the kitchen. The fantasy of creating food excites me; the reality of feeding myself, friends, and family adds a semblance of tranquility. I was first drawn to cooking around the age of 17, when I was simultaneously forging ahead in an altogether different direction. I was spending almost every night at Manhattan gay discos, accompanied by a flamboyant, druggy blond boy who at the time I found extremely exciting. Much of my energy was spent hunting down ball gowns in acid green or shocking pink, or metallic miniskirts with shiny accessories. Juxtaposed with my evenings spent parading in ridiculous costumes and chasing the unobtainable were long afternoons in the family kitchen, re-creating southern Italian family recipes and digging through Italian cookbooks, trying to make myself more Italian than my family ever wanted to be. I didn't realize it at the time, but years later, when I made cooking my life's work, I realized that these seemingly polarized pursuits were fueled by the same drive to blend fantasy and reality in order to create a life I felt comfortable living.

Identifying myself with the people of southern Italy has been a sometimes ambivalent and confusing journey, despite my love of their cooking. They still attach religious symbolism to much of their food, especially in the more remote parts of Basilicata and Calabria, but Catholicism is something that was never pressed on me, and I have long forgotten it. I understand that this, along with my inability to sit still, separates me from a true southern Italian mentality. The religious force behind creating food for celebrations such as on feast days is strong, but although that force eludes me, I do celebrate the arrival of fruits and vegetables at my farmers' market by organizing asparagus or garlic feasts, or strawberry theme dinners. So instead of making cream puffs for St. Joseph's Day, I might mark the first blizzard of the season with a celebratory lasagne. I find that that works.

While choosing recipes to include in this book, I came to realize a few things about the way I cook. I like dishes that are clean and bold. This doesn't necessarily mean simple, but I tend to go through recipes and streamline them, taking out ingredients that are not absolutely imperative for the flavor of the dish. Quick can be delicious, and quite a few of my recipes can be completed in about twenty minutes, especially some of the pasta sauces and sautéed fish dishes. But that's not always what I'm aiming for. Slow and easy is a wonderful way to cook too, and many southern Italian dishes fall naturally into this category, such as leisurely simmered meat ragùs. What I've done is remove clutter and update recipes so you can easily make many of them after work, often with ingredients you may already have in your refrigerator and pantry. I do this not for novelty's sake but because they taste good this way. And since this is a book devoted to home cooking, I have not included foods Italians generally do not make at home, such as elaborate baked desserts like the Sicilian cassata, one of the triumphs of the southern Italian kitchen but nowadays almost always purchased from a pastry shop. The elaborate pasta-and-meat-filled *timbale*, a legacy of Neapolitan and Sicilian baroque court cooking made famous recently in the movie *Big Night*, is reserved for weddings and other special occasions and is usually made by a caterer. I offer in its place several recipes for home-style savory tarts, like *pizza rustica*, some filled with vegetables. My pizza recipes are mostly creative interpretations, using classic Neapolitan flavors but designed to be baked in a home oven. Above all, I've concentrated on southern Italian dishes that taste best when made at home.

Italians are a little more strict than I am about when certain foods should be eaten and how a meal should progress. In this book, I suggest ideas for antipastos and first courses, but I've decided against an antipasto section, instead listing the small dishes at the beginnings of the chapters on vegetables, fish, and meat. Within each chapter the recipes flow from appetizers and little things you'd offer with drinks, to salads and side dishes and then more substantial little dishes, and then on to formal dishes suitable for a proper main course. This is a contemporary concept, an organizing principle I see more and more on restaurant menus. It gives the diner the chance to make a meal of several traditional appetizers, if so inclined. At home I often offer guests a selection of several antipasto dishes, bringing them out one or two at a time. Pasta I more often than not make into a main course, unless I'm planning a fancy dinner party. In southern Italy, where one dish often makes a home meal, this is common. I've included more main-course salads than a real southern Italian might, because for an American they're so often the kind of easy, light thing you want to fix and eat after a long day.

Confidence in the kitchen comes from repetition. You need drive too, but I've found that drive builds with experience. Once you find yourself turning out a better-than-decent tomato sauce, you'll want to make it again, maybe with a small variation. Cooking good food makes me want to cook even better food, and my abiding desire to keep on cooking has gotten me though some kitchen disasters and kept me moving toward a solid sense of creative freedom. For me, there is no better feeling than that of losing myself in the kitchen, sometimes not even thinking about why I'm doing it or who I'm cooking for.

If you know the flavors you love best, you already have the makings of an excellent cook. A good teacher or a good book can help channel your love of food into a desire to create gorgeous meals in your own home. I hope my love of southern Italian flavors and eating and cooking will rub off on you.

ACKNOWLEDGMENTS

THIS BOOK COLLECTS RECIPES AND THOUGHTS on southern Italian flavors that I've accumulated over many years. My mother, Maureen, my sister, Liti, my friend Hester Furman, and my husband, Fred, have sat around my tables tasting and sharing their thoughts about my culinary creations, sometimes sampling zucchini parmigiano, for instance, four nights in a row, and I thank them all for their enthusiasm and for the bottles of wine they brought with them. I'd like to thank my friend Jay Milite for periodically dragging me away from my stove and taking me out to dinner, so I could taste-test all the fine Italian cooking Manhattan has to offer. Thank you also to my longtime friend Barbara Calamari for her emotional support and dedication to the saints of southern Italy.

Thank you Natalia Ravidà and Wolfgango Jezek for introducing me to your first-class Sicilian olive oils and inviting me into your homes. Thank you Alessio Planeta for showing me how amazing Sicilian wine can be. I also want to thank Kyle Phillips, of www.italianfoodabout.com, who has been a longtime fan of my recipes and of my particular point of view on Italian cooking. Thank you Phil Karlin, a fisherman who supplies me with the freshest local catch year round, and Migliorelli Farm, in Tivoli, New York, for your fabulous plums, basil, broccoli rabe, cantaloupes, five varieties of eggplants, and much more, that you transport weekly all the way down to the Union Square Greenmarket in Manhattan, so city girls like me can enjoy just-picked local produce.

I want to say a very special thank you to my charming and extremely intelligent agent, Angela Miller, who grows tomatoes and makes goat cheese in addition to listening to every far-fetched project idea I come up with. Thank you to all the people at John Wiley & Sons who have made this book possible: My editor Pamela Chirls, who has been so supportive of all my work; my production editor, Monique Calello; and my wide-awake copy editor, Carolyn Miller. Thank you also to Vertigo Design NYC for the beautiful artwork.

I also want to thank my father, Dick De Mane, who passed away three years ago. He was my connection to my Italian world and is an ongoing inspiration for my dedication to the flavors of southern Italy.

THE FLAVORS OF THE
SOUTHERN ITALIAN
KITCHEN

I first began finding southern Italian flavors in my family's home cooking. Castelfranco in Miscano, the hill town on the border of Campania and Puglia where my father's mother was born, is home to a few thousand short, curly-haired people, many with sky-blue eyes like my father's. They cook with limited ingredients, among them lamb and pork (including the blood), boldly flavored with fennel or oregano. The town's caciocavallo and pecorino cheeses, with which they season their very al dente pastas, have been singled out by the organization Slow Food as high-quality indigenous foods worth preserving. They flavor chickpeas and favas, two ancient beans, with pancetta or cured pork sausage, and they stud their *taralli*—hard little bread rings—with black pepper. They use a broad assortment of vegetables, heavy on the leafy greens and often seasoned with garlic and olive oil. Not that they have much choice, but local ingredients are what the cooking of Castelfranco's region is all about. They give it its strength.

Campania is the region that encompasses Castelfranco and also Naples, and it is where much that Americans recognize as southern Italian cooking comes from. In Campania, tomatoes, garlic, oregano, basil, and mozzarella play a large part in flavoring classic dishes like eggplant parmigiano and baked pastas like the ziti baked with mini meatballs that my grandmother frequently made. Anchovies, pine nuts, raisins, and capers figure just as prominently, giving Campania's cooking real sparkle. For me, one of the genius dishes of Naples is spaghetti *puttanesca* (what my family called marinara), which contains just about all the boldest flavors of the region: tomatoes, garlic, anchovies, olives, and capers. You'd think a mix like that would be chaos on the plate, but the flavors balance so perfectly that the dish winds up tasting almost mellow. The Amalfi coast, also in Campania, produces the most lemony lemons I have ever tasted. Their famous limoncello liqueur is hard to duplicate at home with our perfectly fine lemons (the results always seem too sweet somehow), and I've tried many times. Grilled fish seasoned with sea salt and the juice from one of those huge, lumpy lemons is a dish I've ordered often in and around Amalfi, and I find myself dreaming about it on cold New York nights.

The region of Puglia, the heel of Italy's boot, is rich in olive and almond trees, and their two flavors figure in much of my improvisational cooking. Puglia's coastal cooking is characterized by impeccable seafood—especially oysters, mussels, and clams—vegetables, and herbs, and it has been an ungoing source of inspiration for me. I love their dishes of mussels or octopus flavored with white wine, olive oil, and tomatoes, a simple idea but one often executed without finesse in Italian restaurants in America. In southern Puglia, they use onions more often than the garlic that is so important in Castelfranco and neighboring inland towns. Many of Puglia's vegetable-and-pasta combinations, which attracted me immediately, are made without tomatoes and instead get their flavor from bitter greens, green olives, artichokes, or chickpeas. Sun-dried tomatoes adorn

Puglia's antipasto tables, and tomato paste, with its burnished, sharp taste, strengthens its ragùs.

The biggest surprise for me in my discovery of southern Italian flavors was the depth of Sicilian cooking. The tastes of this island have been influenced by its many invaders over the centuries, primarily Greek, Arab, Spanish, and French. An Arab-influenced scented watermelon pudding poured into a pastry crust and flavored with cinnamon and jasmine flowers was one of the first desserts I ate in Palermo, and I remember it vividly years later, not only for its lovely flavor but for its very formal presentation. Many of the island's pasta dishes are just as complex, involving sweet and sour flavors and local products such as wild fennel and sardines. Sicily's baked pastas are typically seasoned with spices and nuts. Not all the island's cooking is that exotic, though. Grilled swordfish brushed with olive oil and finished with a scattering of floral salt-packed capers is a dish of intense, pure flavor that I re-create at home often now that I can buy Sicily's beautiful capers in New York. Campania and Sicily have in common a history of court cooking, heavily influenced by French culture, which gives them creations like *pasticcio*, a pastry-covered pie lushly filled with pasta, meat, and cheese. The blending of the regal and the rustic gives the cooking of these two areas a complexity not found in the rest of the south.

Basilicata, the instep of the boot, is poorer and less populous than the other southern regions, so its cooking tends to be simpler. Its ingredients are assertive, including hot chilies, garlic, onion, anchovies, and cured pork sausage in abundance. When I first sampled *bucatini di fuoco* there, a pasta sauced with hot chilies (see page 346 for my version of it), it was spicier than I expected southern Italian food to be, and the chilies had a deep, complex taste that almost reminded me of Mexican cooking. I was served one of the boldest dishes of my life in a trattoria in the gray but lively Basilicata hill town of Pisticci. It consisted of extremely sharp aged pecorino topped with a pesto made from mashed anchovies and very hot dried chilies. It was an after-dinner cheese course of such startling intensity that I couldn't even think straight while eating it. It actually occurred to me that the chef might be making fun of me, but he sat down with great pride and ate along with me, explaining how it paved the way for a digestive liqueur. I have to say, the flavor grew on me after a few bites until it became addictive. After finishing it, I was presented with a half cup of espresso mixed with a half cup of their local bitter amaro cordial.

The cuisine of Basilicata will keep you on your toes. Wild mint frequently flavors the meat and pasta. Their caciocavallo is sharp, but a local cow's milk mozzarella I sampled was tender and creamy. Their cured pork products are justifiably famous, many of them flavored with hot chilies, but I've also eaten antipasto platters at restaurants in Basilicata that were composed entirely of sturdy vegetables like cabbage, roasted potatoes, big meaty mushrooms, and mounds of sweet and hot peppers.

Neighboring Calabria, the toe of the boot, is a region where many Americans have their ancestry. Like Basilicata, it is a poor area with uneven farmland. Wheat is its biggest crop, and hot chilies are even more prevalent there than in Basilicata. Eggplant, sweet pepper, tomato, and onion are its most popular vegetables, turning up often in pasta dishes flavored with basil, oregano, or fennel seeds. I've been served eggplant marinated with vinegar and hot chilies on several occasions in the region, usually as part of an antipasto. It's one of the dishes Italian-Americans from Calabria immediately recall, and it seems always to miraculously appear on the table when there's unexpected company (see page 120 for my interpretation of this classic dish). Calabria's tuna and swordfish are of the highest quality, just like neighboring Sicily's, and its sheep's, cow's and goat's milk cheeses are examples of southern Italian cheesemaking at its best (too bad we can't find more of them in the United States). They love dried figs in the region and sometimes stuff them with almonds and orange zest or candied citron, or dust them with cinnamon or cloves, or dip them in chocolate, or even all of the above (I've included an easy recipe for stuffed figs on page 398).

I have been thrilled to travel through the different regions of southern Italy and sample their food, and eager to come back and try cooking it at home, but I always try to keep in mind that you can never truly duplicate the flavors of a place outside of that place, especially when you're relying on memories from miles away and maybe years ago. Still, culinary recall is deeply ingrained in all of us. Tastes and aromas come flooding back when you least expect them. This happens to me often when I cook. I might be braising chicken, for instance, and almost absent-mindedly throw in a handful of fennel seeds, a pinch of red pepper flakes, and some dry white wine, and as the aroma comes wafting up I'll recall a flavor from a lunch in Puglia or a summer dinner at my grandmother's in Westchester. It's not that I'm cooking the same exact dish, but a core flavor or maybe just a hint of a past aroma has been unleashed. You may notice this when you eat at restaurants—a scent bringing you back to another time and place. Flavors won't ever be exact, and striving to re-create exactness is not only futile but can make your cooking rigid.

Our flavor memories are imperfect, and the lamb, fish, herbs, and even some vegetables here have different tastes from those in southern Italy. Yet the process of adapting flavors is for me what makes cooking most rewarding. At the heart of all good cooking is personal style and a drive to create the flavors you dream about. It's what I strive for when I cook southern Italian food in my own home.

NOTE   All the southern Italian products mentioned in the following essays are available in the United States. See Sources, page 436.

BITTER, SWEET-AND-SOUR, AND SALTY

FUNDAMENTAL TASTES, SOUTHERN ITALIAN STYLE

THE SOUTHERN ITALIAN LOVE OF BITTERNESS

NOT TOO LONG AGO a guy at a cooking class I was teaching asked me what the difference was between bitter and sour. I actually thought he was joking, but it is true that many people in this country don't focus on bitter, or don't have enough of it in their diets to recognize it as a distinct taste. Southern Italians love bitter. They are passionate about gathering wild greens so bitter that they make our supermarket arugula taste like iceberg lettuce. Dandelions, cicorielle (a wild chicory), rucola selvatica (wild arugula), and other greens make their way into soups, salads, and pasta, and many bitter cultivated vegetables like eggplant and broccoli rabe are much loved by southern Italians here and in Italy. I can find some cultivated bitter greens at my farmers' market, such as mustard, dandelion, and different types of chicory. They're all relatively mild by Italian standards, but delicious to me.

I grew up eating wild, spiky Italian arugula (*rucola selvatica*) on Long Island, because our neighbors Gloria and Lou Mastellone smuggled plants back from a family visit to Sorrento in the early 1960s and planted them in their backyard. They've been growing like weeds there for forty years. I've taken cuttings from their arugula and transplanted them to my Manhattan window boxes, but I haven't had much luck keeping them going. I can sometimes find a cultivated form of wild arugula at my farmers' market, but it is less special than the true wild stuff the Mastellones grow. This year, I brought back a package of cultivated *rucola selvatica* seeds from Puglia, and they've sprouted nicely on my windowsill. With some luck, I may actually succeed in growing something edible. If you're at all interested in growing wild arugula or other southern Italian vegetable varietals like *zucca lunga* (mentioned on page 316), San Marzano tomatoes, wild fennel, Sicilian cauliflower and zucchini varieties, Neapolitan basil, various types of *cima di rape*, or Brindisi chicory, check out a company called Seeds From Italy, in Winchester, Massachusetts. They have a large variety of things to try (see page 438).

I discovered amaro liqueur in my family's den bar when I was a kid, and its bittersweet taste appealed to me right away. It was so much more interesting than the syrupy anise-flavored after-dinner drinks my parents usually brought to the table. Amaro, which actually means "bitter" in Italian, is the *digestivo* of choice for much of southern Italy. Many towns make their own distinct amaros, but they all have a characteristic, deep bittersweet taste from a variety of herbs. Averna, from Sicily, is the one we always had around the house, and it's still the easiest to find in this country. I like to taste each town's amaro as I travel through southern Italy; some are terribly bitter and deep green, while others, like most of the ones I tasted in Sicily, have more sweetness and a rich amber hue. Most of them are local and aren't exported, but there are some good amaros available here, like Lucano, from Pisticci, Basilicata, whose bottle is decorated with an drawing of a beautiful woman with black hair, big gold earrings, and a tight red and green dress. I've noticed that it has become fashionable in some southern Italian restaurants to cook with amaro. At Baccosteria, in Barletta, Puglia, I had a dessert of prickly-pear mousse with a sauce that was a syrup of reduced amaro. The sauce had such a concentrated bitterness that it tasted almost like poison to me, but my husband absolutely loved it, and the waiter told me it was one of their most popular desserts.

Campari, a lightly bitter aperitif, is sort of a junior version of amaro. Cynar is similar to Campari but is made with artichokes; it's slightly sweeter but still bitter. Fernet Branca is Italy's *digestivo* of choice for *agita* (indigestion) and hangovers, primarily, I think, because Italians like its taste. It's not a hard medicine to get down.

There are other bitter notes in the southern Italian diet: bitter almonds used in desserts, bitter red wine made from Puglia's Negroamaro (bitter black) grapes, thick black espresso, bitter olives, and maybe the most bitter thing I've tasted in southern Italy, a tiny wild onion called *lampascioni*. *Lampascioni* are a seasonal delicacy in Puglia, the season being the fall. Imagine a little cocktail onion, with its pungent but vaguely sweet flavor, but shot through with strong bitterness. That's the taste. I tried eating them over and over and just couldn't break through to enjoyment. (I tried them puréed into a paste to top *crostini,* vinegared as an antipasto, and bathed in olive oil and herbs.) Many people in Puglia are passionate about them, so maybe if I lived there and ate them often I'd be too. If you have any interest in trying them, Sapori del Salento in Puglia exports them in jars (see esperya.com in Sources, page 436).

BACCOSTERIA'S CAMPARI AND WHITE WINE APERITIVO

Baccosteria, the same elegant restaurant in Puglia that's responsible for the amaro dessert sauce my husband was so crazy about, serves this refreshing, delightfully bitter drink as its house aperitif. It, I love. It's a great change from Champagne for a formal dinner party.

Fill wineglasses with a very cold, dry white wine (if you'd like to use a Puglian wine, try a Locorotondo white). Add a tablespoon or so of Campari. The wine will turn a lovely orangey pink, like a rosé. Add a strip of orange zest. Serve very cold.

SWEET AND SOUR:
THE TASTE OF AGRODOLCE

AGRODOLCE IS A BLEND of sweet and sour tastes that characterize many of my favorite southern Italian dishes. This bold taste is usually achieved by reducing sugar or honey with something sharp like vinegar or wine or lemon into a syrup with a fairly even balance of both. *Agrodolce* dishes are exciting to cook, with pungency wafting up into your face as the sweetened vinegar evaporates in the skillet. Despite their Mediterranean feel, I appreciate these dishes best in the winter, when my kitchen is closed in and heated and the aromas are more easily contained. You'll taste this flavor in various areas of southern Italy, but especially in Sicily, where eggplant, sardines, rabbit, pumpkin, onions, meatballs, and yellow squash are all made sweet and sour. Caponata, usually made with eggplant, is a classic *agrodolce* preparation and so loved by Sicilians that it borders on an island obsession. Sometimes, there are touches of chocolate, candied lemon or orange, or raisins to underscore the sweet element in an *agrodolce* dish. Sometimes, *vincotto* (grape must; see page 413) or balsamic vinegar is added. Sweet-and-sour meatballs is a dish my mother's Sicilian grandmother used to make in New York, always adding raisins and sometimes, inexplicably, grape jelly, which according to my mother she viewed as an *agrodolce* shortcut.

To get the best taste from this concoction, it's best to add the sweetener and the vinegar together toward the beginning of cooking, so their flavors can meld. Some cooks make a syrup separately and then pour it over cooked onions or eggplant, simply mixing it in. This works well enough, but I prefer cooking the flavor directly into the dish so it permeates everything. If when I taste the finished dish it doesn't taste *agrodolce* enough, I usually cook a little vinegar with sugar in a separate small skillet to make a little syrup, then stir that into the dish (just pouring on vinegar or adding dry sugar will make the dish klutzy).

Sugar is a neutral sweetener; honey is a different story. When you add honey to a dish, you taste it. I never thought much about varieties of honey until I started traveling to southern Italy, where they revere *miele*, honey, more than we do in the United States. I always pick up a jar of local honey when I travel through southern Italy. Since bees don't travel very far from their hive, I know I'm buying a truly local product, and the taste can differ from town to town. I grew up eating orange-blossom honey, since I spent most of my childhood winters in Florida, and it has a special floral flavor that I love. Acacia honey, with flavor from the acacia tree, is a kind I discovered in Italy and is now my favorite for cooking, since it has real character but not overwhelmingly so. Eucalyptus honey is popular in Italy, but I find it too medicinal tasting to cook with. Chestnut honey is deep brown and strongly flavored. If you use it in your cooking, know that it will leave its mark on all but the boldest flavors. At my New York farmers' market, they sell upstate honey that's usually mild clover or mixed wildflower. I use such local honey frequently, but when I want to purchase good Italian honey in this country, I usually buy ones labeled Azienda Agrimontana, the name of a fine Italian honey packager.

Some men in my family can eat whole jars of extremely vinegary preserved vegetables. Learning to tolerate pure vinegar seems to be a southern Italian man's rite of passage. I remember my grandfather instructing growing boys on the importance of eating this stuff without wincing. I actually have a low threshold for vinegar and sometimes even prefer my salads with only olive oil, but a good vinegar makes a real difference in your cooking. Truly first-rate vinegars are less sharp and taste more like the wine they're made from. Try, for instance, Caloquiri red wine vinegar from Puglia. It is known as Aspretto and available through Buon Italia (see page 436). Spanish sherry vinegar has an oaky mellowness that I find perfect for Italian cooking, especially since its acid is tamed. I often find myself using it instead of red wine vinegar in many dishes. Several good ones are imported here, and one I particularly like is made by Sanchez Romate and sold by Zingerman's. Vinegars made from a single type of wine tend to have more character. Look for Chardonnay or Chianti varieties instead of stuff labeled simply white or red wine vinegar. A French company called Martin Pouret makes high-quality Chardonnay and Champagne vinegars that I find in my supermarket.

Real balsamic vinegar is an artisanal product of Modena and Reggio Emilia. It's more of a condiment than an actual vinegar, since it's made from the cooked down juice of wine grapes. (It is called *saba* in the north *vincotto* in the south. For more on using *vincotto* in Southern Italian cooking, see page 413.) The long-aged versions are used to drizzle over Parmigiano-Reggiano and to flavor certain foods with its complex sweet-and-sour taste, perfect for many southern Italian dishes. There are many imitation balsamic vinegars sold in supermarkets here to use on salads and for cooking, usually made by sweetening red wine vinegar with caramel. Cavalli brand is made in a more traditional way than other supermarket brands, and has excellent flavor.

I never used vinegar in cooking until I started working in restaurants and noticed chefs using it to "correct" dishes. Soups and stews would get tasted, and if one was declared a little flat, a splash of good vinegar was often added to "wake it up." It works, with meat stews, vegetable soups, and some fish preparations. I've also added it to poached fruits. Start by adding only a few drops, stir it in, and see how it affects the taste. Sometimes a tiny bit can transform a dish, adding acidity the way wine does, but with vinegar you have the luxury of being able to add it anytime you want, even right before serving, since there's no alcohol to cook out. Vinegar is also helpful when you want to deglaze a skillet to form a little sauce for the meat or fish you've sautéed. After I sauté chicken pieces, I take them out of the skillet, pour in a splash of sherry or good white wine vinegar, let it bubble for a few seconds, then add a splash of chicken broth, let it reduce for a few seconds, add a chopped herb, and pour it over the chicken.

A SIMPLE AGRODOLCE SYRUP

MAKES ONE-HALF CUP. ENOUGH FOR FOUR SERVINGS OF VEGETABLES. MEAT. OR FISH.

To give a dish of braised onions or sautéed eggplant, zucchini, or squash a quick *agrodolce* treatment, add this syrup to it. Or, pour this over grilled fish with a handful each of raisins and toasted pine nuts added to the syrup. For a more integrated approach to this style of cooking, see Caponata (page 122) or Chicken Agrodolce (page 250).

$^3/_4$ cup dry white wine
$^1/_4$ cup Champagne vinegar
$^1/_4$ cup sugar

Pour the wine and the vinegar into a small saucepan. Bring to a boil over high heat and cook to reduce it by half. Add the sugar and cook to reduce to about $^1/_2$ cup; the surface will have large bubbles (this means it's gotten to a lightly syrupy stage, which is what you want).

SOUTHERN ITALY AND SEA SALT

I NOW USE SEA SALT FROM SICILY OR PUGLIA for all my cooking. I don't know if my taste for it is psychologically or chemically based, but when I season with southern Italian sea salt, a dish tastes to me more clearly flavored, with each ingredient popping out and seeming more distinctly southern Italian. Sea salt tastes saltier to me than regular salt, so I've been interested to learn that the Sicilian salt I love so much has more magnesium and potassium and less sodium chloride than regular table salt, which I suppose means it's actually less salty. I love the smell of this salt, especially when it's a type that is slightly moist. Using it makes me feel like I'm doing something special for my food, coddling it a little. For my everyday dishes, I buy Sicilian sea salt from Trapani, which is oddly easy to find here now and inexpensive. I have visited the salt flats of Trapani, in Sicily, a surreal vast coastal landscape of rectangular beds of water and high gray mounds of drying sea salt punctuated by rickety wooden windmills. There's even a little salt museum decorated with old photos of Sicilian salt workers from days gone by (and since it is in Italy, there's a small bar and café attached). Terranova is the brand of Trapani salt I usually find; I get it in big bags from Buon Italia, an Italian food importer in New York. The Ravida Sicilian olive oil estate packages a sea salt from Marsala that is moister and has more sea flavor than the Terranova brand. Another good manufacturer is Ittica d'Or. I'll use either of these, which are very fragrant, for special seafood dishes and for some seasonal vegetables that I really want to show off, like the spring asparagus that appears at my farmers' market in May. I keep finely and coarsely ground salt on hand all the time, using the fine salt for salads. I love coarse sea salt sprinkled over thin slices of *pesce crudo* (raw fish) that have been drizzled with really fine olive oil (that's better than wasabi, to my taste). Sale Margherita di Savoia is a sea salt from Puglia, and I made my way down to those salt flats recently as well. I understand that wouldn't be everyone's idea of a Italian dream destination, but any food-related journey has its rewards for me. However, I must admit that the Puglia flats were not as dramatic as the Sicilian landscape; they looked more industrial. The scene was disappointingly less eerie, and I didn't see any of those adorable windmills, but the salt is lovely.

SHRIMP WITH COARSE SEA SALT

SERVES TWO. I sometimes like to give sea salt center stage, and briny shrimp are a perfect vehicle for this. I add the salt to the skillet at the last minute so it stays crunchy, which to me is a big part of its appeal.

Shell and devein about 1 pound of jumbo shrimp, but leave the tails on. In a large skillet, heat 2 tablespoons of good olive oil over high heat until it is almost smoking. Add the shrimp and 2 sliced garlic cloves at the same time (the moisture from the shrimp will prevent the garlic from getting too dark). Sear the shrimp quickly, turning them once, until they are evenly pink, about 3 minutes. Sprinkle them with a generous amount of coarse Sicilian sea salt, shaking the skillet to disperse it. Eat right away.

ESSENTIAL SOUTHERN ITALIAN FLAVORING INGREDIENTS

SOUTHERN ITALIAN OLIVE OIL

WHEN YOU LOOK THROUGH THESE RECIPES, you'll notice that almost every one of them, even including some desserts, is made with olive oil. If you think good cooking contains a heart, and I'll say it does, then olive oil is the heart of my southern Italian–style cooking.

Olive oil is not only a distinct flavor itself but a carrier of flavor. Tomatoes, with their sweet and acidy juices, marry naturally with the oil's slightly biting lushness, whether raw or cooked. The oil mingles with the tomatoes' juices, extending their essence and making them more tomatoey. Linguine with clam sauce is the great dish it is not only because of the clams but also because the abundant amount of olive oil used in the sauce makes the clam flavor travel and coat every strand of pasta. The same with *aglio e olio,* a simple dish of pasta perfumed with the sweetness of garlic, where olive oil tames the garlic's pungency and also distributes its flavor throughout the pasta in a warm, soothing way, while at the same time adding its own flavor to the mix. The marriage of olive oil and local fish, vegetables, meat, and herbs is the flavor base for southern Italian cooking. As every southern Italian cook knows, olive oil, especially slightly warmed, when blended with chopped fresh basil or parsley or any other herb, creates a powerful perfume that the herb alone would have trouble revealing. Heat diminishes olive oil's pure olive flavor to a certain extent, but what it gives back in the process is worth the sacrifice. I use olive oil in different ways throughout the cooking process: initially, with heat, to release the flavors of garlic, onion, spices, or herbs so that these flavors can become the underpinning of the dish. Then I'll use it to sauté meat or fish or vegetables, sealing in and intensifying their flavors. Finally, at the end of cooking, I'll often add olive oil raw, not only for a flavor boost, but to bring all the components of the dish together.

I use a lot of olive oil. My mother watched me once while I was making a pasta sauce and yelled at me, "That's too much. It's so fattening." Now, I don't let her watch, and she always says everything tastes good. I think many home cooks have a shyness about really coating the skillet or pouring a little into a dish at the end of cooking. I don't see this as an indulgence. It may be a calorie issue for some, but the flavor extra-virgin oil gives to good Italian cooking can't be underestimated.

Over the years, as I've focused my cooking style, I've made the decision to use extra-virgin olive oil for all my cooking, even for deep-frying. I'm not saying you have to do this, but it does make cooking a huge pleasure. I do, however, use different qualities of extra-virgin oils for different purposes. I break extra-virgin oils into two categories: estate-bottled and inexpensive supermarket-quality oils.

Estate oils are made from olives grown and harvested on a single farm, and great care is usually taken to make sure the olives are harvested at the optimum time and quickly pressed so that the oil's acidity level is kept very low and the taste is as fresh as it can be. Extra-virgin oils are made by cold pressing the olives, which means pressing them without heat or chemicals. This gives oil its purest taste. Estate-bottled oils usually contain an olive harvest date on the label. Sometimes you'll see the words *prodotto ed imbottigliato,* which means the oil was produced and bottled on the estate. The newest harvest is the best, and any oil with a date more than about three years old is not as fresh as it should be; even when sealed, oil can become rancid, especially if it's exposed to light. If olive oil tastes like linseed oil, it's rancid. Bitterness, however, is not necessarily a bad sign. A peppery bitterness is normal and desirable in some oils, especially those made with underripe green olives (if you've ever tasted a vivid green Tuscan oil, you'll recognize this taste and aroma right away). Most southern Italian oils are traditionally made with riper olives and are lush and golden, but some of the new estates in Sicily are pressing their oils from greener, underripe olives these days, producing oils with fresh grassy tastes and bright green color. I love both types. I use estate-quality oils for salads and to drizzle raw on finished dishes. Sometimes I cook with a really first-rate oil, usually when I'm cooking something very special, for instance a seasonal wild mushroom, where the oil's flavor will be showcased and the cooking time will be short, so the oil stays flavorful. But since heat does diminish the flavor of any olive oil, for the most part I tend not to heat the best ones.

For most of my cooking, I use inexpensive supermarket-quality extra-virgin oil. It's usually made by larger manufacturers with olives purchased from various growers. Generally speaking, it has less character than estate oil, but some brands are much better than others, and some are truly superior. It really depends on the care taken by the manufacturer.

I try to use southern Italian olive oil for all my cooking so I can come as close as possible to authentic taste. Luckily, many of these oils are of the highest quality, and in my biased opinion they're some of the best in all of Italy.

Sicily is now producing absolutely delicious high-quality estate-bottled extra-virgin olive oil, especially in the western part of the island. Three estate labels that I love are Ravida, U Trappitu, and Gianfranco Becchina's Olio Verde. U Trappitu has fresh grassy tones, while Ravida is more complex. Ravida actually smells like underripe bananas, but it has a long finish and opens up on your tongue, revealing layers of flavor. Olio Verde is vivid green and made with slightly underripe olives, giving it a very grassy taste with a lovely bite. The three big oil-producing olives in western Sicily are Nocellara del Belice, Biancolilla, and Cerasuola. Both U Trappitu and Ravida blend these olives, but in different ratios to produce oils with distinct character. Olio Verde, from an estate in Castelvetrano, is made exclusively with unfiltered Nocellara olives. I once had the opportunity to cook with the Ravidà family, creators of my favorite estate-bottled Sicilian oil. Their eighteenth-century estate in Menfi, Sicily, has a semi-open stone kitchen furnished with huge ceramic jugs of this exquisite oil, and when I was there I was encouraged to ladle it out with a casualness that made me a feel a little guilty. For a cook, it was a luxurious experience, one I may never be able to repeat. The aroma of zucchini and artichokes or tuna and shrimp sautéing in this lovely oil is one I won't soon forget. At home, I treat Ravida and these other fine oils like gold.

Esperya.com, a first-rate Italian food website, carries several fine Sicilian estate oils. Ogghiu Sanacore, from Trapani, in western Sicily, is one I've tried and found to have a beautiful, grassy flavor. Geraci, an unfiltered oil made from only Nocellera olives, is powerfully perfumed.

Disisa is another brand I've ordered from Esperya, and both it and Geraci are fruity and delicious. I periodically check Esperya's website to see if they've added any new oils.

Many of the Sicilian estate oils are unfiltered and have a somewhat translucent appearance and a bit of sediment on the bottom. Some producers feel that unfiltered oils give you the best flavor, though when I spoke with Wolfango Jezek about his U Trappitu oil, which he does filter, he seemed to think that unfiltered oils were a gimmick designed for American and British buyers, allowing the producers to claim that they're "natural." But Gianfranco Becchini doesn't filter his Olio Verde, because, he says, he feels that the chlorophyll suspended in the sediment acts as a natural preservative.

Driving through Puglia from the Gargano in the north down past Bari, you'll notice that the region is covered with olive trees, and if you go there at the end of October or early November, as I've done, you'll see the ground covered with orange nets to catch the olives for harvest. It makes for a strange mix of colors, gray green and electric orange, that gives the countryside a somewhat surreal quality. Puglia devotes so much land to olive production that it produces more oil than any other region of Italy. Much of it is sold to large producers for blending, some outside the region, but recently they've been producing many really fine estate oils as well. Most of the oil I tasted in Puglia was rich, thick, and golden in color, lusher in a way and less grassy than the Sicilian oils, sometimes with an almond or artichoke taste. There are many oil-producing olives in the region, but most Puglian oil is produced from the Coratina and Ogliarola varieties.

Zingerman's, a store and mail-order company in Ann Arbor, Michigan, carries several first-rate Puglian oils. La Spineta is one I order; if you like a more delicate oil, try one called Caricato. Petraia is a very grassy-tasting one, maybe too grassy for my taste, but some friends loved it when I used it to dress sliced fennel. Masserie di Sant'Eramo is an estate-quality oil produced with great care from olives purchased from local growers. It is a blend of Coratina and Ogliarola olives, like most of Puglia's best oils. Ciro Federico is another fine producer in Puglia; his oil is available through Esperya.

While in Puglia I purchased a bottle of fine Caligiuri olive oil. It is hard to find here, but so many good oils are now being imported into this country, it may be only a matter of time. It is available through a company called Latina Gourmet Foods, but for some reason only as part of a big gift basket. While in Puglia, I also tasted oils from Torremaggiore in the northern Gargano that were made from Peranzana and Rotondella olives. They were golden and fruity. I've spent some time roaming the Internet trying to find sources for these Torremaggiore oils, but the only place I've been able to locate is The Bio Shop at bioshop.org, an organic-food website out of England. If you visit their part of Puglia, these oils are worth seeking out.

I'm always on the lookout for great supermarket-priced extra-virgin southern oil, and in my experience some of the ones from Sicily are outstanding. Two I really love are Don Luigi, to my knowledge available only from Teitel Brothers on Arthur Avenue in the Bronx, and Frantoio-Barbera, which I've found at many supermarkets in my area. Both are bold and grassy, with little bitterness. If I didn't know better, I'd think the Frantoio brand was a much more expensive oil. I use these for all my cooking, including raw on salads. La Giara, from Calabria, is another good oil at a very good price. There are many supermarket oils from southern Italy, but sometimes you have to study the bottle to know it. In my experience, just about anything from Sicily or Puglia in the supermarket price range is worth trying. Occasionally, I find something extraordinary.

OLIVES IN SOUTHERN ITALIAN COOKING

TO ME, THE MOST IMPORTANT THING when choosing olives to cook with is distinguishing between black and green ones. They impart distinctly different flavors to food. Green olives are underripe and, firm, and have a pleasant astringent taste that really wakes up a dish. I reach for green olives when I need a sharp punctuation point. As olives ripen they darken, going from green to purplish or brown to pitch black. A dark, ripe olive will be relatively soft, rich, and lush tasting. One of my favorite tomato sauces for pasta is flavored with black olives and a splash of cream. There is a luxuriousness to this sauce you wouldn't get with green olives. On the other hand, a Sicilian dish called *stemperata,* made with hare or rabbit or even swordfish, is flavored with celery, green olives, and splash of vinegar. It is a typically bracing Sicilian flavor combination that would lack punch if made with lush black olives. I've chosen green olives for the Chicken Agrodolce on page 250 because their puckery quality balances out the sweetness in the sauce. *Puttanesca,* a vibrant tomato-based pasta sauce, contains anchovies and capers and olives; I usually add green olives because their tartness lets them hold their own amid the other strong flavors. I love adding black olives to dishes that include a rich cheese, such as the stuffed tomatoes with goat cheese and black olives on page 111. I sometimes think of black olives as a winter taste and green olives as a warm-weather taste, but this is just a personal perspective and not something I make into a rule.

All olives are strongly flavored, and you have to keep this in mind when deciding whether to include them in a dish. They will assert their presence, but there are certain ways to treat them in cooking so they reveal their best attributes. I try not to let olives simmer in a dish for very long. Prolonged exposure to heat can bring out bitterness. Add olives in the last moments of cooking to keep them fresh. I'm also in the habit of taste-testing olives before I buy a quantity. Even an olive variety you buy all the time can be different from batch to batch or from store to store. Some can be bitter or absurdly salty, which you don't want in your food. Occasionally, black olives can be mushy and have an almost moldy taste that can really ruin a dish. The salt can be tamed somewhat by blanching the olives in a large pot of boiling water for a few minutes.

I love the look and taste of whole olives studding a dish, and you encounter that all the time in southern Italy. It can be a charming and voluptuous culinary touch but shocking if unexpected (as when they're baked into a closed tart or calzone, for instance). I only use unpitted olives where they'll be clearly seen, for instance scattered over a roast fish or tossed into a dish of spaghetti (not in a baked pasta). They look beautiful and are much juicier when left whole, so you can experience a burst of olive flavor instead of a generalized olive taste in a dish. One of my favorite pastas contains a handful of whole green olives that have been sautéed to plump them. If you'd like to try it, take a look at Fusilli with Sautéed Green Olives and Bread Crumbs (page 346). Chopped pitted olives also have their virtues. Olive pesto, sometimes called olivata or olivada, is a sumptuous treat for olive lovers. It can be made easily in a food processor with green or black olives. I love it tossed with pasta or spooned onto grilled fish or over lamb chops (see page 80 for an olivata made with black olives). For the best flavor and highest quality, I always buy unpitted whole olives, regardless of how I plan on using them. The best way to pit olives is by crushing them lightly with the side of a large knife just until the flesh splits; then the pits will pull away easily. You can split a bunch at once by placing the olives under a kitchen towel and pressing on them lightly with a large pot.

The selection of first-rate southern Italian olives available in this country is not wonderful. Gaeta olives, named after a port town in northern Campania and grown in various places in southern and central Italy, are the easiest to find here. They are picked fairly ripe, so their color ranges from brownish to deep purple and sometimes almost black. The ones I've bought in New York always seem sharper than the ones I've tasted in Italy (maybe there's a psychological element to that), but they can still be delicious. The last time I visited Puglia, I made note of all the different varieties of eating olives I saw in the markets and the ones used to make oil in the area around Ostuni where I was staying: Frantoio, Ogliarola, Nociara, Cima di Melfi, Corotina, Pasola, Nociara da Tavola, Dolce di Cassano, Naradola, Mela, Pecholine, and Leccina are some of the names I jotted down. The table olives I ate there were some of the best I've had anywhere, but I have yet to locate a source for interesting olives like them in America. Huge, mild Cerignolo olives, usually green, are the Puglian variety I most often find in my markets. They are pleasant enough in an antipasto buffet, but they don't add much character to food and they are very hard to pit. I don't consider them really representative of the olives I've eaten in Puglia, which have mostly been more flavorful. The large green, sweet Ascolane olive from Ascoli Piceno in the central Italian Marche region is much more interesting and in my opinion makes a better show when cooked into a dish. You can order it from Manicaretti Foods. I often see olives labeled Sicilian in gourmet shops; they tend to be cracked green olives, usually flavored with hot chilies and garlic or fennel seeds. They're fine for an antipasto, but for cooking purposes you want something without additional flavors that can interfere with the flavors you've chosen for your dish. I often substitute olives from France, Spain, and Greece in my southern Italian recipes. Kalamatas from Greece are a good substitute for Gaetas. Green picholines from southern France remind me of olives I've been served in Lecce in southern Puglia. Brown Arbequinas from Spain are a good choice when you want an olive that has some bite but is not as pungent as a green olive. The little black niçoise olives that I find in upscale supermarkets these days seem always to have good flavor, and they blend effortlessly with most southern Italian flavors (these little olives are actually more likely to be from North Africa than from Nice these days). Shrivelled sun-dried black Moroccan olives have a sweet flavor that I love; I use these when I want a really rich, deep flavor.

Olives in southern Italy are often flavored and served as part of an antipasto selection, sometimes sautéed, and sometimes just tossed with a few raw ingredients such as garlic or chilies or herbs. You can buy preflavored olives easily enough, but it's satisfying and quick to make them yourself. Preflavored ones are often bathed in second-rate olive oil, and ingredients like raw garlic can develop an off taste from sitting around too long. When you make them yourself, you know the ingredients are fresh and bright tasting.

SAUTÉED CERIGNOLO OLIVES WITH FENNEL AND MINT

MAKES ABOUT TWO CUPS

1 tablespoon extra-virgin olive oil
8 ounces green Cerignolo olives
Palmful of fennel seeds
1 large shallot, thinly sliced
1 bay leaf, preferably fresh
$1/4$ cup dry white wine
Pinch of coarse sea salt
1 handful fresh mint leaves, chopped

Heat the olive oil in a large skillet over medium-high heat. Add the olives, fennel seeds, shallot, and bay leaf and sauté, shaking the skillet frequently, until the olives are warm and tender and coated with flavor, 3 or 4 minutes. Add the white wine and let it bubble for a few seconds. Add the sea salt and mint leaves; give the olives a little toss, and transfer them to a serving bowl. Serve warm or at room temperature.

OVEN-ROASTED GAETA OLIVES WITH ROSEMARY, GARLIC, AND ORANGE

MAKES ABOUT TWO CUPS

8 ounces Gaeta olives
2 garlic cloves, thinly sliced
Leaves from 3 or 4 rosemary sprigs, finely chopped
Grated zest of 1 large orange
Coarsely ground black pepper to taste
1 tablespoon brandy or Cognac
2 tablespoons extra-virgin olive oil

Preheat the oven to 400°F.

Put the olives in a baking dish, approximately 9 in. round or equivalent square, so the olives can spread out in more or less one layer. Scatter on the garlic, rosemary, orange zest, and pepper. Add the brandy or Cognac and drizzle on the olive oil. Mix everything around with your hands so the olives are well coated. Roast, uncovered, until the olives are plump and fragrant, about 20 minutes. Serve warm.

COOKING WITH GARLIC

SOUTHERN ITALIANS HAVE a deft touch with garlic, especially in Sicily, where they use it with creativity and discretion and often pair it with something that imparts a touch of sweetness. I've found that in northern Puglia and Campania cooks use garlic in a more forthright way, but they still cook it only until golden and are careful not to let it turn dark and bitter. Garlic mixed with spicy notes characterizes some of the cooking of the Basilicata and Calabria regions. This food has great power, but the garlic is always used in a balanced way, so it doesn't knock you out. The bad reputation for garlic overload in Italian cooking comes from, I'm afraid, old-fashioned Italian American restaurant cooking. As much as I dislike degrading my own people, I believe it's the Italians over here who are responsible for a lack of finesse in the garlic department. Southern Italians often don't combine garlic with onion; I've noticed this especially in Neapolitan cooking. They hold garlic in such high esteem that they just don't add it haphazardly to a dish.

The quality of garlic flavor you wind up with depends on the type of garlic you choose and how you treat it. Fresh green spring garlic shoots, which look like scallions and haven't even formed their cloves yet, have a sweet and seductive, slightly oniony aroma. I find this very young garlic in my farmers' market at the beginning of June, but I look forward to its appearance and start thinking about it toward the end of winter. I use it raw in salads and vegetable dishes, just thinly sliced and tossed in like a scallion. It's great for sautéing and adds a very sweet garlic taste to seafood. You can use a fair amount and it won't overpower a dish; if you choose to cook it, do so briefly so it retains its moist, sweet flavor. It lasts only a few weeks before it matures. The recipe for Mussels with Mascarpone, Green Garlic, and Spring Herbs (page 186) shows how easy these garlic shoots are to cook with. As summer approaches, garlic develops cloves and its more recognizable bulb shape. At this point, it's fresh and juicy and at its peak of flavor. I don't add quite as much to a dish as I would with the June shoots, but this is when garlic tastes most like its ideal: pungent and gorgeous.

I had no idea there were so many garlic varieties until I started attending summer garlic festivals in upstate New York. I counted at least twenty-five at the last festival I attended. My favorite garlics are the hardneck varieties, especially the rocambole strains (these varieties are recognizable by a hard stalk that runs up through the center of the bulb). They're strong and juicy, but with little bitterness, and their cloves are very easy to peel. Hardneck varieties are thought to be related more closely to wild garlic, and maybe that's why they have so much flavor. One I always look for is Italian Red. I find its fat, purple-tinged bulbs at my farmers' market throughout the summer. Look for this variety or any other fresh summer garlic you can find (some are a lot stronger than others—a variety called Temptress I purchased at the festival last summer nearly knocked me out—so taste a bit raw to judge its strength before showering your food with it). A bonus of the summer garlic crop is the skinny dark green scapes, the graceful, long flower stalk of the garlic plant. You can chop the scapes and add them raw to salads just like spring garlic, but they're not as delicately flavored, so I only use a little bit (and sometimes the scapes are a touch stiff, so I chop them finely, as I would chives). I frequently visit upstate New York garlic farms throughout the growing season. La Terre farm, in Clinton Corners, New York, is a beautiful place with long fields of garlic bordered by fresh herbs. You can imagine the amazing smell it has during the summer harvest. They grow only hardneck varieties, and they sell them mainly to restaurants and to farmer's markets. It's a wonderful place to stand and stare out onto the fields and contemplate all the dishes you could make with that beautiful garlic. I'm always sad when summer garlic disappears from my market. It leaves a gap in my cooking that can't be filled no matter how I coddle winter garlic. Luckily, there's next summer's crop to look forward to.

The garlic you find in the supermarket in winter has been dried to preserve it a little longer (that's why the skin is white and papery). A lot of it is the softneck variety (without the center stalk), which is mass produced in California. The drying concentrates the flavor but can also make it harsh. Winter garlic never has the same fresh, clear taste as summer cloves, and I'm very careful not to use too much. I seldom use garlic raw in the winter, unless the cloves are very firm and have a sweet smell when I cut into them. And drying doesn't mean it lasts forever. When the cloves feel soft, they're probably beginning to sprout, at which point the taste can become acrid. If they deteriorate further, they'll start to show brown spots. At that point, I try not to use them at all.

The more you chop garlic, the more intense its flavor. Thinly sliced is my choice for sautéing when I want pronounced garlic flavor, for instance when I'm making *spaghetti aglio e olio* (with garlic and olive oil). I use minced garlic much less often these days than when I first began cooking. I now find it too strong, with the garlic taste dispersed all over the dish. I use minced garlic only in a stuffing or in meatballs, where it has to be finely chopped (and there I use very little of it, maybe half a clove for $1^1/_2$ pounds of chopped meat). In uncooked sauces, I may use a bit of minced garlic only because I don't want people eating big slices that won't be tempered by cooking, but usually I just crush a clove, toss it with the uncooked sauce or salad, let it sit to release some flavor, and then take it out before serving. Generally speaking, I use garlic sparingly. For a tomato sauce for a pound of pasta I'll sauté one or possibly two sliced smallish cloves. If it's harsh winter garlic, I'll use less, or decide on a different flavoring, maybe leeks, for instance. Sweet, fresh summer garlic I use more freely, or even raw. People say raw garlic is very strong. That is and isn't true. Sweet, raw spring garlic to my palate is much gentler than dry, shrivelled, sprouting winter garlic; in fact, I never use the latter raw and try not to use it for much of anything.

I always use gentle heat when sautéing garlic, so it doesn't burn. And it can burn surprisingly quickly, going from white to golden to smoking black before your eyes. My timing in adding sliced garlic to a hot skillet has a lot to do with how much moisture there is in the other ingredients I'm adding. For instance, if I'm sautéing juicy tomatoes, I'll sauté the garlic gently in olive oil, just until it takes on the slightest color, and then add the tomatoes. If I added the tomatoes and garlic at the same time, the juice from the tomatoes would prevent the garlic from sautéing, giving it a boiled taste, rather than disseminating a good rich, sweet undertone. Once the garlic is sautéed and the moist ingredient added, you can turn the heat up a bit if you need to evaporate liquid to concentrate the sauce. Vegetables that have little moisture, like sliced raw artichokes, you can add to the dish at the same time as the garlic, letting both sauté a minute or so and then adding a splash of white wine or broth to prevent too much browning. An *aglio e olio* (garlic and olive oil) sauce for pasta needs to be cooked gently. I often put the oil and garlic in the skillet cold at the same time (as opposed to adding garlic to hot oil), turn the heat to medium low, and let everything warm and cook together until the garlic turns the slightest shade of golden. Then I may introduce a splash of white wine or water to stop the cooking. You can make *aglio e olio* different ways. Another approach, one popular in restaurants because of its quickness, is to heat the oil on relatively high heat, drop in the garlic, and watch it carefully for the few seconds it takes to get from raw to golden. This gives a nice nutty flavor with a strong, raw edge, because the garlic doesn't really cook through. This results in a less mellow taste than the first method. I like both, but the second requires you to be very attentive.

Roasting garlic in its skin has become very popular in this country. This produces a concentrated, burnished garlic taste, which I have to admit I'm not always crazy about. To my knowledge, it's not a flavor used in southern Italian cooking, and I don't often find myself including it in my cooking.

SPAGHETTI AGLIO E OLIO THE SLOW-SAUTÉED WAY

MAKES TWO GENEROUS SERVINGS. I generally make this only in the summer, when I can get fresh garlic.

Put 5 thinly sliced moist summer garlic cloves and about $1/2$ cup of olive oil in a cold skillet. Turn the heat to low. The garlic will sauté slowly as the heat comes up. Let it go, stirring it frequently until very fragrant and very lightly golden, about 5 minutes. Add a splash of white wine to stop the cooking and deglaze the skillet, stirring to scrape up any little bits of sautéed garlic from the bottom so they can become incorporated into the sauce. Add 8 ounces of al dente cooked spaghetti and toss over low heat until the pasta is well coated, adding a sprinkling of red pepper flakes, salt, and a generous handful of chopped flat-leaf parsley. Serve right away.

TOMATOES

A QUICK TOMATO SAUCE made with high-quality canned tomatoes is one of my all-time favorite things in the world. It's easy to prepare and comforting to eat, and it really comes down to just buying a good brand of tomatoes. San Marzano is the name of a town in Campania, but it's also the name of a tomato variety grown there, a type of plum tomato that's different from the Roma plum we're more used to here. The San Marzano is longer, thinner, and pointy at one end. It's also less juicy and less sweet but meatier, all qualities that make it great for sauce. Two favorite brands of canned peeled whole San Marzano tomatoes available here are L'Antonella (from esperya.com) and La Valle San Marzano. Muir Glen Organic is a brand of canned tomatoes from California that I love. Muir Glen tomatoes produce a very light, refreshing sauce that when briefly cooked can taste a little like fresh summer tomatoes. If I want a deep, more complex sauce, I'll use San Marzano; if I want a fresh taste, I'll go for the Muir Glen. The people at Muir Glen thoughtfully pack their tomatoes in cans that are lined, so you don't get any of that metallic taste that can occasionally be a problem even with imported Italian brands. Muir Glen's canned diced tomatoes are pleasing for a chunky sauce with little effort, but I generally never buy chopped or puréed tomatoes from other companies; they tend to be packed in thick tomato paste, making them heavy tasting and adding an unwanted smoothness to the sauce. Muir Glen packs theirs in a light tomato broth.

In my recipes you'll notice I call for using 35-ounce cans of plum tomatoes, either whole or chopped. This is, generally speaking, the right amount to make a tomato sauce for a pound of pasta. Many of the San Marzano brands I buy come in 35-ounce sizes, but I've noticed that several of the more easily available supermarket brands are packed in 28-ounce cans, such as Muir Glen, so if you're using a 28-ounce can for one of my recipes, you'll want to add 7 ounces more tomatoes, about half of one of the standard smaller 15-ounce cans.

In the summer, I'm always tempted to make sauces with the large, round, juicy tomatoes that smell so beautiful, but their voluptuous juiciness in fact makes them difficult to cook with. If you don't drain them well, you wind up with a watery sauce. I drop them into boiling water for a few seconds so I can slip off their skins, then seed and chop them, give them a sprinkling of sea salt, and let them sit in a colander over a bowl for at least 20 minutes. Fresh plum tomatoes make a very good sauce. I generally peel them too, and depending on their juiciness, drain them either just briefly or longer. To make a sauce with fresh tomatoes, even well-drained ones, it's best to use a wide skillet so you have lots of surface from which liquid can evaporate quicky. When I don't want to bother with all that peeling and cooking, I make a raw tomato sauce, simply chopping up summer tomatoes, draining them, and then mixing them with good olive oil, garlic or scallions, and a handful of summer herbs. This is an exquisite, almost effortless sauce for pasta or grilled fish, or just eaten on its own with hunks of bread.

TOMATO PASTE AND SUN-DRIED TOMATOES

Tomato paste has always played a part in southern Italian cooking. Its presence in ragùs and stews is what gives those dishes their rich taste and deep color. I'm not always its biggest fan, though, partly because most of the canned tomato paste available here has a metallic taste from the can and a general sourness. *Estratto di pomodoro* is a very concentrated paste made in Sicily from sun-dried tomatoes that's darker and richer than the tomato paste we get here. The taste is more sweet than sharp, in keeping with Sicily's taste buds. Similar sun-dried tomato concentrates are made in Puglia. In Sicily, I've seen *estratto di pomodoro* molded into huge pine-cone shapes and sold at food markets such as Palermo's Vucciria. When you buy it the vendor scoops a small portion from the pine cone and wraps it in paper, so it never sees a can. I've seen shoppers in southern markets purchase *estratto* and spread it on a piece of bread, right on the spot, for an instant snack, something I couldn't imagine doing with most canned tomato pastes. You can order Sicilian *estratto* from Zingerman's (where it's spelled *strattu,* in Sicilian dialect), but you can also approximate that rich concentrated tomato taste by throwing a few oil-packed sun-dried tomatoes and a drizzle of good olive oil into a food processor and puréeing them. This makes a strong flavor, so if you include it in a sauce, use very little. I sometimes find good imported tomato paste in tubes in the supermarket; to my palate it has better taste than the stuff in the little cans. It's not as sweet or concentrated as sun-dried *estratto,* but it has a balanced flavor that's not too sharp. Mutti is a good brand to look for.

Tomato paste is best used in long-simmered dishes, where its strong flavor can soften and mellow with the other ingredients. My mother always used tomato paste in her Sunday meat sauce, but never in a tomato sauce made without meat, and I think she was right in her thinking. You want to reinforce the tomato presence when you pair tomato with pork, beef, or lamb, as they release such hearty juices, so a little concentrated jolt of tomato can be welcome in the final sauce. I often include a bit of tomato paste in a meat stew that's flavored primarily with red wine. It seems to round out the sauce's acidity and enrich it. Braised Beef with Primitivo Wine (page 268) is a good example of this. Whenever I'm using tomato paste, I always sauté the paste in olive oil, along with garlic or onion or other vegetables such as celery or carrot, at the start of cooking. (This initial sautéing of aromatic vegetables is known as a *soffritto* in Italian cooking. See page 69 for more on this.) This tempers its sharpness so the finished stew or sauce won't have an obvious tomato-paste edge. Adding it at the end of cooking will only sour the dish. In many traditional southern Italian dishes that traditionally include tomato paste, such as the lamb and red pepper ragù on page 384, I leave it out, feeling that the long cooking of the meat and the addition of roasted peppers provide enough depth of flavor. In general, I like a fresher taste in many traditional dishes, so I use tomato paste only when I feel it will deepen the taste in a very positive way.

I love the rich smell and taste of sun-dried tomatoes, and I'm always happy to see them on an antipasto table. Eating whole ones is bracing and good, but when I want to use them in cooking I'm aware that their pungency can easily dominate. I tend to chop them into little bits and use only small amounts, pairing them either with other strong flavors, like olives, or with a soothing counterpoint, like pasta or ricotta (see Tomato Pesto and Ricotta Bruschetta, page 112). They also add depth to simple bean or rice salads. Good sun-dried tomatoes are made by Sapori di Salento in Puglia and sold by esperya.com. When I can only find domestic ones, I opt for the ones that are packed dry, not in any type of oil, since I never know what kind of oil or how old it is. I soak the dried ones in warm water, drain them, and then steep them in my own olive oil.

For a rich, concentrated tomato taste, but one not as pungent as you get from sun-dried tomatoes, you can make your own oven-roasted tomatoes. The results are moister, not as leathery as sun-dried tomatoes but still condensed. There is a recipe in Tomato Pesto and Ricotta Bruschetta, page 112.

SUMMER TOMATO SAUCE

MAKES ABOUT TWO CUPS, ENOUGH FOR ONE POUND DRIED PASTA Here's how I make a very fresh-tasting, lightly cooked sauce from juicy summer tomatoes.

2½ pounds large, round summer tomatoes, peeled, seeded, and cut into medium dice
Sea salt to taste
2 tablespoons extra-virgin olive oil, plus more for drizzling
2 large, moist summer garlic cloves, very thinly sliced
4 scallions, including tender green parts, cut into thin rounds
2 or 3 scrapings of freshly grated nutmeg to taste
Small handful of fresh basil leaves, chopped
Small handful flat-leaf parsley leaves, chopped
Freshly ground black pepper to taste

Put the diced tomatoes in a colander over a bowl and sprinkle on a little sea salt. Let them drain for ½ hour. Reserve the tomato juice.

In a large, wide skillet, heat the 2 tablespoons olive oil over medium heat. Add the garlic and sauté for about 1 minute to release its flavor. Add the scallions and sauté until the garlic and scallions are fragrant and the garlic is just starting to turn very lightly golden, about 1 minute longer. Add the tomatoes, turn the heat to high, and sauté for about 5 minutes, stirring a few times. Even well-drained summer tomatoes should give off enough juice to form a good sauce, but if they seem dry, add a splash of the reserved tomato juice to the skillet. The sauce should be chunky, a little juicy, and bright red. Add the nutmeg (which really brings up the tomato's sweetness), fresh herbs, a few turns of pepper, and a drizzle of fresh olive oil. Taste to see if it needs more salt.

PEELING AND SEEDING TOMATOES: In a large pot of boiling water, blanch tomatoes for about 30 seconds, or until skins start to split. Using a large slotted spoon or skimmer, transfer the tomatoes to a colander and run cold water over them to stop the cooking. Slip off their skins and cut the tomatoes in half crosswise. Hold each half upside down over the sink and squeeze to remove the seeds.

NOTE If you would like to make this with summer plum tomatoes, you'll want to skin and seed them as above, but since their flesh is drier, they probably won't need draining.

UNCOOKED TOMATO SAUCE

MAKES ABOUT TWO CUPS. ENOUGH FOR ONE POUND PASTA. OR SAUCE FOR MEAT OR FISH FOR FOUR *Pomodoro crudo,* a sauce of uncooked tomatoes, is something I make throughout the summer to use on pasta, or as a sauce for grilled fish or meat, or just for eating out of the bowl with a piece of bread. The only thing you really need to remember is to drain the tomatoes so you get a lush, concentrated flavor.

2½ pounds ripe, round summer tomatoes, seeded and cut into small dice (no need to skin them, since they won't be cooked)
Sea salt to taste
¼ cup estate-bottled extra-virgin olive oil
1 small, moist garlic clove, minced
Leaves from 3 to 4 marjoram sprigs, chopped
Leaves from 3 to 4 mint sprigs, chopped
1 palmful salt-packed capers, soaked and drained
Freshly ground pepper to taste
Few drops balsamic vinegar if needed

Put the chopped tomatoes in a colander, sprinkle them with sea salt, and let them drain for about 45 minutes. Transfer the tomatoes to a large bowl. Add the olive oil, garlic, herbs, and capers. Add a few turns of pepper and mix everything well. Let sit for 20 minutes to develop the flavor. Now, taste the sauce. Add a little more salt, if needed, and taste again. If it seems slightly flat, add a few drops of balsamic vinegar (not more, though) to bring up the acidity.

CAPERS

ON MY FIRST VISIT TO SICILY many years ago, I discovered the aromatic capers grown on the islands of Salina and Pantelleria. Sicily turns out the most floral-tasting, sweet capers, or *caperi,* in the world. When you taste them, it becomes apparent that they are actually flower buds, from a Mediterranean shrub that loves dry, hot weather (which is why those two Sicilian islands are just right for their well-being). Sicilian capers are picked more mature and a little larger than the French vinegar-packed ones you see in little bottles and called nonpareil, and because of their size they are much riper and sweeter. Curing and packing them in sea salt preserves their firm texture and sweetness. I'm convinced that people who say they don't like capers have only tasted the vinegar-packed ones, which taste like pickles and whose aggressiveness has always made them a challenge for me to cook with.

Capers have been used in Sicilian cooking since the time of the Greeks. They're still a signature flavoring in many Sicilian dishes, and they're also used lavishly in the cooking of the Naples area. As Sicilian chefs have discovered, they blend beautifully with slightly sweet flavors; I can't imagine a sweet-and-sour eggplant caponata without them. I use the blending of sweet with capers in Carrots with Sicilian Capers (page 99), which incorporates a bit of sugar. The combination of capers and lemon might sound sharp, but it can be utterly refreshing on a cool shellfish salad or as a little skillet sauce poured over a sautéed fish fillet, especially when tempered by an abundant amount of fruity olive oil. It works especially well on rich, oily fish, such as sardines, mackerel, anchovies, and salmon. In Sicily, grilled swordfish is often garnished with nothing but a scattering of capers, making a simple yet fragrant and quite special dish. I love capers added to a potato salad that's been tossed with olive oil and possibly a few sliced shallots. Pan-seared pork chops finished with a sprinkling of capers, white wine, and a lump of butter is one of my favorite quick dinner dishes. And a salad of olive-oil-packed Sicilian tuna, ripe tomatoes, and capers is something I make all summer long; its trio of ingredients produce a fabulous flavor.

I've never seen this in Sicily, but many American chefs deep-fry capers so they burst into little opened flowers and become crunchy. I love those in a fritto misto of seafood, and I use them as a garnish for Veal and Yellow Peppers with Fried Capers (page 240). If I'm not deep-frying them, I tend to add them toward the end of cooking or right before serving, to preserve their delicate floral fragrance and firm texture.

I rejoice in having recently become able to find these great capers in my local markets (I used to smuggle as many bags as I could back on the plane from Italy with me). My favorite capers are the ones produced by Antonio Caravaglio on the island of Salina. They're available through Manicaretti Italian Food Imports. He also harvests caper berries, the fruit of the caper bush, which are larger and more mellow in flavor than capers but can be used more or less the same way. Capers from Pantelleria are available in big bags at my local markets. They last unopened for a few years. Once you open a bag, keep it refrigerated.

SOAKING AND DRAINING SALT-PACKED CAPERS: To remove excess salt, soak the capers in several changes of cold water for about 30 minutes, then rinse in cold water again and drain well.

SICILIAN CAPER AND WALNUT SAUCE

MAKES ABOUT ONE CUP Here is a classic *salsa di caperi* to spoon over grilled fish or meats. I also like it on fried eggs. Parsley is the standard herb added to this sauce and I have added some, but I've also included a few untraditional leaves of tarragon because it blends so well with capers.

$\frac{1}{2}$ cup salt-packed Sicilian capers, soaked and drained (see above)
2 oil-packed anchovy fillets, minced
Handful of very fresh walnut halves, lightly toasted and chopped (see note)
1 small garlic clove, minced
About $\frac{1}{2}$ teaspoon Dijon mustard
Juice of $\frac{1}{2}$ lemon
Freshly ground black pepper to taste
3 or 4 tarragon sprigs, chopped
Leaves from 3 or 4 flat-leaf parsley sprigs, chopped
Pinch of salt
Pinch of sugar
$\frac{1}{2}$ cup extra-virgin olive oil

Chop the capers coarsely with a large knife and put them in a nice-looking small serving bowl. Add all the remaining ingredients. Mix well and let stand at room temperature for about 1 hour before serving so the flavors can blend and mellow. To store, cover and refrigerate for up to 4 days, but return it to room temperature before serving for the most vibrant flavor.

TOASTING WALNUTS My favorite way to toast walnuts, or any nuts, is to spread them out on a sheet pan and place them in a preheated 400°F oven until they're just turning golden, usually about 12 minutes, but start watching them after 6 or 7 minutes to make sure they don't burn. This method produces an all-over golden toastiness as opposed to toasting them in a skillet over a flame burner, which often produces dark spots on the nuts.

ORANGES AND LEMONS

I USE SO MUCH LEMON ZEST in my cooking that my sister once called my kitchen the house of the bald lemons. But the use of grated lemon zest in savory dishes is more a trick of American chefs than it is traditionally southern Italian. Southern Italians use grated zest in pastries and cakes, but not often in stews and pasta sauces the way I love to. There, they're more likely to employ lemon peel or juice. But grated zest gives food a direct hit, and if you're careful not to scrape up any of the white pith, you can use it to impart the essence of lemon with no bitterness.

As a kid, I was crazy about the smell of Lemon Pledge furniture spray, and I think it somehow set it in my head what a lemon should smell like. Not that Pledge had real lemon in it, but it smelled like lemon oil, from the peel, where the most intense lemon essence lies. The California lemons in our markets year round were somehow not lemony enough. One year when I was a child, my parents took a trip to Naples and the Amalfi Coast and brought back a bottle of the region's famous limoncello liqueur, which is flavored with the skin of large, lumpy Amalfi Coast lemons. The liqueur got me very excited, but not until years later, when I traveled to Amalfi myself and tasted those glorious lemons in the raw, was my dream of lemon realized. As special as those lemons are, though, I think the cachet of lemons in southern Italian cooking also has to do with how they are glorified. If you go to pottery shops in Palermo or on the Amalfi Coast, you'll find lemons painted on plates and pitchers and cups even more often than religious symbols. Our lemons are perfectly fine, but their presence doesn't create that kind of drama.

For the freshest flavor, I add lemon zest toward the end of cooking a dish, or even right before taking it to the table. It's like a jolt of sunshine. If you've cooked a stew or a soup that tastes a little lackluster, sometimes a quick grating of lemon zest can be just the thing to bring it into focus. I love to grate zest over a roast duck right when I take it from the oven. When I make traditional southern Italian pork sausages with roasted peppers, I often grate lemon (and sometimes orange) zest over the dish just before bringing it to the table; the zest brightens it up and cuts through the fattiness. And lemon zest is a helpful acidic ingredient for a fish marinade, where lemon juice might whiten or cook the fish's surface, making it mushy, or make the marinade too liquid, leading to steaming instead of browning. Try including lemon zest in vegetable and ricotta fillings for ravioli or *tortas* where you feel the creaminess needs a little reining in. I've never been a big fan of cream sauces, but I occasionally make one for a first-course pasta with hints of lemon zest and nutmeg—both sharpness and warmth. I use lemon zest in *pasta e fagiole* to break through the sea of starch, making the dish feel contemporary.

I occasionally find Sicilian lemons in my markets, imported by AgriNature, a co-op in Avola, Sicily, around late January. They are small, perfectly round, and a lovely pale yellow. I find them a little less acidic then our local California varieties, but not sweeter. When I see them I always buy them, not because they're so very different from our lemons, but just for the romance of having the beautiful, fragrant Sicilian-grown things in my kitchen.

Limoncello liqueur is wonderful poured over ice cream or added to a lemon *sorbetto* to boost its lemon flavor. I occasionally also use a tiny splash of it in sautéed mussels or clams; it adds interesting flavor, the way a brandy would but with a lemon edge. It is very sweet, so a little goes a long way in a savory dish. Caravella is a good brand of limoncello you can find in the United States. Lemon verbena is another great way to add lemon to your cooking. This herb has an almost pure lemon essense that blends in easily in a gelato or a fruit tart or as a garnish for poached fruit. You can add a few leaves to a fish stew to good effect, but too much will make the dish taste like air freshener. Lemon balm, another lemon-scented herb I find at my farmers' market in summer, is not as interesting; to my palate it makes food taste a little musty.

I grew up in New York, but each winter we shared a house in Hollywood, Florida, with my paternal grandparents (my father was a golf pro and needed to follow the sun). It was an odd little house with a ramshackle open quality that made me feel I wasn't completely sheltered, but the small backyard was dotted with lemon and orange trees that grew mountains of fruit. One of the orange trees produced large brownish green, bumpy fruit that when cut into revealed a brilliant orange interior with a sweet orange taste. My grandfather used to squeeze them for juice, and the taste was amazing. Real orange juice and real oranges with deep flavor were such a big part of my childhood taste memory that when I first started visiting Sicily I was drawn immediately to the ways they used oranges in cooking, and when I discovered their famous savory orange salads I couldn't believe a culture had come up with a dish that mixed sweet oranges with sea salt, black pepper, olive oil, green olives, sometimes anchovies, fennel, and red onion in one dish. Such salads have become a Christmas Eve tradition in my house and have inspired me in finding ways to blend orange into fish and meat dishes.

Blood oranges are the pride of Sicily, loved for their deep red to purple insides and their slightly tart but berrylike flavor. I've encountered three types of blood oranges in Sicily: Tarocco; Moro, with a deep red-black color; and Sanguinello. Tarocco is my favorite. Though not as deeply colored as the others (usually they have deep orange insides with streaks of red running through), they are sweet and richly flavored. I occasionally find imported Tarocco oranges in this country, but most of the blood oranges here are grown in California, and they tend to be the Moro variety, which can be very tart. In the past few years I've purchased Taroccos at the Whole Foods chain that were from Beck Grove in Fallbrook, California (see page 436). These make a gorgeous and sweet Sicilian orange salad. Blood oranges are generally available in California from December through June. Bitter oranges, also called Seville oranges, are grown in Sicily and in Spain, but most of ours come from Florida and California. They are more sour than bitter; I use them like lemons. Sweet oranges such as the Valencia juice orange; navel oranges in different varieties, mostly from California; and mandarins (also called tangerines) are all wonderful to cook with. Florida Honeybells are incredibly sweet and juicy and available only in January, but they're worth looking out for. I use them in Honeybell-and-Lillet Gelatina (page 420). An orange liqueur like Grand Marnier is sweet, and I use it only in desserts. When I want an orange flavor in a savory dish, I more often add a touch of Lillet, which tastes like an orange-scented vermouth.

Orange flower water is used in southern Italy to flavor ricotta and cream desserts, fruit, and occasionally savory dishes. It imparts an exotic perfume aroma, more floral than citrus. A few drops will suffice to flavor an entire ricotta cheescake. Orange flower water is packed in little bottles; the ones I find are usually imported from France. I love this flavor, but if you're looking for pure orange essence, I'd go with the zest.

A surprising way to liven up a tomato sauce is by adding a little grated orange zest, and orange zest paired with a sweet and nutty cheese like Parmigiano-Reggiano makes a stunning blend. I've used it to season asparagus in a recipe on page 82. Orange blended with hot chilies, with fennel, and with garlic are other favorite pairings of mine; you'll find them in several of my recipes.

LIMONCELLO AND CHAMPAGNE COCKTAIL

SERVES ONE Here's a refreshing *aperitivo* to serve on its own or with a simple raw fish appetizer, like Salmon Carpaccio with Mint and Celery Leaves (page 158).

Drizzle about 1 tablespoon limoncello into a Champagne glass and fill the glass with very cold Champagne, Prosecco or another sparkling wine. Add a lemon twist and serve right away.

ANCHOVIES AND BOTTARGA

I HAVE LOVED PRESERVED ANCHOVIES since I was very young. As a child, I could—to the horror of friends and even myself—eat a whole tin of them in one sitting. I still love eating them straight, but now I know that they show their true reason for being when you cook with them. Southern Italians sometimes treat anchovies the way they would salt, as a seasoning that heightens the taste of everything around it. They add anchovies to dishes such as lamb stew, beef *braciole*, sautéed broccoli, and eggplant, where the fish taste may not even be detectable but brings out every other taste. Anchovies are mixed with green olives to powerful effect in Sicily, in pastas and in rabbit dishes. Anchovies mixed with softened butter and melted is my favorite sauce for a steak. Anchovy butter is also wonderful tossed with egg tagliatelle, and anchovies melted in olive oil produce one of the most enticing sauces for spaghetti I have ever eaten. If you start a tomato sauce with garlic and a few anchovies melted in olive oil, add a splash of white wine, then add a can of chopped tomatoes and let it bubble for about 10 minutes, you'll have a sauce that's quick and sublime.

The preserved anchovies I grew up with were packed in olive oil, usually in tins or little jars. I still love them on antipasto plates and just for eating as is, but for cooking you'll get the best flavor from anchovies packed in salt. Flott is a Sicilan brand I really love. It's available through Buon Italia. The fish are whole and just need to be filleted, which is very easy, believe it or not.

> **FILLETING AND SOAKING SALT-PACKED ANCHOVIES:** Run the anchovies, one at a time, under cold running water and, starting from the head end, work the fillet free from the backbone with your fingers. After doing a few, you'll get the hang of it (it doesn't matter if you mutilate a couple, since they're probably going to dissolve in the sauce anyway). Soak the fillets in a bowl of cold water for about 15 minutes to remove the excess salt, then drain them and pat them dry.

Oil-packed anchovies are not bad for cooking, and I use them when I don't have the salt-packed ones. Flott makes good ones, and I also like Bel Aria brand. With oil-packed anchovies, I always go for bottled. They taste better than the ones packed in tins. Marinated fresh anchovies, like the ones on page 154, are a dish in their own right, and not what you want for cooking.

Anchovies can stand a little heat. They dissolve and release more flavor with cooking, which is a wonderful characteristic if you want to hide the fact that you've added them from some guest who thinks he's made his mind up about them. For salad dressings, you can mince them or purée them in a mini food processor; on the other hand you can garnish a dish with whole uncooked ones. Anchovies give you a lot of leeway.

Bottarga is pressed dried fish roe. In Sicily, it's made from tuna roe; in Sardinia, they use gray mullet eggs, whose flavor is more subtle and a little less salty. I always try to find Sardinian bottarga. Sicilian cooks like to shave it into pasta with garlic and olive oil, and sometimes with tomatoes and herbs as well, or scrape it over salads of fennel and celery, or cherry tomatoes. I've also had it just sliced and served as is, drizzled with olive oil. I especially like it shaved over a mozzarella and tomato salad (see the recipe below). The Sicilian stuff comes cut into little blocks; the Sardinian is a whole roe that looks like a tongue. It's firm but somewhat moist and usually covered with wax to preserve it. To use it, all you need to do is peel off the wax coating and shave off as much bottarga as you need, using a sharp vegetable peeler, directly onto the dish. You can also use a grater with large holes.

Always add bottarga to a dish raw and right before serving. Cooking ruins its flavor and texture, which is why it's best on salads or tossed with hot pasta at the last minute. Once you start using it, you'll discover that it's very strongly flavored and salty, somewhat like caviar but more concentrated, so a little goes a long way. I have bought bags of pregrated bottarga in Sicily, mainly because it was inexpensive, but I haven't been happy with the taste or the texture; it was dry and very fishy. They use it in pasta dishes in Sicily, but I find that so much of bottarga's appeal comes from its moist, melting texture that the powdery stuff isn't worth buying. Lately, I've seen this powder in gourmet shops here, but I'm not tempted by it. Many Italian shops now carry bottarga, and you can also order it from Italian food websites (see page 436).

MOZZARELLA AND TOMATO SALAD WITH BOTTARGA

SERVES FOUR

> 1-pound ball mozzarella, thinly sliced
> 2 large summer tomatoes, sliced
> About 10 shavings bottarga, preferably Sardinian gray-mullet bottarga
> Extra-virgin olive oil for drizzling
> Freshly ground black pepper to taste
> Handful of fresh mint leaves

Arrange the mozzarella slices and tomato slices alternatively on a large serving platter. Shave the bottarga over them with a sharp vegetable peeler. Drizzle with olive oil and grind on a little pepper. Garnish with the mint leaves and serve right away.

MOZZARELLA AND ANCHOVY PANINI

MAKES TWO SANDWICHES This is my all-time favorite sandwich. Made with the classic Italian pairing of mozzarella and anchovies, it's gooey and salty at the same time.

6 thin slices fresh mozzarella
4 slices firm, white sandwich bread (Pepperidge Farm makes a good one)
6 oil-packed anchovy fillets
Leaves from 3 or 4 marjoram sprigs, chopped
Freshly ground black pepper to taste
About 2 tablespoons extra-virgin olive oil

Divide the mozzarella between 2 pieces of bread. Lay the anchovies on top. Scatter on the marjoram and add a few grindings of pepper. Close the sandwiches with the other 2 pieces of bread.

In a large skillet, heat the olive oil over medium heat. Add the sandwiches and sauté, pressing down on the bread with a spatula to flatten them. When they're nice and brown on one side, about 3 minutes or so, flip them over and brown the other side, flattening them with the spatula and adding a little more olive oil if the skillet seems dry. The cheese should now be melted and the sandwiches fairly thin. Transfer them to a cutting board and cut them in half on an angle. Eat right away, preferably with a glass of cold white wine.

SWEET PEPPERS AND HOT CHILIES

THERE ARE POCKETS of very spicy cooking in southern Italy, especially in the regions of Calabria and Basilicata. Hot chili pastes and fresh chilies can turn up in almost anything there, from sausages to green salads. Campania and Puglia like a little heat now and then as well. My father used fiery amounts of red pepper flakes on *pasta e fagioli* and pizza, and even thought these foods were incomplete without it. *Peperoncini* is the word used in most of southern Italy for hot chilies, but I've heard the hottest ones called *diavoletti*—"little devils" (which is also what my grandfather used to call me and my sister).

There isn't a wide variety of hot chilies in southern Italian cooking, so you don't get the range of chili flavors that exists in Mexican food, for instance, but roasted and sautéed dried chilies give the hot dishes of the south real character. Chili pastes, like the one I ate in Pisticci, in Basilicata, are made with dried chilies that have been sautéed in a skillet with garlic, olive oil, and sometimes anchovies to intensify their flavor (see Bucatini with Dandelions, Tomatoes, and Basilicata Chili Sauce, page 144). Italian Americans, especially ones of Calabrian decent, can recognize little jars of vinegary, hot round cherry chilies as an emblem of their heritage. I find imported jars of them and other Calabrian chilies, some stuffed with anchovies or just packed in vinegar, at Buon Italia, my local Italian food shop, but most of the time I cook with dried chilies or my own local fresh chilies (if I want vinegar in my food, I'd rather add it myself). The long, skinny fresh chilies I find in my supermarket that are usually called *peperoncini* can give cooking an authentic southern Italian taste and a moderate amount of heat. They can be green or red or somewhere in between, depending on how ripe they are. Even with hot chilies, the riper they are the sweeter they are, so if you want a spiciness that's less sharp, go for a red chili. I often find fresh cherry chilies, and they tend to be very hot but also a good choice for flavor. Fresh chilies will always give you heat, juiciness from their moist skins and flesh, and a clear flavor. They'll also add pretty specks of bright red or green color. In July, my farmers' market offers a huge variety of hot and sweet fresh chilies. I've experimented with several varieties. Cascabella, a medium hot red Spanish chili, gave a good Italian flavor to a spicy tomato sauce. I don't often use poblanos, because I feel they add a distinctly un-Italian flavor to food. Jalapeños, if they're all you can find, are not bad, being basically heat with not much flavor.

Whole dried small red chilies, when crumbled into a dish, give an earthier, toastier taste than when used fresh. Dried red pepper flakes (actually dried seeds), the type you often see in plastic containers in pizza parlors, provide a lot of heat and some roasted flavor if they're really fresh. Ground cayenne is really straight heat, and I use it when I want to add a hint of spiciness to flour to coat fish or meat, mainly because it's so finely ground. Even better than cayenne for a finely ground pepper is Aleppo, from Syria. It has a sweeter, almost fruity heat. I often add a pinch of it when I'm sautéing garlic or onions for a pasta or a ragù.

Hot chilies paired with fennel seeds is a typical Calabrian flavor duo that turns up again and again, especially in lamb and pork recipes. It's a flavor melding that works well with both meat and fish. I use it in Sautéed Shrimp with Celery, Fennel Seeds, and Chilies (page 184) and Rigatoni with Spicy Pork and Fennel Ragù (page 382). The blending of chilies with other flavors is what gives spicy food character. Garlic and chilies is a time-honored classic, and most chili pastes I've encountered in the south have contained some garlic. It's a fine blend for dressing sturdy dried pasta. For a lighter touch I often blend chilies with mint or basil. Orange zest and chilies is a combination I particularly love, and I use it in Big Shrimp Gratin (page 182). Astringent touches like lemon juice or white wine seem to amplify chilies' heat, which is sometimes just what you want. I love that in a fish stew. Oregano blended with chilies produces a bold flavor that works well as a marinade for grilled meat or swordfish steaks.

If you ever make your way to Calabria in early September, try to get to the annual *peperoncino* festival in the beachfront town of Diamante. To find out more about this, contact Centro Gastronomico Sapore Calabria by fax at 0985/87168 (I have yet to make it there myself, but I've heard it's pretty wild, with food tastings, chili-eating contests, and erotic art as well).

PEPERONI (SWEET PEPPERS)

AN EASY WAY TO MAKE a simple chicken or veal dish or a ragù taste southern Italian is by adding roasted sweet peppers and a little garlic. That's is how most Italian Americans flavor chicken *alla cacciatora*. Lamb ragù simmered with sweet roasted peppers is a dish I learned about when visiting my grandmother's birthplace on the border of Puglia and Campania, near Foggia. It is now one of my all-time favorites (I include it in Lasagne with Lamb and Red Pepper Ragù and Caprino, page 384, but it can easily stand alone as a sauce for ziti). Veal and peppers, and pork chops with vinegar peppers, are two other southern Italian classics; they're made around Naples and in other regions as well.

Sweet Italian frying peppers were a staple in Italian markets when I was a child; they seem to be harder to find these days. Corno di Toro (horn of the bull) is a sweet pepper variety I find in July at my farmers' market. It seems to be the same sweet light green frying pepper my father grew in his little garden (although never by that name), which was the kind my mother always used for her veal and peppers. He picked it when the peppers were lightly specked with red; if he had let them ripen, they'd have turned a beautiful shade of crimson. Cubanelle, a sweet pepper you can find at Spanish markets, looks similar and tastes close enough that I often use it when I can't find the real thing. Bell peppers come in a fabulous range of colors. When I buy them from local farmers during the summer, their taste is warm and alluring and they're delicious raw, but in the winter they can be harsh or flavorless or both, or even have a slight gasoline flavor when eaten raw.

Roasting deepens the taste of any sweet pepper. I almost always roast and peel sweet peppers when I'm using them in a sauce or stew; otherwise the skins detach and float around in the dish, which looks unappealing. Roasting can turn even out-of-season bell peppers into something smoky and sweet. You want to lightly cook the flesh while roasting the skin, which is why doing it over a gas burner doesn't work so well. The gas flame sears the skin so quickly that the pepper remains raw.

ROASTING AND PEELING PEPPERS Roast peppers on an outdoor grill 5 to 6 inches from low heat until charred on both sides. Or, preheat the broiler and put the peppers on a baking sheet. Roast about 5 inches from the heat on each side until charred. Put the peppers in a paper bag for about 15 minutes, then peel. Remove the seeds by cutting a slit in one side if using the pepper whole; otherwise, halve, seed, and chop or slice as called for in the recipe. Hot chilies can be roasted the same way.

OLIO SANTO

MAKES ONE CUP Olio santo, which means holy oil, is a traditional sauce of hot chili and olive oil that southern Italians love to drizzle over *pasta e fagioli* and other pasta dishes and into soups. I don't generally love flavored olive oils, but this one has a special place in the cooking of the southern regions.

7 small dried red chilies
1 cup inexpensive extra-virgin olive oil

Lightly grind 5 of the chilies in a small spice grinder or a mortar to make a coarsely crushed mass (you just want to open them up so their flavors can be released into the oil). Put the ground peppers in a glass jar or some type of container that has a lid, and pour on the olive oil. Cover and let this stand, unrefrigerated, overnight. Strain out the chilies and return the oil to the jar (it will now be a light pink color). Add the remaining 2 whole chilies and close up the jar. I sometimes funnel the oil into a small wine bottle and cork it, which looks pretty on the table. It's now ready to use.

Olio santo, traditionally made with dried chilies, will last several months because there is no moisture in it. I keep it covered but unrefrigerated since refrigeration can cause some moisture to build up in the oil, making it rancid. Olio santo made with fresh chilies will only keep about a week.

SOME THOUGHTS ABOUT BLACK PEPPER

PLACE A FEW BLACK PEPPERCORNS in a mortar and give them a good grind with the pestle. Take a sniff. Black pepper has a sharp, deep aroma that makes food come alive. The smell and taste of freshly ground black pepper is almost intoxicating to me, but I don't feel I need to use it on every dish. That would diminish its specialness. When a waiter comes hovering with a pepper grinder and asks, "Freshly ground black pepper?" I try to think about it, and I often say no. In southern Italy, black pepper is added as a main seasoning to specific dishes such as *pepata di cozze* (mussels with black pepper), spaghetti *cacia e uovo*, certain cheeses like Sicily's sheep's milk pepato, or coarsely ground to flavor *taralli*. Some foods, especially those containing basil (pesto, for instance), are traditionally not seasoned with black pepper. The rationale is that basil is innately peppery, so adding another peppery element will confuse the palate. Tomato salads in southern Italy are usually seasoned only with salt and olive oil. In fact, most of the green salads I've eaten there also contained no black pepper.

I use black pepper in cooking much more than most southern Italians do. I've grown up with the taste and have gotten used to it making an appearance in many foods, but still my use of it is quirky. Sometimes I can explain why I add or omit it in a certain dish, but sometimes I just have the feeling it doesn't belong. Whatever my decision, my taste is my guide. If I'm adding a hot chili, either dried or fresh, I'll probably not add black pepper, for its taste may be drowned out in all the heat. I've noticed that southern dishes that contain chilies almost never include black pepper as well.

It's good to weigh the innate pepperiness of your ingredients. I find arugula very peppery and often omit black pepper from a dish that includes it, unless I'm going for a very peppery taste. If I'm adding a fresh herb, such as marjoram, and I want its flavor to stand out, I may feel that black pepper would compete with it. Certain seasonal vegetables, I find, taste purer without it, especially fresh peas, zucchini, and bell peppers, yet I love black pepper on winter squash dishes, and I always add it to eggplant and artichokes. I wouldn't think of eating a nice rare steak without freshly ground black pepper, but squid and many other mild seafoods have a delicacy that I sometimes feel would be compromised by black pepper (although I love it on just about any crab dish). Spaghetti tossed with olive oil, grated pecorino and abundant black pepper is a simple but elegant dish where each component plays an important part. Lemon juice and zest and black pepper make an elegant but surprisingly bold flavoring for shellfish and rich fish like swordfish.

Puglia and Campania share a dish called *pepata di cozze*, which is simply mussels steamed with a little wine and abundant black pepper. When I had it at Ristorante Zaccaria on the Amalfi Coast, I realized just how much heat black pepper really has, previously thinking it was a somewhat mild seasoning. Black pepper is a wonderful thing on a Sicilian-style orange salad dressed with olive oil, and it shines in some desserts too, especially ones containing chocolate, where a play of sweet and spicy can be very appealing. Strawberries tossed with balsamic vinegar and a grinding of black pepper make a haunting and delicious dessert. I like to add a touch of black pepper to a fruit sorbet, too, especially one made with berries, where the spice will highlight both the sweetness and the acidity of the fruit.

Black pepper loses its strength after being cooked for a few minutes. I'll sometimes add a little at the beginning of cooking, knowing it won't provide much impact later on, just for subtle flavor (actually, if you add a large amount at the beginning of cooking, it can turn bitter). I'll add a more generous amount right before serving so it stays potent. For the freshest flavor, I always use whole peppercorns and grind them myself when I'm cooking. When I want a strong taste of black pepper in a dish, I'll grind it coarsely. A gentle showering of finely ground pepper is good for fine-tuning a dish, as it will blend easily with other flavors. Tellicherry peppercorns from India have the most complex flavor. I buy big bags of them at an Indian market in New York.

FENNEL AND SAFFRON

Fennel blended with saffron is one of the classic flavor combinations of Sicily, the saffron being a legacy of long-ago Arab occupation, and the wild fennel growing like a weed all over the island. If you've ever tasted *pasta con le sarde*, a famous dish from Palermo consisting of bucatini pasta tossed with fresh sardines, wild fennel, raisins, pine nuts, and saffron, you'll know how beautiful this flavor combination can be. It's a taste that stays in your memory. I find the aroma so alluring that I'm ever grateful and honored by its existence. Fennel and saffron are also used as accent seasonings in Provençal bouillabaisse. In fact, this blending is not exactly a secret around the Mediterranean.

I love mussels cooked with fennel seeds, a few threads of saffron, white wine, and a touch of cream. Fennel seeds and saffron added to a plain tomato sauce produce an unexpected sauce for spaghetti, and it's great poured over fish fillets for baking. I've also found that fennel with saffron makes a superb flavoring for white meats such as chicken and veal. I like adding it to a veal ragù, and I often braise chicken pieces with saffron, tomatoes, bulb fennel, and a splash of fennel-flavored liqueur. Sautéed zucchini with fennel and saffron is another dish I've had success with. I sauté sliced zucchini together with sliced fennel and a bit of sliced onion until tender, adding a pinch of saffron (dissolved in a few tablespoons of warm water) at the end, along with a few chopped tarragon leaves, which have a fennel-like taste. And of course, both fennel and saffron are used independently and in conjunction with other flavors in many southern Italian dishes.

You can bring fennel flavor into your cooking in various ways. The skinny wild fennel with bushy, long fronds that is so prevalent in Sicily is hard to find in the United States unless you live on the West Coast (where you can yank it up along the highways).

It's used more like an herb than a vegetable. I sometimes find it at my greenmarket in the summer and always grab a bunch when I do. If you have a garden, it's pretty easy to grow.

Cultivated fennel, also called Florence fennel, has a rounded bulb base that is sliced and used as an aromatic vegetable. Its fragrance is gentle compared with that of the wild variety, but it adds a crunchy texture and subtle flavor to a sauce. Its short fronds don't have a wonderful taste. I'll add a small amount or chop some for garnish, but if you add too much it'll make your dish taste grassy. Sliced bulb fennel sautéed with a few toasted and ground fennel seeds will give you a strong but sweet fennel flavor and makes a fine substitute for wild fennel (I use this combination when I make *pasta con le sarde*).

Fennel seeds give dishes a sweet, very appealing fennel flavor. I often sauté a few whole in olive oil along with garlic or onion as a flavor base for a sauce. The seeds are traditionally used to season pork sausages, sometimes with the addition of hot chili, in various parts of southern Italy, and it's hard to find Italian pork sausages in this country without them. Fresh tuna coated with lightly crushed fennel seeds and then grilled is a dish I've eaten in Palermo and it is a good example of how the southern cook will use a few ingredients to produce vibrant flavor. I'll sometimes sauté a bunch of seeds whole in a little olive oil until crisp and fragrant and scatter them over grilled sardines, squeeze on a little lemon, and that's the dish: perfect summer cooking. Dried wild fennel branches, available at some gourmet shops, can be steeped in a fish-stew broth or stuffed inside a whole fish before baking or grilling it. This is more of a Provençal technique and I don't believe I've ever seen this done in southern Italy.

Fennel and anise are flavors I often use interchangeably. I sometimes opt for aniseeds over fennel when I want a sweeter, less vegetable flavor, but since they're very anisey, I'll only use a few to flavor a big pot of fish soup. Fennel-flavored liquor such as French pastis (Ricard and Pernod are good brand names) or Italian anise-flavored Sambuca or anisette can be added to a fish dish to boost its fennel or anisey flavor. Sambuca and anisette are sweeter than pastis, so unless you want a sweet note in your dish, I would opt for the latter.

Tarragon is not an herb used a lot in southern Italian cooking or in Italy in general, but I love it and consider it an extension of the fennel-anise flavor. It's overwhelming in large quantities (I would never make an all-tarragon pesto, for instance), but I will often add a few sprigs to a fennel-flavored dish to underscore this flavor. Chervil, although not a popular herb in southern Italian cooking either, fits into this world of fennel-anisey-tasting things. I've had the most success using it in salads or as a garnish for soup. Somehow I'm not crazy about it cooked; it turns a little soapy. Star anise has an absolutely beautiful aroma. I'll add a pod to a fish-stew broth or use it for poaching fruit (see Pears Poached in Malvasia and Star Anise, page 414). Licorice is popular in southern Italy for candies and to make very powerful breath fresheners, and you will often see old men sucking on licorice sticks. This is a strong, bitter flavor and something I've not found a place for in my cooking.

Basil blends very well with fennely flavors, and I often include basil in a dish where I've also added bulb fennel or fennel seeds to create a more complex flavor. A salad of thinly sliced fennel bulb tossed with red onion, basil, and olive oil is simple and perfectly balanced. Sliced fennel, olive oil, lemon juice, and shaved pecorino is my idea of another great little salad. I love bulb fennel tossed with roasted red peppers. Fennel goes extremely well with pork (see Pork Loin with Bay Leaves and Caramelized Fennel, page 242), and a pasta sauce of little chunks of pork sausage, bulb fennel, and tomato is my idea of cold-weather comfort food.

Deep red saffron threads are the stigmas—the tips of the styles—of a variety of crocus common to Mediterranean countries. In Italy, saffron is grown in Abruzzo, Sardinia, and recently in San Gimignano in Tuscany. It is thought that saffron was introduced to Sicily by the Arabs (although the Greeks may have known of it earlier), but the saffron business did not survive in Sicily, being costly and labor-intensive, though it did hang around long enough to influence their cooking. Piacentinu, one of Sicily's best-loved cheeses, is scented with saffron, and the island has recently started to reestablish its saffron crop, but it is in the early stages. I usually buy Spanish saffron. I buy one-ounce amounts of Spanish saffron threads in colorful tins in Middle Eastern or Indian spice shops. I know this sounds like a lot of saffron to buy at one time, but I keep it in the freezer so it stays moist, and it lasts about a year that way. You can buy tiny amounts at a time, but this is very expensive. Check the packaging date on the tin; it should be no older than two years for optimum freshness. You really shouldn't bother with powdered saffron, which is often sold mixed with other ingredients like turmeric.

To get the most bang for your buck from saffron threads, you'll need to grind them to a powder. Adding whole threads to a sauce is wasteful, because they won't dissolve completely. The threads are often a bit moist, making them hard to grind, so it's a good idea to toast them first. Then they can be dissolved easily in a few tablespoons of warm water (it will turn the water a deep orangey yellow), or just added directly to a warm, liquidy dish, where their flavor will blossom. I sometimes grind toasted fennel seeds together with saffron threads to use as a spice base.

> **TOASTING AND GRINDING SAFFRON THREADS:** Put the saffron threads in a small, dry skillet and stir them over very low heat until brittle, about 30 seconds. Transfer to a mortar and grind with a pestle.

When I first started experimenting with saffron in my cooking, I wasn't always thrilled with the results. Saffron can be tricky. I've discovered I need much less to produce a beautiful flavor and deep golden color. When you smell saffron, you'll notice a slight floral fragrance with an underlining hint of what to me smells like iodine, but in a good way. This is what gives saffron its alluring depth of flavor, which can be delicate and almost elusive. If you add too much saffron, its flavor can swing toward medicinal and become bitter. Adding saffron in small amounts (about 6 ground threads will perfume a big pot of fish stew to serve 6) and adding it toward the end of cooking so it is in contact with heat only briefly, will preserve its sweet tones and not allow the bitter ones to come forward.

I often add saffron to a stew or sauce as a single flavoring, so I can really show it off. It blends effortlessly into a base of tomatoes and white wine, and is carried and enlivened by olive oil. In addition to pairing it with fennel, Sicilian cooks will blend it with a discreet amount of garlic to produce a warm, rounded aroma; this is especially enticing in a lamb stew or ragù. Saffron with basil is a marriage made in heaven, and I use these flavors in Calamari and Artichoke Rice Salad (page 168). If you're looking for an unusual and delicious seasoning for a fish soup, try saffron mixed with orange zest, added to a white wine and fish broth base. Ground saffron can be mixed into soft goat cheese or ricotta to fill scooped-out summer tomatoes.

FISH MARINATED WITH FENNEL AND SAFFRON

SERVES FOUR AS A MAIN COURSE

MARINADE

> 1 tablespoon fennel seeds, toasted and coarsely ground with a mortar and pestle
> 3 garlic cloves, crushed
> $1/4$ cup extra-virgin olive oil
> $1/4$ cup Pernod or another brand of pastis
> Large pinch of saffron threads, toasted, ground, and dissolved in a few tablespoons of warm water (see page 42)
> Leaves from 5 or 6 large thyme sprigs, chopped
> Grated zest of 1 lemon
> Grated zest of 1 lime
> Freshly ground black pepper to taste
> Salt to taste
>
> 4 skinless fish fillets, about 8 ounces each (sea bass is a good choice)

Mix all the marinade ingredients together in a small bowl. Put the fish fillets in a glass or ceramic baking dish large enough to hold them in one layer. Pour on the marinade, turning the fish over in it several times until well coated. Cover with plastic wrap and refrigerate for at least 1 hour so the fish can develop flavor.

Preheat the oven to 500°F.

Season the fish well with salt, and roast until tender and just starting to flake when you poke into it with a knife, 6 to 8 minutes, depending on the thickness of your fillets.

NUTMEG AND CINNAMON

THE FLAVOR OF NUTMEG-SCENTED RICOTTA has been etched in my memory since childhood as pure pleasure. My mother always added a bit of nutmeg to her ricotta filling for lasagne or stuffed shells. She used the preground stuff from a bottle, but its sweet aroma shot through the air to fill the kitchen. I'm now a bit of a nutmeg fiend. As they do in southern Italy, I add it to many preparations that contain ricotta, such as cannoli filling. Nutmeg is what gives pancetta its suaveness, and it's used to flavor some dried pork sausages.

I also use nutmeg in ways not traditional to southern Italian cooking—in salad dressings, for instance. When I want to tame a vinaigrette, especially if I'm going to use it on a seafood salad, where I don't want anything too sharp that might compete with the delicate sea flavors, I sometimes add a few scrapings of nutmeg, and it seems to bring the oil and vinegar together in a mellower bond. I love it rubbed into fish, usually along with lemon zest, before baking for a mellow marinade. Sometimes, when a tomato sauce cooks up a bit acidy, I'll grate a little nutmeg into it (the southern Italian grandma's equivalent to a pinch of sugar). A few scrapings of nutmeg added to a fish stew give it a warm tone, softening any overt brininess from shellfish. I also include a few scrapings to soften the bitter edges of cooked escarole or broccoli rabe. If the wine I've added to a fish stew tastes a little obvious, I sometimes add a pinch of nutmeg to cut its acidity. Nutmeg underscores the sweetness in lobster or shrimp, and one of my favorite ways to cook squid is in a slow braise with white wine, tomato, and pinches of both nutmeg and cinnamon. I also add a pinch of nutmeg to *olivata* (olive paste) and to roasted red peppers, just to introduce warmth. When I make spaghetti dressed with anchovies and olive oil and the result is too assertive, a few gratings of fresh nutmeg will usually bring it into balance.

I tend to add nutmeg early, putting it into the olive oil while I'm sautéing onions or garlic, for instance, when its flavor can really open up. If I need to add it later, into a liquidy stew or a soup, for instance, as a flavor adjuster, I grate it in and let it sit for at least twenty minutes so it can integrate itself into the dish. Otherwise, it can taste a touch medicinal. Pregrated nutmeg loses its aroma very quickly, so I always buy whole nutmeg and grate it myself.

Mace is the lacy skin of the nutmeg, and often the nutmeg I buy has the mace covering still attached; I'll pull it off and grind it in a spice grinder (it is brittle and hard to grate with a hand grater). Mace smells like nutmeg, but more so. You can use it the same way, but you should add a little less.

I was amazed when I learned how a pinch of cinnamon can transform a dish. When I recreated a cinnamon-scented ravioli my mother had described from her childhood memories, I was unsure how much cinnamon to add, since she had said things like "It was cinnamony but not too cinnamony." I decided to add just a pinch to a pound of ricotta, and the result was a sweet, exotic taste that came through in the ravioli even after it was covered with tomato sauce. Cinnamon adds warmth to eggplant and lamb, and it's a traditional addition to the crust of a Neapolitan *pizza rustico* (a cheese and meat pie). I added a cinnamon stick to a wine-and-tomato-based calamari stew and it produced a mouthwatering aroma that filled the kitchen; this is now one of my favorite recipes.

In Sicily, I've tasted cinnamon in things where no cinnamon had been added, in bread and in lamb dishes, for instance. It's hard to say what accounts for this, but I have a feeling it's something in the soil or herbs eaten by animals, or maybe just my own romancing of a place I love.

My mother's grandmother made a cinnamon-laced pig's blood pudding called *sanguinaccio* that was sweet, and my mother remembers it not unfondly. You can still find it at certain pastry shops on Arthur Avenue in the Bronx, and when I've tasted it there I found it deep, rich, and heavy with cinnamon, chocolate, and candied fruit. It's not something I want to eat every day, but it shows how this spice can even make something as unappealing as blood taste good (the chocolate doesn't hurt, either).

I keep whole cinnamon sticks in my kitchen to throw into stews. One stick simmered in a stew or ragù for an hour or more will release a pronounced cinnamon flavor, which is sometimes what I want. I'll break a stick in half if I want less. Being ground is what really gives cinnamon a strong flavor. It's easy to overdo it, so always add less than you think you need, let the dish sit for a few minutes so the flavor can open up, and then taste. You can always add a little more. Cinnamon sticks are hard to grate with a hand grater, so I usually buy small packages of ground cinnamon to use in pastry doughs or ricotta fillings where a whole stick would be awkward.

VINAIGRETTE WITH NUTMEG, ANCHOVY, AND MARJORAM

MAKES ABOUT ONE-HALF CUP OF VINAIGRETTE, ENOUGH FOR A LARGE HEAD OF ESCAROLE, CAULIFLOWER, OR BROCCOLI I use this slightly sweet and savory vinaigrette on green salads, especially ones containing a bitter green such as escarole, but it's also wonderful tossed with vegetables such as cauliflower or broccoli that have been cut into florets, boiled until tender, drained, and dressed while still hot so they can soak up all the flavors.

1 garlic clove, crushed
2 oil-packed anchovy fillets, minced
Juice of $1/2$ small lemon
Tiny pinch of sugar
Pinch of salt
6 scrapings of fresh nutmeg
$1/3$ cup extra-virgin olive oil
Freshly ground black pepper to taste
Leaves from 3 to 4 small sprigs marjoram, coarsely chopped

In a small bowl, place the garlic clove, minced anchovy, lemon juice, sugar, salt, and the nutmeg, and stir everything around until well blended (the lemon juice will dissolve the sugar and salt and soften the nutmeg, gently releasing their flavors). Add the olive oil in a slow stream, whisking it the entire time. Add a few gratings of pepper and the marjoram and whisk briefly to blend. Taste for seasoning, adding extra salt if needed, or more oil or lemon to get a good balance of mellow to acid. Use right away, but remove the garlic clove before you do.

PANCETTA AND SALUMI

MY SISTER CLAIMS THAT I put a little bit of pork in everything. That's not quite true, but I do use pancetta a lot. A secret southern Italian cooks have for boosting the flavor of soups, stuffings, vegetables, and sauces is the addition of little bits of pancetta, salami, or fatty prosciutto end to produce big flavor at little cost. This creative technique was developed to provide flavor that could be missing in a poor region with little access to opulent cuts of meat. I often find dishes with touches of meat flavoring more appealing than roasts or other large cuts. Pancetta is a cured but not smoked bacon cut that was made for cooking. The flavor is subtle and sophisticated, with hints of nutmeg, and lots of fat streaked with slivers of meat. American bacon, with its heavy smoke flavor, can never really be a substitute.

Pancetta needs relatively slow cooking to render its fat. I use it as an underpinning for many pasta sauces and stews, adding it even before onion or garlic so the fatty part can melt and the meat part can crisp up into savory nuggets. I usually chop it into small dice. Pancetta is also good for giving deep flavor to out-of-season vegetables. It does wonders for mushrooms, and I always add a little when I'm sautéing green beans. Fatty prosciutto ends are also good for that, and several of my local Italian markets sell the little chunks, which are unsuitable for slicing but excellent for cooking. Ask if you don't see them; it just might be that they routinely get thrown away. My markets make me pay for them, but you may get a chunk for free. If you see something called guanciale in your Italian market, it's cured pork cheek. It's used like pancetta, but to my palate has much more flavor.

Lardo, a cured pork fat, is something that health concerns seem to be driving out of style in southern Italy, and it's not particularly popular here either. But it does have its place, and I sometimes prefer it to pancetta for flavoring (it's really just the fatty part of pancetta without the meat section). I use it when I don't want little bits of crisp pork floating around in a dish, since lardo melts beautifully. I find slabs of it at my local Italian shop, usually seasoned with rosemary, black pepper, salt, and garlic, which gives food it's cooked in a lovely flavor. Real Italian lardo is not yet available here, but look for domestic brands in Italian specialty shops. Niman Ranch, a first-rate organic meat farm, makes a very good slab lardo (see Sources, page 436).

I remember big tubs of rendered lard from my grandmother's kitchen, and it's still used in Sicily for traditional renditions of cannoli pastry and pie crusts, but I don't find much use for it, preferring butter or olive oil in pastries. Prosciutto cotto—cooked ham—goes into Neapolitan calzones and is a good choice for pasta dishes where salt-cured prosciutto might turn rubbery with cooking.

Almost every area in the south has its own local cured hams and salumi, some flavored with black peppercorns, some with hot chilies, or more subtly with nutmeg, fennel, cinnamon, or wine. Soppressata, a fatty sausage made throughout the south, is different in each region and sometimes from town to town; capocollo, cured pork shoulder or neck, is famous in Calabria and in the area of Martina Franca in Puglia for its suave flavor, but unfortunately neither is available here (except domestically made), nor are any other cured pork products from southern Italy.

As of this writing, only several types of prosciutto from northern Italy and mortadella from Bologna are allowed into this country, since nothing else has yet met our FDA requirements. This is sad, because most of the domestic stuff has a slightly sharp taste that lingers at the back of my throat. My guess is that it has to do with the American overuse of preservatives. I'm always pretty happy though with the salami made by Faicco's Pork Shop in Greenwich Village in New York. (Unfortunately, Faicco's is too small to do mail order, but if you're in the city, it's a great old-fashioned Italian food shop to visit. See page 437 for its address.) Zingerman's carries fine salamis made by Francois Vecchio that all have excellent flavor but are not strictly southern Italian style. Volpi and Oldani are good brands you can find in Italian specialty shops. You don't want to cook with salami, since heating destroys its flavor and texture, but just add it toward or at the end of cooking. I like to add slivers of capocollo or soppressata as an accent to pasta, salad, or vegetable dishes.

ARUGULA SALAD WITH SOPPRESSATA, SUN-DRIED TOMATOES, AND PECORINO

SERVES ONE AS A MAIN COURSE SALAD Here's a southern Italian–inspired pantry salad I often make myself for lunch or dinner when I'm home alone.

1 small bunch arugula, stemmed
Leaves from 1 small endive
2 very thin slices red onion
5 thin slices soppressata, cut into matchsticks
4 oil-packed sun-dried tomatoes, cut into thin strips
6 generous shavings aged pecorino cheese
6 whole fresh basil leaves
2 tablespoons extra-virgin olive oil
Few drops red wine vinegar
2 or 3 scrapings freshly grated nutmeg
Salt and freshly ground black pepper to taste
1 small handful pine nuts, toasted (see page 61)

Put the arugula and endive in a salad bowl. Add the red onion, soppressata, sun-dried tomatoes, and pecorino. Scatter on the basil leaves. Drizzle on the oil and give the salad a toss. Add the red wine vinegar, a little nutmeg (very nice with the salami), salt, and black pepper. Give it another gentle toss and scatter on the pine nuts. Eat right away.

BUYING SOUTHERN ITALIAN CHEESE IN AMERICA

ONE THING I'VE LEARNED from eating and cooking with southern Italian cheeses is that many of them are basically variations of mozzarella. Caciocavallo and scamorza are two types of aged mozzarella. So is provolone, but it's usually aged longer, giving it a sharper flavor and firm texture. They all belong to the *pasta filata* family, cheeses that are pulled and stretched like taffy and then molded, giving them a slightly layered texture and, most important, the ability to melt beautifully when heated, making them perfect for use in classic southern Italian baked ziti, eggplant parmigiano, and lasagne.

Mozzarella is the glory of the Campanian table. The most delicious mozzarella is made from buffalo milk. It is pillow soft but firm enough to hold its shape, and creamy white, and has a slight tang to it. If you go to the Caserta, Battipaglia, Aversa, or areas around Salerno where the finest cheese comes from, the sellers will tell you it's best the day it's made. Volpetti, a fabulous cheese shop in Rome, makes a big deal out of getting its cheese as soon as it's made, and therefore carries it only a few days a week.

I was skeptical when I first started noticing imported buffalo mozzarella in New York markets. I tried it several times and found most of it too sour, just a little over the hill. After shopping around I did finally find a place that carries it as fresh as it can be. But you should always ask when the cheese arrived and how long it took to ship (not that you'll always get an honest answer). Any type of mozzarella is very perishable, especially after being flown across the ocean. As special as buffalo mozzarella is, I feel freshness is more important, so more often I buy cow's milk mozzarella (usually called fior di latte in Italy to distinguish it from buffalo mozzarella), from cheese shops in my neighborhood that make it on the premises. DiPalo's, on Grand Street in New York's Little Italy, makes the best mozzarella in the city, and the long lines on weekends attest to this. Although Little Italy long ago collapsed into one big tourist trap, DiPalo's cheese shop has only gotten better. It has been run for years by the DiPalo family, originally from Basilicata. You can mail-order aged cheeses from them; they're not comfortable mailing out their fragile homemade ricotta and mozzarella, but if you're in town, their shop is well worth visiting.

Burrata is a type of mozzarella that's a specialty of Puglia. It is a ball of semifirm mozzarella with a core of very soft mozzarella mixed with heavy cream. It is exquisite and luscious. I've been served it in Puglia as part of antipasto assortments, one time decorated with pomegranate seeds and almonds. It is made in the towns of Andria and Martina Franca in southern Puglia, where they produce regular cow's milk mozzarella as well. Several cheese shops in Manhattan have it flown in from Puglia. I've bought it in New York when it was sweet and delicious and also when it was way past its prime. One time when I spoke to Lou DiPalo (the owner of DiPalo's on Grand Street), he told me that he had temporarily stopped ordering it because a heat wave in southern

Italy had made it less than perfect. Manteca is a drier version of burrata, with a center made from heated ricotta whey instead of soft cream mixed with mozzarella. This cheese is less delicate than burrata, and you can find good imported versions that are consistently fresh. Burrini is a similar type of aged mozzarella with a core of butter. As for smoked mozzarella, I've never been a big fan of it, and I have to say I never use it in cooking. I find its smokiness overpowering.

Caciocavallo, scamorza, and provolone are flavors from my childhood. They remind me of the opulent antipasto platters my father used to assemble when my parents had big parties (which was often). They are cow's milk cheeses, often formed in big waxy-looking balls or long logs and tied with rope. American versions of them have long been available, and they are for the most part what I grew up with, but now that I've tasted the real thing, I find most of the American ones too salty and lacking in finesse. It can take a little hunting to find imported ones, but they are definitely worth seeking out.

I sometimes find a caciocavallo called ragusano (Ragusa is a lovely Baroque town in eastern Sicily), a famous high-quality cheese that is worth looking for. Caciocavallo silano is originally from the Sila mountain region of Calabria and now made in other areas of the south as well; caciocavallo Podolico is made from the milk of the Podolico cow and is manufactured in many parts of southern Italy. I can find all three of these cheeses at my local markets on a fairly regular basis. Scamorza from the Abruzzi region is what I most often run across. Good, sharp imported provolone with real flavor is harder to find in this country. The few really good ones I've found have all been from Calabria. Provola is yet another of these aged mozzarella-type cheeses. The ones I've eaten in Campania have been made from buffalo milk and have had a complex, tangy flavor. Buon Italia sometimes carries them.

Pecorino, which is made from sheep's milk, is southern Italy's grating cheese (although firm aged caciocavallo is also good for grating). Pecorino crotonese from Calabria is pungent and salty, and I love it grated over a sausage ragù or over a dish of sautéed eggplant. Pecorino siciliano, which can be mild, or sharper with age, is very hard to locate in this country; the only one I regularly see in my market is pepato, which is studded with black peppercorns. I occasionally find Sicilian primo sale, a delicious young pecorino, and I love it drizzled with honey. Canestrato pugliese, shaped like a basket, is sharp, pleasantly salty, and excellent for grating over pasta. DiPalo's cheese shop carries a pecorino from the family's home region of Basilicata.

I've always loved ricotta. I love southern Italian ricotta cheesecake scented with orange flower water. A bowl of cannoli filling can occasionally be my idea of an excellent meal (I even like the candied citron most people pick out and put aside). I find hot pasta tossed with ricotta, aged pecorino, and a few grindings of coarse black pepper to be one of the most delicious dishes imaginable. I think of ricotta as a gentle pillow that cushions the bold flavors of the southern Italian kitchen.

Ricotta is traditionally made from the whey left over after cheesemaking (*ricotta* actually means "recooked," or "cooked again," and it's considered not so much a cheese as a cheese by-product). In Campania, they make ricotta from the whey of buffalo mozzarella. That, in my opinion, is the best ricotta. I sometimes find imported buffalo ricotta in my markets, but often it's a little past its prime after its flight over. Ricotta made from cow's milk mozzarella is also very good. Many Italian shops in this country that make their own mozzarella also make ricotta, and you know it's fresh. In Sicily, I've mostly been served sheep's milk ricotta, made from the whey of pecorino cheese. It's creamy, with a sweet, tangy taste. Sheep's milk ricotta goes into cannoli fillings in Sicily, giving the pastries a slightly sheepy flavor that took me some time to get used to (not too much time, though). Old Chatham Sheepherding Company in Old Chatham, New York, makes a wonderful sheep's milk ricotta that's sold at many supermarkets in the United States (see page 437). When I can't find, or don't have the time to search out, shop-made or another special mozzarella, I'll buy a supermarket brand, like Calabro, which is fine for cooking. Supermarket brands can sometimes be watery. If any ricotta you purchase seems very loose or has liquid floating on the top, I suggest draining it in a colander for about half an hour before using it, especially if you plan to cook it.

Ricotta salata is dried, salted ricotta. It's used as a grating cheese in Sicily, and I often reach for it when I want a bold cheese accent in a dish. *Ricotta informata*, baked ricotta, is another Sicilian specialty. It's slow-baked until it's golden brown on the surface and the inside is dry and crumbly. Cacioricotta is an aged ricotta that is used to grate over pasta in Puglia, and ricotta forte is another specialty of Puglia, a very peculiar one: a strong aged ricotta that looks like a beige paste you might use to fill in floor tiles. It tastes something like whipped, extremely pungent blue cheese, not, in my opinion, in a completely appealing way. Maybe you have to grow up eating it. When I first tasted it, in Puglia, it did make some sense stirred into the pasta with chickpeas I had ordered, along with the very acidic white wine I was drinking. Its taste was manageable then, but when I bought an imported container of it from DiPalo's, the taste was so startling, I just couldn't fit it into my life.

There are big industrial cheese producers and small artisanal cheese makers in southern Italy. Generally speaking, the stuff you find in the United States is from the larger producers. This doesn't mean the cheeses you find here aren't good; it just means that when you travel to southern Italy and sample local cheeses, you'll be in for a great treat, like when I tasted the sharp, complex, tangy, and sweet caciocavallo made in the area of Castelfranco in Miscano where my grandmother was born. Many local cheeses never make it out of their neighborhoods.

The best way to find out which southern Italian cheeses are available to you is just to ask at a good cheese shop if they have any cheeses from Puglia, for instance, or if they have any cheeses from Sicily. I do this routinely, and it's how I've discovered that many cheeses I had eaten in southern Italy, such as burrata, were available here. Also, Italian food websites like Esperya.com tend to carry a changing selection of Italian cheeses, usually listed by region, so you can just look up cheeses from Calabria or Basilicata and see what they have.

As much as I love finding southern Italian cheeses to use in my cooking, I don't always want to run all over town looking for a Puglian pecorino (although the preceding paragraphs may make it sound like I do). So, I may substitute a Sardinian pecorino or an aged Tuscan pecorino, which are much easier to find. Spanish Manchego is a great sheep's milk cheese that I find aged and young in my supermarkets, and its flavor works very well in most pasta or baked dishes. Parrmigiano-Reggiano and grana padano, two famous cow's milk cheeses from in and around Parma, are obviously not southern Italian, but southern Italians know a good thing when they taste it, and both of these cheeses are used periodically in southern Italian dishes (especially at fancy restaurants). When I want a sweeter, mellower flavor than a pecorino can give me, I use one of these fine cheeses. In my opinion, the pecorino romano exported into this country is too sharp and clunky tasting and throws southern Italian dishes out of balance.

COOKING WITH SOUTHERN ITALIAN CHEESES

An interesting thing about cooks in southern Italy is that they don't go in for the strict no-cheese-with-fish thinking that prevails in most other parts of Italy. They've found great ways to blend the two. You'll find cheese in stuffings for fish, in savory fish tarts, in fish casseroles, and baked with fish in pastas. You'll taste tuna with caciocavallo, mozzarella mixed with anchovies, pecorino with mussels, and swordfish *involtini* from Sicily, which almost always has a touch of cheese in the filling. A traditional dish from Puglia called *tiedda,* or *tiella,* is a baked casserole of mussels and potatoes. Sometimes, rice, zucchini, or tomatoes are added, but grated pecorino is a must; it melts in the heat of the oven and sharpens all the flavors. This is a very successful blending of seemingly incongruous elements, where cheese and seafood meet and mingle effortlessly.

For a simpler version of the mussels and cheese concept, see the recipe for baked mussels on page 164. For another traditional example of this pairing, take a look at Swordfish Pie with a Sweet Orange Crust (page 52), which blends swordfish, oranges, olives, raisins, pine nuts, and pecorino to spectacular effect. To me, clams are too briny to handle any type of cheese, and I can't recall one time I've been served clams with cheese anywhere in southern Italy. And even though baked pastas or tarts containing seafood often include cheese, nowhere, to my knowledge, will you find grated cheese sprinkled over a pasta containing seafood. Bread crumbs usually replace the cheese in that case. When cheese and seafood are combined, it is not done in a haphazard way but with a sure culinary spirit that guarantees its worthiness.

One thing to keep in mind when cooking with most southern Italian cheeses is that even the good exported stuff can be a little salty. I always taste a piece of cheese to check for salt. Some caciocavallo and provolone can be very salty, and you might want to include only a very little bit of it in your dish.

HOMEMADE RICOTTA

MAKES ABOUT TWO CUPS You can make ricotta at home using whole milk. The result may not be as rich tasting as when made from whey, but the flavor is very good.

3 quarts whole milk
¼ teaspoon sea salt
⅓ cup fresh lemon juice

Pour the milk into a large saucepan. Add the sea salt and stir to blend it into the milk (the salt is very important for bringing out the flavor in the finished ricotta). Bring to a very low boil over medium heat. Add the lemon juice and stir briefly to blend. Bring back to a very low boil and cook for about 1 minute. You will start to see little white particles coagulate on the surface. This means the curds are starting to form. Don't let the milk cook any longer than about 1 minute or you may wind up with hard, dry curds instead of the soft, creamy texture you are after. Remove the pan from the heat and cover. Let the ricotta sit for about 20 minutes, untouched. This will allow bigger, more substantial curds to form.

Line a colander or a tightly woven wicker basket with cheesecloth or a muslin dish cloth. Gently pour the ricotta into the cloth, being careful not to break up the curds too much (the best approach is to tilt the pot against the colander or basket right up at the rim; free-fall pouring may be too violent). Let this drain at room temperature for about 1 hour. You will now have a rather moist ricotta, the way I like it. If you prefer it drier, you can tie and hang the cheesecloth over the sink or a bowl so the ricotta can drain more thoroughly. The ricotta is now ready to use. You may refrigerate it, but it will stay really fresh and sweet only for about 2 days. If you plan on baking with the ricotta, drain it well.

Note that ricotta is best served either freshly made and still slightly warm or at room temperature, but not straight from the refrigerator.

1. Put the ricotta in a large shallow serving bowl. Surround it with black olives (Gaeta and niçoise are good choices), drizzle with your best olive oil, and season with ground black pepper and a scattering of minced fresh rosemary or thyme. Serve with simple bruschetta (Italian bread slices toasted, rubbed with garlic, and brushed with olive oil).

2. Put the ricotta in the center of a serving platter. Surround with roasted red pepper slices or oven-roasted tomatoes, French breakfast radishes (the long kind), and thin slices of soppressata or other salami. Season with a grating of fresh nutmeg and a generous drizzle of olive oil. Serve with a loaf of good Italian bread.

3. Serve the ricotta in small bowls, drizzled with wildflower honey and dusted with ground cinnamon. Surround it with sliced fresh figs, if you like. Or, top the ricotta with a sprinkling of finely ground espresso coffee or cocoa and confectioners' sugar. Serve with plain sugar cookies.

4. Serve *crostini* (little toasted bread rounds made from a baguette), each topped with 1 tablespoon ricotta, 1 or 2 marinated fresh anchovies, which you can buy in many Italian specialty stores (or see Marinated Anchovies on Mozzarella Crostini, page 154), and a scattering of chopped fresh herbs such as parsley, basil, or marjoram.

5. Place a generous dollop of ricotta on top of hot pasta dressed with a tomato sauce or a southern Italian–style ragù.

BASIL, MINT, AND PARSLEY

MINT, BASIL, AND FLAT-LEAF PARSLEY are the fresh, leafy herbs my culinary mind registers as the flavors of casual summer cooking. They are the "scattering herbs" I'm more likely to add to a dish in the last minutes of cooking or shower over the top right before bringing the dish to the table, so their flavors remain bright. The charms of these three herbs can be fleeting, easily lost to heat, so I don't often actually cook with them. Rawness is their appeal. I chop them lightly, with a few quick, precise strokes, or I add leaves whole (for more on chopping fresh herbs, see page 57).

A tomato and mozzarella salad is a wonderful thing, but it approaches perfection when you add fresh basil leaves, making it the classic *caprese* salad from the island of Capri, off the coast of Naples. Throughout the Naples area, basil and tomatoes have an intimate association, and I always find that when I need to throw together a summer meal on the spur of the moment, if I make a big bunch of basil and some juicy tomatoes the main components, I can satisfy anybody's desire for summer flavors. Linguine and clam sauce is incomplete without the abundant parsley I always add at the last minute, which mixes with the clams' briny juices to create an entirely new flavor. I associate parsley so much with seafood that even when I taste a leaf on its own I imagine I discern a slight sea taste. The marriage of white wine, parsley, and seafood is a classic southern coastal flavoring and one that brings memories of my family's own vacation and holiday cooking.

These leafy herbs have the ability to lighten up a rich dish but also can add complexity to a simple one. Fresh mint is what gives Sicily's sweet-and-sour (*agrodolce*) sauces their finishing touch, lifting their richness. Often in summer, I make salads of nothing more than a pile of whole fresh basil, mint, and parsley leaves lightly dressed with good olive oil and sea salt—altogether a wonderful bed for grilled meat or fish. Basil leaves alone tossed with a thinly sliced fennel bulb and coated with olive oil make a beautiful match of flavors. Fresh mint, basil, or parsley scattered over a tomato and mozzarella pizza hot from a wood-burning oven provides an intense burst of flavor that exemplifies southern cooking at its most brilliant. I was surprised to discover that mint is a flavoring in a classic Sicilian pesto (see Baked Mussels with Sicilian Nut Pesto on page 164). Since travelling to Sicily, I've used mint more and more in my cooking. It makes a nice change from basil in a tomato sauce (especially if you throw in a few capers or green olives as well), and I love mint and basil with fresh fruit. I've added mint to my fig crostata (page 402), and I include basil in Peach and Basil Pizza (page 410).

None of these herbs dries successfully, so I don't bother with that at all (dried mint does have an interesting aroma and is used in some Middle Eastern cooking, but its taste strikes me as out of place in southern Italian dishes). You can usually now find fresh herbs year-round (although they will not be as fragrant and abundant as in the summer). But I seldom use basil in the winter—mainly because I want to keep it special and save it for the summer.

I usually use one principal herb at a time, since I like to streamline my cooking down to essential flavors, but sometimes a combination of two or more herbs is just what I'm looking for. When I want the taste of mint but don't want its chewing-gum-like quality, I'll mix it with a few basil leaves, which soften its strident tones. Parsley is one of my favorite herbs, and I often let it shine on its own, but it can also round out other flavors. Parsley mixed with a few mint leaves is a taste I often use to flavor fish when I think parsley alone would be too predictable. Parsley and basil together have a surprisingly complex taste that stands up to intense meat dishes; they're delicious scattered over a platter of grilled pork sausages. Southern Italy has a wild mint called *mentuccia* that I've tasted on artichokes, fava beans, wild mushrooms, and fish, and in a tripe dish. It has a complex but more subtle taste than our spearmint and peppermint, which are bold but can be a little one-note. By mixing spearmint with a few leaves of basil and a few sprigs of marjoram leaves I get a taste somewhat like my memory of *mentuccia*.

PESTO WITH THE TASTE OF MENTUCCIA

MAKES ABOUT THREE-QUARTERS OF A CUP Here's a bright green mixed-herb pesto with a taste somewhat like southern Italy's wild mint. It contains no cheese, so it's loosely textured and also quite versatile. I sometimes add a dollop of it to a seafood salad or a bowl of boiled new potatoes, or I spoon a little over roasted asparagus or into a skillet of sautéed artichokes. It's also pleasing tossed with rice or pasta or used as a dressing for grilled fish or chicken.

As you've probably noticed, pesto can turn from bright green to a drab olive in no time, due to oxidation. If you blanch the herbs for a few seconds, as here, the problem disappears.

1 packed cup fresh flat-leaf parsley leaves
½ cup loosely packed mint leaves, preferably spearmint
Leaves from 3 marjoram sprigs
½ cup whole blanched almonds
1 small summer garlic clove
1 small green chili, such as a jalapeño, seeded and coarsely chopped
Salt to taste
Pinch of sugar
½ cup extra-virgin olive oil

In a medium pot of boiling water, blanch the parsley, mint, and marjoram for about 30 seconds. Using a large skimmer, transfer the herbs to a colander. Run cold water over them until they're cold and their bright green color has come up. Squeeze out all the water with your hands.

In a food processor, combine the almonds, garlic, and chili and pulse several times until everything is well ground. Add the blanched herbs, salt, sugar, and olive oil. Pulse again several times until the pesto is smooth, but not puréed (you want a bit of texture). Use right away, or cover and refrigerate for up to 2 days. After that, its flavor begins to fade (but its color shouldn't).

HOW TO CHOP HERBS

My first cooking job was at an all-night bistro in the meat-packing district of Manhattan. I was the assistant lunch cook, arriving at about 6:30 A.M. along with the local transvestite hookers, who waited for me to open the door so they could use the bathroom to freshen up. You might think this morning scene would set the tone for the restaurant, and in a way it did, but the kitchen was strictly run. Many repetitive tasks had to be done constantly. My most tedious duty was what our Ecuadorian prep cooks accurately called "parsley ball." It consisted of picking and washing huge bunches of parsley, mounding the wet leaves on a work space, and chopping them into minuscule bits, which would take at least twenty minutes of relentless knife work. Then I'd scrape the pulverized green mush off the counter, dump it onto a kitchen towel, and wring all the moisture and flavor out of it by twisting and twisting the towel in opposite directions at both ends. The result was a big ball of moss that got jammed into little bowls and distributed to the various cooking stations, to be sprinkled on just about everything that came out of the kitchen.

This abuse of healthy herbs really irked me, and I have since made it a point to treat herbs kindly and gently. Fresh herbs, I feel, should be chopped as little as possible, just enough to release their fragrance. One or two clean chops with a big chef's knife should do it. Overchopping bruises the leaf and deposits much of its flavor on the cutting board.

And sometimes I don't even bother to chop them at all. I love adding whole leaves of a tender herb to a dish right before serving it. To me, the whole leaves of some herb varieties have a different flavor from chopped ones, especially leaves of flat-leaf parsley, which have a slight sea-salt taste that blends beautifully with cold seafood salads. Whole basil leaves seem spicier to me than chopped ones, and I often include a handful of small ones in a green salad just to wake it up.

Herbs don't need to be scrupulously stemmed unless the stems are very woody or thick. You can be a bit casual about picking tender leaves from parsley, tarragon, chervil, mint, or other soft, feathery herbs; their stems have incredible flavor and are easy to bite into. Thyme, rosemary, and sometimes basil and oregano, if they are mature, can have tough or thick stems which are fine in a slow-cooked dish where they will eventually be fished out, but which should be removed before scattering them raw.

Try to cut fresh herbs right before you use them, to capture all their potential.

OREGANO, ROSEMARY, AND BAY LEAVES

ROSEMARY, OREGANO, AND BAY LEAVES are robust herbs that give an earthy character to much southern Italian cooking. Oregano is most commonly recognized in Neapolitan food, but it's used in Sicily and throughout the south, often paired with tomato or garlic, or used alone to season grilled meat or fish. They prefer dried oregano, because fresh oregano can be a little harsh on the tongue. Drying brings out a sweetness in the herb that is not apparent when it's fresh. When you visit a food market in Sicily or Campania, you'll see large branches of dried oregano hanging upside down. Many cooks also dry their own. High-quality dried oregano has a lovely, powerful perfume that I've tasted many times in my travels through southern Italy. I've purchased imported dried oregano on the branch, usually from Sicily, in food shops in New York, but I've never been completely happy with it; it always seems harsh to me. Oregano's flavor varies from area to area in southern Italy, in some places sweeter, in others more bitter, and I think they usually export the bitter stuff. As a result I don't find myself using much dried oregano in my cooking.

When I can find very young, fresh oregano with little bitterness I use it, sparingly, but for the most part I almost always reach for fresh marjoram over any oregano I can find in this country. Marjoram is similar in taste to oregano but much more floral and sweet. Southern Italian cooks do sometimes use marjoram interchangeably with oregano, and it's a very popular herb in the cooking of Capri. It's powerful enough that I generally use only a few sprigs in a dish, sometimes tempering them with parsley. When I want that classic Neapolitan pizza taste in a dish (if I'm making a steak *pizzaiola,* for instance), I may mix a pinch of dried oregano with a few sprigs of fresh marjoram. Unfortunately, most of the dried oregano you buy here in little bottles is terribly harsh, and in my opinion can overpower and even ruin your cooking.

I never realized how special bay leaves were until I began buying them fresh. The dried ones in little bottles are always musty, even before they get to sit in your pantry for a few years. It would never have occurred to me I'd want this flavor to stand out in a dish. Fresh leaves are another story completely. Their aroma is powerful and intoxicating. When I'm looking for a complex, deep flavor in a stew or a sauce, I often include a fresh bay leaf. Sometimes, one is all I want to mingle with other flavors; sometimes I want bay in abundance, so I'll add a lot of leaves so their flavor can really take over. I love the latter approach with a pork roast. Sometimes I line a serving platter with fresh bay leaves and pile sautéed shrimp right on top so that the heat from the shrimp releases the bay aroma, allowing it to waft up into the shrimp and into the air. I also love the scent of bay with stewed calamari. I use fresh leaves as a bed for soft cheeses, so they can very gently flavor the cheeses. In Sicily, fresh bay leaves are often abundantly used to flavor baked ricotta. And they blend beautifully with orange and lemon for a fish soup. And I love one added to the poaching liquid for dried figs.

Culinary bay doesn't grow particularly well in the Northeast where I live and I hardly ever find it at my greenmarket, but I buy hothouse leaves year-round from my supermarket. The two types of bay leaves in our markets are California, which are long and narrow, and Turkish, with a pointed, more oval shape. I find both varieties fresh, but usually go for the Turkish leaves since, to my palate, they have a more subtle flavor. California bay leaves seem to impart a slight curry taste, which I don't want in my Southern Italian dishes.

I don't often find recipes using rosemary in southern Italian cookbooks, but home cooks in southern Italy use it all the time. It grows well there, and every house I've been to in Puglia or Sicily or Campania has had a few big, fat rosemary bushes that have been going strong for years. Rosemary is strong and oily. It almost reminds me of eucalyptus when I chew on a sprig. Cooking softens it, releasing its sweeter side, but it remains a powerful herb. Yet that strength is exactly why it's so appealing. Rosemary can become medicinal tasting if you overdo it. A few small sprigs thrown into a ragù or stew will release their oils slowly to develop a rich mellowness. When I want a quick hit of rosemary, I chop the spiky leaves and add some at the beginning of cooking and a tiny bit more at the end, for lively flavor. California bay leaves seem to impart a slight curry taste, which I don't want in my Southern Italian dishes.

Lamb and rosemary is a classic coupling in many cuisines, and southern Italians have certainly discovered this perfect match. In Sicily, I've noticed, many cooks also use rosemary to flavor chicken and rabbit (along with white wine and garlic). If you add a few chopped tomatoes to that you get a traditional chicken *alla cacciatora* of the Campania region (see page 254). I once was served wild mushrooms sautéed with rosemary and tossed with penne in Foggia, Puglia, and now I make it at home all the time. Lately I find myself slipping it into dishes where years ago I would have thought it improper, such as in fish preparations. Rosemary and anchovies sounded strange on paper when I first read about their coming together in Sicilian cooking, but when I tried them on a roasted fish, the taste was beautiful, the flavors brought together by olive oil and the fish roasting juices. The blending of rosemary, hot chilies, and orange zest is something I've been playing with lately, and I've found it wonderful for skillet-seared duck breasts.

Some throughts about thyme: southern Italy's preoccupation with oregano has led its cooks to overlook thyme. I use fresh thyme quite a bit in my cooking. For me it is an anchoring herb that usually somehow underscores the natural flavor of what I season with it. For instance, if I begin sautéing lamb chops or broccoli and add a few pinches of fresh thyme, I somehow don't taste the thyme as much as I taste the lamb and broccoli intensified. In Cavatelli with Zucchini, Potatoes, and Ricotta Salata (page 337), I sauté the zucchini with a little thyme just to deepen its flavor, but I finish the dish at the end with fresh basil. What you taste is the basil; the thyme is there to add depth of flavor. I tend to use it in vegetarian dishes the way I would anchovies or a bit of pancetta in nonvegetarian ones. It has a similar strong flavor but doesn't take over. Where oregano dominates other flavors, thyme works with them.

BRUSCHETTA WITH MARJORAM

SERVES SIX AS AN ANTIPASTO OFFERING Grilled bread brushed with olive oil is offered as a starter at many southern Italian restaurants. One that came to my table at Zaccaria, near Amalfi, was rubbed with garlic and sprinkled with dried oregano. I love a slice of bruschetta to start a meal when it's simple and you can really taste the bread and the olive oil. Here's my version.

Six ½-inch-thick slices crusty Italian bread
1 large garlic clove, halved
Extra-virgin olive oil for brushing
Sea salt for sprinkling
Leaves from 3 or 4 large marjoram sprigs, chopped

Grill the bread slices on both sides, either on an outdoor grill or on a stove-top grill pan or griddle. Quickly rub them on one side with the cut garlic clove. Brush the garlic-rubbed side liberally with olive oil, sprinkle on sea salt, and scatter on the marjoram. Serve right away.

PINE NUTS AND RAISINS

THIS FLAVOR DUO IS OFTEN MY ANSWER when I want a dish that is sweet but savory, maybe with a Sicilian feel to it, and I'm not sure how to pull it together. The combination of pine nuts and raisins turns up just about everywhere Arabs have left their footprints around the Mediterranean, including in Sicily and Naples, where this opulent combination can tranform sautéed eggplant, meatballs, or a grilled swordfish steak into something really special. It's used in *agrodolce* dishes and in conjunction with sharp flavors such as capers and green olives. Some dishes studded with pine nuts and raisins, such as Sicilian caponata (page 122), also include many other flavors, resulting in true complexity. I love those, but pine nuts and raisins added alone to a vegetable or atop a piece of fish can create a balanced dish that stands as a testament to Mediterranean creativity.

The most flavorful pine nuts I've found in this country come from Portugal. They're long, skinny, and costly. Sometimes, the package says that the nuts are Italian, but I've been told that they really came from Portugal. Chinese pine nuts are bigger and fatter, not bad when toasted, but not as flavorful as the Portuguese ones or the Spanish ones I occasionally find. A lot of restaurants in the United States use the Chinese. Kulustyan's, a really fine Middle Eastern food shop in Manhattan, carries Lebanese pine nuts, which have very good flavor. I've noticed that Zingerman's stocks piñon, or pine nuts from New Mexico that they say are incredibly flavorful, but I've yet to order any.

TOASTING PINE NUTS Whatever kind of pine nut you buy, its flavor is always improved by a light toasting. After burning many skillets of pine nuts, I've found that the best way to toast them to a uniform golden is by spreading them out on a baking sheet and putting them in a 400°F oven for 8 minutes or so. Check on them every few minutes, as they can go from golden to black in no time. I occasionally sauté them in a dry skillet if I'm in a rush, but this usually results in nuts with black spots and not the great roasted taste the oven method gives you.

American-grown raisins are much sweeter than the ones I've eaten in Sicily. I've bought *pasoli* or *pasolina* raisins at the Vucirria market in Palermo (*passoli e pinoli* is what the combination of raisins and pine nuts is called in Sicily); they are small, dark, and only slightly sweet, closer in taste and size to our dried currants. I often choose dried currants instead of raisins for fillings for meatballs or baked vegetables, because their small size keeps them put and their sweetness is more subtle. (Actually, most of the dried currants we buy are not currants at all, but a variety of mini-grapes.) Golden raisins look very pretty in some dishes, and I use them for their color. They're quite sweet, but I often plump them in a little white wine, which not only softens them but washes away some sugar while infusing them with a touch of welcome acidity (if you're using red wine in your dish, go ahead and soak them in that). I do the same with dry sweet dark raisins or dried currants.

SWISS CHARD WITH CURRANTS AND PINE NUTS

SERVES TWO AS A FIRST COURSE OR SIDE DISH Here's a recipe that lets you easily create a raisin and pine nut flavor. You can substitute spinach or another fairly quick-cooking green. If you want to try it with cauliflower or broccoli, blanch the vegetable first.

1 large bunch green Swiss chard, thick center ribs removed, leaves coarsely chopped
2 tablespoons extra-virgin olive oil, plus more for drizzling
2 garlic cloves, thinly sliced
Salt to taste
1 small dried red chili, crumbled (seeds removed if you like less heat)
2 or 3 scrapings of freshly grated nutmeg
Handful of golden raisins soaked in ¼ cup dry white wine
Handful of pine nuts, lightly toasted (see page 61)

Rinse and drain the chard, but let the leaves remain slightly (not dripping) wet. In a large skillet, heat the 2 tablespoons olive oil over medium-low heat. Add the garlic and sauté until it just starts to turn golden. Add the Swiss chard, a generous pinch of salt, the red chili, and nutmeg. Turn the heat to medium and sauté until nicely wilted and all the water has evaporated (the chard should be tender but still green). Add the raisins and their soaking wine and cook until the wine evaporates. Add the pine nuts and a drizzle of fresh olive oil, and stir this into the chard. Taste and adjust the seasoning. The dish should have a nice balance of sweet, spicy, and mellow.

ALMONDS AND PISTACHIOS IN SOUTHERN ITALIAN COOKING

UNSALTED, UNCOLORED, FRESH PISTACHIOS are hard to find on this side of the ocean. Pistachios are a Sicilian specialty, grown in a few small towns around Mount Etna. They're smaller, greener, and more flavorful than the ones grown here (which may be why we usually salt and dye ours). One of the most memorable food experiences of my life was when I first tasted fresh pistachio ice cream in the Sicilian town of Noto. It was pale green in color and tasted genuinely like pistachios. Pistachios find their way into many Sicilian desserts, and they also show up in savory cooking. They're a key ingredient in Sicilan pestos (see page 164). They're chopped and sautéed with shrimp or calamari, or tossed whole into seafood salad.

In keeping with the Sicilian way, I never use pistachios just for a garnish; I make them a flavor element that I try to work into the structure of a dish. When I discovered that Buon Italia, in New York, sells imported Sicilian pistachios in airtight bags (they sell almonds the same way), I was delighted. They're bright green and very fresh and have so much flavor that I never bother to toast them. A quick sauté in olive oil along with the other ingredients of a dish sets their flavor. Try a handful of pistachios instead of pine nuts in a pasta with broccoli or cauliflower, or in a skillet of sautéed chicken, especially if you've added a good amount of lemon; they'll add richness, making an everyday dish special.

The taste of really fresh, moist almonds can be shocking in its subtlety if you're accustomed to almond extract, as I was after growing up with typical Italian American desserts. I now find almond extract very off-putting, and have a hard time relating it to real almonds.

Almonds play a big role in Sicilian and Puglian cooking, and also in dishes from Basilicata. Roasted sweet peppers sautéed with almonds is a dish from Basilicata that I find so beautifully conceived that I've added it to my list of the genius flavor combinations of Italy (see page 129 for a recipe). Really fresh almonds make a wonderful addition to a fruit salad, especially with peaches or apricots. They're a beautiful match for mild fish like cod or calamari too. *Latte di mandorle* is an almond milk popular in Puglia and Sicily that is made by letting ground almonds macerate in hot water and then putting them through a strainer. I guess it's a luxury you'd come up with if you had a ton of fabulous almonds lying around. You can order glasses of it at espresso bars as a midday pick-me-up.

I've been told that southern Italian almonds have more oil in them than the ones we buy here, making them more flavorful. I think the problem may be just that we're too tempted by packaged sliced and ground almonds. I love a shortcut, but buying whole almonds and toasting and coarsely chopping them yourself doesn't take very long (you can use a food processor to grind them), and the flavor is much better. If American almonds taste a little bland to you, a better boost than almond extract is *orzata* syrup, the kind you add to seltzer to make soft drinks, just a drop or two. Amaretto liqueur also works, especially in baking, since it's not too sweet. If you want to try very moist blanched whole Italian almonds, exported in airtight bags, order them through Buon Italia (see page 436).

WINE IN COOKING

SOUTHERN ITALIANS USE A LOT OF WINE in their cooking and so do I. It may seem obvious, but it's always good to remember that the taste of any wine you cook with will be transferred to your food. A light red will give a ragù or a stew a light fruitiness; a powerful red like a Primitivo from Puglia will inpart richness and also deeper color. I use all sorts of wine for cooking, but I almost never buy a bottle just for that purpose. Generally speaking, what I drink is what I cook with. I keep a lot of southern Italian wine around the house (see pages 434-435 for information about choosing southern Italian wines to go with food), but I'm also partial to Beaujolais, Rhône wines, and light whites like Vernaccia and Frascati from central Italy. These are my everyday drinking wines.

For cooking, I often mix odds and ends of wines of the same color together in one bottle and try to use it within a day or two. I do taste the concoction to make sure I haven't created some hideous hybrid, but usually the mix is fine. Personally, I very much dislike a strong taste of oak in any wine I drink, such as you find in some California Chardonnays, and I'm not crazy about this taste in food either, so no oaky wines make their way into my cooking. Turned, or corked, wine, as tempting as it is to find a use for, I also keep out of my cooking. Corked wine gives a stew a mildew taste. I know. I've tried it.

I use wine in cooking basically in two ways: in little splashes to deglaze skillets for creating quick sauces, or in large quantities when I'm making a stewed meat dish or a ragù of some sort. The longer something takes to cook, the more wine you can use, since it will have time to reduce, mellow, and lose its alcohol. Fish stews, with their short cooking time, are best made with only a small amount of wine. Sometimes an entire bottle of wine can go into a pot of beef or lamb, but if I'm also including tomatoes, which is often the case, I'll add a smaller amount of wine, let it bubble away to release much of its alcohol, and then add the tomatoes. Tomatoes and wine make an acidic combination that requires a good balance of ingredients to keep from being too sharp. I often choose a slightly sweeter wine, rather than a drier one, for a sauce or stew if I'm also planning on using a lot of tomatoes. For instance, I might use Marsala.

Dry and sweet Marsala are fortified wines that have been famous since around 1800, when they were created in Sicily by an Englishman looking to develop something that tasted like his beloved port and sherry. In Sicily, Marsala is held in high esteem and there are several reserve grades—dry, semidry, and sweet—that are just not imported to the United States. For cooking, you can find very good Marsala, both dry and sweet, here, but some brands are much better than others, and you really get what you pay for. Florio, an old established producer, is the one I always use for cooking. (If you'd like to try a very good Marsala to sip after dinner, look for the sweet Vecchio Samperi produced by Marco De Bartoli.) Marsala does wonders for a pastry crust, making it lushly flavored but lighter in texture. I use both dry and sweet Marsala to poach fruit in and, of course, to make zabaglione.

But it's in savory cooking that Marsala can really surprise you. Dry Marsala added to a lamb or pork stew, especially one that's flavored with strong herbs like sage or rosemary, will add a rich earthiness you just can't get from regular wine. It mellows the acidity of tomatoes and adds depth to fish stews and sautés, dishes where you might expect to use dry white wine. Try adding a splash of dry Marsala to a skillet of sautéed shrimp in the last seconds of cooking, and finish the dish with a scattering of chopped mint leaves. You'll have a warm dish with sophisticated flavor. A slow-simmered calamari stew flavored with Marsala and tomatoes is surprisingly sweet and full bodied. Just use the wine the way you would sherry or port. (I also use sweet and dry vermouth in my cooking when I want something a bit more herby than Marsala.)

Moscato, made on the island of Pantelleria from the Zibbibo grape, and Malvasia, from Lipari, one of the Aeolian islands, are two famous sweet wines from Sicily. Hauner is an excellent producer of both. I've also sampled a Malvasia produced by Cantine Colosi that was delicious. These are fine after-dinner sipping wines. I don't usually buy a bottle just to cook with, but when there's a bit left over, I always find a place for it in my cooking. I've come to love shellfish steamed in sweet wine, often mixing it with a bit of lemon juice, or adding something sharp like capers or green olives to cut the sweetness and create an enticing blend of flavors. For a good example of using sweet wine with seafood, see Calamari Filled with Ricotta and Herbs and Sautéed in Malvasia Wine (page 194). Other sweet wines, such as the French Muscat Beaumes-de-Venise or the California Muscat made by Bonnie Doon, are fine to drink and to use in cooking.

RECIPES

COOKING SOUTHERN ITALIAN STYLE

After years of cooking southern Italian style in New York City, I've come to realize that I get the best results when I adapt regional recipes or just improvise using the best local produce I can find. The quality of meat, fish, and vegetables available in America is excellent—sometimes, especially with chicken and beef, better than you'll find in most southern Italian markets. If you always start with the best, you've got a much better chance of turning out something wonderful, even if you make a few mistakes along the way. That's why you'll find recipes here using such un-Italian ingredients as avocado, fresh corn, salmon, Maine lobsters, endive, Long Island bluefish, sheep's milk ricotta from Connecticut, and shiitake mushrooms.

In most cases, when I take a chance on a local ingredient, such as an upstate New York goat cheese in place of an unavailable Calabrian import, the results are ones that southern Italians would relate to in spirit and I hope find delicious. Luckily, many excellent southern Italian imports such as olive oil, Sicilian capers, and anchovies, and artisanal pasta are now more available, so I can cook New York Italian in a fashion my grandmother only dreamed of (she was stuck with mushy American spaghetti, third-rate olive oil, and characterless cocktail olives stuffed with pimientos). When choosing ingredients for your own cooking, choose local and seasonal when you can, and go for the best. All my recipes have an improvisational quality, because for me that is the most enjoyable way to cook. Successful improvisation comes with experience, but you've got to start somewhere, so feel free to substitute what is best in your markets. You might surprise your-self by creating a great new dish.

My goal when preparing southern Italian dishes is to reach a balance between preserving the basic taste of the ingredients and adding savor to them. I think of aiming for intensity of flavor with no heaviness. This is the philosophy for all southern Italian cooking, regardless of region. Linguine with clam sauce, one of the great dishes of Naples and the Amalfi Coast, is flavored with white wine, garlic, and abundant parsley, all ingredients that elevate the brininess of the clams. A Sicilian dish of sautéed cauliflower includes the time-honored duo of raisins and pine nuts, transforming a somewhat bland vegetable into an exotic treat. My mother's veal-and-pepper stew, gently simmered with red wine, onions, and a pinch of oregano, is another example of the South's way of creating big flavor with few ingredients.

Cooking with a sense of style is for me meditative and repetitive, two feelings I've grown to love when I'm in the kitchen. There's a pattern to all southern Italian dishes that is varied only by your imagination. When, for instance, I want to make myself a good tomato sauce I start by thinking about it as a classic but one full of possibilities. Olive oil is my anchor, and I reach for it first as a cooking fat and again later as a flavoring agent. A splash of olive oil goes into a hot skillet first thing. I then add a choice of savory ingredients to create what Italians call a *soffritto*. There is no exact English equivalent to this word, but it refers to a selection of sautéed ingredients such as garlic, onion, celery, carrot, fennel, and herbs or spices, that become the underpinning of your sauce. It's what will give your sauce character and depth of flavor. Anchovies or pancetta can be added to sway your sauce in a desired direction. For instance, if I want to include sharp flavors like capers or green olives toward the end of cooking, I might include a touch of anchovy in my *soffritto* to support these sharp notes. But on the other hand, if I want to create a woodsy tomato sauce, maybe with a hint of rosemary, I might decide to sauté a little chopped pancetta along with my *soffritto*, to add suaveness.

Once my *soffritto* is nicely sautéed and all the aromas are released into the warm oil, I'll add the tomatoes, letting them simmer on heat that might be a little higher than you would expect for a tomato sauce. Tomatoes, whether canned or fresh, need quick cooking to stay tasting like tomatoes, which is the ultimate goal of any really fine tomato sauce. The myth of Italian mamas simmering tomato sauces for hours and hours is not really accurate; it comes from the reality of long-simmered meat sauces—Sunday sauces—that contain tomato but are slow-cooked to tenderize the *braciole*, sausages, and other large chunks of meat floating in them. Fine-tuning my sauce with salt, pepper, chopped fresh herbs, and of course that final drizzle of oil, comes last, after a tasting to determine how the flavor needs to be balanced out.

The recipes in this book have many sub-recipes that you can extract for use in their contexts: an easy tomato sauce similar to the one described above; a Sicilian pesto of almonds, pistachios, and mint leaves; a sweet ricotta cream; a hot pine-nut vinaigrette; a basic recipe for *crespelle* (Italian crepes made with olive oil); a pear marmalade; and many more. These components can be adapted to many other dishes. Mix and match is a game I often play in the kitchen, and it's a great way to create new flavor combinations.

There is much overlapping of flavors and styles in Italy's deep south, and different regions have ingredients, weather, and to a certain extent temperament in common. That's why a sauce from Sicily can often blend effortlessly with a fish-cooking technique from Naples. Working with the flavors of these regions can give you great creative leeway. I hope you'll use the recipes in my book as ideas and not as inflexible set formulas. Pull them apart, taking a little of this and an idea from that to have fun and to create your own dishes with southern Italian style.

VEGETABLES

SHOPPING FOR VEGETABLES

COOKING IS MY FANTASY ESCAPE from the sometimes not so lovely realities of life. It brings me into a world of good smells and beautiful colors. As much as I love to cook, I get almost as much enjoyment from shopping for food. I don't know how I'd live in Manhattan without the Union Square Greenmarket, the biggest farmers' market in the city and luckily very close to where I live. It seems every season I notice new varieties of vegetables. Now, with so many farmers growing heirloom tomatoes, there are at least twenty types available toward summer's end. Many upstate and New Jersey farmers grow Mediterranean vegetables that I've previously seen only in southern Italy. I can find wild arugula, San Marzano tomatoes, unusual mints that taste like the wild kinds I've found in Sicily, and *zucca lunga,* the long, curled Sicilian zucchini, including its *tenerumi,* or much-prized runners (see page 316 for more about cooking with this vegetable). At the peak of the season, I often buy huge bunches of everything that looks beautiful, take them home to spread out on my counter, and stare at them in amazement, sometimes bursting into tears. Maybe I've been cooped up in the city for too long.

As inspiring as the greenmarket is, it's not much help to me in the winter, when it's pretty much reduced to wool, candles, and dried flowers. Winters can get pretty grim in Manhattan, and as much as I believe in the seasonal swing of things, I can't be a slave to it. I'm grateful to the commercial hothouses that bring marjoram, tarragon, and arugula to my supermarket all year long. I can buy blood oranges from Italy for Christmas and artichokes from California (New York is not artichoke country). I tend not to buy basil in winter, not necessarily because it won't taste good but because I'm very involved in the drama of seasonal cooking, and basil to me means summer. Winter tomatoes are awful, and I never buy them (although hothouse cherry tomatoes can be pretty good when you need a tomato fix). Winter corn is the worst. But the big black industrial eggplants I find at the supermarket in January aren't so bad, and I'll use them if I just have to have eggplant (as sometimes happens). Generally speaking, in winter I gravitate toward chicories, root vegetables, canned tomatoes, and vegetables grown in Central America and California that have a good smell to them and feel ripe (though you never really can tell until you taste one; sometimes they can be mealy and tasteless inside).

COOKING VEGETABLES

SOUTHERN ITALIANS APPROACH VEGETABLE COOKING a little differently from Americans. One of the fascinating but at times oppressive aspects of eating in southern Italy is that when a vegetable, say green beans, is in season, you inevitably consume it three times a day. It's on every menu, in every household, prepared in a myriad of ways, until you're sick to death of it. This also means that when it goes out of season, it won't be seen again until same time next year. There is a sense of completion about this kind of eating, and it is, I believe, one of the reasons for the southern Italian creativity with vegetable cooking (Sicilian cooks have a hundred ways of preparing eggplant, for instance). I try cooking this way in New York, following the rhythms of my greenmarket, but there are so many choices here that I'm not always successful. Also, being a true American, I'm easily bored and antsy and crave variety. If I served my husband green beans every night for four weeks, he'd probably shoot me.

Southern Italian cuisine is not as protein based as ours. Pasta and vegetables take center stage. You'll often find vegetables served as a separate course, not as a side dish, either before or after a small serving of meat or fish. Can you imagine eating at a friend's house in America and being offered a dish of mashed potatoes, alone on a plate, before you've had your steak or pork chops? But I've been served sautéed artichokes or asparagus or roasted peppers this way in private homes in southern Italy. I find it helpful to view vegetable preparations in isolation. It forces me to give their preparation a lot of thought.

Ciambotta, a traditional Neapolitan vegetable stew that in my family usually contained eggplant, zucchini, peppers, tomatoes, onions, and sometimes potatoes, is something we had often when I was a kid. I liked it well enough, but now when I buy small, tender summer zucchini, I generally like to show it off solo, maybe flavored only with sweet onion and basil. Tomatoes are often used in southern Italy to support other single vegetables. My family always cooked potatoes or green beans in tomato sauce, and I loved it (see page 119 for Romano Beans with Pancetta and Rosemary). Potatoes often take the place of pasta in pairings with artichokes, arugula, sweet peppers, or mushrooms. I think this was originally done to stretch the flavor of a more costly vegetable with the cheaper, more neutral-tasting potato. It's an excellent technique worth experimenting with.

Americans consider textures very important in a meal. The crust on a fried potato and the crispness of quick-cooked vegetables are things I've come to expect. Growing up with my grandmother's cooking, I thought all vegetables were gray and soft. That's how she cooked broccoli, green beans, spinach, and in fact just about anything naturally green. Traditionally, southern Italians cook vegetables well to deepen their flavor, sacrificing color. Indeed, my grandmother's vegetables were deliciously steeped in garlic, herbs, olive oil, wine, and broth, but my American self wants color and crispness. I often go for a compromise solution, cooking vegetables enough to take off their raw edge, but not enough so they're completely lacking in bite. Blanching and shocking in cold water, something my grandmother would have found ridiculous, preserves their color so vegetables can then be sautéed with savory flavors, combining the best of both worlds. Recently, I've noticed vegetable cooking moving toward a lighter approach in many of the fancier restaurants in cities like Naples and Palermo (the small trattorias tend to hold more tightly to tradition).

When I'm looking to add flavor to a vegetable, the first thing I consider is its instrinic delicateness or robustness. There exist many elaborate treatments for vegetables in the southern repertoire (Sicilian eggplant caponata comes to mind, with its pine nuts, olives, raisins, and sometimes even chocolate). Eggplant, even in the south, where it is almost the national vegetable, is considered something that needs all the help it can get. But you won't see this approach with wild mushrooms or spring asparagus (often the skinny, wild variety); they are treated simply, to showcase their special flavors.

I tend to prepare seasonal local produce much more gently than I do winter supermarket fare. I'll choose onion or garlic as a seasoning, but usually not both. This is common practice in southern Italy, but not a strict rule by any means. Winter zucchini I'll stuff and bake or make with some sort of gratin using an imported caciocavallo or pecorino or a good locally made mozzarella. Sometimes, if I'm slow-cooking winter vegetables for a stew or a pasta sauce, I'll include both garlic and some type of onion, since their flavors mellow and blend in a delicious way with long cooking. I love the southern Italian habit of adding little bits of cured meats to robust vegetables such as beans or bitter greens; it adds subtle flavor and makes the dish more substantial. Pancetta, slab lard, or *lardo* (basically the fatty part of pancetta without the meat), fatty prosciutto ends, or soppressata can be diced and sautéed in olive oil and used as a flavor base for many types of vegetables.

The flavors of some vegetable dishes are more intense when they're served at room temperature, and southern Italians know this better than anybody. They often eat minestrone, caponata, roasted peppers, stuffed tomatoes, frittata, zucchini parmigiano, and even pasta at room temperature. Americans tend to think it's not dinner if it's not boiling hot. I always felt that way until I was served a minestrone in Campania, almost cool against the summer heat, and was amazed at how the flavors just burst forth. I now routinely taste dishes hot and at room temperature to see how their flavors change. Serving some dishes at room temperature is also, needless to say, a great gift to the cook.

GREEN SALADS IN THE SOUTHERN ITALIAN KITCHEN

SALADS IN AMERICA have become awfully elaborate. Order a green salad on a restaurant menu and it will likely be a mesclun of arugula, red and green leaf lettuces, frisée, and maybe sprouts tossed with an elaborate vinaigrette. Ask for a green salad in a restaurant in Puglia or Sicily and you'll get lettuce, usually only one kind. An *insalata mista*—mixed salad—on a menu in Rome and southward tends to mean lettuce and tomato, frequently with the addition of what in my opinion are weird things like shredded carrots or, as I've noticed lately, canned corn kernels. Olive oil and vinegar come to the table and you dress the salad yourself. Most southern Italian natives don't bother much with salads at restaurants. They're not something you pay for but something you make at home.

There is, however, one salad that's a staple of southern Italian trattoria menus, *ruchetta e pomodorini*—spiky wild arugula with halved cherry tomatoes, usually dressed only with good olive oil and salt. People do order that one. Extra-virgin olive oil and salt is a popular dressing on bitter greens where lemon or vinegar would fight the gentle bitterness; on acidy little tomatoes, southern Italian cooks conclude, vinegar would pitch the flavor too high. The dressing was a revelation to me when I first tasted it, since I come from a vinegar-happy family (my father would dress salads with practically all vinegar and just a drizzle of oil, which made my nose run). I often now dress chicory and arugula salads with no acid at all. This is especially nice if you're serving the salad as a first course. I've always found vinegar hard to take on an empty stomach.

Although our home salads were too astringent for me, there were times I welcomed them. My mother served a simple green salad to accompany meatballs, or *polpettini*. Pasta with the meatball cooking sauce was a first course, the meat coming after. This is classic southern Italian style, and with these rich meat dishes a salad with a bit more acidity makes a lot of sense, especially when two dishes with the same flavored sauce have already been served. (Generally speaking, salads come first in restaurants in southern Italy but often toward the end of the meal in homes.)

A composed salad of lettuce with the addition of meat, vegetables, eggs, cheese, or fish, so popular in French and American cooking, is relatively new to southern Italy except in a few classic dishes, such as one of arugula with grilled shrimp that is very popular in Sicily. I present several contemporary composed salads, here and in the meat and fish sections of the book, that combine southern Italian ingredients and flavors in ways that would seem unfamiliar to most southern Italians—for example, Grilled Shrimp with Fresh Shell Beans and Sopressata (see page 166) and Steak and Celery Salad with Capers and Romaine (see page 228). I love these meal-in-a-bowl salads and often find them supremely convenient to throw together for a healthful and substantial dinner.

I've arranged my vegetable recipes more or less in the order in which the vegetables come into season. So, for instance, fava beans, asparagus, and artichokes, the Italian springtime vegetables, are grouped together.

SERVES FOUR AS AN ANTIPASTO OR A FIRST COURSE. Favas, along with chickpeas, were known in the ancient world and have played a big part in southern Italian cooking for centuries. They show up in pasta dishes and in purées, salads, and fritters. Favas are a favorite vegetable in Puglia, in both fresh and dried form, and nowadays I find them fresh in my own markets. The pairing of raw fava beans and pecorino is an Italian springtime classic, but I like adding a few extra ingredients, turning it into a real salad. And since favas are a bit of work to shell and peel, it's nice to stretch them a little with greens and herbs.

RAW FAVA BEAN SALAD WITH PECORINO, DANDELION, AND MINT

1 bunch young dandelion greens, stemmed

1 small chunk aged pecorino (Sicilian or Sardinian)

2 pounds fava beans, shelled and peeled (see note)

Leaves from 3 or 4 mint sprigs

Sea salt and freshly ground black pepper to taste

Extra-virgin olive oil for drizzling

Put the dandelion greens in a large salad bowl. Shave a generous amount of pecorino into the salad bowl with a sharp vegetable peeler. Add the fava beans and mint leaves. Season with sea salt, a few grindings of pepper, and a generous drizzle of your best olive oil. Toss gently and serve right away.

NOTE The sharpness of the cheese mingling with the slight bittersweet taste of the favas makes the addition of vinegar or lemon unnecessary, especially since the mint adds so much freshness.

PEELING FAVA BEANS Remove the beans from their pods. In a medium pot of boiling water, blanch the fava beans for about 30 seconds. Drain the beans into a colander and run cold water over them to stop the cooking. Slip the outer skins off the beans (this may seem tedious, but the skin, unless the beans are extremely young and just harvested, can be bitter and tough).

Serves four as a first course. The restaurant Al Fornello da Ricci, in Ceglie Messapico, Puglia, serves a beautiful antipasto assortment. One November night when I was there, one of the little dishes the kitchen brought out was mozzarella sprinkled with pomegranate seeds. I was made so happy by the look and taste of the dish, it inspired me to put together this salad.

ARUGULA SALAD WITH ALMONDS, POMEGRANATE SEEDS, AND MOZZARELLA ✓

2 large bunches arugula, stemmed

1 large shallot, very thinly sliced

Handful of whole blanched almonds, lightly toasted and coarsely chopped (see note)

Seeds of ¹/₂ pomegranate

DRESSING

1 tablespoon fresh lemon juice

4 tablespoons extra-virgin olive oil

¹/₂ teaspoon Dijon mustard

Pinch of sugar

Salt and freshly ground black pepper to taste

1 small baguette, cut into 12 thin rounds

1 ball fresh mozzarella (about 8 ounces), cut into 12 slices

In a large salad bowl, combine the arugula, shallot, half of the almonds, and half of the pomegranate seeds. In a small bowl, whisk together all the ingredients for the dressing. Taste and adjust the balance of oil to lemon juice if you need to.

TO SERVE THE SALAD, preheat the broiler. Toast the baguette slices on one side. Turn them over and place a slice of mozzarella on each one. Put them under the broiler for a few seconds to warm the cheese.

Toss the salad with the dressing and divide it up onto the plates. Place three mozzarella toasts on each salad and garnish the salads with the remaining almonds and pomegranate seeds. Give each one a grinding of pepper and serve right away.

NOTE   Arugula soaks up oil and wilts quicker than many other types of lettuce, so it's always a good idea to wait to dress it until the moment you're ready to take the salad to the table.

TOASTING ALMONDS   Preheat the oven to 400°F. Place the almonds in a small skillet or baking dish and toast in the oven until the almonds are golden and fragrant, 6 to 8 minutes, but check them often to make sure they're not getting too dark.

MAKES TWO EIGHT-INCH FRITTATAS, ENOUGH FOR FOUR TO SIX AS AN ANTIPASTO OR TWO AS A LUNCH DISH. Bread crumbs are often added to frittatas in southern Italy as an economy measure to stretch the eggs, a pointless concept in this case, where I've also included fancy morel mushrooms, but in fact the bread crumbs add a lot of flavor and good texture. Years ago, when I cooked at Le Madri, a Tuscan style Italian restaurant in Manhattan, I learned to make frittatas very thin and crisp, with more filling and less egg. They were often cut into wedges and included on antipasto plates, usually served at room temperature. They were so different in texture from the relatively thick, eggy frittatas I had been making, I at once realized that the Le Madri version was far better, and now I always cook them that way.

Ramps are foraged wild leeks. They look like very skinny scallions but have a stronger, almost garlic-like taste. They show up in East Coast markets in early spring. If you can't find them, substitute about half the amount of scallions, plus a small garlic clove, minced.

FRITTATA WITH MORELS, RAMPS, AND BREAD CRUMBS

2 to 3 tablespoons extra-virgin olive oil

About 10 ramps, chopped, including some green leaves

12 morels or other wild or cultivated mushrooms, cleaned and quartered lengthwise

Salt and freshly ground black pepper to taste

1 tablespoon or so dry white wine

4 large eggs

2 tablespoons grated aged pecorino

2 tablespoons homemade dry bread crumbs (see page 308)

In a medium skillet, heat 2 tablespoons of the olive oil over medium heat. Add the ramps and morels and sauté until tender and fragrant, about 4 minutes. Season with salt and pepper. Add the white wine and let it boil away.

In a small bowl, beat the eggs lightly. Add the morel mixture, pecorino, and bread crumbs. Season with a bit more salt and pepper.

Heat an 8-inch skillet over medium heat for a few seconds. Add about a tablespoon or a little more of the olive oil. Let the skillet heat a few seconds more and then add half the egg mixture, tilting the skillet to make sure it spreads out evenly. Let it cook undisturbed until it starts to brown lightly at the edges, 3 or 4 minutes. Shake the pan to see if the frittata is loose. If not, let it cook a few seconds longer. When the frittata is loose, lightly browned on the bottom, and somewhat set on top, flip it over, either in the air or by placing a plate on top, inverting it onto that, and then sliding it, cooked side up, back into the skillet. (It's actually a lot easier than you think to flip a frittata in the air. What you need to do is just do it without thinking about it, putting any anxiety out of your head.) I don't like just running the top under a broiler to finish cooking, because a good frittata should have a fried crust that has come into contact with olive oil, which adds so much flavor. Give the second side a few seconds of cooking, just to color it lightly. Slide the frittata out onto a flat surface. Make another frittata with the remaining egg mixture, adding a little more olive oil if needed to coat the skillet. Let sit for a few minutes to firm up before slicing. Serve warm or at room temperature.

TO SERVE AS AN ANTIPASTO, cut into thin pie-shaped wedges and arrange on a serving platter. For a lunch dish, slide each frittata onto a plate and serve with a green salad.

SERVES TWO AS A FIRST COURSE OR BRUNCH DISH. This dish should be voluptuous, so keep the eggs very soft and runny, letting the yolks mingle with the saltiness of the olives and the rich olive oil. Choose thick, juicy asparagus and peel the stem ends so they're tender all the way up.

Olivata (or olivada) is Italian olive pesto, very similar to French tapenade. This recipe makes more olivata than you'll use, but it keeps well for about week in the refrigerator and it tastes great on many things. You can use it on grilled or roasted seafood, or on grilled lamb chops, or spooned onto *crostini*—little toasted bread rounds—as an appetizer. I especially like to toss it with spaghetti. To do so, cook the spaghetti al dente and place it in a warmed serving bowl. Add a generous spoonful of olivata, a drizzle of olive oil, and a splash of the spaghetti cooking water. Add a handful of chopped basil leaves and toss.

ASPARAGUS WITH POACHED
EGGS AND OLIVATA

OLIVATA

1 cup black olives such as Gaeta, pitted

1 garlic clove, coarsely chopped

Small palmful of salt-packed capers, soaked and drained (see page 29)

2 salt-packed anchovies, filleted and soaked (see page 33)

Grated zest and juice of 1 small lemon

Leaves from 4 or 5 thyme sprigs

1 tablespoon grappa or brandy

1 teaspoon Dijon mustard

Freshly ground black pepper to taste

1/3 cup extra-virgin olive oil

10 fairly thick asparagus stalks, trimmed, stems peeled

Salt to taste

Extra-virgin olive oil for drizzling

Squeeze of lemon juice

Freshly ground black pepper to taste

2 very fresh eggs, preferably organic

Handful of fresh basil leaves, cut into thin strips

TO MAKE THE OLIVATA: In a food processor, combine the olives, garlic, capers, anchovies, lemon zest and juice, and thyme. Pulse for a few seconds until you have a coarse paste. Add the grappa or brandy, mustard, a few grindings of pepper, and olive oil as needed to moisten all the ingredients. Pulse a few more times until everything is mixed but the texture is slightly chunky and luxuriously oily. Because of all the salty things you've added here, you won't need extra salt, but taste for balance; depending on your preference, you might feel you need a little more garlic or lemon. Use now, or transfer the olivata to a small bowl and refrigerate for up to 1 week (but serve at room temperature).

In a large pot of boiling water, blanch the asparagus until crisp-tender, 3 or 4 minutes. Using a large skimmer, transfer to paper towels to drain. Arrange the asparagus on 2 small plates, all going in the same direction. Sprinkle with salt and drizzle lightly with olive oil.

Meanwhile, fill a wide, shallow saucepan with water, bring to a boil, and reduce the heat to a very gentle simmer. Add a pinch of salt. Gently crack an egg into a small coffee cup and slip it into the water smoothly, so the yolk is not jarred. Do the same with the other egg. Poach until the whites are set but the yolks are still runny, about 3 minutes. Using a slotted spoon, transfer eggs to paper towels to drain. Place 1 egg on each serving of asparagus.

Spoon a generous spoonful of olivata onto each egg. Give each dish a squeeze of lemon juice and a grinding of pepper. Garnish with the basil and serve right away.

SERVING SUGGESTION Serve with thinly sliced prosciutto and good Italian bread, toasted if you like (and if you choose to toast it, you might as well go all the way and rub the toast with raw garlic, brush it with olive oil, and finish it with a pinch of salt).

SERVES **FOUR**. Orange and Parmigiano-Reggiano both have sweet and sharp notes, and I find that they complement each other extremely well. Combine often with green vegetables, especially asparagus and artichokes. Parmigiano is not a southern Italian cheese, but they use it a lot in their cooking, especially where a gentle sweetness is desired.

ROASTED ASPARAGUS WITH ORANGE ZEST AND PARMIGIANO

1 large bunch fairly thick asparagus stalks (about 5 per person), trimmed

Extra-virgin olive oil for drizzling

Salt and freshly ground black pepper to taste

Grated zest of 2 large oranges

1 small chunk Parmigiano-Reggiano cheese

Preheat the oven to 450°F.

Lay the asparagus on a baking sheet. Drizzle with a generous amount of olive oil. Season with salt and pepper, and toss the stalks with your hands until they're well coated with oil and the seasoning is distributed.

Place the asparagus in the oven and roast until fragrant, tender, and just starting to brown at the tips, about 15 minutes, depending on how thick they are. When the asparagus are about a minute or so away from being done, take them from the oven and sprinkle on the orange zest, and grate a thin layer of Parmigiano evenly over them. Return the asparagus to the oven just long enough to melt the cheese, about 1 minute (watch them to make sure the cheese doesn't get too dark).

Place the asparagus on a large serving dish and serve immediately (They also taste good at room temperature, but the cheese won't be as soft.)

SERVES FOUR AS A FIRST COURSE. Asparagus and fennel, as I recently discovered, go very well together. I first improvised this salad in early April, before local asparagus was available in New York. I had a strong desire for spring tastes and made this with California asparagus and a juicy spring onion I found at my supermarket. It raised my spirits.

ASPARAGUS, FENNEL, AND SPRING ONION SALAD

12 thick asparagus stalks, trimmed and peeled

2 small fennel bulbs, trimmed, cored, and very thinly sliced

1 small spring bulb onion, including tender green part close to the bulb, very thinly sliced, or 3 scallions, including tender green parts, thinly sliced

Handful of fresh basil leaves, chopped

1 bunch arugula, stemmed

DRESSING

Grated zest and juice of $1/2$ lemon

3 tablespoons extra-virgin olive oil

Pinch of sugar

Salt and freshly ground black pepper to taste

Small chunk pecorino cheese, not too sharp

In a large pot of boiling water, blanch the asparagus for about 4 minutes, or until crisp-tender (when they start smelling like asparagus, they're usually cooked enough). Drain into a colander and rinse under cold water to preserve their green color. Drain and slice, on the diagonal, into 1-inch pieces.

In a salad bowl, combine the asparagus, fennel, onion, and basil. Arrange a small bunch of arugula leaves on each of 4 salad plates.

In a small bowl, whisk together all the dressing ingredients. Taste for a good balance of lemon to olive oil, adjusting it if you need to. Pour the dressing over the asparagus and toss gently. Divide the asparagus salad over the arugula. Top each salad with a few shavings of pecorino and serve right away.

Serves two as a first course. Several upstate New York farmers grow a tiny cultivated strawberry that becomes available at Manhattan's Union Square greenmarket in late spring. This sweet little strawberry is much like the fragoline di bosco you find on many restaurant menus in Italy in the spring, a variety cultivated from the wild. If you can find such an American version, choose it for this salad; otherwise use very sweet larger strawberries cut in half.

STRAWBERRY AND WATERCRESS SALAD WITH PINE NUTS

SALAD

1 large bunch watercress

About 2 dozen small spring strawberries (see headnote), hulled

6 or 7 fresh chives, chopped

Small handful of pine nuts, lightly toasted (see page 61)

DRESSING

1 teaspoon balsamic vinegar

$1/2$ teaspoon Spanish sherry vinegar

Salt and freshly ground black pepper to taste

2 tablespoons extra-virgin olive oil

1 tablespoon walnut oil, or 1 more tablespoon olive oil

In a salad bowl, combine all the salad ingredients. In a small bowl, whisk all the dressing ingredients together. The dressing will be a bit sweet from the balsamic vinegar, but make sure you've added enough salt to balance it out. Toss the salad with the dressing. Divide between 2 salad plates and serve right away.

ARTICHOKES AND SOUTHERN ITALIAN FLAVORS

In this country, most home cooks aren't very creative when it comes to artichokes. I think this has more to do with the varieties available to us than with culinary skill. We boil the large ones whole and serve them with a bowl of melted butter. It's not a bad dish, but it can get clunky and one-note after you've scraped the first dozen leaves against your teeth. And then there's the mammoth Italian American artichoke of my childhood, stuffed to overflowing with sausage, garlic, and bread crumbs. I have to say I've never liked that one very much. It's so huge, and where's the artichoke flavor? Is it a main course or an appetizer? My grandmother used to serve that as a first course before an American Thanksgiving dinner (and I lived to tell about it). Until I was about nineteen, those two artichoke preparations were the only ones I ever ate or knew about. Then I started traveling to southern Italy.

Rome is famous for its crisp-fried flattened Jewish-style artichokes, which look like sunflowers on a plate, and I love them, but it is southern Italy, especially in Sicily, whose artichoke preparations are close to my heart, filling a large culinary void. Artichokes baked with capers and anchovies, artichokes braised with olives and white wine, artichokes sautéed with orange and lemon, artichoke gratins topped with pecorino and wild mint . . . those are just a few of the amazing versions I've been served in Sicily. Italy does have more interesting varieties of artichokes than we have, and I'm sure they inspire creativity. I especially love the small, spiny, purplish Sicilian ones, which are very tender. Working with what is available here, I've come up with southern Italian–inspired artichoke recipes that I'm happy with. Our "baby" artichokes can stand in for the little Sicilian ones (actually, they're not babies; they're just miniature offshoots from the globe artichoke plant). They have no fuzzy choke and no thorns, so they can be eaten whole, requiring only a minimum of trimming.

Serves four or five as an appetizer. You can buy little jars of artichoke pesto in food shops in many places in southern Italy. They're often very good, but they're never as good as when you make it yourself. Since everything in it gets puréed, you don't even have to do a real tidy job cleaning the artichokes, so the cooking is easy. Some artichoke pestos I've sampled have contained green olives, which I like, but here I've gone for a lusher approach, adding pecorino, mascarpone, and a splash of vermouth.

BRUSCHETTA WITH ARTICHOKE PESTO

ARTICHOKE PESTO

2 lemons, halved

4 large artichokes

3 tablespoons extra-virgin olive oil, plus more for drizzling

2 garlic cloves, thinly sliced

Salt and freshly ground black pepper to taste

1 tablespoon dry vermouth

1 tablespoon warm water, plus more if needed

1 tablespoon grated young pecorino cheese

1 tablespoon mascarpone cheese

Leaves from 3 or 4 large mint sprigs, chopped

1 baguette, cut into thin rounds

Extra-virgin olive oil for brushing

Shavings of pecorino cheese

To make the pesto: Fill a bowl with cold water and add the juice of 1 of the lemons. Peel the artichokes down to the tender light-green leaves. Trim the bottom of the stems, leaving as much tender stem as possible. Peel the stems. Slice off about 1 inch from the top. Quarter the artichokes lengthwise and cut out the chokes and any prickly inner purple leaves. Drop each piece in the water as you finish working on it.

In a large skillet (avoid cast iron—it might turn the artichokes slightly gray), heat the 3 tablespoons olive oil over medium heat. Add the garlic and artichoke pieces, season with salt and pepper, and sauté just until they start turning golden. Add the vermouth and let it boil away. Add the warm water, turn the heat down a bit, and simmer, covered, until the pieces are very tender, adding more water if the pan dries up. This should take about 15 minutes.

Put the artichokes and any pan juices in a food processor. Add the pecorino, a generous drizzle of fresh olive oil, a squeeze of lemon juice, the mascarpone, and mint. Pulse briefly to make a coarse but slightly fluffy paste. Taste and adjust the seasoning.

Toast the baguette slices and brush them lightly with olive oil. Spoon a generous amount of the artichoke pesto on top and garnish with a few shavings of pecorino.

VARIATION   This pesto makes a great pasta sauce for two. Simply cook about 8 ounces penne or ziti until al dente, saving a little of the cooking water. Drain the pasta and toss with the artichoke pesto, thinning it out with a little of the cooking water. Garnish with chopped fresh mint leaves.

Serves four as a first course or a side dish. For the last few years, I've been making this Sicilian spring vegetable stew as part of my Easter dinner. Artichokes, fava beans, peas, and spring onions are always present in it; asparagus can be added or substituted, if you like. In Sicily, this stew is sometimes flavored in the *agrodolce* style—with a sweet-and-sour sauce—but I prefer a gentle approach so the vegetables can really show off, adding just a touch of vinegar, basil, and chervil.

LA FRITELLA

Juice of 1 large lemon

2 dozen baby artichokes

3 tablespoons extra-virgin olive oil, plus more for drizzling

1 large spring onion, including tender green part, thinly sliced

Salt and freshly ground black pepper to taste

3 or 4 scrapings freshly grated nutmeg

1/4 cup dry white wine

1/2 cup warm water

1 pound fava beans, shelled and peeled (see page 76)

1 cup fresh green peas

1/8 teaspoon white wine vinegar

5 or 6 fresh basil leaves, cut into strips

Small handful chervil, stemmed

Fill a large bowl with cold water and add the lemon juice to it.

Pull off all the tough outer leaves on the artichokes until you get down to the tender, light green ones. Cut and trim the stems and slice a bit off the top. Slice the artichokes in half lengthwise. As you work, drop the artichokes into the bowl of water.

In a large skillet or flameproof casserole, heat the 3 tablespoons olive oil over medium heat. Add the onion and let it cook for a few minutes without browning. Drain the artichokes well and add them to the skillet. Season with salt, pepper, and nutmeg, and sauté until they are just starting to turn golden, about 10 minutes. Add the white wine and let it boil away. Add the warm water (adding cold water would lower the temperature and slow down cooking, and you want this to cook quickly so the vegetables retain brightness of flavor and color). Add the fava beans and peas and cook, uncovered, at a brisk simmer until the vegetables are moist and just tender and all the liquid has evaporated, about 10 minutes. Add splashes of warm water if the skillet starts to dry up.

When finished, you should have a nice moist glaze on all the vegetables but they shouldn't be sitting in liquid. Turn off the heat. Add the white wine vinegar and mix it in. Taste for seasoning. Add the basil, chervil, and a generous drizzle of olive oil (the fresh oil will help blend all the flavors). Toss to mix. Transfer to a serving bowl and serve hot or, preferably, just slightly warm or at room temperature.

VARIATION   To make a nice pasta Primavera, toss this dish with about 12 ounces penne pasta, cooked until al dente, adding a little pasta cooking water to loosen the sauce and a drizzle of fresh olive oil. This serves 4 as a first-course pasta.

SERVES FOUR OR FIVE AS A SIDE DISH OR AS PART OF AN ANTIPASTO OFFERING. In Sicily, you find tiny, spiky artichokes labeled *spinelli* (meaning spiny) at many markets. I've yet to see anything like them in New York, even at fancy gourmet shops, but our baby artichokes can be prepared in many of the same ways. Artichoke with mint is common throughout Sicily and also in Rome, and it is a beautiful combination, even using our none-too-subtle spearmint (for information on the types of mint used in southern Italian dishes, see page 54). The braised artichokes are soft and infused with flavor. I think this tastes best at room temperature.

BRAISED BABY ARTICHOKES WITH MINT, WHITE WINE, AND OLIVE OIL

Juice of 1 lemon
3 dozen baby artichokes
4 tablespoons extra-virgin olive oil
5 or 6 garlic cloves, peeled
½ cup dry white wine

Salt and freshly ground black pepper to taste
Small handful of fresh mint leaves, chopped
5 or 6 fresh basil leaves, chopped

Fill a large bowl with cold water and add the lemon juice to it.

Pull off all the tough outer leaves on the artichokes until you get down to the tender, light green ones. Cut and trim the stems and slice a bit off the top. As you work, drop the artichokes into the bowl of water.

Drain the artichokes. In a large skillet, heat the olive oil over medium-low heat. Add the garlic and artichokes and sauté for about 3 minutes. Add the white wine and cook to reduce by half. Add the lemon water, cover, and cook, shaking the skillet occasionally, until the artichokes are fork-tender. Check every few minutes to see if the liquid has evaporated, adding more water when it does.

When the artichokes are tender, uncover the skillet and let the liquid boil down to a glaze. The artichokes and garlic should be lightly golden and there should be no liquid left in the skillet, just a nice, moist sheen on the artichokes. Sprinkle with the salt, pepper, mint, and basil. Serve warm or at room temperature.

SERVES FOUR AS A FIRST COURSE OR SIDE DISH. Here, I've combined my two favorite southern Italian vegetables, fennel and artichokes, into one dish, coming up with a lighter, more manageable version of the Italian American stuffed artichoke. Lemon and crème fraîche add a touch of tartness.

BAKED ARTICHOKES FILLED WITH FENNEL AND PECORINO

2 fennel bulbs, cored, trimmed, and finely diced (fronds reserved)

3 large leeks (white part only), rinsed and cut into thin rounds

Extra-virgin olive oil for drizzling

2 tablespoons unsalted butter

Salt and freshly ground black pepper to taste

Large pinch of fennel seeds, ground

$^{1}/_{2}$ cup crème fraîche

1 large egg, beaten

$^{3}/_{4}$ cup grated pecorino cheese

4 large globe artichokes

Juice of 1 small lemon

Preheat the oven to 400°F. Place the chopped fennel and leeks on a large baking dish. Drizzle with olive oil and dot with the butter. Sprinkle with salt, pepper, and ground fennel seeds. Roast, stirring occasionally, until the vegetables are tender and lightly browned at the edges, 20 to 25 minutes. Transfer to a large bowl. Add the crème fraîche, egg, and half the pecorino. Mix well.

Meanwhile, in a large pot of boiling water, cook the artichokes until tender, about 20 minutes. They are ready when you can easily pull off a large leaf. Drain, run briefly under cold water, and drain again, upside down, on paper towels. Remove all the large leaves from the artichokes until you reach the very tender inner leaves. Trim and peel the stem, leaving about $^{1}/_{2}$ inch. Cut the artichokes in half lengthwise and scoop out the fuzzy chokes and any small spiky leaves.

Coat a large baking dish with olive oil and lay the artichoke halves in it, cut side up. Sprinkle with salt and pepper to taste.

Fill each artichoke half with the fennel mixture. Sprinkle with the remaining pecorino and drizzle with the lemon juice. Drizzle lightly with olive oil. Bake until the tops are lightly browned, about 15 minutes. Mince some of the fennel fronds and scatter them over the top. Serve hot or warm.

SERVES FOUR OR FIVE AS AN ANTIPASTO OFFERING. When I was a kid, our neighbor Gloria Mastellone, an excellent cook whose family is from Sorrento in Campania, fried up a batch of stuffed zucchini blossoms and brought them to the table one night when my family was eating over. My father took a bite of one of the hot blossoms and a big, mad bumblebee flew out and buzzed around the dining room. Since then, I always check the insides of the blossoms for any bugs that might be hiding in them.

Zucchini blossoms should be very fresh and unwilted when you buy them. They are quite perishable and will only keep for about a day, so plan on using them right away. Sticking their stems in a small glass of water in the refrigerator will sometimes prolong their freshness for an extra day. A classic filling for these beautiful yellow blossoms is mozzarella and anchovy. This version includes sun-dried tomatoes, which add their own brand of saltiness, and fresh marjoram.

FRIED ZUCCHINI BLOSSOMS FILLED WITH MOZZARELLA, MARJORAM, AND SUN-DRIED TOMATOES

1 small ball mozzarella (about 8 ounces), cut into $\frac{1}{2}$-inch dice

About 20 fresh zucchini blossoms, cleaned (see note)

8 oil-packed sun-dried tomatoes, cut into strips

Leaves from 3 or 4 marjoram sprigs, chopped, plus several sprigs for garnish

BATTER

1 cup all-purpose flour

Scant $\frac{1}{8}$ teaspoon baking powder

Generous pinch of salt

Freshly grated nutmeg to taste

$\frac{3}{4}$ cup cold water

Inexpensive extra-virgin olive oil for deep-frying

Gently place a piece of mozzarella in each blossom. Add a few slices of sun-dried tomato and some chopped marjoram. Twist the tops of the blossoms to close them up. Use now, or refrigerate for a few hours.

TO MAKE THE BATTER: In a medium mixing bowl, combine the flour, baking powder, salt, and nutmeg. Stir well to blend. Add the cold water and whisk until smooth (it should be a little thicker than heavy cream). Set aside.

Fill a large sauté pan with about 2 inches of oil. Heat over medium heat until the surface shimmers (360° to 365°F is the ideal frying temperature, but I honestly never use a thermometer). To test, add a few drops of batter. If the batter bubbles and turns golden right away, the oil is ready.

Dip the blossoms in the batter, letting the excess drip off. Fry in batches, about 5 at a time. Turn them when they look golden and crisp, about 2 minutes on each side. Using tongs, transfer to paper towels to drain for a moment. Transfer to a serving dish. Sprinkle with salt and pepper and garnish with marjoram sprigs. Serve right away.

CLEANING ZUCCHINI BLOSSOMS   Open each blossom and pinch off the stamen, checking while you do this for any dirt (or bugs) that might be trapped inside. Wipe the blossoms inside and out with damp paper towels. If they are really dirty, dunk them very briefly in a sink full of cool water, lift them out right away, and drain on paper towels.

SERVES FOUR AS A MAIN COURSE OR SIX AS A SIDE DISH. I loved my mother's eggplant parmigiano, which was light and fresh, layered with tomatoes, thin slices of mozzarella, and sometimes sliced hard-boiled eggs. While discussing this dish with my friend Jay Milite, whose family comes from around Gaeta, in Campania, he remembered that his mother made zucchini the same way.

Parmigiano-style layering and baking is one of the classic treatments for vegetables in the Campania region. I've played with the zucchini idea, adding scamorza, which is basically an aged mozzarella, and a generous amount of fresh basil. The scamorza adds a little more depth of flavor than fresh mozzarella and gives the dish a slightly smoky taste.

ZUCCHINI PARMIGIANO WITH SCAMORZA AND BASIL

2 tablespoons extra-virgin olive oil, plus more for deep-frying

2 garlic cloves, thinly sliced

One 28-ounce can plus one 15-ounce can plum tomatoes, drained and chopped

1 bay leaf, preferably fresh

3/4 cup all-purpose flour for dredging

3 or 4 scrapings freshly grated nutmeg

Pinch of ground cinnamon

Salt and freshly ground black pepper to taste

5 zucchini, cut lengthwise into 1/4-inch slices

One 8-ounce piece scamorza cheese, thinly sliced

About 12 fresh basil leaves, chopped

1/2 cup grated pecorino cheese

In a large skillet, heat the 2 tablespoons olive oil over medium-low heat. Add the garlic and sauté until very lightly golden. Add all the tomatoes and the bay leaf. Increase the heat to high and cook at a lively bubble for about 10 minutes, just until the sauce thickens slightly. Season with salt and pepper.

Preheat the oven to 400°F.

In a large sauté pan, heat 1 inch olive oil over medium heat. While it is heating, pour the flour onto a large plate and mix in the nutmeg, cinnamon, salt to taste, and a generous amount of pepper. Dredge the zucchini pieces in the flour. Test to see if the oil is hot enough by dipping the edge of one of the zucchini pieces in it. If it sizzles, it's hot enough. Fry the zucchini in batches, turning them when golden to cook the other side. The smell of the cinnamon-coated zucchini frying in good olive oil is for me almost as enticing as eating the finished dish. As they are ready, use tongs to transfer the zucchini to paper towels to drain.

Spread a thin layer of the tomato sauce in the bottom of a 9-by-13-inch baking dish. Add a layer of zucchini and a layer of scamorza. Scatter on about half of the basil and top with a sprinkling of pecorino. Pour on another layer of tomato sauce and then make another layer of zucchini. Scatter on the remaining basil. Pour on the remaining tomato sauce and top with the rest of the scamorza. Grate on a very thin layer of pecorino and grind a little pepper over the top.

Bake, uncovered, until bubbling and lightly golden, about 20 minutes. Remove from the oven and let stand for about 10 minutes before serving warm, or serve Neapolitan style, at room temperature.

SERVES FOUR AS A FIRST COURSE OR SIDE DISH. Whole wheat berries are used in southern Italy to make all sorts of salads and soups and for *cuccia*, a mix of wheat berries, ricotta, and sugar or honey. Make sure to buy hard-wheat berries (usually labeled hard spring wheat); soft winter wheat ones cook up a little too mushy. You can find wheat berries at natural foods stores and Middle Eastern markets.

WHEAT BERRIES WITH ZUCCHINI, PINE NUTS, AND RICOTTA

1½ cups hard-wheat berries

1 bay leaf, preferably fresh

Extra-virgin olive oil, for drizzling, plus 3 tablespoons

Salt and freshly ground black pepper to taste

3 thin slices of pancetta, finely diced

4 or 5 scallions, including tender green parts, thinly sliced

5 tiny, young zucchini, finely diced

2 tablespoons dry white wine

Handful of pine nuts, lightly toasted (see page 61)

Grated zest of 1 lemon

Generous handful of fresh basil leaves, chopped

Squeeze of fresh lemon juice, if needed

1 cup whole-milk ricotta cheese, sheep's milk if available

Put the wheat berries in a large pot and add cold water to cover by about 4 inches. Add the bay leaf and bring the water to a boil. Reduce the heat to medium-low and cook the wheat, uncovered, at a low boil for about 45 minutes. Add hot water if the water level shrinks to less than 1 inch above the wheat. When done, the grains will have swelled to about twice their size and be tender to the bite, with just a bit of resistance. Some of the grains will have started to burst, but this is normal. Drain well and pour into a large serving bowl. Remove the bay leaf. Drizzle with a few tablespoons of olive oil and season lightly with salt and pepper. Give it a gentle mix.

In a large skillet, heat the 3 tablespoons olive oil over medium heat. Add the pancetta and sauté until crisp, about 4 minutes. Add the scallions and zucchini and sauté until the zucchini is just tender, about 5 minutes. Season with salt and pepper. Add the white wine and let it bubble for a few seconds (the wine will loosen juices on the bottom of the skillet so they can be incorporated into the dish, adding a lot of flavor). Add the zucchini with all the skillet juices to the wheat berries. Add the pine nuts, lemon zest, and basil. Add a drizzle of fresh olive oil and toss everything gently. Taste for seasoning. You might want to add a little fresh lemon juice to pick up the flavors. Serve warm in small pasta bowls with a dollop of ricotta on top of each serving.

SUMMER WHEAT BERRY SALAD WITH TOMATOES AND BASIL Drain the cooked wheat berries, pour them into a large serving bowl, and drizzle with a little olive oil. Halve two large summer tomatoes and seed them. Chop the tomatoes and let them drain in a colander for about 15 minutes to get rid of excess juice. Add the tomatoes, a handful of chopped fresh basil, a few gratings of grana padano cheese, and a thinly sliced garlic clove. Season with salt and black pepper, add a fresh drizzle of oil, and toss gently. Serve at room temperature. This salad tastes best made fresh and not refrigerated, as chilling flattens the taste of beautiful summer tomatoes. Serves 4 as a light lunch or first course.

SERVES FOUR OR FIVE AS A FIRST COURSE OR A SIDE DISH. I'm always look-ing for ways to make baked vegetable dishes without having to fry the vegetables before baking them—not to cut calories, necessarily, but to cut time and mess. Here, I layer the vegetables in a gratin dish and bake them dry before pouring on a flavored custard. This ensures that the vegetables will be cooked tender and your gratin will not be watery.

Mixing fresh oregano with another herb mellows it without masking its pungent flavor. Here, I've paired it with thyme.

ZUCCHINI AND PLUM TOMATO GRATIN WITH OREGANO

Extra-virgin olive oil for drizzling

4 zucchini, cut into thin rounds

About 6 plum tomatoes, cut into rounds a bit thicker than the zucchini

Salt and freshly ground black pepper to taste

$\frac{1}{2}$ cup pasteurized (not ultra pasteur-ized) heavy cream

2 large eggs

$\frac{1}{4}$ cup grated mild pecorino or grana padano cheese

1 garlic clove, minced

Leaves from 3 or 4 small oregano sprigs, chopped

Leaves from 5 thyme sprigs, chopped

Preheat the oven to 425°F.

Choose a gratin dish that will hold all the vegetables snugly (I use a round 11-inch enam-eled tart pan). Brush it lightly with olive oil. Make a row of slightly overlapping zucchini slices. Add a row of tomato slices (make a circular pattern for a round dish and straight rows for a square or rectangular dish). Alternate zucchini and tomato rows until you've filled the dish. Drizzle with a generous amount of olive oil and season with salt and pep-per. Bake, uncovered, until the vegetables are about halfway cooked and starting to become fragrant, about 20 minutes.

In a small bowl, whisk the cream, eggs, pecorino, garlic, and herbs together. Season generously with salt and pepper. Pour over the vegetables and bake until the custard is firm and the edges of the gratin are lightly browned, about 20 minutes longer. Serve warm or at room temperature.

SERVES FOUR AS A SIDE DISH. Here's a treatment for carrots that plays up their sweetness. This, to my knowledge, is not a traditional southern Italian dish but just something I came up with one night as an Italianate accompaniment to a pork chop dinner. The excellent Sicilian salt-packed capers from the islands of Lipari, Salina and Pantelleria have a special floral note that marries perfectly with the carrots.

CARROTS WITH SICILIAN CAPERS

3 tablespoons unsalted butter

1 large bunch carrots (about 12 slender ones), peeled and cut into $1/8$-inch rounds

Generous pinch of sugar

2 or 3 scrapings freshly grated nutmeg

Salt to taste

$1/4$ cup dry Marsala

Palmful of salt-packed capers, soaked and rinsed (see page 29)

Freshly ground black pepper to taste

Small handful of fresh flat-leaf parsley leaves, chopped

Choose a wide skillet with a lid that will hold the sliced carrots in more or less one layer for easy cooking (they can overlap, as long as you don't have them piled several inches deep). Melt the butter in the skillet over medium heat until it foams. Add the carrots, sugar, nutmeg, and salt. Sauté for about 1 minute or so to lightly caramelize the sugar. Add the Marsala and let it bubble until reduced by half. Reduce the heat to medium-low, cover, and simmer until the carrots are tender, about 5 minutes.

When the carrots are about a minute away from being tender, uncover the skillet and cook to let the liquid evaporate to a moist glaze on the carrots. Add the capers and pepper. Taste and adjust the seasoning. Add the parsley and serve right away.

SERVES FOUR OR FIVE AS A FIRST COURSE OR LIGHT MEAL, OR EIGHT AS PART OF AN ANTIPASTO OFFERING. The day after the World Trade Center disaster, when gray soot and a burning electrical smell filled the air outside my downtown Manhattan apartment, I found myself numbly flipping through Richard Olney's cookbook *Provence the Beautiful,* with its gorgeous photos of that region's cookery. I wanted badly to relate to those photos, but it wasn't easy. So I decided to cook something from the book. This recipe is my southern Italianized departure from Mr. Olney's fine recipe, which calls for stuffing onion layers and then baking them in a light tomato sauce. You can serve it as a side dish, but I find it rich enough and interesting enough to stand as a first course or as a vegetarian meal, with a green salad and good Italian bread.

VIDALIA ONION ROLLS STUFFED WITH RICOTTA AND SWISS CHARD

4 large Vidalia onions, sliced in half lengthwise (through root ends)

STUFFING

1/2 cup chopped reserved onion centers

1 cup whole-milk ricotta cheese, drained if watery

1 bunch Swiss chard, central ribs removed, blanched, well drained, and chopped

1 tablespoons extra-virgin olive oil

1 garlic clove, minced

Generous pinch of grated nutmeg

Leaves from 5 or 6 thyme sprigs, chopped

1/2 cup grated pecorino cheese

2 egg yolks, beaten

Salt and freshly ground black pepper to taste

TOMATO SAUCE

2 tablespoons extra-virgin olive oil

2 garlic cloves, very thinly sliced

1 tablespoon dry white wine

One 35-ounce can Italian plum tomatoes, well chopped, with juice

Salt and freshly ground black pepper to taste

Leaves from 5 or 6 thyme sprigs, chopped

Leaves from 5 or 6 fresh flat-leaf parsley sprigs, chopped

Extra-virgin olive oil for drizzling

1/4 cup grated pecorino cheese, to sprinkle on top

Cook the onions in a pot of boiling water until tender, about 20 minutes. Using a large skimmer, transfer the onions to cold water. Drain briefly. Trim the root ends and separate the layers. Lay all the onion layers out on paper towels to drain. Chop the center layers that are too small for stuffing (You'll only need ½ cup).

In a small bowl, combine the chopped onion centers and all the remaining stuffing ingredients. Mix well. Taste and adjust the seasoning.

To make the tomato sauce: In a medium skillet, heat the olive oil over medium heat. Add the garlic and sauté until very lightly golden. Add the white wine and let it boil away. Increase the heat to high and add the chopped tomatoes. Cook at a lively bubble until just starting to thicken, about 10 minutes. Add the salt, pepper, thyme, and parsley.

Preheat the oven to 350°F.

Pour a few tablespoons of tomato sauce into a low-sided 10-by-12-inch baking dish and spread it out to form a thin coating. Place 1 heaping tablespoonful of stuffing in each onion layer and roll them up (they should look like little torpedoes). Place the rolls, seam side down, in the dish. Pour on the remaining tomato sauce and add a drizzle of olive oil. Cover the dish with aluminum foil and bake for about 30 minutes. Uncover and sprinkle on the grated pecorino. Continue baking, uncovered, until the onions are very tender and lightly browned, about 20 minutes. Serve hot or at room temperature.

MAKES ABOUT TWO CUPS. Little pickled vegetables are popular throughout southern Italy, where they're usually eaten alongside something rich and fatty like soppressata. *Giardiniera*, which means "garden style," is the name for a pickled vegetable assortment that usually includes cauliflower, carrot, sometimes celery or fennel, and hot or sweet peppers. My grandfather bought jars of Progresso *giardiniera* and ate it in the morning. I got the feeling that along with raw eggs, which he sucked out through little holes in their shells, *giardiniera* was his idea of a hangover remedy.

I like *giardiniera* not only with cured meats like soppressata or capocollo, but as an accompaniment to strong cheeses, like provolone, or even with meat stews to cut the richness. The jarred versions from my childhood were none too subtle. My own is a kinder, gentler version. This recipe is scented with saffron. That's not traditional, but saffron's aromatic bitterness blends well with vinegar, so I think it's a good addition.

GIARDINIERA WITH SAFFRON

2 carrots, peeled

2 celery stalks

1 large fennel bulb, trimmed and cored

1 large red bell pepper, seeded and deribbed

½ small cauliflower, cut into small florets

2 garlic cloves

1 cup dry white wine

1 cup high-quality white wine vinegar, such as Champagne vinegar

2 tablespoons sugar

Large pinch of saffron threads, dried and ground to a powder (see page 42)

1 bay leaf, preferably fresh

About 10 fennel seeds

Salt to taste

Cut the carrots, celery, fennel, and bell pepper into bite-sized pieces. Cook all the vegetables, including the garlic, in a large pot of boiling water for about 3 minutes. Drain in a colander and run cold water over them to stop the cooking and to bring up their colors. Drain well, then transfer to a large bowl.

In a medium saucepan, combine the white wine and vinegar. Add the sugar, saffron, bay leaf, fennel seeds, and a generous pinch of salt. Bring to a boil over high heat, reduce the heat to medium, and let the mixture simmer for about 5 minutes.

Pour the vinegar mixture over the vegetables and toss well. Taste and adjust the seasoning. This should be highly seasoned and, because of all the other strong flavors, it can take a fair amount of salt. Cover the bowl with plastic wrap and refrigerate overnight before serving. Store in the refrigerator for up to 1 week.

SERVES FOUR OR FIVE AS A SIDE DISH. Potatoes sautéed in a skillet with sweet peppers and sometimes onion (and maybe even a little hot chili) is a homey Calabrian classic. I've taken potatoes, peppers, and onion and given them a more formal structure by layering them in a tart pan, so you can cut the result into wedges. *Gatto* is a southern Italian word for "cake," usually a savory one, derived from the French word *gâteau*.

POTATO AND SWEET PEPPER GATTO, CALABRIAN STYLE

2 tablepoons extra-virgin olive oil, plus more for drizzling

4 red bell peppers, seeded, deribbed, and cut into strips

1 large onion, thinly sliced

Salt and freshly ground black pepper to taste

1 tablespoon dry vermouth

1½ pounds unpeeled Yukon Gold potatoes, thinly sliced

Leaves from 3 or 4 rosemary sprigs, chopped

Leaves from 3 or 4 marjoram sprigs, chopped

½ cup grated pecorino cheese

½ cup grated caciocavallo cheese

In a large skillet, heat the 2 tablespoons olive oil over medium heat. Add the peppers and onion, season with salt and pepper, and sauté until tender and very lightly browned, about 15 minutes. Add the vermouth and let it bubble a few seconds, stirring to scrape up the cooked-on pan juices. Set aside.

Preheat the oven to 375°F. Brush an 8- or 9-inch tart pan lightly with olive oil (I use one with a removable bottom so any excess oil will leak out during cooking).

Place the sliced potatoes, rosemary, and marjoram in a medium bowl. Add a drizzle of olive oil and season with salt and pepper to taste. Toss the potatoes well so they're well coated with oil and seasoning.

Make a layer of half of the potatoes in the tart pan, in a slightly overlapping circular pattern. Cover with about three-fourths of the sautéed peppers. Sprinkle on a generous layer of pecorino and caciocavallo (you can mix the cheeses together if you like). Add a layer of the remaining potatoes and top with the remaining peppers (you want fewer peppers on top, because they might burn). Top with the remaining cheeses. Drizzle any remaining oil and herbs that might be left in the bowl over the top. If using a pan with a removable bottom, place the tart on a baking sheet (it will leak a little oil).

Bake until the top is nicely browned and the potatoes are tender when pierced with a thin knife, about 1 hour. Let stand for about 10 minutes before cutting it into wedges.

SERVES FOUR AS A SIDE DISH. In my thinking, the best way to start flavoring a potato salad is by steeping hot sliced potatoes in white wine. Its fruity, acidic base is far preferable to overloading the dressing with vinegar or lemon juice, which can drown out the gentle potato flavor and make the salad taste more like deli fare than something lovingly assembled with seasonal summer produce.

WARM FINGERLING POTATO SALAD WITH WHITE WINE AND PARSLEY

1½ pounds fingerling or Yukon Gold potatoes, halved lengthwise

Salt to taste

¼ cup dry white wine

2 tablespoons extra-virgin olive oil, plus more if needed

Freshly ground black pepper to taste

1 young summer garlic clove, minced

2 small red shallots, very thinly sliced

2 oil-packed anchovy fillets, minced, or 1 salt-packed anchovy, filleted, soaked, drained, and minced (see page 33)

Generous handful of fresh flat-leaf parsley, chopped

⅛ teaspoon Spanish sherry vinegar

Put the potatoes in a large pot and add cold water to cover by 1 inch. Add a little salt and bring to a boil over high heat. Reduce the heat to medium and cook the potatoes until fork-tender, about 8 minutes (try not to let them go to the point that the skins start pulling away; they look prettier with their skins intact). Drain well and place in a large serving bowl. While the potatoes are still hot, pour on the white wine and gently mix. Let the potatoes stand to absorb the wine for about 10 minutes.

Add the 2 tablespoons olive oil to the potatoes and toss gently. Add all the remaining ingredients and toss gently again. Add a little more olive oil, if needed, to coat the potatoes well, and taste for seasoning. You might need a pinch more salt to pull all the flavors together. Serve warm.

VARIATION   A traditional Puglian dish of warm new potatoes tossed with wilted arugula is one I've always loved: Add arugula leaves instead of parsley to this salad. The heat from the just-cooked potatoes will wilt it slightly.

SERVES FOUR AS A FIRST COURSE. In late summer, when tomatoes are at their peak, I sometimes get a little anxious that I'm not going to get enough of them while they're around. I start concocting recipes that use tomatoes doubly, such as this tomato salad with a dressing made from tomatoes. Its intense taste calms my fear of missing out.

Heirloom, or old-style, tomatoes are grown by caring farmers from long-forgotten seed varieties. They have much more personality than the perfectly round red hybrid tomatoes we are used to. Every summer, it seems, I see more varieties at my farmers' market. Look for Brandywine, Green Zebra, Purple Calabash, and Old German. I've seen a long yellow variety called Banana Legs. I think sometimes the farmers who resurrect these varieties simply make up the names, but that's okay. It's the taste the counts. For the best flavor, keep them out of the refrigerator. It can make them mealy and deaden their fragrance.

HEIRLOOM TOMATO SALAD WITH TOMATO VINAIGRETTE

VINAIGRETTE

1 small, ripe summer tomato, peeled and chopped (see page 26)

1/4 cup extra-virgin olive oil

1 teaspoon Spanish sherry vinegar, plus more to taste if needed

Sea salt and freshly ground black pepper to taste

SALAD

5 or 6 heirloom tomatoes (a mix of yellow, green, and purple is nice), cut into 1/4-inch rounds

1 small red onion, cut into very thin rounds

Small handful of fresh basil leaves, cut into thin strips, plus sprigs for garnish

Handful of pine nuts, lightly toasted (see page 61)

TO MAKE THE VINAIGRETTE: Press the tomato through a fine-mesh sieve with your fingers or the back of a large spoon, letting the juice run into a small bowl. (I tried puréeing it in a food processor, but the texture was too thick. What you want is the juice, what chefs call tomato water.) You should have about 1/4 cup juice. Add the olive oil and the 1 teaspoon Spanish sherry vinegar to the tomato juice. Season with salt and pepper. Let the vinaigrette stand for about 1 hour before using (this will allow it to thicken and develop more flavor). Now taste it, adding more salt or a few drops more vinegar if needed. (To let the flavor of the tomatoes really shine, try not to add too much vinegar. You want to appreciate the natural acidity of the tomatoes.)

Arrange the tomato slices on a large serving plate in a pretty circular pattern, alternating colors, if you've got them. Scatter on the sliced onion and basil strips. Drizzle with the vinaigrette and garnish with the pine nuts and basil sprigs. Sprinkle on an extra pinch of salt and some fresh pepper before bringing the salad to the table.

SERVES FOUR AS A FIRST COURSE OR A LIGHT LUNCH MAIN COURSE.
Sweet corn is not commonly grown or eaten in southern Italy. But we have such wonderful corn on the East Coast in the summer that I'm always looking for ways to incorporate it into my Italian-inspired dishes.

Little Green Zebra tomatoes, with their streaky green and white skins, start showing up at my farmers' market in early August. They're juicy and slightly tart.

ZEBRA TOMATO AND CORN SALAD WITH CACIOCAVALLO AND DANDELION

3 ears fresh corn, shucked

5 or 6 Green Zebra tomatoes, quartered

1 small red onion, very thinly sliced

Leaves from 3 or 4 large marjoram sprigs, chopped

Small handful of fresh flat-leaf parsley leaves, chopped

VINAIGRETTE

1 garlic clove, lightly crushed

1 tablespoon Champagne vinegar

Tiny pinch of sugar

Tiny pinch of ground allspice

Salt and freshly ground black pepper to taste

3 tablespoons extra-virgin olive oil, plus more if needed

1 large bunch young dandelion greens, stemmed

1 chunk caciocavallo cheese

In a large pot of boiling water, cook the corn until just tender, about 4 minutes. Drain and let cool to the touch. Cut off the kernels with a sharp knife. In a large bowl, combine the corn, tomatoes, red onion, and herbs.

TO MAKE THE VINAIGRETTE: In a small bowl, combine the garlic, vinegar, sugar, allspice, salt, and pepper. Whisk in the 3 tablespoons olive oil. Taste and add more olive oil if needed (it shouldn't be too sharp).

Pour the dressing over the vegetables and toss gently. Taste and adjust the seasoning.

Divide the greens among 4 salad plates and top with the corn mixture. With a sharp vegetable peeler, shave a generous amount of cheese over each salad and serve right away.

VARIATIONS A handful of matchstick-sized strips of soppressata or capocollo can be added for a more substantial main course. Or, omit the cheese and toss in grilled shrimp or scallops.

SERVES FOUR AS A FIRST COURSE. This is not a traditional Sicilian salad, but I've taken several common Sicilian ingredients (tomatoes, melon, mint, and sweet Moscato wine) and combined them to produce a sweet and pungent taste very much in the traditional Sicilian style. Without the chicory, the salad makes a good sauce to spoon over grilled strongly flavored fish such as sardines, mackerel, or swordfish.

TOMATO AND CANTALOUPE SALAD WITH MOSCATO VINAIGRETTE

1/3 cup Moscato di Pantelleria or other sweet dessert wine such as Muscat Beaumes-de-Venise

1 teaspoon Spanish sherry vinegar

1/4 cup extra-virgin olive oil

Salt and freshly ground black pepper to taste

3 round summer tomatoes (a mix of red and yellow is pretty), cut into wedges

1/2 small, ripe cantaloupe, peeled and cut into 1/2-inch dice

1 large shallot, very thinly sliced

Small handful of pine nuts, toasted (see page 61)

Handful of fresh mint leaves, chopped

Leaves from 1 small head chicory

Pour the Moscato into a small saucepan and boil it down over high heat to about 1 tablespoon. Let it cool for a few minutes and then pour it into a small bowl. Add the Spanish sherry vinegar, olive oil, salt, and pepper. Blend well.

In a salad bowl, combine all the remaining ingredients except the chicory. To serve, pour on the dressing and toss. Divide the chicory among 4 salad plates and top with the salad. Serve right away.

SERVES FOUR AS A SIDE DISH OR FIRST COURSE. Halved plum tomatoes filled with all sorts of nice things and baked are a favorite on antipasto tables in southern Italy. They are especially popular in southern Puglia, where they're usually filled with bread crumbs, cheese, herbs, olives, or anchovies. I like to serve my goat cheese–filled version (*caprino* is the Italian word for goat cheese) as a side dish with lamb or plopped on top of a green salad as a first course.

PLUM TOMATOES BAKED WITH CAPRINO, ROSEMARY, AND BLACK OLIVES

8 ripe plum tomatoes, halved length-wise

One 11-ounce log fresh goat cheese, such as an Italian caprino, a French Montrachet, or an American goat cheese, at room temperature

1 tablespoon dry white wine

1 garlic clove, minced

Leaves from 3 or 4 rosemary sprigs, minced

Leaves from 3 or 4 fresh flat-leaf parsley sprigs, chopped

Handful of black olives, such as Gaeta, pitted and halved

Salt and freshly ground black pepper to taste

Extra-virgin olive oil for drizzling

Preheat the oven to 425°F.

Scoop out the insides of the tomatoes with a small spoon. Drain them, upside down, on paper towels for a few minutes.

In a small bowl, mix the goat cheese with all the remaining ingredients except the olive oil until well blended. Fill each tomato half with 1 tablespoon of the goat cheese mixture. Place on a sheet pan or in a shallow baking dish and drizzle with olive oil. Bake until the tomatoes are tender and the tops are lightly browned, about 20 minutes. Serve hot or warm.

VARIATION   To serve as a sit-down first course, dress a mixed green salad and serve 2 hot tomatoes on each serving.

Serves five or six as an appetizer. *Patè di pomodori secchi* (sun-dried tomato pesto) is a specialty of the Salento area of Puglia, south of Bari. I've purchased it at various food shops there in little jars, but it is very easy to make at home, either with your own oven-dried tomatoes (you can also use oil-packed sun-dried tomatoes). It makes a wonderful pasta sauce or topping for roast chicken or tuna, but since it's so highly flavored I often serve it as part of an antipasto. This version is a bit more jazzed-up than the relatively plain ones I've sampled in Puglia.

It's a good idea to double the amount of tomatoes you're drying, since it's pleasant to have some extra on hand for tossing with pasta or serving on an antipasto platter.

TOMATO PESTO AND RICOTTA BRUSCHETTA

TOMATO PESTO

10 plum tomatoes, halved lengthwise
2 tablespoons extra-virgin olive oil
Salt to taste
1 garlic clove, chopped
Small handful of capers
2 oil-packed anchovy fillets, chopped
Leaves from 4 or 5 marjoram sprigs

Grated zest of ½ orange
1 tablespoon extra-virgin olive oil
Freshly ground black pepper to taste
Very tiny splash grappa

1 baguette, cut into thin rounds
1 cup whole-milk ricotta, drained if watery

To make the pesto: Preheat the oven to 225°F. Put the tomatoes on a baking sheet. Drizzle on the olive oil, sprinkle with salt, and toss with your hands until well coated. Arrange cut side up and bake for about 3 hours, until slightly shriveled but still moist in their centers. Let cool.

In a food processor, combine the tomatoes and all the remaining pesto ingredients. Pulse a few times until you have a coarse paste. Taste and adjust the seasoning. Use now for the liveliest taste, or cover and refrigerate for up to 2 days; return to room temperature before serving.

To serve, toast the baguette slices on both sides, spread with a dollop of ricotta, and top each with 1 teaspoon tomato pesto. Serve right away.

SERVES TWO AS A BRUNCH, LUNCH, OR LIGHT SUPPER. This Neapolitan dish is sometimes called "eggs in purgatory," I suppose because the eggs are trapped in sauce only until they reach heaven in your mouth. I make it often for myself when I'm home alone at night or for lunch. I'm drawn to it not only because I almost always have a can of tomatoes and a few eggs in the house but also because my father, who rarely cooked, used to scramble eggs, tomato, and basil together and serve it to me and my sister for weekend breakfasts. This is a more formal arrangement of those ingredients, but the taste is similar.

BAKED EGGS WITH WINTER TOMATO SAUCE

2 tablespoons extra-virgin olive oil, plus more for drizzling

2 garlic cloves, thinly sliced

2 oil-packed anchovy fillets, chopped, or 2 salt-packed anchovies, filleted, soaked, drained, and chopped (see page 33)

1 tablespoon dry white vermouth

One 35-ounce can diced tomatoes with juice

Salt and freshly ground black pepper to taste

Leaves from 3 or 4 large marjoram sprigs, chopped

4 large eggs at room temperature

1 small chunk pecorino cheese for grating

6 or 7 fresh basil leaves, chopped

Preheat the oven to 425°F.

In a large skillet, heat the 2 tablespoons olive oil over medium heat. Add the garlic and anchovies and sauté until the garlic is very lightly golden and the anchovies have dissolved, 2 or 3 minutes. Add the vermouth and let it boil away. Add the tomatoes, salt, and pepper. Increase the heat to medium-high so the tomatoes cook at a lively bubble. Cook for about 5 minutes, just long enough to concentrate some of the tomato juices, but not so long that it loses its fresh taste and bright red color. The sauce now should be fairly thick. Stir in the marjoram.

Pour the sauce into an 8- or 9-inch round or square baking dish or 2 shallow ramekins. Make 4 depressions in the sauce with a spoon and crack an egg into each one. (Keeping the eggs far apart so they don't run into each other too much is ideal, but it's not a problem if you can't manage it.) Sprinkle with salt and pepper to taste and drizzle with olive oil. Grate a small amount of pecorino over the eggs and bake until the egg whites are firm but the yolks are still runny, about 5 minutes. Scatter on the basil and serve right away.

SERVING SUGGESTION   Serve with chunks of crusty Italian bread and a glass of red wine, if you like.

VARIATIONS   The quickly cooked tomato sauce for this dish can be tossed with pasta or poured over fish fillets or chicken, or you can personalize it by adding capers, olives, different herbs, or a little chopped prosciutto (omit the anchovies if you add prosciutto).

When I make this for myself, I often just crack the eggs into the skillet on top of the tomato sauce, cover the skillet, and cook the eggs on top of the stove over low heat until the whites are set, usually about 5 minutes. I then slip the whole thing into a pasta bowl, or more often than not, I just eat it from the skillet.

SERVES FOUR AS A SIDE DISH. The southern Italian way with broccoli is to cook it long and relatively slowly, infusing it with flavor, usually including garlic. The result is the classic gray broccoli my grandmother brought to the table. The taste was good, but the color and mushiness didn't appeal to me. My compromise is to blanch it first, then sauté it just enough to soak up all the garlic and wine flavors.

In my opinion, the best part of broccoli is the stems. I always slice them thinly and include them in the dish (peeling them if they look tough). I also use the leaves, leaving them whole so they wilt into the dish.

Look for rocambole garlic. These fat, purple-tinged hard-necked bulbs are available at farmers' markets throughout the summer. They are strong and juicy, but with little bitterness. Variety is not as important as freshness for this recipe. You want young, moist summer garlic that hasn't been dried and turned papery.

BROCCOLI WITH WHITE WINE AND SUMMER GARLIC

1 large head broccoli, cut into florets, stems trimmed and sliced, leaves left whole

3 tablespoons extra-virgin olive oil, plus more for drizzling

3 or 4 large, fresh garlic cloves, very thinly sliced

Salt and freshly ground black pepper to taste

$1/2$ cup dry white wine

Leaves from 5 or 6 thyme sprigs, chopped

Grated zest of $1/2$ lemon

In a large pot of boiling water, blanch the broccoli florets, stems, and leaves for about 4 minutes, or until crisp-tender. Drain and run cold water over it to stop the cooking and preserve its bright green color. Drain well.

In a large skillet, heat the 3 tablespoons olive oil over medium heat. Add the broccoli and garlic at the same time (the moisture from the broccoli will prevent the garlic from burning). Season with a generous amount of salt and pepper. Sauté just until the garlic starts to turn golden. Add the wine and let it bubble for 1 minute, leaving a bit of liquid in the skillet. Add the thyme, lemon zest, and a drizzle of fresh olive oil. Sauté 1 minute longer to blend all the flavors. Taste for seasoning. Serve either hot or at room temperature.

SERVES FOUR OR FIVE AS A SIDE DISH OR AS PART OF AN ANTIPASTO
OFFERING. I made this gratin when I worked at a French bistro in Manhattan years
ago. The original was seasoned with brown butter, but I've southern-Italianized it by
adding anchovies, garlic, and olive oil.

CAULIFLOWER GRATIN WITH CAPERS AND EGGS

2 salt-packed anchovies, filleted,
soaked, and drained (see page 33)

1 large garlic clove

3 tablespoons unsalted butter at room
temperature

2 tablespoons extra-virgin olive oil

Salt and freshly ground black pepper
to taste

1 large cauliflower, cut into small florets

2 hard-cooked eggs (see note), yolks
crumbled, whites reserved for another
dish

Handful of salt-packed capers, soaked
and drained (see page 29)

$1/2$ cup homemade dry bread crumbs

Handful of fresh flat-leaf parsley leaves,
chopped

Preheat the oven to 450°F.

In a mortar or a mini food processor, combine the anchovies and garlic. Grind to a
paste. Add the butter and olive oil. Season with a tiny amount of salt and a more generous amount of pepper. Mix until everything is creamy.

Cook the cauliflower florets in a large pot of salted boiling water for 3 minutes, or until
crisp-tender. Empty into a colander and drain well.

Put the still-warm cauliflower in a 12-inch round baking dish or an equivalent square-
dish. Add all but about 1 tablespoon of the anchovy mixture and toss until the cauliflower
is well coated. Bake uncovered until lightly browned and fragrant, about 15 minutes.

Take the dish from the oven and scatter on the crumbled egg yolks, capers, and bread
crumbs. Dot the top with the remaining anchovy mixture and return it to the oven until
the top is lightly browned, about 5 minutes. Scatter on the parsley. Serve hot.

TO HARD-COOK EGGS   Put the eggs in a saucepan. Add cold water to cover by 1 inch. Bring the water
to a rolling boil over high heat. Turn off the heat, cover the pan, and let it sit on the turned-off
burner for 10 minutes. Run the eggs under cold water and peel.

SERVES FOUR OR FIVE AS A SIDE DISH. Here's a classic Sicilian treatment for cauliflower. I often toss it with bucatini pasta, but it's lovely served as is, as a vegetable side dish.

CAULIFLOWER WITH SAFFRON, RAISINS, AND PINE NUTS

1 large cauliflower, cut into florets, tough stems trimmed

3 tablespoons extra-virgin olive oil, plus more for drizzling

2 medium shallots, thinly sliced

Salt and freshly ground black pepper to taste

Pinch of ground cloves

Generous palmful of raisins soaked in dry white wine to cover until plump

Generous pinch of saffron threads, toasted, ground (see page 42), and dissolved in 2 tablespoons warm water

Palmful of pine nuts, lightly toasted (see page 61)

3 to 4 fennel fronds or dill sprigs (see note), chopped

In a large pot of salted boiling water, blanch the cauliflower for about 3 minutes, or until crisp-tender. Drain in a colander and run cold water over it to stop the cooking. Drain.

In a large skillet, heat the 3 tablespoons olive oil over medium heat. Add the shallots and sauté for 2 to 3 minutes. Add the cauliflower and season with salt, pepper, and ground cloves. Sauté until the cauliflower is tender and fragrant, about 5 minutes. Add the raisins and wine and let the wine boil down to almost nothing. Add the saffron water and pine nuts and simmer for 1 minute. Add the fennel or dill. Taste for seasoning, adding a few fresh grindings of pepper and a drizzle of fresh olive oil. Toss gently. Serve warm or at room temperature.

NOTE   This dish is traditionally flavored with wild fennel fronds. Look for them at farmers' markets or, in California, growing along the highway.

SERVES FOUR AS A FIRST COURSE. Dress this just before serving so everything stays crisp. A few chopped anchovies are a classic addition, but here I've used bottarga, the pressed tuna or gray mullet roe famous in Sicily and Sardinia, which gives this simple summer dish an exciting, salty bite. For more information on buying and cooking with bottarga, see page 32.

GREEN BEAN AND TOMATO SALAD WITH CELERY AND BOTTARGA

12 ounces tender green beans or haricots verts, trimmed

3 tender inner stalks celery, thinly sliced, plus leaves from 5 stalks, chopped

1 large red shallot, thinly sliced

2 cups red cherry tomatoes, halved

Leaves from 3 or 4 marjoram sprigs, chopped

3 tablespoons extra-virgin olive oil

1/2 teaspoon Champagne vinegar

Pinch of salt

Freshly ground black pepper to taste

About 12 scrapings bottarga (preferably gray mullet roe from Sardinia)

In a medium pot of boiling water, blanch the beans for about 3 minutes. Using a large skimmer, transfer the beans to a colander and run cold water over them to preserve their color. Drain.

In a large salad bowl, combine the beans, celery and celery leaves, shallot, cherry tomatoes, and marjoram. Pour on the olive oil and Champagne vinegar. Add the salt (remember the bottarga is very salty) and a few grindings of pepper. Toss everything gently. With a sharp vegetable peeler, shave the bottarga into the bowl and give it another gentle toss.

Divide the salad among salad plates and serve right away.

SERVING SUGGESTION I like serving this salad with *taralli,* the hard ring biscuits from Puglia (see page 307 for more on *taralli*).

SERVES FOUR AS A SIDE DISH. I have a nostalgic fondness for Romano beans. My father grew them in his small garden, and many other Italian American families I knew grew them. This is my version of an old family recipe. I've substituted rosemary here for the basil or parsley or dried oregano my mother would have used. The flavor combination of pancetta and rosemary is a wonderful one, warm and deep. I use it in winter, when I make this with canned tomatoes. For a summer version, use fresh tomatoes and basil.

ROMANO BEANS WITH PANCETTA AND ROSEMARY

1 pound Romano beans

2 tablespoons extra-virgin olive oil, plus more for drizzling

2 thin slices pancetta, chopped

2 garlic cloves, thinly sliced

Sprinkling of red pepper flakes

Leaves from 3 small rosemary sprigs, chopped

Salt to taste

5 or 6 canned plum tomatoes, chopped, with a little of their juice

1/8 teaspoon Spanish sherry vinegar

In a large pot of salted boiling water, blanch the Romano beans for about 3 minutes, or until crisp-tender. With a large strainer, transfer the beans to a colander and run cold water over them to preserve their color. Drain well.

In a large skillet, heat the 2 tablespoons olive oil over medium heat. Add the pancetta and cook until crisp, about 4 minutes. Add the garlic, red pepper flakes, rosemary, and Romano beans. Season with salt and sauté until the beans are coated with flavor, 3 or 4 minutes. Add the tomatoes and cook until they start giving off juice, another 3 or 4 minutes. Add the Spanish sherry vinegar and stir it in. Taste for seasoning, adding extra salt, if needed. Add a drizzle of fresh olive oil and serve either hot or warm.

VARIATIONS   For a summer version, substitute fresh basil for the rosemary and 2 large, round summer tomatoes, chopped and drained for the canned plum tomatoes.

Although it gives these beans an entirely different taste than the rosemary, mint is excellent used as a substitute, but add it at the end of cooking so the flavor stays bright.

SERVES FOUR AS A SIDE DISH, SIX AS AN ANTIPASTO OFFERING. *Scapece* is a pungent vinegar-and-mint-seasoned dish I've tasted in Campania, Sicily, and also in Puglia. It has remained popular with Italian Americans. It's often made with zucchini, but eggplant stands up to the strong vinegar and mint seasoning better, especially when hot chilies are also included. The dish should be sharp, but not piercingly so. I like to use Champagne vinegar in it; it's a bit milder than regular white wine vinegar and gives a mellower result.

EGGPLANT WITH VINEGAR, MINT, AND CHILIES

2 unpeeled eggplants, cut into thin rounds (the long Italian ones are better for this than the rounder varieties)

Salt to taste

Extra-virgin olive oil for frying, plus 2 tablespoons

1/4 cup Champagne vinegar

1/4 cup water

Small handful of fresh mint leaves, chopped

5 or 6 fresh basil leaves, chopped

2 large garlic cloves, very thinly sliced

1/2 small, fresh red chili such as a peperoncino, minced (including seeds if you like some heat)

Lay the eggplant slices on paper towels and sprinkle them lightly on both sides with salt. This will draw out some of the water so they brown more easily and don't become soggy. Let stand for 1 hour and pat them dry.

In a large, heavy skillet, heat 1 inch olive oil over medium-high heat. Test the oil by dipping the edge of one of the eggplant pieces into it; it will sizzle immediately if it's hot enough. Fry the eggplant in batches until golden, about 3 minutes on each side. Using tongs, transfer to paper towels to drain. (The smell of vegetables frying in extra-virgin olive oil is one of my favorite culinary experiences, and worth the extra pennies it costs.)

In a small saucepan, combine the vinegar, water, and 2 tablespoons of olive oil. Bring to a boil over medium heat and cook to reduce by half, about 5 minutes.

In a shallow, wide serving bowl or dish (a 9-inch round), layer half of the eggplant. Scatter on half of the herbs, garlic, and chili, and a sprinkle of salt. Pour on half of the hot vinegar mixture. Repeat with a second layer. Cover the dish with plastic wrap and let it stand at room temperature for 1 hour. Or, refrigerate overnight, but return it to room temperature before serving.

SERVING SUGGESTIONS   Serve this as part of an antipasto platter that includes soppressata, or caciatorini, and maybe a few sharp southern Italian cheeses, like provolone and caciocavallo. It also makes a great sandwich if you layer the eggplant with a few slices of mozzarella.

SERVES SIX AS AN ANTIPASTO OR A FIRST COURSE. Caponata is made all over Sicily, and in my opinion it is one of the genius dishes of Sicilian cooking, blending the much-loved eggplant with pine nuts, green olives, raisins, capers, and the sweet-and-sour flavors that derive partly from Arab cooking. The sweet-and-sour taste is achieved by cooking sugar with vinegar and reducing it to a syrup. At its most elaborate and festive, caponata can be decorated with sautéed baby octopus, calamari, shrimp, or other seafood and dusted with powdered cocoa or cinnamon. A real Baroque treatment.

I came across an unusual recipe in an old cookbook I bought in Palermo that added pear to caponata, and this is my version of that combination. The pear adds another layer of sweetness but also fruitiness, lightening what can sometimes be an overly intense taste experience. I've left out the traditional green olives, preferring to highlight the capers instead. *Caponatina* is a simpler version of caponata, with a more delicate appearance because the vegetables are more finely chopped. It is usually served unadorned or garnished simply with chopped almonds or pistachios. Serve it with toasted bread.

CAPONATINA WITH PEARS AND GOLDEN RAISINS

4 tablespoons extra-virgin olive oil, preferably Sicilian

2 small celery stalks with leaves, stalks cut into medium dice, leaves chopped

1 large onion, finely diced

1 firm pear, peeled, cored, and cut into medium dice

1 tablespoon high-quality white wine vinegar or Champagne vinegar

1 teaspoon sugar

2 unpeeled eggplants, cut into medium dice

Salt and freshly ground black pepper to taste

Pinch of ground cinnamon

2 medium tomatoes, peeled, seeded, and cut into medium dice (see page 26), or 4 canned plum tomatoes, chopped

Small handful of pine nuts, lightly toasted (see page 61)

Small handful of golden raisins

Palmful of salt-packed Sicilian capers, soaked and drained (see page 29)

About 10 fresh basil leaves, chopped

In a large skillet, heat 2 tablespoons of the olive oil over medium heat. Add the celery, celery leaves, and onion and sauté until soft, about 4 minutes. Add the pear and sauté until it is soft but the pieces are still intact, about 4 minutes. Add the vinegar and sugar and cook a minute or so to dissolve the sugar. You should smell a pungent sweet-and-sour aroma and have a liquidy glaze left in the skillet. Pour the celery mixture and pan liquid into a large serving bowl.

Add the remaining 2 tablespoons olive oil to the skillet over medium heat. Add the eggplant and season with salt, pepper, and cinnamon. Sauté until softened and lightly browned. Add the tomatoes and cook until they start to give up their juices, about 5 minutes. Add the pine nuts, raisins, capers, and basil. Transfer to the serving bowl. Give everything a good mix. Taste for seasoning. The caponata should have a pronounced but not too aggressive sweet-and-sour flavor. Taste and adjust the seasoning by adding a drizzle more vinegar, a pinch of sugar, or more salt, if needed.

Let cool to room temperature. Caponata keeps well for about 5 days in the refrigerator, but always return it to room temperature before serving.

VARIATIONS For a more traditional caponata, leave out the pear and add a small handful of chopped green olives along with the pine nuts, raisins, and capers. Another addition, giving the dish a Spanish touch, is to sprinkle 1 teaspoon unsweetened cocoa over the eggplant as you sauté it.

SERVES SIX AS A FIRST COURSE OR A LIGHT SUPPER. The southern Italian's love for rolling and stuffing just about any type of food extends to vegetables. This eggplant dish has been a favorite of mine since my childhood when my father first ordered it for me at Angelo's, on Mulberry Street in New York. This rendition includes prosciutto and sage, an herb that wasn't present at my first tasting. It's a simple dish, with few ingredients, but it has a polished, almost formal presentation that makes it seem celebratory.

EGGPLANT INVOLTINI WITH RICOTTA AND PROSCIUTTO

Extra-virgin olive oil for brushing and drizzling

3 unpeeled large eggplants

Salt and freshly ground black pepper to taste

1½ cups whole-milk ricotta, drained in a colander for about 20 minutes if it seems loose

1 egg, beaten

Pinch of ground nutmeg

1 cup grated Parmigiano-Reggiano cheese

4 ounces prosciutto di Parma, thinly sliced

Handful of fresh sage leaves

Preheat the oven to 425°F. Coat a baking sheet and a 9-by-13-inch baking dish with olive oil.

Cut off the top and bottom of the eggplants so they can stand upright. With a very sharp knife, cut the eggplant into ¼-inch-thick vertical slices, discarding the first and last pieces that are all skin. Brush the eggplant slices with olive oil on both sides and sprinkle them with salt and pepper. Lay the eggplant slices on the prepared pan and bake until lightly browned and tender, about 20 minutes. Let cool to the touch (this will also firm them up a bit, making them easier to roll).

In a small bowl, mix the ricotta, egg, nutmeg, 2 tablespoons of the grated cheese, and salt and pepper to taste.

Gently pull the eggplant off the sheet pan (if they stick, gently wedge a spatula under them). Lay them out on a work surface (if one side is browner, lay them brown side down). Lay a piece of prosciutto on each slice, cutting it to fit if necessary. Place 3 or 4 sage leaves on the prosciutto. Place a heaping tablespoonful of the ricotta at one end of each of the eggplant slices. Roll up the eggplant and place them, seam side down, in the prepared baking dish. Sprinkle with a thin coating of grated cheese. Grind fresh pepper over the top and drizzle with olive oil. Bake, uncovered, until bubbling hot and lightly golden, about 15 minutes. Serve warm or at room temperature.

VARIATION   To serve with tomato sauce, accompany with Winter Tomato Sauce (see page 113), served hot in a bowl alongside.

SERVES FOUR OR FIVE AS A SIDE DISH. If you really love parsley, as I do, make a parsley pesto, where its flavor can really shine. I rub the pesto into the flesh of halved eggplants and bake them in a hot oven. For something so simple, the dish has really rich flavor.

BAKED EGGPLANT WITH PARSLEY PESTO

PARSLEY PESTO

1 large garlic clove

3 oil-packed anchovies or 2 salt-packed anchovies, filleted, soaked, and drained (see page 33)

1 shallot

Large handful of fresh flat-leaf parsley leaves

$1/4$ cup extra-virgin olive oil

Salt and freshly ground black pepper to taste

4 small (about 4 inches long) globe eggplants or Asian eggplants, halved

Preheat the oven to 425°F. Lightly oil a baking sheet.

TO MAKE THE PESTO: In a food processor, combine the garlic, anchovies, and shallot. Pulse to a paste. Add the parsley, olive oil, salt, and pepper. Pulse a few times until just blended but still coarse.

With a thin, sharp knife, score the cut side of the eggplants in a large diamond pattern, cutting about halfway down (be careful not to cut into the skin). Spread a generous amount of pesto on each eggplant, working it down into the cuts. Place them on the prepared pan and bake until lightly browned and tender, about 30 minutes.

You can serve these hot, but the flavors seem more vibrant to me when they're eaten at room temperature.

SERVES FOUR. This is my interpretation of a dish I like to order at Bar Pitti, a trattoria near where I live in Greenwich Village. A whole, soft buffalo mozzarella is plopped down in the middle of a warm bell-pepper compote. It's a great cold-weather lunch dish (I always drizzle the cheese with a good amount of extra olive oil). I've flavored my *peperonata* more elaborately than Bar Pitti does, adding a generous pinch of clove and fresh rosemary.

If you can't find buffalo mozzarella, one made with cow's milk is a fine substitute, especially if you know a place that makes it fresh on the premises. (See page 49 for more information on mozzarella.)

BUFFALO MOZZARELLA WITH WARM, SPICED PEPERONATA

PEPERONATA

2 tablespoons extra-virgin olive oil

2 garlic cloves, thinly sliced

5 red bell peppers, roasted, peeled, and cut into strips (see page 36)

Generous pinch ground cloves

Small pinch ground nutmeg

Leaves from 3 to 4 small rosemary sprigs, chopped

1 bay leaf, preferably fresh

Salt and freshly ground black pepper to taste

1 tablespoon dry red wine

2 tomatoes, peeled, seeded, and chopped (see page 26)

Warm water, if needed

Two 1-pound balls buffalo mozzarella at room temperature, halved

Handful of fresh flat-leaf parsley sprigs, stemmed and chopped

TO MAKE THE PEPERONATA: In a medium skillet, heat the 2 tablespoons olive oil over medium heat. Add the garlic and sauté for a few seconds to release some flavor. Add the sliced peppers, cloves, nutmeg, rosemary, and bay leaf. Season with salt and pepper and sauté until the peppers are tender, about 4 minutes. Add the red wine and cook for a few seconds to cook off some alcohol. Add the tomatoes and simmer for about 4 minutes to soften the tomatoes and release some of their juice. You should have some liquid in the skillet. If the consistency seems dry, add a little water. Taste for seasoning.

Spoon the *peperonata* onto 4 small plates. Place half a cheese ball in the center of each. Drizzle on a little olive oil and scatter the parsley on top. Serve warm. You can make this a day ahead, if you like, and reheat it, adding a little warm water if necessary to bring back a moist consistency.

VARIATIONS   The cloves and rosemary are my additions to this southern Italian classic, but they are not usual seasonings. For a traditional flavor, omit the cloves and rosemary and add a few chopped anchovies or a palmful of capers, and a small handful of chopped fresh basil or some chopped fresh oregano.

This *peperonata*, with slices of mozzarella, makes very nice, if a little sloppy, *panino* on a traditional long Italian loaf.

NOTE   This version of *peperonata* is simmered longer and is more saucelike than the one on page 129, which is sautéed quickly and served cool. Both styles are traditional.

SERVES FIVE OR SIX AS AN ANTIPASTO DISH OR A FIRST COURSE. *Mandorlata di peperoni*—almond-flavored sweet peppers—is a classic dish from Basilicata, in my opinion another one of those genius dishes of the southern Italian kitchen. The flavor combination is truly opulent, and whenever I serve it, guests comment on how beautiful it looks and how luscious it tastes.

The amaretto liqueur is not traditional, but I like the way it heightens the almond flavor and underlines the sweetness of the peppers.

PEPERONATA WITH ALMONDS, BASILICATA STYLE

$^1/_4$ cup extra-virgin olive oil, plus more for drizzling

2 garlic cloves, very thinly sliced

1 small dried red chili, crumbled (seeded if you like less heat)

Pinch of ground nutmeg

5 red bell peppers, roasted, peeled, and cut into thin strips (see page 36)

Salt to taste

$^1/_2$ cup whole blanched almonds, lightly toasted (see page 77)

1 tablespoon amaretto liqueur

Leaves from 3 to 4 large sprigs flat-leaf parsley, chopped

In a large skillet, heat the $^1/_4$ cup olive oil over medium-low heat. Add the garlic, the dried chili, the nutmeg, and bell pepper strips, seasoning with a little salt. Sauté until the peppers are soft and fragrant and the garlic has turned very lightly golden. Add the almonds and sauté for about 1 minute. Add the amaretto and let it boil away. Add the parsley and a drizzle of fresh olive oil. Serve at room temperature.

VARIATIONS   Many *peperonata* variations exist throughout southern Italy. The almonds are specific to Basilicata. Anchovies are typical of Campania. One I was served in Palermo included basil, garlic, and anchovies, a particularly good mix of flavors.

SERVING SUGGESTION   One of my all-time favorite dinners is roasted leg of lamb served with this *peperonata*. The flavors marry beautifully.

SERVES FOUR AS A FIRST COURSE. I recall eating beets only once in southern Italy, in a restaurant in Lecce, Puglia, where they were dressed with mint, vinegar, and olive oil. They are plentiful at my farmers' market in late summer, though, and with their saturated colors ranging from golden yellow to brilliant crimson, their beauty intrigues me. I always take bunches of them home, and think a little harder than usual to figure out what to do with them.

Here, I've reached into my southern Italian flavor bag for citrus and nuts, a touch of anchovy, and fruity olive oil to create an interesting salad whose ingredients complement the beets' sweet and slightly bitter notes.

ROASTED BEET SALAD WITH CANDIED LEMON AND PISTACHIOS

2 lemons

1 tablespoon sugar

5 crimson or golden beets, beet greens trimmed to 1 inch and reserved for another use, beets scrubbed

1 oil-packed anchovy fillet, minced

1 garlic clove, crushed

2 or 3 scrapings freshly grated nutmeg

1 tablespoon Spanish sherry vinegar

Salt and freshly ground black pepper to taste

$1/4$ cup extra-virgin olive oil

1 large bunch arugula, stemmed

1 small red onion, very thinly sliced

Large handful of unsalted pistachios

Peel the zest from the lemons in long, thin strips with a zester, cutting off as little of the white pith as possible (if you don't have a zester that will do this, remove the skin with a sharp vegetable peeler and then cut it into thin strips). Put the strips in a small saucepan, and add the sugar and cold water to cover. Over medium heat, bring the water to a boil and simmer until the water has evaporated and the zest is sticky. Spread the zest out on a counter or cutting board to dry for about 30 minutes.

Preheat the oven to 400°F. Wrap the beets in aluminum foil and place them on a baking sheet or in a shallow baking dish. Roast until tender and fragrant, about 1 hour (a thin knife should pierce the biggest one easily). Let the beets cool a few minutes, then trim and slip off their skins. Cut the beets into thin slices.

In a small bowl, combine the anchovy, garlic, nutmeg, Spanish sherry vinegar, salt, and pepper. Whisk in the olive oil and taste for seasoning (the sweetness of beets can take a little extra salt).

Put the arugula in a salad bowl and toss it with a drizzle of the dressing. Divide it among 4 salad plates. In the same salad bowl, combine the beets, red onion, pistachios, and candied lemon zest. Pour on the rest of the dressing and toss very gently so the slices don't break up (I do this with my fingers). Divide the beets onto the arugula. Serve right away.

VARIATIONS Orange is another citrus fruit that goes well with beets. I sometimes include a few slices in this salad (if I use golden beets, blood oranges are a good contrast). Crumbled young goat cheese is delicious scattered over the top right before serving. If you'd like to include an herb, basil, tarragon, or mint marries especially well with beets.

SERVES FOUR AS A LIGHT LUNCH OR SIDE DISH. Neapolitan-style stuffed cabbage was never cooked in my family, but I had it with friends' families when I was a kid and always liked its flavor. Rice and pork sausage are the standard stuffing; this recipe uses a soft goat cheese and substitutes pancetta for the sausage, making the filling lighter.

STUFFED SAVOY CABBAGE WITH CAPRINO, RICE, AND PANCETTA

1 head savoy cabbage

1½ cups long-grain white rice

3 cups water

2 tablespoons extra-virgin olive oil, plus more for drizzling

4 thin slices pancetta, cut into small dice

5 scallions, including tender green parts, thinly sliced

2 inner celery stalks, finely diced

1 garlic clove, thinly sliced

Leaves from 3 to 4 small rosemary sprigs, minced

Salt and freshly ground black pepper to taste

One 11-ounce log caprino or other fresh goat cheese, crumbled

1 large egg, lightly beaten

Large handful of Gaeta or niçoise olives, pitted and coarsely chopped

Handful of fresh flat-leaf parsley leaves, chopped

½ cup dry white wine

TOMATO SAUCE

2 tablespoons extra-virgin olive oil

2 garlic cloves, thinly sliced

3 to 4 small rosemary sprigs

1 tablespoon brandy or Cognac

One 35-ounce can of plum tomatoes, well chopped, including juice

1 tablespoon heavy cream or crème fraiche

Salt and freshly ground black pepper to taste

Remove 12 large leaves from the savoy cabbage, discarding any outer leaves that seem tough or bruised. Blanch the leaves in a large pot of boiling water for 3 minutes. Drain into a colander and run cold water over them to stop the cooking. Transfer to paper towels to drain.

Preheat the oven to 400°F. Coat a 9-by-13-inch serving dish with olive oil.

Put the rice in a medium pot and add the water. Bring to a boil, then reduce the heat to low, cover, and cook until tender, about 15 minutes. Set aside to cool.

In a large skillet, heat the 2 tablespoons olive oil over medium heat. Add the pancetta and sauté until it begins to crisp. Add the scallions and celery and sauté until the vegetables are soft, 3 or 4 minutes. Add the garlic and rosemary and cook for 1 or 2 minutes. Remove from heat and let cool briefly. Add the rice to the skillet, season with salt and pepper, and gently stir. Add the goat cheese, egg, olives, parsley, and a drizzle of olive oil. Gently stir and taste for seasoning. (The rice should be well seasoned, so add a little more salt if necessary.)

Place about $1/4$ cup of rice filling on each cabbage leaf, positioning it toward the root end of the leaf. Pull the end up over the rice and then tuck in the sides. Roll the leaf closed, forming a little package. Place the cabbage rolls, seam side down, in the prepared baking dish and pour the white wine over. Generously drizzle with olive oil and sprinkle with a little salt and pepper to taste. Bake, uncovered, until hot, bubbly, and very lightly browned on top, about 30 minutes.

WHILE THE CABBAGE IS BAKING, MAKE THE SAUCE: In a medium skillet, heat the olive oil over medium heat. Add the garlic and rosemary sprigs and sauté for 1 or 2 minutes. Add the brandy or Cognac and let it boil away. Add the tomatoes, increase the heat to high, and cook, uncovered, to reduce slightly, about 5 minutes. Turn off the heat, add the cream or crème fraîche, and season with salt and pepper.

When the cabbage is done, pour the sauce into a serving bowl, reheating it gently if you need to. Bring everything to the table and present the cabbage with a ladle of sauce on top of each serving.

SERVES TWO AS A FIRST COURSE. Pan-seared scamorza or caciocavallo cheese is often presented as a main course in southern Italy, an alternative to a meat dish. It's served unaccompanied, on a big plate, hot and gooey, to eat quickly with a knife and fork before it cools. I like it in a smaller portion on top of greens, as a first course. And I use a sweet-and-sharp yellow-pepper vinaigrette with fresh marjoram, whereas in Sicily the hot cheese is traditionally seasoned with vinegar and dried oregano when it's pulled from the skillet.

SEARED SCAMORZA WITH CHICORY AND YELLOW PEPPER VINAIGRETTE

1 yellow bell pepper, roasted, peeled, and finely diced (see page 38)

Salt to taste

1 small garlic clove, lightly crushed

1 teaspoon Spanish sherry vinegar

5 tablespoons extra-virgin olive oil

1 small head chicory, cut into bite-sized pieces

Two 1/2-inch-thick slices scamorza cheese

Leaves from 5 or 6 large marjoram sprigs, chopped

Freshly ground black pepper to taste

Put the diced pepper in a small bowl. Add the salt and garlic. Add vinegar and 2 tablespoons of the olive oil. Stir.

TO SERVE, put the chicory in a medium bowl and toss with a little over half of the vinaigrette. Divide between 2 plates.

In a medium skillet, preferably nonstick, heat the remaining 3 tablespoons olive oil over medium-high heat. When the oil is very hot, add the scamorza, leaving a tiny space between the slices so they don't stick together. Sauté the cheese until it is golden on one side, about 1 minute. Flip the slices over and sauté the other side. Lift the cheese from the skillet with a slotted spatula (so the oil can drain off) and place 1 slice on each salad. Drizzle with the remaining vinaigrette, sprinkle on the marjoram, and give each one a few turns of pepper. Serve right away.

NOTE   I've designed the recipe for only 2 servings, making it easier to manage. You can double it if you like, but if you do I'd suggest using 2 skillets to sear all the cheese at once.

SERVES SIX AS A SIDE DISH. I like mayonnaise-based coleslaw well enough, but in my ongoing campaign to southern-Italianize American foods I've come up with a coleslaw with pine nuts, raisins, basil, a touch of fresh chili, and fruity extra-virgin olive oil. It goes very well with an Italian-style barbecue of sausages and peppers. Ruffly savoy cabbage is more tender than purple and green cabbage, and I like it better for a raw salad.

COLESLAW WITH SICILIAN FLAVORS

1 small savoy cabbage, trimmed of tough outer leaves, cored, and very thinly sliced

5 scallions, including tender green parts, cut into thin rounds

Large handful of pine nuts, lightly toasted (see page 61)

Handful of golden raisins, soaked in dry white wine to cover

1 small red peperoncino chili, seeded and minced

Pinch of sugar

Pinch of freshly grated nutmeg

Salt to taste

$1/3$ cup extra-virgin olive oil

2 teaspoons high-quality white wine vinegar or Champagne vinegar

Generous handful of fresh basil leaves, chopped

In a large serving bowl, combine the sliced cabbage, scallions, pine nuts, golden raisins with their wine, chili, sugar, nutmeg, and a generous amount of salt. Toss briefly. Add the olive oil, vinegar, and basil. Toss well. Let stand at room temperature for about 30 minutes (to give the flavors time to develop and meld).

Taste and adjust the seasoning. Serve now, or make it a few hours ahead and refrigerate, but return it to room temperature before serving so all the flavors can really shine.

SERVING SUGGESTION I love this served as a sit-down first course on salad plates that have been lined with thin rounds of soppressata or cacciatorini. Spoon some of the coleslaw into the center of each plate and garnish with basil sprigs.

Serves five or six as a first course or to serve after a main course. Blood oranges have fantastic color, ranging from just slightly rose tinted to dark burgundy throughout the skin and the flesh, and their taste is sweet, like a regular orange, but with a pleasant sharp edge—perfect for a savory salad (for more on varieties of blood oranges and cooking suggestions, see page 30). Varieties of orange salad are served throughout Sicily, sometimes pairing the fruit with sliced fennel or celery, and often with red onion, which I've chosen for my version. Salt, abundant freshly ground pepper, and extra-virgin olive oil make up the classic dressing. Anchovies or preserved herring are also common additions. Oranges go with salty, preserved fish much better than you'd imagine, especially when dressed with good olive oil and finished with a scattering of basil.

BLOOD ORANGE SALAD WITH FENNEL AND A HINT OF ANCHOVY

7 or 8 blood oranges, peeled and cut into thin rounds

2 fennel bulbs, trimmed, cored, and thinly sliced

1 small red onion, cut into very thin rounds

Handful of Gaeta or kalamata olives, pitted and halved

3 oil-packed anchovy fillets, minced, or 2 salt-packed anchovies, filleted, soaked, drained, and minced (see page 33)

Estate-bottled extra-virgin olive oil for drizzling

Sea salt and freshly ground black pepper to taste

3 or 4 fresh basil leaves, cut into thin strips

Arrange the orange slices in a circular pattern on a large, pretty serving platter. Scatter on the fennel and red onion. Top with the olives and scatter on the anchovies. Drizzle with a generous amount of olive oil. Season with salt and pepper. Garnish with the basil strips and serve at once.

SERVES FOUR OR FIVE AS A SIDE DISH. Thanksgiving dinner at my grandparents' always involved a brazen mix of dishes: Waldorf salad with canned tangerine sections and marshmallows; artichokes filled with sausage; lasagna with ricotta and tomatoes; sweet potatoes baked with pineapple chunks; cranberry sauce; a huge overcooked turkey; a big bowl of raw fennel and olives; pumpkin pie; and fried *struffoli*.

Now, when I work out my Thanksgiving menu, it tends to fall naturally into turkey and a few southern Italian–style vegetable dishes. Endive is not a vegetable I recall ever eating anywhere in southern Italy, but it is a member of the chicory family, with that bitter quality so beloved in the south. It marries beautifully with sweet, slow-cooked garlic, and together they've become a new addition to my Thanksgiving table.

BRAISED ENDIVE WITH GARLIC CREAM

2 cups nonultrapasterized heavy cream

1 large garlic clove, minced

Salt and freshly ground black pepper to taste

2 or 3 scrapings freshly grated nutmeg

2 tablespoons unsalted butter

Extra-virgin olive oil for drizzling

8 Belgian endives, bruised outer leaves removed

Leaves from 3 or 4 thyme sprigs, chopped

3 tablespoons freshly grated young pecorino cheese

Handful of fresh flat-leaf parsley leaves, chopped

Preheat the oven to 375°F.

In a small bowl, mix the cream with the garlic. Season with salt, pepper, and nutmeg. Set aside at room temperature. In a large skillet, melt the butter with a drizzle of olive oil over medium heat. Add the endives, thyme, and a pinch of salt and sauté until the endives are golden all over.

Place the endives in a 9-by-13-inch baking dish. Pour the garlic cream over the top, cover with aluminum foil, and bake for 45 minutes. Uncover the dish and spoon some of the cream over the endives. Sprinkle with the pecorino. Put the dish back in the oven, uncovered, and bake until bubbling and lightly browned, about another 15 minutes. By now the cream will have reduced and the endives will be very tender. Garnish with parsley and serve.

Serves four. Here, figs are paired with the bitter and sharp notes of arugula, celery, pepper-studded pepato cheese from Sicily, basil, fennel, and lemon. Green figs to me have a better-tasting skin than the dark variety, which can sometimes be musty.

GREEN FIG SALAD WITH PEPATO, FENNEL, AND BASIL

1 bunch arugula, stemmed

1 large fennel bulb, trimmed, cored, and thinly sliced (handful of fronds reserved and chopped)

4 inner celery stalks with leaves, stalks thinly sliced, leaves left whole

1 large shallot, thinly sliced

10 green figs, halved lengthwise

Small handful fresh basil leaves

Grated zest of $1/2$ lemon

1 tablespoon lemon juice

Pinch of salt

3 tablespoons extra-virgin olive oil

1 chunk pepato cheese

In a large salad bowl, combine the arugula, fennel and chopped fronds, celery and celery leaves, shallot, and figs. Add the basil leaves. In a small bowl, whisk the lemon zest and juice, salt, and olive oil. Taste for a good balance of olive and acid, adjusting it if you need to. Pour over the salad and toss gently. Divide the salad among 4 salad plates and shave a generous amount of the pepato over each one. Serve right away.

SERVES FOUR AS A FIRST COURSE. This is a simple composed salad with a good balance of sweet and salty, inspired by a similar one served at Grano Trattoria, in Greenwich Village. The spice in the walnuts is my own addition.

SPINACH SALAD WITH PEARS, SPICED WALNUTS, AND RICOTTA SALATA

WALNUTS

A few drops of extra-virgin olive oil

1/2 cup very fresh walnut halves

Pinch of salt

4 scrapings freshly grated nutmeg

Pinch of ground cinnamon

Pinch of sugar

Pinch of cayenne pepper

DRESSING

1 garlic clove, crushed

1 tablespoon fresh lemon juice

Salt and freshly ground black pepper to taste

3 tablespoons extra-virgin olive oil

SALAD

2 unpeeled ripe pears, cored and thinly sliced (red Anjou are especially pretty for this)

2 cups baby spinach leaves

1 shallot, very thinly sliced

1 small chunk ricotta salata

Heat a medium sauté pan over medium-low heat for 1 minute. Add all the spiced-walnut ingredients and sauté until the walnuts are fragrant and lightly toasted, 3 or 4 minutes.

TO MAKE THE DRESSING: In a small bowl, combine the garlic, lemon juice, salt, and pepper. Whisk in the olive oil.

Decorate the rims of 4 salad plates with the pear slices.

Put the spinach and shallot in a medium salad bowl. Remove the garlic from the dressing. Add the dressing to the salad and toss. Divide the salad among the 4 plates. Shave or crumble some ricotta salata over each salad and garnish with the walnuts. Serve right away.

SERVES SIX AS A SIDE DISH OR FIRST COURSE. Gigante beans look like huge white limas, but they're actually a Mediterranean heirloom variety originally from Greece. I find them at Buon Italia, my neighborhood Italian food importer, in Manhattan's Chelsea district, and I also buy them from Phipps County Store and Farm, a farm in Pescadero, Californa (see the Sources, page 436). You may find similar beans labeled Corona at your market.

Sun-dried tomatoes have strong flavor. I like using them in small amounts, chopped into tiny flecks, so they punctuate a dish with hints of flavor and don't overwhelm.

GIGANTE BEANS WITH SAGE, LEEKS, AND SUN-DRIED TOMATOES

2 cups Gigante or Corona beans, soaked overnight in cool water to cover by 4 inches

2 bay leaves, preferably fresh

Extra-virgin olive oil for drizzling, plus 2 tablespoons

Salt to taste

2 leeks, including light green parts, rinsed and cut into thin rings

Pinch of ground cloves

2 celery stalks, thinly sliced, plus leaves from 4 stalks

2 tablespoons dry white wine

6 fresh sage leaves, cut into thin strips

5 oil-packed sun-dried tomatoes, finely chopped

Freshly ground black pepper to taste

Drain the beans and put them in a large pot. Add cold water to cover by about 6 inches. Add the bay leaves and turn the heat to high. When the water starts to boil, reduce the heat to a simmer, partially cover the pot, and cook at the lowest bubble until the beans are tender, about 1½ hours. (The cooking time really depends on the dryness of your beans, so taste one after about an hour to see how far along they are.) Add additional water to the pot at any time if the level gets low. Resist the temptation to stir the beans while they cook; this could cause them to break up. Also, don't add salt or anything acidy to the water while they're cooking because it might toughen their skins.

When the beans are tender, turn off the heat and let them sit in the water, uncovered, for about 30 minutes (this seems to further tenderize them without overcooking). Drain the beans and put them in a large serving bowl. Drizzle with a generous amount of olive oil, season with salt, and give them a gentle toss (I like doing this with my hands because you can feel when you're starting to break up with beans and judge better how gentle you should be).

In a large skillet, heat the 2 tablespoons olive oil over high heat. Add the leeks, cloves, and chopped celery (not the celery leaves, though). Sauté for about 1 minute. (You don't want to cook these vegetables, just take the raw edge off and coax out their flavors to coat the beans.) Add the white wine and let it bubble for a few seconds.

Pour the vegetables with the skillet juices over the beans. Add the celery leaves, sage, sun-dried tomatoes, and a generous drizzle of fresh olive oil. Season with a little more salt and a few grindings of pepper. Toss gently and taste for seasoning.

Serve at room temperature. (You can refrigerate them overnight, but take them from the refrigerator about 1 hour before serving. You also might want to recheck the seasoning. Sometimes refrigeration can subdue certain flavors like salt or acid, and you might need to fine-tune the dish again.)

NOTE   Many cooks add vinegar to beans, dressing them like a salad. I prefer a mellow approach to seasoning, and especially in this case, where I've added sun-dried tomatoes, which are sharp, I wouldn't include any.

SERVES FOUR AS AN APPETIZER OR FIRST COURSE I saw this salad being served at a table next to mine at a restaurant in Palermo; I wanted it, but it was made with porcini mushrooms, which happen to be the one thing on earth I'm seemingly allergic to. I tried making it back home, using our relatively bland cremini mushrooms, and was surprised by how much flavor they had raw. The trick is to make sure all the ingredients are very thinly sliced, so the texture is delicate and all the flavors blend effortlessly.

RAW MUSHROOM AND CELERY SALAD WITH PECORINO AND LEMON VINAIGRETTE

8 cremini mushrooms, very thinly sliced

4 celery stalks with leaves, stalks thinly sliced, leaves chopped

2 scallions, including tender green parts, cut into thin rounds

3 or 4 fresh tarragon leaves, chopped

VINAIGRETTE

Grated zest and juice of $1/2$ lemon

Salt

Freshly ground black pepper to taste

3 or 4 scrapings freshly grated nutmeg

Pinch of sugar

Extra-virgin olive oil

1 small head frisée lettuce, cut into bite-sized pieces

1 chunk aged pecorino cheese

In a large salad bowl, combine the mushrooms, celery and leaves, scallions, and tarragon.

TO MAKE THE VINAIGRETTE: In a small bowl, mix the lemon zest and juice, salt, pepper, nutmeg, and sugar. Whisk briefly. Whisk in the olive oil. Taste for seasoning. You want a fairly pronounced lemony taste and a balance that is a bit sharper than a vinaigrette you might make for a plain lettuce salad.

Distribute the frisée among 4 salad plates.

With a sharp vegetable peeler, shave a generous amount of pecorino into the salad bowl. Pour on the vinaigrette and mix gently, trying as best you can not to break up the cheese. Add a drizzle more olive oil if needed to coat everything evenly. Divide the salad over the frisée. Serve right away.

VARIATION   Just because I can't eat porcini doesn't mean you can't use them in this salad. Look for ones that are firm and woodsy smelling.

SERVES FOUR AS A FIRST COURSE OR SIDE DISH. One of the puny injustices of my life is that I am allergic to porcini mushrooms. Southern Italy in November is filled with the huge, fragrant things, and cooks sneak them into everything. Every single time I've been in Italy in the fall, I've found I couldn't help but test myself and eat a tiny bite, and I've always gotten ill. But thankfully I can eat other kinds of mushrooms with no problem, so I've used other varieties here. But if you have the good fortune to be able to, include a few porcini.

BAKED WHOLE WILD MUSHROOMS WITH HONEY AND PECORINO

Extra-virgin olive oil for drizzling

1½ pounds whole wild mushrooms, or a mix of wild and cultivated (see note), trimmed and wiped with a damp cloth

1 teaspoon acacia honey or mixed wildflower honey

½ cup dry white wine

3 tablespoons grated pecorino cheese, such as cacia di Roma

½ cup homemade dry bread crumbs, not too finely ground (see page 308)

1 garlic clove, minced

Leaves from 4 or 5 thyme sprigs, chopped

Leaves from 3 or 4 rosemary sprigs, chopped

Leaves from 4 or 5 fresh flat-leaf parsley sprigs, chopped

Salt and freshly ground black pepper to taste

Preheat the oven to 425°F.

Coat a good-looking 9-by-13-inch baking dish with a little olive oil. Put all the mushrooms, stem up, in the dish (they should fit snugly).

In a small saucepan, heat the honey and wine until the honey has dissolved. Pour this over the mushrooms. In a small bowl mix the pecorino, bread crumbs, garlic, and all the herbs together. Season with salt and pepper and sprinkle evenly over the mushrooms. Drizzle the mushrooms with a generous amount of olive oil and bake, uncovered, until they are tender and lightly browned, about 20 minutes. Serve hot.

NOTE   A mixture of wild and cultivated mushrooms works well here. Try using a few chanterelles, a handful of shiitakes, and more cremini. The addition of a few chanterelles or other wild mushrooms such as porcini is important for their rich flavor. The only mushroom I've found that doesn't bake well is the morel, which is too porous and just seems to get soggy when baked.

SERVES FIVE OR SIX AS PART OF AN ANTIPASTO OFFERING. Tony Molinaro was my grandmother's cousin whom I visited in the late 1980s in Campolattaro, an ancient town in central Campania. He had lived for many years in New York and moved back to Italy in his eighties with his life's savings. He had acquired the nickname Tony Millionaire in New York because he was always broke, but when he returned to Campania he was actually rich for the town and was treated like the mayor. He bought a two-story house, the biggest in town, with a sloping garden and a color TV. He had a passion for putting up pickled vegetables, and he gave me many jars to take back with me, most of which my sister proclaimed probably contained botulism and made me throw out (some did make a weird hissing noise when I opened them), but his little lemony mushrooms were the best I've ever tasted, herby and mushroomy and not too acidic. I detected wine, lemon, fennel, and bay leaf, so I created this recipe along that line.

Tony put up large quantities of these in sterilized jars. I'm not interested in mass production and storage, so I make only enough to last for about a week in the refrigerator.

MARINATED MUSHROOMS TONY MILLIONAIRE

1 cup dry white wine
Juice of 2 lemons
One 3-inch strip lemon zest
Small palmful of fennel seeds
1 bay leaf, preferably fresh
5 black peppercorns
Generous pinch of salt

12 ounces white button mushrooms, tough stem ends trimmed
1 fennel bulb, trimmed, cored, and finely diced
2 garlic cloves
Extra-virgin olive oil for drizzling
Handful of fresh flat-leaf parsley leaves, chopped

In a large saucepan, combine the white wine, lemon juice and zest, fennel seeds, bay leaf, peppercorns, and salt. Bring to a boil over medium heat and cook for about 5 minutes. Add the mushrooms, diced fennel, and garlic cloves and simmer for 3 or 4 minutes longer. Turn off the heat and let stand for about 30 minutes.

Transfer the mushrooms and all the pan liquid to a large bowl. Cover and refrigerate them overnight (this will help to develop flavor). Serve now, or keep refrigerated for up to 1 week.

To serve the mushrooms, let them come to room temperature. Scoop the amount you need out into a small bowl with a slotted spoon so all the liquid drains off. Add a generous drizzle of olive oil and the parsley and toss.

SERVING SUGGESTION   I always serve these mushrooms with an antipasto plate of capocollo, soppressata, and maybe thinly sliced prosciutto as well. The fatty, rich meat and the slight acidity of the mushrooms are a perfect match.

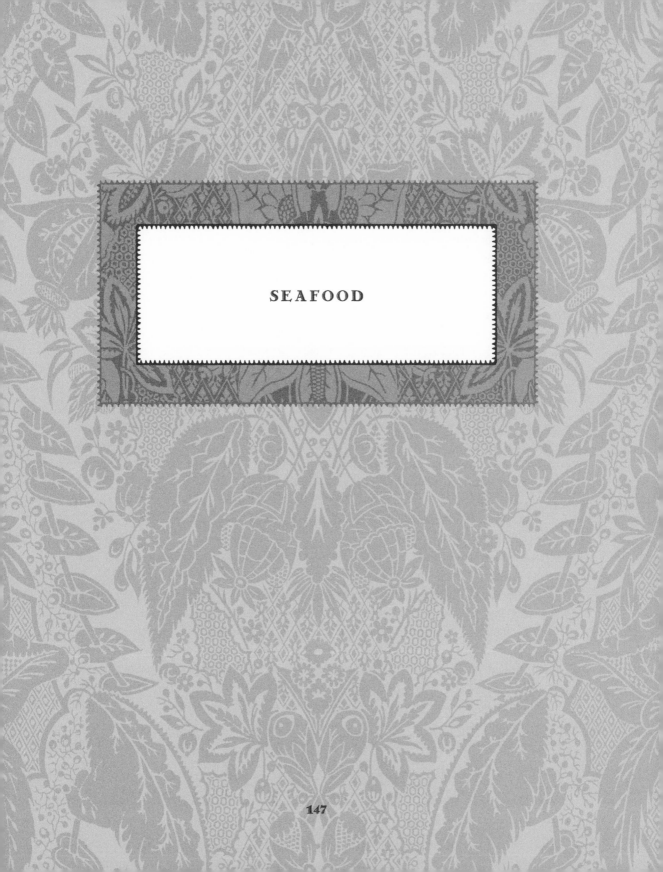

SEAFOOD

BUYING SEAFOOD

THE ATTENTION TO FRESHNESS GIVEN SEAFOOD in the coastal areas of southern Italy is remarkable. The Mediterranean doesn't teem with fish the way it once did, but the attitude toward the local catch is one of deep respect. Eating seafood is a born right of southern Italians who live along the Mediterranean and Adriatic coasts; however, Italians who don't live near the sea in southern Italy don't have much fish in their diet. Aside from salt cod, there is absolutely no fish available in my grandmother's village of Castelfranco, in inland Campania.

Most people in America want some fish in their diet, regardless of where they live. From my dismal experiences trying to buy acceptable fish during summer vacations in mountainous upstate New York, I have to say that sometimes it's almost impossible. The supermarket is the only place it's even available, and aside from the occasional piece of decent salmon, everything has been frozen and thawed and refrozen and rethawed until it's mealy or even smelly. Luckily, I live in a more populous place, where attention is paid to these things, but the price for quality can be discouraging, especially when you want fish a lot, like I do.

Eating and buying fish in southern Italian coast towns has put me on a relentless search for the freshest fish I can find here (though I haven't actually broken down and gone fishing). When I was a kid, my father and his friends used to go clamming at Sea Cliff Beach, which was very near our house in suburban Long Island. This beach is about a mile from a power plant that used to send a pink-purple, fluorescent oily film onto the water on a fairly regular basis. The thought of all the clams and mussels I consumed from that spot now sends shivers down my spine (my father and his buddies used to actually eat them raw). I can't say it wasn't fresh, but I suspect that even now, if I were examined under an ultraviolet light my body might glow.

My own source, which is even better than fancy Manhattan fish shops, is Phil Karlin of P.E. & D.D. Seafood, who brings fresh fish to the Union Square Greenmarket from Riverhead, Long Island, three times a week. I've become so spoiled by the freshness of his seasonal catch that shopping for fish even at top-notch shops makes me critical. He offers a limited local selection, all caught the night before or that morning in the ocean off Montauk, so it's almost as fresh as the fish I've eaten in seaside restaurants in places like Mazara del Vallo, a port on the west coast of Sicily where you watch the fishermen dock and haul the catch onshore and straight into the restaurant kitchens.

Depending on the season, Mr. Karlin carries blue mussels, littleneck clams, fresh squid (most fish stores carry only previously frozen squid), scungilli (conch), bluefish, tuna, swordfish, sea and striped bass, mackerel, Long Island lobster, monkfish, and huge sea scallops. No salmon and no shrimp, because they're not local. He carries many whole fish, something most American markets don't bother with because people often aren't comfortable cooking them. Look at the recipe for whole sea bass with rosemary oil on page 210, and you'll see how easy cooking a whole fish can actually be. Do it once and you'll want to do it often, for the flavor is much better than you get with fillets. I always try to buy from Mr. Karlin unless I want something that's not local.

In the last few years, imported Mediterranean seafood has started showing up in fish shops in big American cities, iced and flown in overnight, supposedly caught just before. I routinely find fresh anchovies, langoustines, black mussels, orata (sea bream), branzino (bass), red mullet (called *triglie* in Italy), sardines from Portugal, and *vongole verace*, the tiny clams classically paired with linguine or spaghetti. Sometimes the fish is fresh enough, but occasionally I suspect that it has spent too long in transit, and I have to weigh whether or not it's worth sampling. It's always tempting, because the flavor of a real red mullet is far superior to what we call mullet here, but if it's not fresh it's not going to taste good no matter how much expensive olive oil you pour onto it. You always should smell any fish you're thinking of buying, especially if it's imported or is an oily fish like sardines or anchovies, which go off very quickly. I often feel like a real irritant when I ask to smell the goods, but I've purchased truly stinky imported sardines on several occasions when I didn't.

COOKING AND FLAVORING SEAFOOD

I FIND COOKING SEAFOOD to be ceremonial, in a way. It all looks so beautiful (even, to me, octopus, with its grotesque suction-cupped body). I'll break out my best estate-bottled olive oil and use it lavishly, something I wouldn't dream of doing with a slab of steak. I also find sea salt vitally important for enhancing a fresh fish's flavor. I sometimes use two types, a fine-grain salt for cooking and a coarser one to sprinkle over the cooked fish before sending it to the table, for a little sea-tinged crunch.

Certain herbs come right to mind when you think about cooking fish in an Italian Mediterranean way, especially basil and parsley, but I like to use richer, oilier herbs as well. I love rosemary with saltwater fish. Sage, commonly paired with freshwater fish like brook trout, is wonderful with cod and other flaky white fish too, especially when simmered with tomato. Oregano and marjoram are also popular with fish in the south. In Sicily, they like to brush tuna and swordfish steaks with olive oil, sprinkle dried oregano generously over them, and grill them, making them taste a little like pizza. To my palate, the flavor is too strong. I'm more conservative with these herbs, adding a few chopped sprigs after cooking. It's interesting how often I find myself using anchovy, though—just a touch—to flavor fish dishes. You might think fish would be fishy enough and that I must be anchovy-crazed, but this is commonly done in southern cooking, for emphasis. One or two chopped fillets add a flavor boost to mild fish stews made without shellfish or to fish simmered in a tomato-based sauce.

Tomato, white wine, and garlic are a southern trio that turns up again and again for flavoring seafood stews and sautés. One of my favorite three-minute shrimp dishes, one that shows off the southern Italian style as well as anything can, is a sauté of shrimp with garlic, tomato, white wine, and basil, four of the area's key flavors. Here's how you make it: Get a large skillet very hot over high heat. Add 2 tablespoons of olive oil. When the oil is shimmering hot, add 1 pound of large shelled shrimp and 2 sliced garlic cloves at the same time (if you added the garlic first on such high heat, it might burn). Season with salt and pepper and shake the skillet until the shrimp is evenly pink, no more than 2 minutes. Add a large handful of halved cherry tomatoes and sauté a minute longer, just until they start to give off a little juice. Add a tiny splash of dry white wine and pull the skillet from the heat (the wine will evaporate quickly from the hot skillet). Throw in a small handful of coarsely chopped fresh basil, and serve hot. See a variation on this dish on page 184, a sautéed shrimp with celery, fennel seeds, and chilies (they're very different flavors, but the recipe follows the same principle).

Dry white wine is always a safe bet for flavoring fish, but a dry red is excellent for strong, oily fish. I love sweet or dry vermouth with shellfish. A sweet dessert-type wine does wonders for squid (see page 194 for calamari with ricotta and Malvasia). I also love sweet wine with shrimp, especially if you counteract the sweetness with something spicy like fresh hot chilies. Limoncello, the famous lemon liqueur from Amalfi, is another nice thing to have on hand when cooking seafood, as it adds sweet and sharp flavors in one splash.

When you order fish or shellfish in a restaurant in Sicily or on the Amalfi Coast, you generally get fish on the plate and nothing else. Sauces and flourishes are not common additions, but being used to such things myself I do sneak little American touches into my fish recipes. I'll take a classic southern Italian sauce that is traditionally used only on pasta and adapt it for a fish dish because I see the flavors blending well (pan-fried red mullet *puttanesca*, page 215, is an example of this). Fish on or next to a little tossed salad is another American concept that I like, as it gives the seafood a vegetable crunch and counterbalances its richness. I have several such recipes, and I believe they fit in a spiritual if not literal way with the southern Italian culinary mind-set.

It is true that almost all seafood should be cooked briefly (octopus and squid can be exceptions), so attention must be paid from the minute you put it on the heat. This doesn't mean that fish is difficult; it just means it's fast, so the most important thing—actually the only thing you really need to think about ahead of time—is having all your ingredients ready. Do your herb chopping and garlic slicing and have it all prepared before the fish goes into the skillet. Then you'll be in good shape. I almost always pull fish from the heat a minute or two before I think it's done. It continues to cook through gently as it sits and is then perfect when I bring it to the table.

RAW FISH IN THE SOUTHERN ITALIAN DIET

Raw fish is not as commonplace in southern Italy as in America, but raw-fish traditions do exist. Raw shellfish is very popular in Puglia, and I'm always tempted by their mussels, clams, and fabulous-smelling oysters. Guidebooks always tell tourists to avoid such things, and most of the time I obey them, but I certainly wish I had tasted some of those oysters. I noticed chefs slicing raw fish and serving it like sushi in a restaurant in Taranto, Puglia, simply drizzling the thin slices with local olive oil. In Sicily, lightly marinated raw swordfish, soaked in lemon juice like seviche, is a traditional dish at seaside restaurants. On the two occasions when I've tried it, it was exceptionally delicious. I've also had raw sea urchins at Mondello beach, outside of Palermo. They were one of the great seafood experiences of my life. I lived to tell it, and I look forward to eating them again.

Fish carpaccio, or *crudo* ("raw"), as it is sometimes called on Italian menus in America, is really a fusion of Japanese-style sashimi with Italian flavors, sort of an exaggeration of what Italians do with raw fish. But its mix of pure sea flavors and classic Italian ingredients such as extra-virgin olive oil, basil, arugula, olives, and capers, among a myriad of other possible additions, makes so much sense and can be so delicious that the marriage was inevitable. There are several contemporary *crudo* recipes in this chapter.

TIPS FOR BUYING AND SERVING RAW SEAFOOD

I've had a lot of kinds of fish raw at restaurants, including mackerel, bluefish, monkfish, and swordfish, but when I prepare fish carpaccio at home I'm much more conservative, choosing only sushi-quality salmon or tuna or extremely fresh scallops from a seller I know well and trust. Very fresh black sea bass also makes excellent carpaccio, when I can find it. Other types of fish, especially oily ones like mackerel or bluefish, go off very quickly, and I feel less confident about serving them raw at home. That's for restaurants.

Look for cuts without a lot of tough, sinewy white thread running through them, especially when buying tuna. You might see a fish labeled "sushi quality," especially tuna; this is a good starting point for selection, but remember it's really only sushi quality if it's fresh, so make sure to tell your fish seller that you plan on serving the fish raw. Then you'll get a more honest account of its condition.

Keep the fish refrigerated until right before serving. The best way to keep fish really cold is to lay it out on a plate and place the plate on top of a pan filled with crushed ice. I try to serve any fish destined for carpaccio within about 6 hours.

The type of olive oil you use will set the tone for the dish. Estate-bottled Sicilian oils like Ravida or U Trappitu are my first choice. Oils from Puglia tend to be golden and mellower than the Sicilian ones, and they're also wonderful with raw fish, imparting a softer flavor. Since olive oil is such an important component of fish carpaccio, I always use one of my finest oils. See page 14 for more about different types of southern Italian olive oil.

SERVES **SIX AS AN APPETIZER**. Raw sea scallops have a beautiful flavor, texture, and pearly white color when they're extremely fresh. I make this when I find sweet-smelling (and I always smell them) dry scallops in my market. "Dry" is a label you'll see on scallops that haven't been treated with phosphates to artificially plump them up.

SEA SCALLOPS CRUDO WITH FAVA BEANS

1 pound small fava beans, shelled and peeled (see page 76)

Extra-virgin olive oil for drizzling

Pinch of sea salt

1 pound large sea scallops, side muscle removed

Grated zest and juice of 1 large lemon

Freshly ground black pepper to taste

3 scallions, including tender green parts, cut into thin rounds

Small handful of fresh mint leaves, cut into thin strips

1 crusty baguette, cut into thin rounds

Put the beans in a small bowl. Drizzle them with a little olive oil and sprinkle with salt.

Cut the scallops into very thin rounds with a sharp knife. Place the slices on a large serving platter and season them liberally with olive oil, lemon juice and zest, salt, and pepper. Scatter over the fava beans and scallions. Give everything an extra drizzle of olive oil and garnish with the mint. Serve right away, with the baguette slices alongside in a little basket.

VARIATIONS   When fava beans aren't in season (or you just don't feel like bothering with them), the scallops can stand alone (you can garnish the plate with a few toasted pine nuts if you like). I've also made this *crudo* using blanched asparagus tips instead of fava beans.

SERVES FOUR AS AN APPETIZER OR FIRST COURSE. This is an American restaurant–style treatment for tuna tartare. I've given it southern Italian style by adding fresh marjoram, capers, lemon zest, and extra-virgin olive oil.

TUNA TARTARE CROSTINI WITH CAPERS AND AVOCADO

12 ounces sushi-quality yellowfin or bluefin tuna (ask for the belly cut)

1/2 ripe Hass avocado

2 scallions, including tender green parts, finely chopped

Extra-virgin olive oil for drizzling and brushing

1 teaspoon soy sauce

Grated zest and juice of 1/2 lemon

Sea salt and freshly ground black pepper to taste

Small palmful of capers, soaked and rinsed (see page 29)

Leaves from 3 or 4 large marjoram sprigs, chopped

1 baguette, cut into thin rounds

The easiest way to cut raw fish is to have it very cold and make sure you have a sharp knife. First, cut the tuna into thin, wide slices. Cut the slices into thin strips. Now, line up the strips and cut them into very small dice with sharp, quick knife strokes. With any luck, it should look like little red jewels. Place the tuna in small bowl and refrigerate until ready to serve.

TO SERVE THE TARTARE, peel, pit, and finely dice the avocado and add it to the tuna. Add the scallions, a generous drizzle of olive oil, the soy sauce, lemon zest and juice, salt, pepper, capers, and marjoram. Give it a gentle toss. Taste for seasoning (I find raw fish dishes tend to need a little fine-tuning of seasoning and I always wind up adding a little extra lemon, salt, olive oil, or pepper to balance the flavors).

Preheat the broiler. Toast the baguette slices about 4 inches from the heat source on both sides and brush them with olive oil. Spoon a little of the tartare on each slice and serve right away.

SERVING SUGGESTIONS You could, if you prefer, serve the tartare in a bowl with the toasted bread on the side. The Atkins-minded could spoon the tartare into endive leaves.

SERVES FIVE OR SIX AS AN APPETIZER OR AS A SIT-DOWN FIRST COURSE. You can find *alici marinate* on antipasto tables throughout coastal southern Italy. It's made with fresh anchovies, which I'm finding more easily on this side of the ocean these days.

Often, I buy already prepared marinated anchovies at Italian or Spanish specialty stores, but when I can get fresh ones, I fillet and marinate them myself so I can add my own touches, like the thyme and capers included here. Most of the store-bought versions seem very vinegary to me and don't have much character aside from that. I usually wind up doctoring them with good olive oil and fresh herbs.

MARINATED ANCHOVIES ON MOZZARELLA CROSTINI

About 2 dozen fresh anchovies

Juice of 2 lemons

2 or 3 gratings of freshly grated nutmeg

Freshly ground black pepper to taste

Small handful of salt-packed capers, soaked and drained (see page 29)

1 shallot, very thinly sliced

Leaves from 5 or 6 sprigs thyme, leaves chopped

Leaves from 3 or 4 flat-leaf parsley sprigs, chopped

Extra-virgin olive oil, as needed

FOR THE CROSTINI

1 baguette, cut into thin diagonal slices

One 8-ounce ball fresh mozzarella cheese (buffalo or cow's milk), cut into $1/4$-inch slices

Run the anchovies under cold water as you fillet them by running your thumb along the backbone, loosening the fillets. (They come away from the bone easily, and after you do two or three, you'll get the hang of it.) Lay the fillets in one layer in a shallow serving dish. Squeeze on the lemon juice. Cover the dish with plastic wrap and place it in the refrigerator for about 2 hours (this will give the lemon juice a chance to soak into the fillets, cooking them a bit, the same as for a seviche).

Pour off all the lemon juice and reposition the fillets in the dish if you need to. Season with nutmeg and pepper. Scatter on the capers, shallot, thyme, and parsley. Cover the anchovies with a thin layer of olive oil. Cover the dish with plastic wrap and let it sit for at least 1 hour at room temperature before serving so they can develop good flavor. You can marinate them overnight in the refrigerator, if you like, but return the anchovies to room temperature before serving.

TO MAKE THE CROSTINI: Preheat the broiler. Toast the baguette slices about 4 inches from the heat source on one side, turn them over, and place a slice of mozzarella on each one. Broil for a few seconds to lightly melt the mozzarella. Place 2 anchovies on each toast. Serve right away as a passed appetizer or as part of an antipasto offering.

SERVING SUGGESTIONS   You can serve this simply accompanied with good Italian bread, but I like the way the creaminess of mozzarella plays against the pungently flavored fish in these *crostini*. Try it both ways.

VARIATION   Another favorite way of using these anchovies is by hard-cooking a few eggs, cutting them in half, and scooping the yolks into a small bowl. Chop a handful of the anchovies coarsely and add them to the yolks along with a little chopped parsley and a drizzle of olive oil. Mix everything together and fill the eggs with the mixture. These make a good antipasto dish with cold white wine.

To serve the *crostini* as a sit-down first course, dress a salad of arugula or escarole with lemon and olive oil and place 2 or 3 *crostini* on each plate.

SERVES FOUR AS A FIRST COURSE OR LIGHT LUNCH. Tuna is in season in the New York area starting in early June, and Phil Karlin, the man I buy fish from at the Union Square Greenmarket, carries the freshest, most beautiful tuna, not only bluefin and yellowfin but also the lighter-colored albacore, which is often passed over. It's not gleaming ruby red, but it has excellent flavor. Any kind of fresh tuna is fine for this dish.

Sicily has a long history of tuna canning, and though the business is not as vast as it once was, the island still produces some of the best canned tuna in the world. It is slowly cooked and preserved in olive oil and so is very tender. Here is a home version of preserved tuna that takes about 15 minutes and gives excellent results. Use the delicate belly cut, if you can find it. *Ventresca* is what they call this cut in Italy. The best Sicilian canned tuna is often so labeled. Double or triple the tuna recipe if you want extra for other recipes; it will keep, refrigerated, for up to 5 days.

PRESERVED SICILIAN TUNA WITH TOMATOES, RED ONIONS, AND OLIVES

TUNA

1 pound bluefin, yellowfin, or albacore tuna (the belly cut if you can find it), cut into chunks about 1½ inches thick

1 teaspoon sea salt, plus salt to taste

1 garlic clove, lightly smashed

1 bay leaf

2 or 3 black peppercorns

2 small rosemary sprigs or a small palmful of fennel seeds

2 large marjoram sprigs

2 long lemon zest strips

About 1 cup inexpensive extra-virgin olive oil

2 cups cherry tomatoes, stemmed and halved

1 small red onion, thinly sliced

2 celery stalks, thinly sliced, plus a handful of celery leaves

Handful of Gaeta or kalamata olives, pitted and cut in half

Extra-virgin olive oil for drizzling

Generous squeeze of lemon juice

Salt and freshly ground black pepper to taste

To make the tuna: Put the tuna chunks in a deep saucepan. Sprinkle on the 1 teaspoon of sea salt (the salt flavors and preserves the tuna) and give it a good stir. Add the garlic, bay leaf, peppercorns, herbs, and lemon zest. Pour on enough olive oil to cover the tuna by about 1/2 inch. Heat over low heat until bubbles start to form around the edges of the pan, about 5 minutes. Turn off the heat and cover the pan. Let the tuna sit on the turned-off burner for about 10 minutes. The waning heat from the oil will continue to gently cook the tuna through, making it very tender and infusing it with flavor (ideally, it should remain slightly pink at the center). Uncover the pan and let it come to room temperature. You can use the tuna now, or cover it tightly and refrigerate it for up to 5 days Return it to room temperature before serving.

In a large salad bowl, combine the cherry tomatoes, red onion, celery and celery leaves, black olives, and the preserved tuna. Drizzle with olive oil and add a squeeze of lemon juice. Season with salt and pepper. Toss gently. Serve at room temperature.

NOTE Several good brands of Sicilian canned tuna are available in this country. Flott is one I always buy. It has a rich olive oil taste. Tonno Rosso is a brand I've purchased by mail order from the importer Vino e Olio (check the source list on page 436 for more information about purchasing these brands).

VARIATIONS Preserved tuna can be added to all sorts of salads, especially chickpea, potato, or rice salads. It's also great included in a hot or cold pasta dish. If you're adding it to hot pasta or any hot dish, add it at the last minute, off the heat. Cooking preserved tuna spoils its delicate taste and texture.

For a quick summer pasta sauce, finely dice about 5 ripe, round tomatoes and put them in a large serving bowl (if they are very juicy, let them drain in a colander for about 15 minutes). Add a handful of torn fresh basil leaves and a smaller handful of fresh flat-leaf parsley leaves, a handful of capers or chopped pitted olives, a minced garlic clove, a few thinly sliced scallions, and about 1/2 cup good olive oil. Let this stand while you cook a pound of penne or fusilli pasta al dente, drain it well, and then add it to the bowl. Break the tuna into small chunks with your fingers and add it, along with a generous amount of pepper and some salt. Toss gently and serve either warm or at room temperature. Serves 4 as a main course or 6 as a first course.

SERVES FOUR AS A FIRST COURSE. Salmon is often seasoned with dill in the United States, but mint, I've discovered, goes very well with the sweet and rich oils in salmon. It is curious how certain herbs seem to be rejected by certain cultures. This is generally true of dill in southern Italy. I saw wild dill growing in several places in central Sicily, and when I asked a few local women about it, they said they never used it in cooking because it was considered foreign—even though it grew in their backyards.

Unlike seviche, carpaccio is never marinated. The fish in a carpaccio is truly raw, not "cooked" in an acidy liquid such as lemon or vinegar, which is what gives seviche its whitened appearance, sharp taste, and soft texture. Carpaccio is usually dressed in some way, but only right before serving, so its raw taste and texture are preserved.

SALMON CARPACCIO WITH MINT AND CELERY LEAVES

12 ounces very fresh salmon fillet, skinned and pin bones removed

3 scallions, including tender green parts, finely chopped

2 unpeeled inner celery stalks, finely chopped, plus a handful of celery leaves, chopped

1/2 unpeeled cucumber, seeded, finely chopped, lightly sprinkled with salt, and drained for 15 minutes to remove excess water

Grated zest and juice of 1/2 lemon, plus lemon juice to taste

2 tablespoons extra-virgin olive oil, plus more for drizzling

3 or 4 large fresh mint leaves, chopped, plus sprigs for garnish

Salt (preferably sea salt) to taste

Pinch of cayenne pepper

Pinch of sugar

Slice the salmon on the diagonal as thinly as possible, using a very sharp carving knife. Place each slice between layers of plastic wrap and pound the fish very gently with a meat pounder until it is very thin, but not so thin that it begins to tear. Refrigerate the slices, still wrapped in the plastic, until you're ready to serve.

TO SERVE THE CARPACCIO, mix the scallions, celery and leaves, and cucumber together in a little bowl. Add the lemon zest and juice, olive oil, and the chopped mint. Season with salt, cayenne, and sugar. Toss gently.

Unwrap the salmon slices and divide them among 4 salad plates. Drizzle them lightly with olive oil, squeeze on a few drops of lemon juice, and season with salt. Place a small amount of the celery mixture in the middle of each plate. Garnish with mint sprigs. Serve very cold.

SERVES FOUR AS A FIRST COURSE OR A LIGHT MEAL. I love the pungent smell of sardines on a grill, and I always make variations on this when I find really fresh sardines in the market. The ones I use are flown in from Portugal. They are best the day they arrive. If you see them at your market, ask what day they usually arrive (mine come in every Thursday); that way, you'll get them at their best. The creaminess of the pine nuts marries very well with the rich oiliness of these little fish.

GRILLED SARDINES WITH HOT PINE NUT VINAIGRETTE

VINAIGRETTE

1/2 cup very fresh pine nuts

1/2 cup extra-virgin olive oil

Salt and freshly ground black pepper to taste

Pinch of sugar

Grated zest and juice of 1 large lemon

1 tablespoon dry white wine

12 sardines, gutted and scaled, heads left on (see note)

Extra-virgin olive oil for coating

Sea salt and freshly ground black pepper to taste

Juice of 1 lemon

Leaves from 1 head chicory or frisée lettuce

Handful of fresh flat-leaf parsley leaves, chopped

To make the vinaigrette: In a medium skillet, toast the pine nuts over low heat, stirring occasionally, until they are nicely golden. Add the olive oil, salt, pepper, sugar, lemon zest and juice, and wine. Let this bubble for a minute and then turn off the heat, leaving the skillet on the turned-off burner.

Place a grill pan over high heat. Coat the sardines lightly in olive oil and sprinkle with salt, pepper, and lemon juice. Grill until good char marks appear, about 1 minute on each side. This should cook them through, but large ones will take a little longer. Line a large serving plate with the chicory or frisée. Grab the sardines from the grill with tongs and place them on a serving plate. Reheat the pine nut sauce for a few seconds, just until it's hot, adding a splash of water to loosen it up if necessary. Scatter the parsley leaves over the sardines and pour on the pine nut sauce. Serve hot.

CLEANING SARDINES   While holding a sardine under cold water, rub the scales away with your fingers (they come off easily and don't need to be scraped off as with larger fish). Stick a small knife into the middle of the belly and make a 1-inch lengthwise slit. Pull out the insides with your fingers and wash each fish inside and out with water.

SERVES FOUR AS A FIRST COURSE OR LIGHT LUNCH. Squid cooked with potatoes and tomatoes is a Neapolitan tradition. Here, I've substituted octopus for the squid and updated the dish with a tomato vinaigrette. Most Americans don't often think about cooking octopus, perhaps because of its startling looks, but all you really need to do is simmer it in a big pot of water, and it gives off a wonderful sweet aroma as it cooks.

WARM OCTOPUS AND POTATO SALAD WITH TOMATO VINAIGRETTE

One 3-pound octopus, cleaned, thawed if frozen

1 bay leaf

Generous pinch of sea salt

1 cup plus 1 tablespoon dry white wine

Leaves from 3 or 4 flat-leaf parsley sprigs, with stems

2 garlic cloves, lightly crushed

Extra-virgin olive oil for drizzling, plus 2 tablespoons

10 small unpeeled Yukon Gold potatoes, halved

2 leeks, rinsed and cut into thin rounds

2 celery stalks, thinly sliced

Salt and freshly ground black pepper to taste

Small handful of fresh flat-leaf parsley leaves, chopped

Fresh marjoram sprigs for garnish

VINAIGRETTE

4 canned plum tomatoes, very well drained or squeezed of juice

$1/4$ cup extra-virgin olive oil

$1/2$ teaspoon balsamic vinegar

Salt and freshly ground black pepper to taste

Freshly grated nutmeg to taste

3 or 4 large marjoram sprigs, chopped

Put the octopus in a large pot and add the bay leaf, salt, 1 cup of white wine, parsley, garlic, and a drizzle of olive oil. Add cold water to cover and bring to a boil. Reduce the heat to low and simmer, partially covered, until the octopus is very tender, about $1^{1}/_{2}$ hours. Start testing after about 1 hour; it is possible to overcook octopus and make it dry. (Cooking times for octopus can vary; it is done when a knife goes easily into the thick tentacle area closest to the head.) When the octopus is tender, lift it from the cooking liquid and let it cool slightly. (Reserve the octopus cooking liquid for another use; it makes a good broth for a seafood stew, although it is darkly colored and with a pronounced octopus taste. You can boil it down to a manageable amount, strain, and freeze it, if you like.)

Put the potatoes in a small saucepan of cold water. Bring to a boil. Reduce the heat and boil until the potatoes are tender, about 5 minutes. Drain and place in a large serving bowl.

Meanwhile, combine all the vinaigrette ingredients in a food processor and pulse until blended and fairly smooth. Taste for seasoning; it should have a gentle, not aggressive sharpness from the tomato and the balsamic vinegar. Pour 1 tablespoon of the vinaigrette over the warm potatoes and give them a toss.

Cut the octopus by first slicing off the tentacles from the head. You'll notice a soft skin covering the tentacles. This adds good flavor and is, in my opinion, part of its charm. Some cooks, especially in restaurants here (not in Italy, though), remove it. If you don't like its texture, peel some of it away (it will slip right off). Sometimes I'll remove some but not all of it. Cut each tentacle into thin slices. I usually discard the head, but in southern Italy I've noticed it is generally sliced and added to salads. It's up to you.

In a large skillet, heat the 2 tablespoons olive oil over high heat. Add the octopus, leeks, celery, salt, and pepper and sauté until the raw edge of the octopus is warmed through, about 1 minute. Add the 1 tablespoon of white wine and let it boil for a few seconds. Pour into the serving bowl with the potatoes. Add the parsley and the remaining vinaigrette, giving everything another toss. Taste for seasoning, and if needed to balance the flavors, add more salt, pepper, a few drops of balsamic vinegar, or a drizzle more olive oil to coat everything well. Garnish with marjoram sprigs. Serve right away (it will still be slightly warm) or at room temperature.

VARIATION   If the idea of cooking octopus seems a bit challenging (although once you try it, you'll see there's nothing to it) and you'd like to make this with squid, cut about $1^1/_2$ pounds cleaned squid bodies into thin rings and leave the tentacles whole. Bring a large pot of water to a boil, add a generous amount of sea salt, and blanch the squid for about 1 minute, just until it turns opaque. Using a large strainer, transfer to paper towels to drain. Add it to the bowl when you add the celery leaves and parsley. (There's no need to sauté the squid as you did the octopus; it would only make it tough.)

SERVES SIX AS AN APPETIZER. Sicilian nut pesto comes in many variations. I was served one tossed with pasta at the home of Wolfango Jezek, the producer of the wonderful U Trappitu olive oil (from Trapani), and it was just about the most wonderful pasta I ever ate. Sicilian pestos are made with a variety of nuts, some herbs, olive oil, and always a touch of tomato, making them quite different from the Genoese basil pesto most people are more familiar with. I've reproduced the pesto from memory, and although I often serve it in the traditional way, tossed with pasta, I've found that it makes a good topping for baked mussels, which in Sicily and southern Italy would more likely be prepared with some sort of seasoned bread crumb topping. The crunchiness and oiliness of the nuts, I think, really works well with the brininess of the mussels. (For information on buying mussels, see page 370.)

BAKED MUSSELS WITH SICILIAN NUT PESTO

SICILIAN NUT PESTO

½ cup unsalted pistachios

½ cup whole blanched almonds

Handful of pine nuts

1 garlic clove

½ chili, such as a red peperoncino, coarsely chopped

Small handful of fresh mint leaves

Large handful of fresh basil leaves

½ cup extra-virgin olive oil

Generous pinch of salt

1 tomato, peeled, seeded, and cut into small dice (see page 26)

2 pounds mussels, scrubbed and debearded, if necessary

1 cup dry white wine

1 chunk pecorino cheese for grating

TO MAKE THE PESTO: Combine the nuts, garlic, and chili in the bowl of a food processor and grind coarsely. Add the mint, basil, olive oil, and salt. Pulse the mixture a few times until everything is well blended but it still has some texture. Pour the pesto into a small bowl and mix in the tomato.

Preheat the broiler. Put the mussels in a large pot and pour the wine over them. Turn the heat to medium and cook, stirring them frequently, until they've opened, 3 or 4 minutes. Let the mussels cool until you can handle them. Pull off one of the shells and loosen the mussel from its remaining shell, putting it back in the shell after you do. Do this with all the mussels. Strain the mussel cooking liquid and add 1 tablespoon to the pesto (the rest you can use in a fish broth or for a fish soup if you like).

Spoon about $1/2$ teaspoon pesto onto each mussel and top each one with a grating of pecorino. Line the mussels up on a baking sheet. Place them under the broiler about 4 inches from the heat source and broil until the tops are very lightly browned, 2 or 3 minutes. Serve warm.

VARIATIONS   To use this pesto in a more traditional way, simply toss it with 1 pound of spaghetti or bucatini pasta cooked al dente, remembering to thin it out to a creamy consistency with a few splashes of pasta cooking water. Serve with grated pecorino cheese on the side.

NOTE   Most cultivated mussels are quite clean and don't need to be de-bearded, but the wild mussels I buy from my Long Island fish seller usually have the little fuzzy "beard" attached and also, sometimes, a few small rocks and fair amount of sand. I soak them in a large pot of cold water and scrub them, yanking the beard. Any mussels that remain open after soaking in cold water and also being tapped on the shell, should be thrown out.

SERVES FOUR AS A LIGHT MAIN COURSE. Late summer to early fall is when I find fresh shell beans in their pods at my farmers' market in Manhattan. They're available for only a short time, but they cook up so tender and are so much fresher than dried beans that I make sure to use them while they're around. I usually find only cranberry beans, but when I've visited farmers' markets in California I've come across fresh French flageolets, cannellini beans, black-eyed peas, and beans I'd never seen before, fresh or dried. Use whatever looks best in your market.

The trick in balancing the flavors in this dish is to use only a very little bit of soppressata and to cut it into thin strips so you get little tastes and it doesn't overpower the delicate shrimp.

GRILLED SHRIMP WITH FRESH SHELL BEANS AND SOPPRESSATA

1½ pounds fresh shell beans (see headnote), shelled

2 tablespoons extra-virgin olive oil, plus more if needed

Salt and freshly ground black pepper to taste

8 ounces yellow wax beans

Leaves from 1 small head chicory (about 1 packed cup), cut into bite-sized pieces

12 cherry tomatoes, stemmed and halved

3 thin slices soppressata, cut into matchsticks

Leaves from 3 or 4 large tarragon sprigs, chopped

Handful of fresh basil leaves, chopped

1 small red onion, very thinly sliced

DRESSING

1 garlic clove, lightly crushed

1 tablespoon Dijon mustard

1 tablespoon red wine vinegar, or to taste

Salt and freshly ground black pepper to taste

¼ cup olive oil

12 jumbo shrimp, shelled, tails left on

Grated zest of 1 lemon

Put the shell beans in a medium pot and add cold water to cover by about 3 inches. Bring to a boil over high heat. Reduce the heat to medium and simmer, uncovered, until tender, about 30 minutes. Drain and toss with 1 tablespoon olive oil, salt, and pepper.

In a pot of boiling water, blanch the wax beans until crisp-tender, about 3 minutes. Pour into a colander and run cold water over them to stop the cooking. Drain.

In a large, shallow salad bowl or serving bowl, combine the chicory, tomatoes, soppressata, tarragon, basil, and onion. Drain the shell beans and add them to the bowl along with the wax beans.

TO MAKE THE DRESSING: In a small bowl, combine the garlic, mustard, and vinegar and mix well. Season with salt and pepper and the olive oil. Mix everything together until well blended, adjusting the flavors to suit your taste.

Heat a grill pan over high heat until very hot. Toss the shrimp with the remaining tablespoon olive oil, the lemon zest, and salt and pepper to taste. Grill them on one side without moving them until good grill marks appear, about 2 minutes. Turn and grill the other side for about 1 minute, until pink.

Add the shrimp to the salad bowl, pour on the dressing removing the garlic clove, and toss gently, adding a little more olive oil if needed to coat everything well. Serve right away.

VARIATION   If you've missed fresh shell bean season, replace them with 8 ounces green beans (they look lovely mingling with the wax beans), but blanch them separately to make sure both varieties are perfectly cooked.

SERVES FOUR OR FIVE AS A MAIN COURSE, SIX OR SEVEN AS A BUFFET OR ANTIPASTO DISH. Rice salads are more common than pasta salads on antipasto tables in southern Italian restaurants, and I find myself making them more and more too, especially when I need to feed a big group. Rice salads with a mix of fish and vegetables (or just vegetables) have become a staple of my southern Italian–inspired repertoire. In the summer, I serve them at room temperature; in the winter, I prefer them warm. Use a long-grain rice, not Italian risotto rice, which cooks up a little too starchy for this.

CALAMARI AND ARTICHOKE RICE SALAD WITH SAFFRON

About 15 baby artichokes

2 lemons, halved

1½ cups long-grain white rice

5 tablespoons extra-virgin olive oil, plus more for drizzling

Large pinch of saffron threads, toasted, ground (see page 42), and dissolved in a few tablespoons of warm water

2 pounds small squid, cleaned (see page 195), bodies cut into thin rings, tentacles left whole

Salt and freshly ground black pepper to taste

3 tablespoons dry white wine

2 garlic cloves, thinly sliced

4 or 5 scallions, including tender green parts, cut into thin rounds

Large handful of pine nuts, toasted (see page 61)

Small handful fresh mint leaves, chopped

12 fresh basil leaves, chopped

Snap off all the tough outer leaves from the artichokes until you get down to the tender, light green ones. Trim and peel the stems and slice off a bit of the tops. Cut the artichokes lengthwise into thick slices. Put the slices in a bowl of cold water with the juice of one of the lemons as you finish with each one.

Cook the rice as you would pasta in a large pot of salted boiling water, al dente (tender but with a bit of a bite), about 12 minutes (this method keeps the rice grains firm and separate). Drain the rice into a fine-mesh sieve and run cold water over it to stop the cooking. Drain well and transfer to a large serving bowl. Drizzle on 2 tablespoons of the olive oil, add the saffron water, and toss well. The rice will be a light pinky orange color.

Pat the squid dry with paper towels (they will sauté better this way). In a large skillet, heat 2 tablespoons of the olive oil over high heat. Add the squid and sauté just until it turns opaque, no more than 2 or 3 minutes (taste a piece for tenderness). Season with salt and pepper and add 2 tablespoons of the white wine, letting it bubble a few seconds before adding the squid and all the skillet juices to the rice.

In the same skillet, heat the remaining tablespoon olive oil over medium heat. Add the artichokes, garlic, and salt and pepper to taste and sauté until the slices are lightly browned, about 8 minutes. Add the remaining tablespoon white wine to the skillet and let it bubble for a minute to deglaze the skillet bottom. Taste a piece of artichoke to see if it's tender. If not, add a little water to the skillet and continue cooking a few minutes longer. Add the artichokes and any skillet juices to the rice. Add the scallions, pine nuts, mint, and basil. Squeeze on a little lemon juice and a generous drizzle of fresh olive oil. Season with salt and pepper to taste and toss gently.

Let the salad come to room temperature before serving. You can make it a day ahead and refrigerate it (although I think it tastes best freshly made), but let it come back to room temperature before serving.

SERVES FIVE AS A MAIN COURSE. Once when my grandmother was very old, I decided to cook manicotti for her. I made it in standard southern style, filled with ricotta and topped with tomato sauce, but instead of making pasta casings I made *crespelle*. Everyone around the table had a first taste and then there was charged silence. Finally, my grandmother said, "This tastes different." My aunt said, "This *is* different," meaning it wasn't exactly what my grandmother made. There wasn't much room for creativity in her kitchen. I wonder what she would make of this recipe.

Crespelle, the Italian version of crepes, appear in southern Italy on special occasions such as weddings. I've run across them mostly in the Campania region. Usually, they're filled with ricotta and prosciutto or a mix of ricotta and a green such as spinach. They are baked with tomato sauce or béchamel, or sometimes both.

Fish fillings give *crespelle* a lighter feel. Here, I've bathed scallops in the classic southern Italian trio of basil, garlic, and tomato.

CRESPELLE WITH SCALLOPS, ARUGULA, AND BASIL CREAM

CRESPELLE BATTER

1 cup all-purpose flour

3 large eggs

1½ cups milk

3 tablespoons extra-virgin olive oil, plus more for cooking the crespelle

Pinch of salt

BASIL CREAM

1 cup nonultrapasteurized heavy cream

Handful of fresh basil leaves, coarsely chopped

FILLING

2 tablespoons unsalted butter

2 tablespoons extra-virgin olive oil

2 pounds large sea scallops, side muscle removed

2 garlic cloves, very thinly sliced

Salt and freshly ground black pepper to taste

1 tablespoon grappa or brandy

1 large bunch arugula, stemmed and chopped

Small handful of fresh basil leaves, chopped

3 large tomatoes, peeled, seeded, finely diced (see page 26)

½ cup grated grana padano or Parmigiano-Reggiano cheese

TO MAKE THE BATTER: In a food processor, combine all the *crespelle* batter ingredients and pulse until well blended. Pour into a bowl and let stand for about 30 minutes (this gives the batter a chance rest and to thicken, making cooking the crespelle much easier).

TO MAKE THE CRESPELLE: Heat an 8- or 9-inch crepe pan or omelet pan over medium heat. If you like using nonstick, do so, but you really don't need it (the olive oil in the batter makes these crepes quite slippery and stick proof). Pour in a little olive oil and shake it around to coat the pan. Take the pan off the heat and pour in a scant $\frac{1}{4}$ cup batter, swirling it around quickly to coat the surface evenly (if you do this on the heat, the batter will start cooking before you can swirl it and you'll wind up with a lump of cooked batter instead of a crepe). Put the pan back on the heat and let it sit there without touching it for a few seconds.

When the edges of the crepe start to bubble, shake the pan to loosen it (the crepe should move freely; if it doesn't, let it sit there for a few more seconds). Tilt the pan so the crepe slides to one side and you can slip a spatula under it. Now, with seeming confidence, just flip the thing over quickly. (I always mess up a few of them, especially in the beginning before the pan heat is well regulated, so don't worry about it, you've got extra batter.) Stack the crepes on a plate as you make them (there's no need to put plastic wrap between them, they won't stick together). You want to wind up with 10 nice-looking crepes.

TO MAKE THE BASIL CREAM: Pour the cream into a small saucepan, add the basil leaves, and heat over medium heat until little bubbles form around the edges of the pan. Turn off the heat and let stand for about 30 minutes (this gives the basil time to infuse the cream). Strain out the basil. Preheat the oven to 450°F. Brush a 9-by-13-inch baking dish with olive oil.

TO MAKE THE FILLING: In a large skillet, melt the butter with the olive oil over high heat. Add the scallops and garlic at the same time. Season with salt and pepper, and sauté quickly, about 1 minute on each side. Add the grappa or brandy and let it boil away. Turn off the heat and add the arugula and basil. The heat from the skillet will wilt the greens gently. (I like cooking the scallops right before I heat the *crespelle*, to keep their texture fresh and tender.)

Lay out the *crespelle* and fill each one with 4 or 5 scallops per crespelle, plus greens. (They shouldn't be filled to bursting. The beauty of this dish is a good balance between the scallops and the tenderness of the *crespelle*.) Lay them, seam side down, in the baking dish. Scatter on the chopped tomatoes and pour the basil cream evenly over everything. Sprinkle the top with the grated cheese.

Bake, uncovered, for 10 to 15 minutes, or just until the cream bubbles and the top is lightly colored. (You just want to give them a brief blast of heat to crisp the top and warm the tomatoes.) Serve right away.

MAKES EIGHT CAKES; SERVES FOUR AS A LUNCH OR LIGHT SUPPER. Transforming an American classic like crab cakes into a southern Italian–inspired dish is a game I like to play in the kitchen, and I'm especially happy when it turns out really well, as this one did. Lemon, basil, capers, and pine nuts are the flavors that highlight this dish.

CRAB CAKES WITH A NEAPOLITAN FLAVOR, SERVED WITH CHICORY SALAD

1 pound fresh lump crabmeat, picked over for shell

4 scallions, including tender green parts, finely chopped

2 inner celery stalks, finely chopped, plus leaves from 4 stalks, finely chopped

1 garlic clove, minced

1/2 red peperoncino chili, minced

3 or 4 gratings of nutmeg

Leaves from 3 or 4 large flat-leaf parsley sprigs

6 fresh basil leaves, chopped

Grated zest and juice of 1 lemon, plus 1 lemon cut into wedges for garnish

1 large egg, beaten

2 tablespoons mayonnaise (Hellman's or Best Foods is fine)

3 tablespoons homemade dry bread crumbs (see page 308)

1 tablespoon plus 1/2 cup extra-virgin olive oil

Salt to taste

Flour for dredging

SALAD

Leaves from 1 head chicory or frisée lettuce, cut into bite-sized pieces

Generous drizzle of extra-virgin olive oil

Juice of 1/2 lemon

Salt and freshly ground black pepper to taste

Palmful of salt-packed capers, soaked and drained (see page 29)

Handful of pine nuts, lightly toasted (see page 61)

In a large bowl, combine the crabmeat, scallions, celery with leaves, garlic, chili, nutmeg, parsley, basil, and lemon zest and juice. Toss very gently, trying not to break up the crab chunks too much. Add the egg, mayonnaise, bread crumbs, and the 1 tablespoon olive oil. Season with salt and give everything another gentle toss (I like doing this with my hands so I can feel the texture of the crabmeat and know when I'm breaking it up too much). Form the mixture into 8 cakes (the mix will be a little loose, but that's what keeps them tender). Place the crab cakes on a plate and cover them with plastic wrap. Refrigerate for at least 30 minutes before cooking (this will help hold them together).

When you're ready to serve the crab cakes, set up a large skillet and pour in the $\frac{1}{2}$ cup olive oil. Place over medium heat. Dredge the crab cakes in flour seasoned lightly with salt. When the oil is hot, add the crab cakes and sauté without moving them until they're nice and brown on the bottom, 4 or 5 minutes. (You want to sauté them on medium, not high heat, so they brown slowly. Too high a heat will cause the outside to get dark before the inside heats through, especially since you're cooking them cold, straight from the refrigerator.) Turn them over and brown the other side, 4 or 5 minutes more.

MEANWHILE, MAKE THE SALAD: Put the chicory or frisée in a salad bowl. Add the olive oil and lemon juice. Season with salt and pepper and toss (one good thing about chicory and frisée is that they don't wilt quickly, like arugula for instance, so you have some leeway when using them as a component in a dish).

Divide the salad among 4 dinner plates. Using a slotted metal spatula, transfer the crab cakes to paper towels to drain briefly. Place 2 crab cakes alongside each salad. Garnish with the capers, pine nuts, and lemon wedges. Serve right away.

SERVES SIX AS AN APPETIZER. For me, the most delicious seafood salads are simple ones without vinegar, raw green peppers, huge amounts of garlic, red pepper flakes, or any of the other harsh-tasting additions Italian American delis like to throw in. The most important ingredients are gently cooked, very fresh seafood and your best extra-virgin olive oil. I like to include just a few flourishes. Here, I've added pistachios, pomegranate seeds (red and green for Christmas), and a few gentle fresh herbs.

CHRISTMAS EVE LOBSTER SALAD WITH PISTACHIOS AND POMEGRANATE

1 heaping tablespoon sea salt, plus salt to taste

2 bay leaves, preferably fresh

2 live lobsters, about 2½ pounds each

1 pound very fresh small squid, cleaned, bodies cut into rings, tentacles left whole

1 pound large shrimp, shelled (deveined, if desired), tails left on

½ cup extra-virgin olive oil

4 scallions, including tender green parts, cut into thin rounds

1 garlic clove, minced

3 or 4 scrapings freshly grated nutmeg

Grated zest and juice of 1 lemon

1 teaspoon soy sauce

Freshly ground black pepper to taste

Handful of unsalted pistachios

Seeds from ½ small pomegranate

12 fresh basil leaves, cut into thin strips

Leaves from 5 or 6 large tarragon sprigs, chopped

Small handful of fresh flat-leaf parsley, chopped

Bring a large pot of water to a boil. Add the 1 tablespoon sea salt and the bay leaves. When the water returns to a boil, drop in the lobsters and boil them until the meat is opaque throughout, about 15 minutes (cook them one at a time if you don't have a very large pot). Remove the lobsters from the water and set them aside to cool.

Return the water to a boil and add the squid, cooking just until it turns opaque, about 30 seconds (cooking longer will make it tough). Using a large skimmer, transfer the calamari to paper towels. Return the water to a boil and add the shrimp, cooking them until they turn pink and are just tender, about 2 minutes, depending on their size. Transfer them to paper towels. Let cool for about 15 minutes.

When the lobsters are cool enough to handle, crack them open with kitchen scissors and a claw cracker (I cover the claws with a kitchen towel so shards of shell and juices don't get all over the place). Remove and discard the intestines from the tail meat, the tomalley, and any roe. Using your fingers or a small fork, remove all the meat from the tail and claws over a shallow pan so you can catch any juices. Cut the meat into not-too-thin slices.

Put all the seafood in a large serving bowl, along with any juices they've given off. Drizzle the ½ cup olive oil over the seafood and give it a toss. Add the scallions, garlic, nutmeg, lemon zest and juice, soy sauce, and a generous amount of freshly ground pepper. Toss gently. Add the pistachios and pomegranate seeds and toss again. Taste and adjust seasoning. It's best never refrigerated; however, if you need to, you can cook the seafood earlier that day and refrigerate it, but return it to room temperature before adding all the other ingredients to assemble the salad. Right before serving, toss in the fresh herbs.

SERVING SUGGESTIONS   Serve the salad on small plates along with slices of toasted Italian bread brushed with olive oil, or spooned over a bed of lightly dressed arugula or chicory for a more formal first course.

SERVES FOUR AS A FIRST COURSE. There are many variations on fish soup in southern Italy; here is one I was served years ago on the island of Ischia, off the coast of Naples. Its winey broth and razor clams left an impression on me. If you can't find razor clams (in New York they're sometimes flown down from Rhode Island), just add a few extra littlenecks.

A note about the seafood for this stew: I've used a good assortment here, but if you'd like to try a simpler stew, choose only two things, especially if it's the first time you've made a dish like this. Juggling all this seafood and having it all come out nicely cooked can be intimidating, so if you like, use only clams and mussels, or just shrimp and squid. The clams should go in 5 minutes before the mussels, the shrimp 1 minute before the squid. Just double the amount of each to serve 4.

ZUPPA DI PESCE WITH TOMATO-GARLIC MAYONNAISE

MAYONNAISE

3 egg yolks at room temperature

1 large garlic clove, coarsely chopped (choose a moist sweet clove that has no signs of sprouting)

3/4 cup canola oil

2 tablespoons extra-virgin olive oil

3 oil-packed sun-dried tomatoes, well chopped

Salt to taste

Squeeze of lemon juice, to taste

1 pound littleneck clams, the smallest ones you can find, scrubbed

6 razor clams, if available, scrubbed

1 pound small mussels, scrubbed and debearded, if necessary

3 tablespoons extra-virgin olive oil, plus more for drizzling

2 inner celery stalks, chopped

1 onion, finely diced

2 garlic cloves, crushed

1 bay leaf

1 small, fresh peperoncino chili, seeded and minced

2 short strips lemon zest

Pinch of salt

1/2 cup dry white wine

One 15-ounce can diced plum tomatoes, with juice

1 pound large shrimp, with heads if available

1 pound small squid, bodies cut into thin rings, tentacles left whole

Leaves from 3 or 4 large marjoram sprigs, chopped

Handful of fresh flat-leaf parsley leaves, chopped

Warm water, if needed

To make the mayonnaise: In a food processor, combine the egg yolks and garlic. Process until the egg yolks are a light yellow, about 15 seconds. With the machine running, add the canola oil in a very slow trickle. Once the mayonnaise begins to thicken, add the canola oil a little faster. Add the extra-virgin olive oil. (I've found that mayonnaise made with all olive oil is too strongly flavored, but I like adding a little at the end just for a touch of olive essence.) Add the sun-dried tomatoes and pulse a few times to blend them into the mayonnaise (the mayonnaise will be a light salmon color with little specks of red). Season with salt and a generous squeeze of lemon juice. (The lemon juice not only picks up the flavors of the mayonnaise, it also makes it fluffy and less compact and dense.)

Look over the clams and mussels, discarding any that don't close when you tap on the shells (this means they're dead). Choose a large, fairly wide casserole fitted with a lid that will hold all the shellfish after they have opened. Add the olive oil to the casserole over medium heat. Add the celery, onion, garlic, bay leaf, chili, lemon zest, and salt. Sauté until everything is softened and fragrant, 4 or 5 minutes. Add the white wine and let it boil down by about half. Add the tomatoes with their juice and cook at a lively simmer for about 5 minutes, no longer than this; you want to keep the sauce a nice bright red.

Add the littlenecks, cover the casserole, and cook, stirring occasionally, until about half of them have started to open, usually about 5 minutes. Add the razor clams, mussels, and head-on shrimp, if using, and cook, uncovered, stirring until most of the clams have opened, about 5 minutes. Add calamari and shrimp without heads, if using, and stir them so they're covered with sauce. Cover the casserole again and simmer just until the shrimp are evenly pink, about 4 minutes. Turn off the heat and let the casserole sit, covered, for a minute or so on the turned-off burner. (This gives everything a moment to blend together, and also gives any clams or mussels that haven't opened a last chance.)

Uncover the casserole and discard any clams or mussels that have not opened. Add the marjoram and parsley. You should have about 2 inches of liquid in the casserole; if you have less, add a little warm water. Taste for seasoning, adding more salt if needed. Add a generous drizzle of fresh olive oil and stir it into the stew (this is very important for flavor and for texture, since it tends to thicken the broth a bit).

Serve hot, in large bowls with a dollop of the mayonnaise on top so everybody can stir it into the broth.

MAKES ABOUT ONE CUP. Since you have all those shells after a big seafood dinner, you may as well put them to good use. You can add this broth to a fish soup or stew, or to a pasta dish or rice dish that contains some sort of fish.

QUICK SHELLFISH BROTH

3 tablespoons unsalted butter

Extra-virgin olive oil for drizzling

Shells from 2 lobsters, cracked into smaller pieces

Trimmings from 1 pound squid (such as small tentacles you didn't want in the salad)

Shells from 1 pound large shrimp

½ cup dry white wine

1 garlic clove, crushed

2 cups water

Sea salt and freshly ground black pepper to taste

In a medium saucepan, melt the butter with the olive oil over medium heat. Add the lobster and shrimp shells and squid trimmings and sauté them 3 to 4 minutes, or until the shrimp shells turn pink. Add the white wine and cook to reduce by half. Add the garlic and water. Bring to a boil over high heat, then reduce heat to medium and simmer at a low bubble for about 20 minutes. Strain the broth into a clean saucepan. Discard all the shells. Boil the broth over high heat until it has reduced to about 1 cup. Season with salt and pepper.

FLAVORINGS FOR SOUTHERN ITALIAN FISH STEWS

I cook a lot of fish stews and soups, so I'm constantly thinking about new ways to flavor them so they don't all end up tasting alike. This can be a real challenge if you're always combining fish with the southern Italian trilogy of white wine, tomatoes, and garlic. There are many interesting ways to vary fish stews without straying far from classic Mediterranean flavors. Here are a few I particularly like.

FENNEL AND SAFFRON   This time-honored flavor marriage turns up in *pasta con le sarde* (pasta with sardines) and other Sicily seafood dishes. You can use chopped wild or bulb fennel, fennel seeds, or a pastis such as Pernod to get a good fennel flavor. Add the bulb or wild fennel or fennel seeds when you sauté the onion. A tablespoon of pastis and a generous pinch of ground saffron threads are best added in the last 5 minutes of cooking, so that their flavors stay bright.

PANCETTA AND ROASTED RED PEPPER   Cured pork added to seafood is admittedly more of a Spanish concept than it is Italian, but pancetta is so subtle that it adds richness more than any detectable meat flavor. Brown a bit of chopped pancetta in the olive oil before adding the onion. Add 1 roasted red bell pepper, cut into thin strips, in the last 5 minutes of cooking. Basil is a good addition to this dish.

ORANGE ZEST AND MINT   This wonderful flavor combination is another one borrowed from Sicilian coastal cooking. Add a few short strips of orange zest and a few mint sprigs when you sauté the onion. Add a bit more fresh mint right before serving for a double layer of herb flavor.

BLACK OLIVES, SAFFRON, AND CREAM   This luscious combination is especially good with mild white fish. Add a handful of halved pitted black olives (niçoise and Gaeta are good choices), a generous pinch of ground saffron threads, and about $1/2$ cup heavy cream in the last 5 minutes of cooking.

LEEKS AND ROSEMARY   I've borrowed this one from southern Italian meat cooking, but it gives a woodsy aroma to fish, which I find tastes unexpectedly delicious. Replace the onion with 4 chopped leeks. Add a few small sprigs of rosemary when you add the garlic.

SWEET WINE AND STAR ANISE   A tablespoon of sweet dessert wine, such a Malvasia di Lipari from Sicily, added along with the dry white wine, softens the acidity of the broth and adds a delicate, herby sweetness. Star anise is a beautiful spice for fish. Add 1 whole star anise when you add the garlic. Fresh tarragon is the perfect garnish for this stew.

SERVES TWO. The southern Italian love of deep-fried food is one that I share. I order a fritto misto of shrimp, calamari, fish, artichokes, and zucchini just about anytime I see it on a menu. Other fish fries I've sampled on the Amalfi Coast contained little whole fish like anchovies and sardines along with calamari and shrimp. Deep-frying at home can be a lot of work if you do it for a group; you can be stuck in the kitchen turning out batch after batch of whatever you're frying while everyone else is at the table enjoying it. My solution is to fry one thing, make a small amount, and sit down and enjoy it with one friend.

I've tried all kinds of batters for fried fish and vegetables, using beer, cornmeal, eggs, and baking soda. I finally decided on the Italian standby plain flour, which works fine, until I learned that Mario Batali fries calamari in a mix of finely ground flour and cornstarch. I tried it and it made the lightest, crispest crust, so I've implemented his idea here.

The fried lemon slices came from a fritto misto recipe of Jonathan Waxman's; the fried chilies are an idea I picked up from a salt-and-pepper squid dish in Chinatown.

FRIED CALAMARI, LEMON, AND CHILIES

4 cups inexpensive extra-virgin olive oil for deep-frying

1/2 cup cornstarch

1/2 cup Wondra or other "instant" flour

Sea salt and freshly ground black pepper to taste

1 1/2 pounds small squid, cleaned, bodies cut into 1/4-inch rings, tentacles left whole

2 small unpeeled lemons, cut into thin rounds

1 long, skinny fresh *peperoncino* chili, cut into thin rounds

Small handful of fresh flat-leaf parsley leaves

In a large saucepan, heat the olive oil over high heat.

While the oil is heating, mix the cornstarch and flour together in a large bowl and season it with a generous amount of salt and pepper.

Test the oil by adding a small piece of squid. If it sizzles immediately, it's hot enough (the temperature should be 365°F). Pat the squid and lemon slices dry with paper towels. Add the squid to the flour mixture, tossing it around with your hands until it is all well coated. Transfer the squid to a colander over the sink and shake out the excess flour.

Add the squid, lemons, and chili to the oil and fry until the squid is lightly golden, 4 or 5 minutes, stirring it once to make sure it isn't sticking together. Using a large strainer, transfer them to paper towels to drain. Transfer them to a large bowl. Scatter on the parsley leaves and sprinkle on a pinch of fresh salt and a few grindings of pepper, giving it all a quick toss. Eat right away.

VARIATION   I love fried shrimp done this way almost as much as I do squid, and I often make this dish using shelled large shrimp, leaving the tails on for an interesting look and a neat little handle. They take just about a few seconds longer to cook than the calamari.

SERVES FOUR AS A MAIN COURSE. My mother made shrimp scampi at home the way she saw it done in Italian American restaurants, by butterflying jumbo shrimp (opening up their backs), packing them with garlic and bread crumbs, and throwing them under the broiler. She presented this almost every Christmas Eve, and I loved it. My variation on the theme includes orange and hot red chilies, which in my opinion were made to be blended. The orange soothes and lifts the heat of the chilies, and the juices from the shrimp give the dish an almost sweet flavor. True Italian scampi are actually small lobster-like crustaceans with eight skinny legs and long, pointy claws. They are often grilled with garlic and herbs in a similar fashion; the American dish takes its name from them.

I like this as a main course, but it is so easy to throw together and looks so fancy, I also think of it when I'm preparing a buffet or an antipasto offering. Just double the recipe to feed a crowd.

BIG SHRIMP GRATIN WITH SPICY ORANGE BREAD CRUMBS

20 jumbo shrimp, shelled, tails left on

$\frac{1}{2}$ cup homemade dry bread crumbs (see page 308)

Grated zest of 2 oranges

1 small fresh red peperoncino chili, minced (remove seeds for less heat, if you prefer)

2 garlic cloves, minced

6 basil leaves, well chopped, plus 3 to 4 more chopped leaves for garnish

Salt to taste

$\frac{1}{4}$ cup extra-virgin olive oil, plus more for drizzling

Juice of 1 orange

Preheat the oven to 500°F.

Using a sharp paring knife, make a slit down the back of each shrimp, stopping at the tail and cutting about halfway into the flesh; pull out the dark vein and discard it.

In a medium bowl, combine the bread crumbs, orange zest, chili, garlic, and 6 basil leaves. Season with a generous amount of salt and drizzle on the $\frac{1}{4}$ cup olive oil. Mix together until it has a crumbly, oily texture. Add the shrimp one at a time and turn them around in the bread crumbs until coated. Pack some bread-crumb mixture into the slit. Place the shrimp, side by side and slit side up, in a large, shallow baking dish (one that will hold them all in one layer). Scatter any remaining bread crumbs over the shrimp, drizzle them with olive oil, and bake until they turn bright pink and the crumbs are golden, 5 to 8 minutes. Squeeze the orange juice over the dish and scatter on the chopped basil. Serve hot.

FEAR OF HIGH HEAT

Years of work in restaurant kitchens has made me comfortable cooking with very high heat. I'm grateful for the ease with which I do so even at home, sometimes to the horror of my husband, who gets nervous watching high flames coming up around the sides of a skillet. In fact, one thing that separates restaurant cooks from home cooks is their nonchalant attitude toward fire. High heat in a sauté pan can give your fish, chicken breast, or steak the crisp outside and moist inside that is ideal for tender cuts of meat. Cooking a tuna steak on medium heat, for instance, results in an outside with no texture and often a dry inside, whether you grill or sauté. Since low heat takes longer to cook something through, it also allows more moisture to cook away.

The best way to ease yourself into high-heat cooking is by buying a large, even heating skillet. I like the All-Clad brand's large sauté pan without the nonstick coating. Flimsy pans are fine for medium heat, but they'll smoke and burn in no time over a high flame. Olive oil is great for high-heat sautéing because it doesn't burn as quickly as butter. You can use butter, but you have to watch it closely. I sometimes use a mix of butter and olive oil if I want a little butter flavor.

Home cooks like to constantly move food around in the skillet while it's sautéing, whether out of nervousness, because they've got nothing else to do, or just from some feeling that they should be tending to what's in the skillet. Restaurant cooks don't bother, usually because they're busy doing ten other things at the same time. The restaurant cooks are actually right. The more you move stuff around, the less likely you are to get a good crust on it. Moving causes juices to escape from meat or fish, creating steam, which impedes browning. Anything you want to cook on high heat should be well dried so it doesn't steam. Also, leave air space between the things you're cooking. Fish fillets all jammed together in a small skillet will have a very hard time developing a crisp exterior, no matter how high the heat.

SERVES SIX AS AN APPETIZER. FOUR AS A MAIN COURSE. This recipe takes about 5 minutes and has so much flavor that I make variations on it all the time. Sometimes I'll add capers or pine nuts, or a chopped anchovy or two. Its success depends on getting the pan very hot, adding almost all the ingredients at once, and, most important, cooking the shrimp quickly. I serve this as a main course with rice or couscous, but it also succeeds as an appetizer, alongside a glass of cold wine.

SAUTÉED SHRIMP WITH CELERY, FENNEL SEEDS, AND CHILIES

¼ cup extra-virgin olive oil

2 pounds jumbo shrimp, shelled and deveined, and tails left on

Small palmful of fennel seeds

1 small green jalapeño chili, minced

3 inner celery stalks, thinly sliced, plus leaves from 5 stalks, chopped

4 scallions, including tender green parts, cut into thin rounds

2 young garlic cloves, thinly sliced

Sea salt

1 tablespoon Pernod or another pastis (Sambuca or anisette, though a little sweeter than pastis, can also be used)

1 very large summer tomato, seeded, cut into medium dice, and drained in a colander for about 15 minutes if it seems very watery

Handful of fresh flat-leaf parsley leaves, chopped

Heat a large skillet (large enough to fit the shrimp without crowding) over high heat. Add the olive oil and heat until almost smoking. Add the shrimp, fennel seeds, chili, chopped celery stalks, scallions, and garlic. Season with salt and sauté quickly, moving the shrimp around only enough to sauté both sides (too much stirring around will cause liquid to be released from the shrimp and vegetables, causing steaming). Sauté just until the shrimp are evenly pink, about 2 minutes.

Add the Pernod and stir to scrape up the pan juices. Add the tomato, parsley, and celery leaves, toss gently for about 1 minute, and remove from the heat. Finish with a drizzle of fresh olive oil and transfer the shrimp to a large serving bowl, pouring any skillet juices over the top. Serve right away.

Serves two as a first course. In the last year or so I've been finding sea scallops in fish markets with their dark pink roe still attached. It's the way scallops are most often served in Italy—a real treat and a rich one. Serve this first course followed by something light or even uncooked, like a salad.

The most important thing to remember when you're preparing scallops is not to overcook them. Try to take them from the heat a minute before they're completely cooked through, since they'll continue to cook a little even after you pull them from the skillet.

SAUTÉED SEA SCALLOPS WITH ROE AND ANCHOVY BUTTER

6 large sea scallops, with roe attached if possible (the roe will be shiny·and a bright reddish orange when they are really fresh)

2 tablespoons unsalted butter

1 tablespoon extra-virgin olive oil

Freshly ground black pepper to taste

2 oil-packed anchovy fillets, minced, or 1 salt-packed anchovy, filleted, soaked, drained, and minced (see page 33)

1 garlic clove, minced

Juice of 1 large lemon

1 tablespoon of lightly toasted home made bread crumbs

Handful of fresh flat-leaf parsley leaves, chopped

Pat the scallops dry. In a large skillet, melt 1 tablespoon of the butter with the olive oil over high heat. Add the scallops and cook without moving them at all until lightly browned on the bottom, about 2 minutes. Using tongs, turn them over and brown the other side, about 1 minute longer. Season them with pepper but no salt, since you'll be adding anchovies to the sauce. Remove them from the skillet and place 3 scallops on each of 2 small plates.

Reduce the heat to medium-low and add the anchovies and garlic to the skillet, sautéing for about 1 minute. Turn off the heat and add the remaining tablespoon of butter and the lemon juice, swishing it around in the skillet. Pour a little of this sauce over each scallop. Garnish with the parsley. Serve right away.

SERVES FOUR AS A MAIN COURSE. Green garlic, which is immature shoots that haven't yet formed cloves, appears in my farmers' market in early June. It looks like thick scallions and has a mild and sweet garlic taste, with no bitterness. It can be chopped just like scallions and cooked or added raw to salad or sauces. You can use it lavishly, since it's so mild.

MUSSELS WITH MASCARPONE, GREEN GARLIC, AND SPRING HERBS

4 pounds mussels, scrubbed and debearded, if necessary (see page 26 for info. on cleaning mussels)

$1/3$ cup extra-virgin olive oil

3 shallots, thinly sliced

2 green garlic shoots, thinly sliced

$1/2$ cup dry white wine

2 large tomatoes, peeled, seeded, and chopped (see page 26)

2 heaping tablespoons mascarpone cheese

Freshly ground black pepper to taste

Large handful of mixed spring herbs, stemmed and chopped, such as parsley, chives, mint, chervil, and tarragon; avoid strong flavors like rosemary or savory

Salt, if needed

Italian bread for serving

Look over the mussels, throwing out any that don't close tightly when you tap on them (this means they're dead). Choose a very large, wide pot. Place over medium heat and add the olive oil. Add the shallots and garlic shoots and sauté until fragrant, about 1 minute. Add the mussels, along with the white wine and tomatoes, to the pot. Cook, uncovered, stirring the mussels occasionally until they have opened, about 5 minutes. Turn off the heat and add the mascarpone, a few grindings of pepper, and the herbs. Give them a good mixing. Taste the broth, adding a bit of salt if necessary (if your mussels are sufficiently salty, you won't need any).

Serve in large bowls, giving each person a good amount of broth. Italian bread is pretty much essential so you can sop up all the juices.

VARIATION   This recipe is a gentle treatment for mussels, but there is an excellent Puglian dish called *cozze pepato* (mussels steamed with black pepper), which I love. It is another direction to go with steamed mussels. To make it, cook the mussels in white wine with a few sliced garlic cloves as you do for this recipe. When the mussels have opened, add a generous amount of coarsely ground pepper and a handful of chopped parsley and give everything a stir. Serve hot, with sliced Italian bread that has been grilled and brushed with olive oil.

RISOTTO, SOUTHERN ITALIAN STYLE

The risotto technique of preparing rice was created in Lombardy, the region around Milan, but southern Italian chefs have adopted it and turn out great risotto dishes using their local seafood, vegetables, and meats. I had a wonderful sausage-and-artichoke risotto in Sicily, and one of the best risottos I've ever eaten was on Ischia, a small island off Naples not far from Capri. It was piled high with octopus and tiny clams and seasoned with garlic, olive oil, white wine, and tomatoes—just what you'd expect in the area.

HERE ARE SOME TIPS FOR COOKING RISOTTO SOUTHERN ITALIAN STYLE

- Remember that risotto is considered a first course in Italy, so keep it simple, including only one or two main ingredients. Even if you serve it as an entrée, as I often do, less is more. Clear, fresh flavors should dominate.

- Carnaroli, Vialone Nano, and Arborio are the three main risotto rice varieties used in Italy. Arborio is the easiest to find in the United States, and it makes a good risotto, but it can sometimes become gummy if even slightly overcooked. You won't have that problem with Carnaroli, which cooks up with a excellent balance between bite and creaminess. Vialone Nano produces a firmer and slightly looser risotto, which I especially like for southern Italian–style seafood risotto, as it produces a cleaner texture.

- Choose a wide, low-sided heavy saucepan to cook the risotto in. Anything too deep and narrow will impede the evaporation of the liquid, resulting in a mushy risotto. Keep the broth at a simmer. Adding cool broth will lower the temperature of the risotto, slowing down the cooking. Keep it at a constant low bubble during the entire cooking process, so it cooks quickly and the liquid evaporates (this will give you a creamy texture and kernels with a little bite, just as you hope for).

- Start with a well-cooked *soffritto:* All risottos, either northern or southern, start with a gentle sautéing of onion, shallots, or leeks and sometimes garlic in butter, olive oil, or a mixture of both (usually depending on the region). Occasionally, celery, fennel, or carrot is also included. This serves as the aromatic base for the risotto.

- *Rosalare* means "to roast," and in preparing risotto it refers to the technique of lightly cooking the rice in the pan until opaque or toasted before adding liquid. This coats each kernel with seasoning and fat from the *soffritto*, adding depth of flavor to the finished dish.

- The constant stirring of risotto releases the rice's starch and is what gives the finished dish its creamy texture.

◆ *All'onda*, or "wavy," is how the texture of risotto is described in Venice, but Italians in different regions have different ideas about the correct consistency. I prefer risotto loose and unencumbered by too much cheese or cream in keeping with southern Italian style. Even when cooked to perfection, risotto will continue to thicken, so I always add an additional ladle of broth before bringing it to the table, to be sure it stays loose.

◆ *Mantecare* means "to pound," but with risotto it refers to the addition of final ingredients right before bringing it to the table. This could be a few tablespoons of butter or a drizzle of good olive oil or cream. Grated Parmigiano or other hard cheeses are incorporated only at the end, so they don't become heavy. I like to add chopped fresh herbs or citrus zest to certain risottos right before serving, to brighten their flavor.

SERVES SIX AS A FIRST COURSE, FOUR AS A MAIN COURSE. Risotto with a pesto of stinging nettles is a dish I was served in Campania several years ago. It had a grassy, herby taste and bright green color. I occasionally see nettles at my green market in the early summer, but I've found arugula make an interesting pesto alternative, without having to deal with the sting.

RISOTTO WITH ARUGULA PESTO AND MUSSELS

PESTO

½ cup whole blanched almonds

1 large garlic clove

1 large bunch arugula, stemmed

½ cup extra-virgin olive oil

½ cup grated grana padano cheese

Salt and freshly ground black pepper to taste

3 pounds small mussels, scrubbed and debearded, if necessary

½ cup dry white wine

Generous drizzle of extra-virgin olive oil, plus 2 tablespoons

Freshly ground black pepper to taste

4 cups homemade chicken broth (see page 315)

1 cup water, plus hot water if needed

3 shallots

1½ cups risotto rice (see page 187 for the best varieties)

TO MAKE THE PESTO: In a food processor, process the almonds until finely ground. Add the garlic, arugula, and olive oil and process briefly to make a coarse purée. Add the grana padano and process a few seconds to blend. Season with salt and pepper. Transfer the mixture to a small bowl and cover it with plastic wrap. You can make the pesto in the morning and refrigerate it, but make sure to bring it back to room temperature before adding it to your risotto.

Discard any mussels that don't close when you tap them with your finger. Put the mussels in a large pot. Pour on the wine and a drizzle of olive oil. Season with a few grindings of pepper. Turn the heat to high and cook, uncovered, stirring occasionally, until the mussels open, about 4 minutes. Using a large strainer spoon, transfer to a bowl. Strain the mussel cooking liquid through a fine-mesh sieve into a small bowl. Shell about half the mussels, leaving the smallest ones in their shells.

Pour the chicken broth into a saucepan. Add the 1 cup water and bring it to a boil (I like diluting the broth for this dish so the chicken taste doesn't compete too much with the mussels). Turn the heat to low and keep the broth at a low simmer.

In a wide, low-sided, heavy saucepan, heat 2 tablespoons olive oil over medium heat. Add the shallots and sauté until softened, about 4 minutes. Add the rice and stir it for 2 to 3 minutes to coat it well with oil and to toast it very lightly. Add the mussel cooking broth and let it cook down to almost nothing, stirring the rice often.

Start adding the chicken broth a few ladles at a time, stirring the rice almost constantly. The heat should be at an even low boil throughout the cooking (if the heat is too low, the rice may become mushy; what you want is a steady evaporation and absorption of the broth). Keep adding broth as the pan gets dry. Continue adding broth and stirring until the rice is creamy but the kernels still have a nice bite. The entire cooking time will be about 20 minutes. If you run out of broth, add ladles of very hot water.

When the rice is just about ready, add all the mussels and any broth they have given off. Add the pesto and toss everything well. Taste for seasoning. These additions will probably thicken your risotto, so add an extra ladle of broth or water to ensure a nice, loose texture. Serve right away.

SERVES FOUR AS A MAIN COURSE. I've never understood immersing sweet, delicate lobster in an intensely spicy tomato sauce, *fra diavolo* style, either with hot chilies or abundant black pepper; it seems to defeat the lobster's reason for being (or for eating, at least). A Christmas Eve dish my mother's father made was lobster simmered in a rich, boozy tomato sauce with no chilies. Here is my version, as recalled by my mother.

For the best texture, cut-up raw lobster should be added to this sauce, but after working in a restaurant where I was ordered to chop cratefuls of live lobsters, sometimes a hundred at a time, and bursting into tears on one occasion at the overwhelming carnage of the task, I don't think I can ever butcher even one of them live again. Here, I've boiled them, whole, until they're about half cooked, then chopped them up. It is admittedly a compromise solution, but it works pretty well to achieve the velvety, tender texture you want for the dish.

LOBSTER WITH TOMATO AND BRANDY

3 tablespoons extra-virgin olive oil

3 garlic cloves, very thinly sliced, plus 1 whole clove for the bruschetta

2 bay leaves, fresh if possible

4 or 5 scrapings of freshly grated nutmeg

Tiny pinch of ground cloves

One 35-ounce can diced plum tomatoes with juice

$1/2$ cup low-salt canned chicken broth or a very light fish broth

Sea salt to taste, plus 1 tablespoon

Freshly ground black pepper to taste

4 live $1^1/_2$-pound lobsters

4 tablespoons unsalted butter

$1/_4$ cup brandy or Cognac

Leaves from 3 or 4 tarragon sprigs, chopped

Generous handful of fresh basil leaves, chopped, plus a few sprigs for garnish

Large handful of pine nuts, lightly toasted (see page 61)

Set up a very large pot full of water and bring it to a boil.

Meanwhile, in a large skillet, heat the olive oil over medium heat. Add the 3 garlic cloves and sauté briefly until fragrant, about 1 minute. Add the bay leaves, nutmeg, cloves, tomatoes, and broth. Cook, uncovered, at a lively simmer for about 5 minutes (you want the sauce to stay fresh and brightly colored, so don't let it go any longer). Season with salt and pepper. Turn off the heat.

Add the 1 tablespoon sea salt to the water, let it return to a hard boil, and drop in the lobsters, cooking them 2 at a time if you need to. Cover the pot and boil for 5 minutes (they will be almost half cooked). Lift the lobsters from the water and let them cool enough so you can handle them. Pull off their claws, cover the claws with a kitchen towel, and hit each one with a hammer to crack it. Cut the bodies in half lengthwise, quickly so no juices get away. Remove and discard the intestines, but leave the tomalley and any roe you find in the shells.

In a very large skillet that will hold all the lobster pieces and the sauce, melt the butter over medium-high heat (use 2 skillets if you need to). Add the lobster pieces (shell still on), flesh side down, and sauté them for about 1 minute. Season with a pinch of salt and more generously with pepper. Pour on the brandy or Cognac, letting it bubble until it is almost evaporated. Pour on the tomato sauce and stir to blend it. Turn the heat to low and simmer for about 5 minutes to finish cooking the lobster and blend the flavors. Turn the lobster pieces over and add the chopped tarragon and basil. The sauce should be a little brothy and studded with chunks of tomato. Taste for seasoning.

Place the lobster pieces in a wide, shallow serving bowl and pour the sauce over them. Sprinkle with the toasted pine nuts and garnish with basil sprigs. Serve hot.

SERVES FOUR AS A MAIN COURSE. I cook squid gently simmered with tomatoes and white wine year-round. In the winter, I use canned tomatoes and sometimes add celery or leeks or a can of drained chickpeas. In the summer, I use fresh tomatoes and new garlic. In spring, I love adding a green vegetable. Here, I've chosen peas.

The gentle mix of cinnamon, white wine, and basil gives this simple stew a beautiful fragrance as it braises.

BRAISED CALAMARI WITH PEAS, WHITE WINE, AND BASIL

3 tablespoons extra-virgin olive oil, plus more for drizzling

2 shallots, thinly sliced

3 garlic cloves

3 pounds squid, cleaned (see page 195 to clean it yourself), bodies cut into thin rings, tentacles left whole

Salt and freshly ground black pepper to taste

1/2 cinnamon stick

1 bay leaf, preferably fresh

1 tablespoon brandy or Cognac

1/2 cup dry white wine

One 15-ounce can chopped plum tomatoes with juice

1 cup fresh or thawed frozen green peas

Large handful of fresh basil leaves, chopped

Choose a good-looking casserole, fitted with a lid, that you can bring to the table. Over medium heat, add the 3 tablespoons olive oil to the casserole. When hot, add the shallots and garlic and sauté a few minutes so they can release their fragrances. Add the squid, salt, pepper, cinnamon stick, and bay leaf. Sauté for about 3 minutes (this will infuse the squid with flavor). Add the brandy or Cognac and let it boil away. Add the white wine and cook to reduce it by about half. Add the tomatoes and bay leaf.

Cover the casserole, reduce the heat to very low, and simmer for about 30 minutes. Add the peas and cook, uncovered, about 10 minutes, or until the squid is tender (taste a piece for tenderness), the peas cooked through, and the sauce reduced a bit (it will still be brothy, though—squid gives off a lot of water). Taste for seasoning. Add a generous drizzle of fresh olive oil and the basil.

SERVING SUGGESTION   Serve in pasta bowls, accompanied by slices of grilled Italian bread that have been brushed by olive oil.

SERVES FOUR AS A MAIN COURSE. At the elegant restaurant Baccosteria, in Barletta, Puglia, a waiter suggested I order the *calamari ripieni* (stuffed squid). Filled with nothing but the local sheep's milk ricotta, it was creamy, tangy, and sweet all at the same time. This simple but luscious dish was like nothing I'd ever tasted before. I've tried to duplicate it in my home kitchen, even making it with my homemade goat's milk ricotta, but somehow it seemed lackluster. Finally, I figured out how to add a few gentle herbs and a splash of sweet wine to bring it closer to what I remember in Puglia.

CALAMARI FILLED WITH RICOTTA AND HERBS AND SAUTÉED IN MALVASIA WINE

2 pounds large squid, cleaned (see note), bodies and tentacles left whole

1 cup whole-milk ricotta, sheep's milk if available, drained in a colander for about 20 minutes (to get rid of excess liquid so it doesn't ooze out of squid when cooking)

1 large egg, beaten

Handful of fresh flat-leaf parsley leaves, chopped, plus a handful of leaves for garnish

Leaves from 3 or 4 marjoram sprigs, chopped

1 tablespoon grated grana padano or Parmigiano-Reggiano cheese

Salt and freshly ground black pepper to taste

2 tablespoons extra-virgin olive oil

2 unpeeled garlic cloves, lightly crushed

$3/4$ cup Malvasia or other sweet wine such as Baumes de Venise

1 strip lemon zest

Small handful of green olives, such as picholine

Cooked long-grain white rice or couscous for serving

In a large pot of salted boiling water, blanch the squid for about 1 minute. Using a large skimmer, transfer to a colander. Run the squid under cold water, then transfer to paper towels to drain. (Blanching firms up the squid, making it much easier to fill.)

In a small bowl, combine the ricotta, egg, chopped parsley, and marjoram, grana padano or Parmigiano, salt, and pepper. Mix everything together. Using a small spoon, fill the squid about halfway with the ricotta mixture. (If you have a pastry bag with a wide tip, you can use that instead of a spoon.) Close them up with toothpicks. Wipe any ricotta off the outside of the squid.

In a large skillet, heat the olive oil over medium-high heat. Add the stuffed squid, tentacles, and garlic cloves. Season with salt and pepper to taste and sauté until golden on one side. Turn to sauté the other side. Add the sweet wine and lemon zest, reduce the heat, cover, and simmer until the squid is very tender, about 35 minutes, turning them occasionally.

Transfer the squid to a serving platter. Scatter the olives around the squid. Boil the skillet cooking liquid down for about 1 minute to intensify the flavor. You want to wind up with about $\frac{1}{2}$ cup of liquid (if it's already $\frac{1}{2}$ cup, just leave it). Pour the sauce through a fine-mesh strainer over the squid. Garnish with the whole parsley leaves. Serve hot over rice or couscous.

CLEANING SQUID   It's actually easier to find cleaned squid than noncleaned squid in most fish shops today, but when I buy local squid from my fish guy at the farmers' market, it's usually not cleaned. I have to admit, I enjoy cleaning squid. I know this is not everyone's idea of a good time, but in fact it's very easy. All you need to do is run the bodies under cold water while you pull out the insides with your fingers. It pretty much all comes out in one piece: a bit of innards and a long, translucent quill. Now, slip the reddish outer skin off the bodies, which is easily done under running water. (In southern Italy, oftentimes I've been served calamari, especially grilled calamari, with this skin left on. It adds good flavor and looks pretty, but I've never seen this done here and I only do it when I'm grilling it whole.) Give the squid a good rinse, inside and out. If you are using the tentacles, you need to feel for the little hard round beak at the base of each one and cut below that to detach it from the tentacles. That's it.

SERVES FOUR AS A MAIN COURSE. I've hardly ever been to a restaurant anywhere in Sicily and not found some version of these swordfish rolls on the menu. They've become popular even in towns away from the coast. Sometimes they're filled with cheese and herbs, sometimes more elaborately with capers, pine nuts, raisins, and olives mixed together. They can be moist inside, with a crisp crust, or heavily breaded and mushy. I aim for moist and crisp.

SWORDFISH INVOLTINI WITH BAY LEAVES AND LEMON

2 pounds swordfish steak, about 2 inches thick, skinned

3 tablespoons extra-virgin olive oil, plus more for drizzling

3/4 cup homemade dry bread crumbs (see page 308)

Generous palmful of pine nuts, lightly toasted (see page 61), plus about 2 tablespoons extra for garnish

2 heaping tablespoons grated pecorino cheese

2 oil-packed anchovy fillets, well chopped, or 1 salt-packed anchovy,

filleted, soaked, drained, and well chopped (see page 33)

1 garlic clove, minced

Leaves from 5 or 6 thyme sprigs, chopped

Handful of fresh flat-leaf parsley leaves, chopped

Salt to taste

Pinch of cayenne pepper

Juice of 1 lemon, plus 2 lemons sliced into thin half-moons

8 fresh bay leaves (see note)

The size of your swordfish steaks will determine the size of your *involtini*, so I'm not giving you a preferred size. Usually, I can find long steaks that are cut from half the diameter of the fish, but you can also find triangular pieces that are a quarter section of a larger fish. You will need to slice each steak horizontally into thin pieces. It's easiest to do this with a long, thin, sharp knife. Place the palm of your hand on top of the fish and run the knife along the fish slowly to cut a relatively even, thin slice off the top. You will usually get 3 slices from a 2-inch-thick piece of swordfish. Now, with a meat pounder, gently flatten out each slice, working to make it wider rather than longer. Wrap the slices in plastic wrap if that makes it easier, but I find this a bit of a chore, and as long as I'm gentle, I don't tear the fish. If you have a very skinny little tail at the end of your slices, trim it off and chop it finely to add to the stuffing.

Preheat the oven to 425°F.

TO MAKE THE FILLING: In a medium sauté pan, heat 2 tablespoons of the olive oil over medium heat. Add the bread crumbs and sauté until they're lightly crunchy and just turning golden, about 2 minutes.

Pour the bread crumbs into a bowl and add the pine nuts, pecorino, anchovies, garlic, thyme, and parsley. If you have any fish trimmings, chop them finely and add to the filling. Season with salt and cayenne. Add the lemon juice and 1 tablespoon olive oil, and mix everything together. The mixture should be a little moist.

Place about 1 tablespoon filling in the center of each swordfish slice and spread it out to cover all but the edges of the fish, reserving about 2 tablespoons filling. Roll the slices up from the skinny end and close them up with 1 or 2 toothpicks. Season the outsides of the *involtini* with salt and another pinch of cayenne.

Choose an approximately 10-by-12-inch baking dish and coat it lightly with olive oil. Place the *involtini* in the dish and insert the lemon slices and bay leaves among them. Sprinkle on the reserved filling and give everything a drizzle of olive oil. Bake until the fish is just tender and lightly browned, 10 to 15 minutes. Scatter on the pine nut garnish. I like *involtini* served hot, but in Sicily they are often served at room temperature (which is very convenient if you want to offer them as part of an *antipasti* assortment). Don't forget to warn your guests about the toothpicks before they start eating (you can take them out, but it might mess up the presentation).

NOTE If you can't find fresh bay leaves, it's better to omit them than to use dried, which will give the dish a musty taste. Without bay, the lemon will dominate, and that's fine.

Serves four as a main course. *Baccalà* is salt cod, a traditional dish for a Neapolitan Christmas Eve. We never ate it when I was a child, I'm sure because my mother viewed it as embarrassingly rustic, but I've come to love salt cod's unique taste, and I find it worth the day or so of soaking needed for its preparation (in southern Italy you often find it presoaked in the markets). Neapolitan cooks make it with potatoes, with or without tomatoes, with white wine, with peas, cauliflower, or sautéed sweet peppers. They also often add capers and olives. Here's a mellow version, without tomatoes.

BACCALÀ WITH LEEKS, GOLDEN RAISINS, AND PINE NUTS

2 pounds salt cod, preferably *filettone di baccalà,* the center cut, if available

1 tablespoon unsalted butter

2 tablespoons extra-virgin olive oil

2 leeks, including light green parts, rinsed and cut into rounds

2 garlic cloves

Pinch of ground cloves

1 bay leaf

3-inch strip lemon zest

Leaves from 3 or 4 thyme sprigs, chopped

Handful of golden raisins, soaked in $\frac{1}{2}$ cup dry white wine

Freshly ground black pepper to taste

$\frac{1}{2}$ cup canned low-salt chicken broth

Handful of pine nuts, lightly toasted (see page 61)

Salt, if needed

Small handful of fresh flat-leaf parsley leaves, chopped

To soak the salt cod: Put the cod in a large pot of cold water under a faucet and let the water run over it for a few minutes. Let it sit in the pot of water in the refrigerator overnight. In the morning, take it out and put it under the faucet again, letting fresh cold water run over it for a few more minutes. Let it sit in the sink, running fresh water over it from time to time until cooking it in the evening. This is usually long enough to get rid of most of the salt, but taste a little piece to make sure. It should be slightly salty but not overly so.

One thing to remember about salt cod is that once it is desalted by long soaking, it becomes actual fish again, although with a flavor all its own, which means it can easily be overcooked. Gentle simmering for about 20 minutes is all it needs; otherwise it can become tough and dry.

Drain the salt cod and cut it into 2-inch chunks. If the salt cod has its skin, just leave it on (it helps to hold the fish together).

In a large skillet, melt the butter with the oil over medium heat. Add the leeks, garlic, cloves, bay leaf, zest, and thyme. Sauté until the leeks are soft, about 5 minutes. Add the salt cod chunks, skin side up, and sauté them for a minute or two. Turn them over, add the raisins with their soaking wine, and let this bubble for a minute or two. Season the fish with pepper and add the chicken broth. Turn the heat to low, cover, and simmer until the fish is just tender, about 20 minutes.

Add the pine nuts. You should have about $1/2$ inch of liquid in the skillet. Taste for salt and add some if necessary. Transfer the cod to a serving platter. Run your fingers over the top of the pieces to check for bones and pull them out. Also remove any skin that you can pull off easily. If you have more than $1/2$ inch of liquid left in the skillet, boil it down over high heat for a few minutes; otherwise pour everything left in the skillet over the cod. Garnish with the parsley. Serve hot or warm.

SERVES FOUR AS A MAIN COURSE. Serving fish or meat on top of a vegetable is not a southern Italian concept and not something I usually go for, but one night I ordered a roasted codfish on fennel purée at a Sicilian restaurant in New York called Bussola and really enjoyed it. It was lighter and less clinging than the bed of mashed potatoes many American chefs use to prop up a piece of protein. So I borrowed the idea and combined it with skin-on sea bass fillets, cooked by the restaurant method of blasting high heat to crisp the skin and keep the fish moist.

SEA BASS WITH FENNEL PURÉE AND GREEN OLIVES

FENNEL PURÉE

1 tablespoon unsalted butter

2 tablespoons extra-virgin olive oil

1 onion, coarsely chopped

4 fennel bulbs, trimmed, cored, and coarsely chopped, plus a handful of fennel fronds, chopped

1 garlic clove

About 10 fennel seeds

Salt and freshly ground black pepper to taste

1/2 cup warm water

1 tablespoon unsalted butter

2 tablespoons extra-virgin olive oil

Four 6- to 8-ounce sea bass fillets, preferably thick center cuts, skin on

Salt and freshly ground black pepper to taste

Flour for dredging

Juice of 1 large lemon

Large handful of green olives, pitted and coarsely chopped

TO MAKE THE PURÉE: In a medium saucepan, melt the butter with the olive oil over medium heat. Add the onion, chopped fennel, fennel fronds, garlic, and fennel seeds. Season with salt and pepper and sauté until the vegetables are just starting to turn golden and fragrant, 5 or 6 minutes. Add the water and bring to a boil. Reduce the heat to medium-low, cover, and simmer until the vegetables are very soft, about 30 minutes. Check the pan a few times to make sure there is still a little water left; otherwise the vegetables might burn. In a food processor, purée the vegetables and any liquid until smooth. Return to the saucepan. The purée should be thick, not soupy. If it is not, boil it down over medium heat for a few minutes to thicken it. Taste for seasoning, adding a pinch more salt if you need to.

Preheat the oven to 450°F.

In a large skillet, melt the butter with the oil over medium-high heat. Season the sea bass fillets on both sides with salt and pepper, then dredge the skin sides with flour. When the skillet is hot, add the fillets, skin side down, and sauté without moving them. When you notice the edges of the fish are getting nice and brown, after about 4 minutes or so, put the skillet in the oven without turning the fish. This will finish cooking the fish and further brown the skin. Bake just until tender, about 4 minutes. You can check for doneness by poking a thin knife into the flesh side. If it goes in easily but still holds its shape, it's done.

Set out 4 dinner plates and divide fennel purée among them (reheat it if you need to). Place the fillets, skin side up, on top of the purée. Squeeze lemon juice over the fillets and scatter the chopped olives on top. Serve right away.

SERVES FOUR AS A MAIN COURSE. The inspiration for this recipe came from Richard Olney's book *Provence the Beautiful*. His delicious recipe seems southern Italian in concept, like many Provençal dishes; my changes include adding the basil pesto.

BRAISED TUNA WITH ARTICHOKES AND BASIL PESTO

1½ pounds tuna steak (about 1½ inches thick), cut into 2-inch chunks

¼ cup extra-virgin olive oil

1 bay leaf

Grated zest of 1 lemon

3 garlic cloves, crushed

Freshly ground black pepper to taste

Juice of 1 large lemon

5 large artichokes

BASIL PESTO

1 small garlic clove

Handful of whole blanched almonds

Leaves from 3 or 4 mint sprigs

Large handful fresh basil leaves (about 1 cup)

⅓ cup extra-virgin olive oil

Pinch of salt

2 thin slices pancetta, chopped

2 tablespoons extra-virgin olive oil

1 onion, finely diced

Salt to taste

½ cup dry white wine

4 fresh plum tomatoes, peeled, seeded, and chopped (see page 26), or 4 canned tomatoes, chopped

½ cup homemade chicken broth (see page 315) or canned low-salt chicken broth

Put the tuna in a shallow glass or ceramic bowl (metal can give fish an off taste). Pour over the olive oil. Add the bay leaf, lemon zest, garlic cloves, and a generous amount of pepper. Toss with your hands so the fish pieces are well coated. Cover and refrigerate for at least 30 minutes or up to 2 hours.

Fill a bowl with cold water and add the lemon juice. Pull off the artichoke leaves until you reach the tender light-green leaves. Trim the bottom of the stems, leaving as much tender stem as possible. Peel the stems of tough outer skin. Slice off about 1 inch from the top. Quarter the artichokes lengthwise and cut out the chokes and any inner, prickly purple leaves. Drop each piece in the lemon water as you finish working on it.

To make the pesto: In a food processor, combine the garlic and almonds and grind coarsely. Add the mint, basil, olive oil, and salt. Pulse several times to make a coarse paste. Put the pesto in a small bowl and cover it with plastic wrap, pressing the plastic down onto the surface of the pesto (this will keep air out and prevent the pesto from turning dark).

In a large skillet over medium heat, combine the pancetta and olive oil. Sauté the pancetta until it has started to crisp, about 4 minutes. Drain the artichokes and add them to the skillet, along with the onion. Season with salt and sauté a few minutes until the onion has softened and the artichokes are very lightly golden. Add the white wine and boil it to reduce by half. Add the tomatoes and cook for 1 minute. Add the chicken broth, cover, and simmer for 5 minutes. Add the tuna chunks and marinade, spooning some of the skillet liquid over the top. Season with a little more salt, cover the skillet again, reduce the heat to low, and cook until the tuna and artichokes are tender, about 10 minutes. Serve in soup bowls with a spoonful of pesto on top of each serving.

SERVING SUGGESTION Toasted baguette slices that have been rubbed with garlic and brushed with olive oil are a perfect accompaniment.

SERVES FOUR AS A MAIN COURSE. Salmon is not native to southern Italy, but it has become somewhat trendy there, and I've sampled it at upscale restaurants in Sicily and Naples. The southern Italian chef bathes salmon in southern Mediterranean flavors, which makes sense for such a rich, oily fish. Here, I've taken the classic gremolata mix of garlic, lemon zest, and parsley, which is traditionally sprinkled over osso buco (veal shank), and used it for a crust for the fish. The salmon fillets are baked at a high temperature to make them crisp but moist inside, and finished with tomatoes and olives.

BAKED SALMON WITH GREMOLATA CRUST

GREMOLATA

Grated zest of 2 large lemons

2 garlic cloves, minced

1/2 cup chopped fresh flat-leaf parsley

Leaves from 3 or 4 large thyme sprigs, chopped

3 tablespoons homemade dry bread crumbs (see page 308)

Handful of pine nuts, ground in a food processor

3 tablespoons extra-virgin olive oil

Salt and freshly ground black pepper to taste

Four 6- or 8-ounce salmon fillets, cut from the thickest section, skin and pin bones removed

2 tablespoons extra-virgin olive oil

4 scallions, including tender green parts, cut into thin rounds

2 cups sweet cherry tomatoes

2 tablespoons dry white wine

Salt and freshly ground black pepper to taste

Handful of fresh flat-leaf parsley leaves

Leaves from 1 or 2 thyme sprigs, chopped

Preheat the oven to 500°F.

TO MAKE THE GREMOLATA: In a small bowl, combine all the ingredients. Mix well to make a nice, oily paste. (You could grind everything together in a food processor, but I like the hand-chopped texture better; it's less mushy and tends to crisp better when cooked.)

Press the gremolata onto the top of the salmon pieces so it adheres. Lightly coat a nice-looking baking dish (one you can bring to the table) with about a tablespoon of olive oil and place the salmon in it (they shouldn't fit too snugly—you want a little air between the slices so they will bake evenly). Place in the oven to bake until barely translucent in the center, 12 to 15 minutes, depending on the thickness of the fish. (The point of this blasting method is to cook the fish quickly so it sears on the surface, sealing in moisture.)

WHILE THE SALMON IS BAKING, COOK THE TOMATOES: Heat a medium skillet over high heat. Add the remaining tablespoon of olive oil and heat to almost smoking. Add the scallions and tomatoes and sear quickly just until skins crack. This will take only a minute or two. Add the white wine and let it bubble for a few seconds, leaving a little liquid in the pan. Season with salt and pepper.

Remove the salmon from the oven. Add the parsley leaves and thyme to the tomatoes and stir ithem in. Pour the tomatoes, with all their skillet juices, around (not on) the salmon. Serve right away.

NOTE   Farmed salmon is what I generally find in my markets and it's fine, but from late spring into summer wild Alaskan salmon comes into season, and its rich taste and velvety texture can be amazing. Look for Nookta Sound wild salmon or the even richer Copper River King salmon. I also sometimes find wild king, white king, or wild sockeye salmon as well.

SERVES FOUR AS A MAIN COURSE. Grouper is a flavorful and firm-textured fish that is somewhat underrated in this country. When I find large fillets, I like to roast them. I've added rosemary and sage, which I think of as cold-weather flavors, and fashioned a quick sauce from canned tomatoes, making a hearty winter dish.

GROUPER WRAPPED IN PROSCIUTTO AND SERVED WITH A WINTER TOMATO SAUCE

TOMATO SAUCE

3 tablespoons extra-virgin olive oil

2 shallots, thinly sliced

1 inner celery stalk, finely diced

2 garlic cloves, thinly sliced

Leaves from 1 small rosemary sprig, chopped

1 bay leaf, preferably fresh

Salt and freshly ground black pepper to taste

2 tablespoons dry Marsala

One 35-ounce can chopped plum tomatoes, with juice

4 fresh sage leaves, chopped

2 large grouper fillets (1½ to 2 pounds each), skinned

Extra-virgin olive oil for brushing, plus 2 tablespoons, and more for drizzling

Salt and freshly ground black pepper to taste

Juice of 1 large lemon

Handful of fresh basil leaves, plus a few whole sprigs for garnish

7 or 8 fresh sage leaves

8 ounces prosciutto di Parma, very thinly sliced

TO MAKE THE TOMATO SAUCE: In a large skillet, heat the olive oil over medium heat. Add the shallots and celery and sauté until soft, about 5 minutes. Add the garlic, rosemary, bay leaf, salt, and pepper. Sauté a few minutes longer, just until the herbs release their fragrances (the garlic shouldn't brown). Add the Marsala and let it bubble for a few seconds. Add the tomatoes, stir, and simmer at a low bubble, uncovered, until the sauce has thickened slightly, about 15 minutes (a little longer than I usually cook a tomato sauce, but I wanted a deeper flavor for this winter dish). Add the sage. Taste and adjust the seasoning. Turn off the heat and let the sauce sit in the pan while you prepare the grouper (this will allow the flavors to mellow a bit).

Preheat the oven to 400°F.

Brush the grouper fillets lightly with olive oil and season them with salt, pepper, and a generous squeeze of lemon juice. Press the basil and sage leaves onto the fish. Wrap prosciutto slices around each fillet. (The fish doesn't need to be completely covered by the prosciutto, but do the best you can. Sometimes the skinny ends are hard to keep covered.) Hold the prosciutto in place with toothpicks.

In an ovenproof skillet, heat the 2 tablespoons oil over medium heat. Add the fillets, rounded side down, and sauté until the prosciutto is crisp, about 2 minutes on each side. Put the skillet in the oven, uncovered, and roast until the grouper is just tender, about 10 minutes (check by poking a small knife into the center).

Place the fillets on a large serving platter and garnish with basil sprigs. Remove the toothpicks. Reheat the tomato sauce, if necessary, and stir in a drizzle of fresh olive oil. Pour it into a sauce bowl and bring it to the table. With a thin carving knife or a thin serrated one, slice the fish into thick pieces and serve, topping each portion with a generous spoonful of sauce.

SERVES TWO AS A MAIN COURSE. Soft-shelled crabs seem to me the most American of all seafood. We ate them on cottony-centered, shiny rolls every spring at beach restaurants on Long Island, the crunchy crab incredibly greasy and oozing with tartar sauce. Today, thanks to modern fishery technology, their formerly short season extends, at least in New York, from about late March through to the end of the summer. Here I've paired the hot crispy crabs with a cool tomato, cucumber, and basil salad.

Since the crabs need to be sautéed at the last minute and served right away, make this for 2, so you can get it out quickly and sit down and enjoy it with someone you like.

SAUTÉED SOFT-SHELLED CRABS WITH CUCUMBER AND TOMATO SALAD

SALAD

2 small cucumbers, peeled and finely diced

Salt to taste

3 scallions, including tender green parts, chopped

2 large tomatoes, peeled, seeded, and finely diced (see page 26)

Pinch of sugar

Freshly ground black pepper to taste

Extra-virgin olive oil for drizzling

Squeeze of lemon juice

Small handful of fresh basil leaves, cut into thin strips

½ cup semolina flour

Salt and freshly ground black pepper to taste

Pinch of cayenne

4 small soft-shelled crabs, cleaned (see note)

2 tablespoons extra-virgin olive oil

1 tablespoon unsalted butter

Juice of 1 lemon

Handful of pine nuts, toasted (see page 61)

Basil sprigs for garnish

Put the diced cucumber in a colander and sprinkle lightly with salt. Place this over a bowl and let the cucumber drain for about 20 minutes. Transfer the cucumber to a small bowl and add the scallions, tomatoes, sugar, salt to taste, pepper, a generous drizzle of olive oil, and a squeeze of lemon juice. Add the basil strips and toss gently. Taste for seasoning.

Place the flour on a plate and season it with salt, pepper, and cayenne. Coat the crabs in the flour, shaking off the excess.

In a large skillet, heat the olive oil over high heat until almost smoking. Add a table-spoon of butter and let it melt. Add the crabs, shell side down, and sauté until crisp and golden, about 4 minutes (be careful, though, these things can spit at you, so stand back a little if you hear a popping noise). Turn the crabs over and sauté the other side until they are just cooked through and the outside is golden, about 3 or 4 minutes, depend-ing on their size.

Place 2 crabs on each of 2 large dinner plates and season them lightly with a little salt and pepper and the lemon juice. Spoon a generous amount of the cucumber salad between the 2 crabs (not on top—you want the crabs to remain crisp). Scatter on the toasted pine nuts and garnish with basil sprigs. Serve right away.

CLEANING SOFT-SHELLED CRABS   You can have your fish seller clean them for you, but it's not hard to do yourself, as long as you don't mind cutting the eyes out of a live creature. Use scis-sors and snip off the eyes and mouth. Snip off the gills, which are under either side of the shell. That's it. Once they're cleaned, cook them right away or refrigerate them for not more than 3 hours. They become very perishable after cleaning.

SERVES FOUR AS A MAIN COURSE. The mingling of anchovy and rosemary is a quirky Sicilian flavor combination that I love. I use it here to fill the cavity of the sea bass, and also to make a little hot oil for drizzling over the fish after it is filleted. This fish has become a Christmas Eve tradition at my house.

ROASTED WHOLE SEA BASS WITH ROSEMARY OIL

2 tablespoons extra-virgin olive oil, plus more for drizzling

2 lemons, cut into thin rounds

One 3½- to 4-pound sea bass, cleaned and scaled, head and tail left on (if you can't get a large fish, choose 2 smaller ones, about 2 pounds each)

3 or 4 rosemary sprigs

2 garlic cloves, lightly crushed

Salt and freshly ground black pepper to taste

½ cup dry white wine

ROSEMARY OIL

¾ cup extra-virgin olive oil

2 garlic cloves, thinly sliced

Juice of 1 lemon

Leaves from 3 or 4 rosemary sprigs, chopped

4 oil-packed anchovy fillets, chopped, or 2 salt-packed anchovies, filleted, soaked, drained, and chopped (see page 33)

Salt and freshly ground black pepper to taste

Preheat the oven to 450°F. Choose a large baking dish that will fit the fish snugly. Drizzle the 2 tablespoons olive oil into the dish. Place some of the lemon slices inside the fish's cavity, along with the rosemary sprigs and crushed garlic. Season the fish well inside and out with salt and pepper and place it in the baking dish, swishing it around in the olive oil. Drizzle a little extra oil over the top of the fish. Place the remaining lemon slices on and around the fish and pour the wine around it.

Bake the fish, without turning it, until it is just tender, about 25 minutes for a large fish, about 18 minutes for 2 smaller ones. (Check by poking a small knife into the flesh at the backbone to see if it flakes. It might need more time, but it's best to check early so it doesn't overcook.) Baste the fish several times with the juices while it cooks.

While the fish is baking, start preparing the rosemary oil: In a small saucepan, combine the olive oil, sliced garlic, lemon juice, rosemary, anchovies, salt, and a few turns of pepper. Set aside.

Take the fish from the oven. Place the saucepan with the rosemary mixture over medium heat and heat it until the oil is just coming to a boil. Let the oil bubble for about 1 minute. Turn off the heat and whisk the sauce until well blended. Pour into a small sauceboat.

Fillet the fish (see note) and divide it among 4 plates. Pour a little of the hot rosemary oil over each serving and serve right away.

TIPS FOR ROASTING AND FILLETING WHOLE FISH

Roasting whole fish at a high temperature crisps the outside while keeping the flesh moist; you just have to be careful not to let it overcook. When you think a fish is just about done, poke a knife in gently along the backbone; if the flesh pulls away but stays firm, it's done. If it pulls away and flakes very easily, in my opinion it's a little overdone. A fish will continue to cook a bit after you take it from the oven, so it's always better to have it a tiny bit underdone. If the flesh hardly gives at all and is pink looking, it needs more time.

A problem many cooks have when dealing with whole fish is how to fillet it. To start with, you're never going to get a whole side off in one piece, especially when you have a really large fish, as in this recipe. Even when you order a whole fish in a restaurant and it is filleted at the table, the waiter will pull off pieces and put them on your plate.

Start by pulling back the skin from the top (the skin from a large roast fish is never really crisp enough to eat, it just acts as a protective coating to keep moisture in). Then run a fish-boning knife or any long, somewhat flexible knife against either side of the fish, scraping outward, to pull away many of the little bones. Now, working with the knife and a fork, wedge the top fillet up from the backbone. This should come up easily, probably in several large pieces. Look for stray bones and discard them. Now, pull the backbone off with your fingers. It should come right up. Check the bottom fillet for any bones that might run along the top or sides, then lift up the fillet, discarding the bottom skin. Remove the little pockets of meat on the cheeks last.

SERVES TWO AS A MAIN COURSE. This is my reworking of a recipe for sole with orange sauce from Jo Bettoja's book *Southern Italian Cooking*, which is filled with many elegant tomato-free recipes that you might not associate with southern Italian cooking. Bettoja says her recipe came from a restaurant in the hilltop town of Ravello, on the Amalfi Coast. She finishes her version with cream; I've left it out and added butter and wine instead. I've also added basil, which to my palate always makes oranges taste a little more orangy.

I've made this a recipe for only 2, because flounder fillets are so large and take up so much room in a skillet.

SAUTÉED FLOUNDER WITH BUTTER, ORANGE, AND BASIL

1 tablespoon extra-virgin olive oil

5 tablespoons unsalted butter

2 large flounder fillets, about 1 pound total

Salt and freshly ground black pepper to taste

3 or 4 scrapings of freshly grated nutmeg

$1/2$ cup all-purpose flour

Grated zest and juice of 2 oranges

2 tablespoons white Lillet, dry white vermouth, or fruity white wine

Small handful fresh basil leaves, cut into thin strips

In a large skillet, combine the olive oil and 2 tablespoons of the butter. Set over high heat. While this is heating, season the fillets with salt, pepper, and nutmeg, then coat them in flour, shaking off any excess. When the pan is very hot, slip in the fillets and sauté until they are well browned on one side, about 3 minutes. Give them a flip and sauté until lightly browned on the second side, a minute or two longer. (Flounder cooks very quickly and can become dry, so I always undercook it a bit, knowing it will continue to cook after I've taken it from the skillet.) Using a slotted metal spatula, transfer the fillets to paper towels to drain for a few seconds, then transfer to 2 warmed dinner plates.

Pour the excess oil from the pan, and over medium heat add 1 tablespoon of the butter. When it foams, add the orange zest and juice and the Lillet or white wine. Increase the heat to high and cook to reduce the liquid by about half. Pull the skillet from the heat and add the remaining 2 tablespoons butter, whisking it into the sauce until it is emulsified. Scatter the basil over the fillets and pour on the sauce. Serve right away.

SERVES FOUR AS A MAIN COURSE. Bluefish comes into season on the East Coast around May and is available throughout the summer. Its rich oils marry extremely well with southern Mediterranean flavors. This is an easy recipe that, for me, is what summer cooking is all about. All you do is make a little tomato salad with oregano, vinegar, olive oil, orange zest, and garlic, pour it over the fish, and then bake. *Oreganata* is an Italian American spelling that many people are more familiar with.

LONG ISLAND BLUEFISH ARRIGANATE

5 summer plum tomatoes, peeled, seeded, and finely diced (see page 26)

1 tablespoon Champagne vinegar

Leaves from 3 or 4 large marjoram sprigs, chopped

Leaves from 3 or 4 large oregano sprigs, chopped

2 garlic cloves (try to use moist, fresh summer cloves), thinly sliced

Grated zest of 1 large orange

$1/4$ cup extra-virgin olive oil

Salt and freshly ground black pepper to taste

2 pounds very fresh bluefish fillets, with skin

Preheat the oven to 450°F.

In a small bowl, combine the tomatoes, vinegar, marjoram, oregano, garlic, and orange zest. Pour in the olive oil, season with a generous amount of salt and a few grindings of pepper, and stir. (Vinegar is a good addition to dark oily fish, serving to cut the richness.) Put the fish fillets in a 9-by-13-inch baking dish in one layer, skin side down, and pour the tomato salad over them. Bake until the fish is just tender, 10 to 15 minutes, depending on the thickness of the fillets. Test by poking a thin knife into the thickest part of the fish. If it is just starting to flake but still feels firm, it is done. Serve right away.

VARIATION   Spanish mackerel fillets are also great cooked this way.

SERVES FOUR AS A MAIN COURSE. Red mullet is one of my favorite Mediterranean fish. *Triglie* is the word for it in Italian. Whenever I see it on a menu in southern Italy or here, I order it. I've been delighted to find imported red mullet in my markets lately; when I don't, I use whole porgy or sardines.

Puttanesca refers to a sauce for pasta composed of anchovies, tomatoes, olives, and capers. Canned tuna and hot chilies are also customary. My grandmother always called this type of sauce marinara—in fact, she called any tomato sauce that contained anchovies marinara. Both terms seem to be used in Naples, and marinara is an older name. Since the sauce tends to have good body, it makes a nice bed for pan-fried or grilled fish, especially fish with rich flavor.

PAN-FRIED RED MULLET WITH PUTTANESCA SAUCE

PUTTANESCA SAUCE

2 tablespoons extra-virgin olive oil

2 garlic cloves, thinly sliced

3 oil-packed anchovy fillets, chopped, or 2 salt-packed anchovies, filleted, soaked, drained, and chopped (see page 33)

1 small fresh chili, such as a jalapeño, minced, or a pinch of dried pepper flakes

2 tablespoons dry white vermouth or dry white wine

4 large, round summer tomatoes, peeled, seeded, and chopped (see page 26), or one 35-ounce can plum tomatoes, chopped, with half their juice

Handful of Gaeta olives, pitted and coarsely chopped

Generous palmful of salt-packed capers, soaked and drained (see page 29)

½ cup extra-virgin olive oil

12 to 16 whole red mullets (3 or 4 per person, depending on their size), cleaned and scaled, heads left on

1 cup flour for dredging

Salt and freshly ground black pepper to taste

Pinch of ground cloves

Pinch of cayenne pepper

Handful of fresh flat-leaf parsley leaves, lightly chopped

2 lemons, cut into wedges

TO MAKE THE SAUCE: In a large skillet, heat the olive oil over medium heat. Add the garlic, anchovies, and the chili or pepper flakes and sauté for 2 or 3 minutes just to release their flavors (the garlic should color only slightly). Add the vermouth or white wine and let it bubble a few seconds. Add the tomatoes and simmer, uncovered, at a lively bubble for about 10 minutes, or until the tomatoes have softened and given off some juice. Add the olives and capers and let the sauce sit in the skillet while you cook the fish.

In a large skillet, heat the olive oil over medium-high heat. If you want to cook all the fish at once, use 2 skillets.

Pour the flour onto a large plate and season it well with salt, pepper, ground cloves, and cayenne. Coat the mullets with the flour, shaking off the excess. Fry the fish on one side for about 4 minutes, or until the skin is nicely browned. Flip them over to brown the other side for 3 or 4 minutes, depending on their size (check for doneness by poking a little knife into the flesh along the backbone to see if it goes in easily and the fish is just starting to flake). Lift the mullets from the oil with a slotted spatula and let them drain for a moment on paper towels.

Reheat the sauce and taste for seasoning, By now the olives and capers will have had a chance to release their flavors and salt into the tomatoes, but taste to see if you need a little extra. Pour the sauce out onto a large serving platter. Place the fish on top. Garnish with the chopped parsley and the lemon wedges. Serve right away.

MEATS AND POULTRY

MEAT IN THE SOUTHERN ITALIAN HOME KITCHEN

MY FAVORITE SOUTHERN ITALIAN MEAT DISHES blend frugality with creativity. I love well-put-together meatballs and Italian-style meatloaf, which is basically a big meatball. Both of these ground-meat dishes were originally designed to make a little go a long way, and they traditionally contain quite a bit of bread and usually some cheese as filler, giving them a special flavor.

Involtini Sicilian style and *braciole* from Campania are two classic stuffed-and-rolled meat dishes that follow the same principle. Pork, beef, or on a good day, veal, can be filled and rolled with raisins, pine nuts, pecorino, basil, garlic, skinny strips of soppressata, and/or capers, then long-simmered in a wine and tomato broth until tender and fragrant. The intensely flavored cooking broth is used to sauce a pasta that is served first; then the rolls are sliced and served as a second course. I love the continuity in this approach, and anyway I find meat much more interesting when combined with other flavors so everything mingles and becomes one new flavor.

Southern-style ragù, made with large cuts, slow-simmered in wine, herbs, and tomato, is a traditional centerpiece for a Sunday dinner or a special occasion. The southern ragù, with all its variations, is the showcase dish of southern home cooking. Whenever I present it to guests, they seem thrilled and flattered that I made something so seemingly grand for them. I give recipes for ragùs in this chapter and also in the pasta chapter, depending on how meat-centered I think the recipes are, but generally speaking most ragùs and meats that are slow-simmered in plenty of aromatic liquid are paired with pasta in some way. Several—including my braised beef in Primitivo wine, and lamb shoulder with Marsala and cinnamon—I give a choice of serving with pasta or without. Sometimes, the meat and its delicious sauce are best with just good bread and a vegetable or salad.

Cured pork has a strong tradition in southern Italy, served as an antipasto or as a snack at just about any time of day. Soppressata and caciatorini are two dried sausages I've tasted around my grandmother's village of Castelfranco, in Campania; they were first rate, much more nuanced than the versions made here. Puglia is famous for its very suave capocollo. Every area has its own *salume,* or processed pork product, some flavored with fennel, garlic, hot chilies, orange zest, wine, or more delicately with nutmeg. Most restaurant chefs throughout southern Italy like to show off their local *salume* and make it part of any mixed antipasto platter. A plate of capocolla and soppressata, served along with pickled vegetables and maybe a ball of fresh mozzarella, is something my father used to put together for company. Variations on this theme are still the starting point for many of my dinner parties.

There are more chicken recipes here than you'd find in a classic southern Italian cookbook. Traditionally, chickens were saved for their eggs. I've adapted dishes more commonly made with rabbit or hare, like my chicken *agrodolce,* from Sicily. You'll also find recipes for salad greens tossed with bits of meat such as chicken or steak. This is a very American concept, and something most southern Italians would find unusual, maybe even a touch barbaric. I have to say I really enjoy eating meat this way. I feel that it fits into the southern Italian tradition of taking a small amount of meat and stretching it, not with pasta or bread, as is customary, but with raw greens and vegetables.

COOKING FOR A GROUP

WHEN I WAS A KID, festive dinner parties always centered on a huge cut of meat brought to the table with a flourish and maybe a slight sense of embarrassment from knowing it was excessive (if five were invited, my mother always made enough for twelve, a trait I inherited and have been battling to subdue all my cooking life). Long-simmered ragùs and large cuts of meat are the hallmark of special-occasion dinners throughout southern Italy. There is no getting around the fact that they require some effort on the part of the cook, not because they're complicated but because of the sheer quantity you must make to feed a group.

A few years ago on one of my trips to Sicily, I visited a man who makes one of my favorite estate olive oils. I, along with my husband and his parents, was invited to share a midday meal with the man's family. This was a very large meal, with two pastas, two braised-lamb dishes, and many side dishes. Obviously, a huge amount of work went into getting this food ready, but the women (a hip-looking young mom and her teenage daughters) were invisible during drinks and conversation and barely sat down to eat. This is exactly how I remember the atmosphere at my grandmother's house when she served food (even if it was just toast and grapefruit halves for breakfast). She and my aunt never relaxed. They were always hovering over us, looking for an expression of pleasure or disgust, waiting to whisk one dish from under someone's nose and replace it with another. This made me very nervous, and I came to think of it as connected with the southern Italian female mentality.

Things were much more democratic in my mother's kitchen. Everyone helped, and everyone sat down to eat. But when I began cooking in my own home, I felt that frantic tendency surging up in me. I would silently criticize every dish, race around the table, then disappear into the kitchen for long stretches while my guests carried on with their party, wondering, I suspect, what had become of me. When you're in charge of the food and there are people waiting, it's easy to start acting like hired help, especially if, like me, you want everything perfect. This approach to party-giving is so antisocial and exhausting that I knew early on I needed to get a grip.

The truth is that many of these special-occasion meat dishes are make-ahead, low-maintenance dishes. They're basically all stews or roasts—*braciole, polpettone*, ragùs, even festive meat lasagne—and though they may require a little initial work, once they're done, they can sit for hours without losing their charm, something that can't really be said for fish. Another great thing about slow-cooked meat is its improvisational quality. I sometimes have a hard time writing a stew recipe down, since it involves a gradual process where everything blends and morphs and becomes one big, grand flavor in the end. I almost always go for such a dish as the centerpiece for a ceremonial dinner or a party, forgoing the more correct Italian procession of courses and just bringing a lot of food out to the table at once, followed by a big salad accompanied by plenty of wine and a purchased dessert (very typical of southern Italian home entertaining). This approach frees me to act less like my grandmother and to spend more time with my guests.

SERVES SIX AS AN APPETIZER. I've been making a particular Sicilian-inspired chicken liver mousse (or *spuma*, which means "foam," in Italian) for so long, I no longer know where it came from, but when I wanted to include a version for this book I hunted around and found the original in Jo Bettoja's excellent *Southern Italian Cooking*. Her version, which she attributes to a Signor Corleone of Palermo, contains Marsala, gin, and Cognac, a mix I must have decided was too boozy. I dropped the gin and added a few personal flourishes.

CHICKEN LIVER MOUSSE WITH MARSALA AND SAGE

2 tablespoons unsalted butter

1 tablespoon extra-virgin olive oil, plus more for brushing

1 pound chicken livers, trimmed of any tough connecting tissue, cut into 1-inch chunks

1 garlic clove, thinly sliced

1 oil-packed anchovy fillet, chopped

Salt and freshly ground black pepper to taste

3 or 4 scrapings freshly grated nutmeg

1 tablespoon brandy or Cognac

2 tablespoons sweet Marsala

6 fresh sage leaves, finely chopped, plus a few more, chopped, for garnish

Small palmful of salt-packed capers, soaked and drained (see page 29)

1 baguette, cut into thin rounds

In a large skillet, melt the butter with the olive oil over medium-high heat. Pat the chicken livers dry with paper towels (they will sauté better this way). When the butter foams, add the chicken livers, garlic, and anchovy. Season with salt, pepper, and nutmeg, and sauté quickly for about 3 minutes, or until the livers are slightly pink at the center. Add the brandy or Cognac and Marsala and let everything bubble for about a minute. (Sometimes liquor can flame up over high heat. If this happens, just pull the skillet from the heat for a moment.) You should still have a little liquid left in the skillet.

Put the liver, along with any skillet juices, in a food processor. Add the sage and capers and pulse 3 or 4 times to make a coarse paste. Scrape into a small bowl and let it cool a bit. If it's not to be used right away, press a piece of plastic wrap onto the surface of the mousse (this will prevent it from darkening) and refrigerate for up to 2 days (but return it to room temperature before serving).

To serve, toast the baguette slices on both sides and brush them lightly with olive oil. Spoon a generous amount of the mousse on each one and garnish with the chopped sage.

SERVES SIX AS AN ANTIPASTO DISH, FOUR AS A LIGHT DINNER. This is based on an old-fashioned dish from Campania that my mother often made. It was very popular in Italian American households when I was growing up. I still see it on antipasto tables in southern Italy, but it's not made here much anymore, maybe because it can be a little clunky. I thought it was worth updating. I've cut down on the amount of rice used as filler and increased the sausage, making it more of a meat dish. I've always felt the filling needed some sharpness against all the starch and meat, so I've added green olives and mint.

ZUCCHINI FILLED WITH SAUSAGE, GREEN OLIVES, AND MINT

5 green or yellow zucchini (or a mix of both)

1 tablespoon extra-virgin olive oil, plus more for drizzling

4 sweet Italian sausages, removed from casings

2 shallots, minced

1 garlic clove, minced

Small handful of dried currants soaked in $1/2$ cup dry white wine, plus $1/4$ cup white wine for baking zucchini

$1/2$ cup cooked long-grain rice

Salt and freshly ground black pepper to taste

1 large egg, lightly beaten

Handful of green olives, pitted and coarsely chopped

1 tablespoon grated grana padano or Parmigiano-Reggiano cheese, plus 2 tablespoons

Leaves from 4 or 5 large mint sprigs, chopped, plus 4 to 6 whole sprigs for garnish

Cut each zucchini into 3 equal sections. Slice each section in half lengthwise. With a melon baller or a small spoon, scoop the seeds out of each section, leaving a ridge around the edge to form a little boat (this will help hold the filling). Discard the seeds.

Preheat the oven to 350°F.

In a large skillet, heat the 1 tablespoon olive oil over medium heat. Add the sausage and shallots and sauté, breaking the sausage up with your spoon, until lightly browned. Add the garlic and sauté 1 minute longer to release its fragrance. Add the currants with their white wine and let the wine bubble away. Remove from the heat and let cool for about

5 minutes. Add the cooked rice, a little salt and pepper, the egg, olives, cheese, and chopped mint. Mix together well.

Coat a 10-by-12-inch baking dish lightly with olive oil. Fill the zucchini boats with the sausage mixture and place them side by side in the dish. Pour the $^1/_4$ cup white wine over the zucchini and sprinkle it with the 2 tablespoons grated cheese. Drizzle with olive oil and bake, uncovered, until the zucchini is tender and the top is golden, about 40 minutes. Garnish with mint sprigs to serve.

SERVES FOUR AS A FIRST COURSE. Real southern Italian capocollo is not yet available in this country, unfortunately, but here's a nice way to perk up our domestic varieties, making them seem a little richer. The time-honored dish of prosciutto and fresh figs inspired me to create these braised figs, whose winey taste stands up well to the strong, rustic taste of capocollo.

CAPOCOLLO WITH RED WINE–BRAISED FIGS

12 dried Calimyrna figs, stemmed
1 tablespoon sugar
2 cups dry red wine
3 or 4 peppercorns
1 allspice berry

1 long strip lemon zest
5 or 6 thyme sprigs
1 tablespoon red wine vinegar
4 ounces thinly sliced capocollo
4 mint sprigs

In a large pot, combine all the ingredients except the capocollo and mint sprigs. Set over high heat and bring to a boil. Reduce the heat, partially cover, and simmer until the figs are tender and puffy, about 30 minutes. Using a slotted spoon, transfer the figs to a bowl. Boil the liquid down for a few minutes by about 1/4 or until you have a thin syrup. Return the figs to the pot and let them cool in the syrup.

TO SERVE, line a serving platter with the capocollo. Cut the figs in half and arrange them over the capocollo, drizzling on a little of their syrup. Garnish with the mint sprigs.

SERVES SIX AS A SIDE DISH OR PART OF AN ANTIPASTO BUFFET, OR FOUR AS A MAIN-COURSE LUNCH OR SUPPER DISH. When I notice a warm bean dish on an antipasto buffet table I immediately go for it, sometimes even making it my dinner. Since this one contains soppressata, I find it suitable for a main course, almost like a simple southern Italian version of cassoulet. The key to making this kind of dish irresistible is leaving it a little brothy, so the beans are enveloped in flavor.

CANNELLINI BEANS WITH SOPPRESSATA, TOMATOES, AND ROSEMARY

1½ cups dried cannellini beans, soaked overnight in cold water to cover by 2 inches

2 bay leaves, preferably fresh

3 garlic cloves, 1 lightly crushed, 2 thinly sliced

Salt to taste

Extra-virgin olive oil for drizzling, plus 3 tablespoons

Leaves from 3 or 4 large rosemary sprigs, finely chopped, plus a little more for finishing (optional)

2 cups cherry tomatoes, stemmed and halved

Freshly ground black pepper to taste

2 tablespoons sweet red vermouth

2-inch chunk soppressata, cut into matchsticks

Drain the beans and put them in a large pot. Add cold water to cover by about 3 inches. Add the bay leaves and crushed garlic clove. Bring the water to a boil. Reduce the heat to a simmer, partially cover, and cook slowly until tender, at least 1 hour (this depends of the dryness of the beans). When the beans are tender, turn off the heat. Add a generous amount of salt to the pot and a drizzle of olive oil. Cover the pot and let sit on the turned-off burner for about 30 minutes (this further tenderizes them and allows them to drink up some additional seasoning). Drain the beans, saving the cooking liquid.

In a large skillet, heat the 3 tablespoons olive oil over medium heat. Add the sliced garlic and rosemary and sauté to release their flavors, about 1 minute. Add the cherry tomatoes and sauté them for 2 or 3 minutes, adding a little salt and pepper. You want them to soften, but not to lose their shape. Add the sweet vermouth and let it bubble for 1 minute. Add the cannellini beans and sauté for 1 or 2 minutes longer, turning them around in the flavorings. Add enough of the reserved cooking liquid to cover the beans about halfway. Reduce the heat to medium-low and let the beans simmer, uncovered, for about 5 minutes to blend all the flavors. You should have some liquid left at this point, but you don't want the texture overly soupy. Add the soppressata (adding it at the last minute and not allowing it to cook very long will preserve its flavor and texture). Taste for seasoning, adding salt or pepper if needed. You can add a tiny amount of fresh rosemary if you like to heighten that flavor. Give the dish a drizzle of fresh olive oil and serve either hot or at room temperature.

VARIATION This makes an interesting *pasta e fagioli* tossed with al dente penne pasta.

SERVES FOUR AS AN APPETIZER. Here's a Sicilian way to prepare *babaluci*, as they call snails there (*lumache* is the proper Italian term). Tomatoes, wine, garlic, and fresh herbs make it lush and a little soupy, unlike the butter-and-garlic treatment most Americans are familiar with from French restaurants. I like serving this spooned over toasted country bread as a bruschetta, but it's also wonderful tossed with spaghetti. It's specifically a version of *babaluci del festino,* a snail dish traditionally cooked for the Feast of Santa Rosalia, the patron saint of Palermo, in mid-July.

BRAISED SNAILS WITH TOMATOES, GARLIC, AND WHITE WINE

2 tablespoons unsalted butter

1 tablespoon extra-virgin olive oil, plus more for drizzling and brushing

2 garlic cloves, thinly sliced

Two 7-ounce cans snails, drained (see note)

Leaves from 5 or 6 thyme sprigs, chopped

4 or 5 scrapings freshly grated nutmeg

Salt and freshly ground black pepper to taste

2 tablespoons dry white wine

One 35-ounce can plum tomatoes, chopped and lightly drained

Leaves from 4 or 5 marjoram sprigs, chopped, plus sprigs for garnish

Handful of fresh flat-leaf parsley leaves, chopped

Eight $1/4$-inch-thick slices crusty Italian bread

In a large skillet, melt the butter with the 1 tablespoon olive oil over medium heat. Add the garlic and sauté for about 1 minute. Add the snails, thyme, nutmeg, salt, and pepper and sauté for 3 or 4 minutes to coat the snails well with flavor. Add the white wine and let it bubble until almost dry. Add the tomatoes and simmer, uncovered, on medium-low heat for about 5 minutes (canned snails are already cooked, so you really just need to heat them through). Add the chopped marjoram, parsley, a few fresh gridings of pepper, and a generous drizzle of fresh olive oil.

Toast the bread on both sides and brush one side of each with olive oil. Place 2 pieces on each plate and pour the snails with their sauce over them. Garnish with marjoram sprigs.

SERVES TWO AS A MAIN COURSE. I'm not sure why, but I tend to make steak salads when it's snowing. I take out my grill pan and smoke up my small apartment in a very appealing way. A smoky apartment during a blizzard must just make me feel cozy (we don't have a fireplace). You can make a steak salad with leftovers, but hot, juicy, just-cooked meat tossed with cool greens really can't be beat for taste and texture. I love anchovy flavoring with steak, so I've included a few of them in the dressing. Think of this recipe as a guideline for composing your own Italian-inspired steak salad, and when choosing ingredients consider adding a few sharp notes like capers and lemon juice. I've included something crunchy (celery and fennel), and potatoes for a mellow, starchy element.

STEAK AND CELERY SALAD WITH CAPERS AND ROMAINE

1 pound skirt steak

1 garlic clove, crushed

2 bay leaves, preferably fresh

3 or 4 rosemary sprigs

Drizzle of extra-virgin olive oil

1 tablespoon dry red wine

Freshly ground black pepper to taste

DRESSING

2 oil-packed anchovy fillets

1 garlic clove, crushed

Juice of 1/2 lemon

Salt to taste

1/4 cup extra-virgin olive oil

Freshly ground black pepper to taste

Leaves from 1 small head romaine lettuce, cut into small pieces

1 small fennel bulb, trimmed, cored, and thinly sliced (small handful of fronds reserved and chopped)

2 celery stalks with leaves, stalks thinly sliced, leaves left whole

Large handful of fresh flat-leaf parsley leaves

5 red new potatoes, boiled until tender and halved

Salt to taste

Handful of salt-packed capers, soaked and drained (see page 29)

Put the skirt steak on a plate and add the garlic, bay leaves, and rosemary. Drizzle on a generous amount of olive oil and the red wine. Add a few grindings of pepper and turn until the steak is well coated with the marinade. Let stand at room temperature while you prepare the salad.

TO MAKE THE DRESSING: Using a fork, mash the anchovy fillets in a small bowl. Add the garlic, lemon juice, and salt and stir until the anchovies are pretty much dissolved. Add the olive oil and a few grindings of pepper and stir to blend.

Choose a large salad bowl (I prefer wide and shallow instead of deep for steak salads, so the ingredients don't get buried at the bottom). Put the romaine, fennel and fronds, celery and leaves, parsley, and potatoes in the bowl.

Heat a grill pan over high heat. Season the steak with salt. When the grill is hot, put on the steak and grill it until nicely charred on one side, about 4 minutes. Turn and grill the other side for 3 or 4 minutes longer for rare to medium-rare (skirt steak cooked past medium-rare is a little tough). Transfer the steak to a cutting board and let it rest a few minutes before slicing it thinly. Add the steak and capers to the salad. Pour on the dressing and toss gently. Taste for seasoning, adding more olive oil, lemon juice, salt, or pepper to taste. Serve right away.

SERVES FOUR OR FIVE AS A LUNCH OR LIGHT SUPPER. The only time I've ever been served a chicken salad in southern Italy was as part of a very extensive antipasto buffet at a seaside restaurant in Trapani, and I got the feeling the chef there periodically came up with new, nontraditional dishes just to keep things lively. His salad was garnished with chopped almonds. Here is my slightly more elaborate version.

CHICKEN SALAD WITH PINE NUTS, CURRANTS, AND BASIL

4 chicken breast halves, with bones and skin

1 cup canned low-salt chicken broth

1 bay leaf, preferably fresh

2 celery stalks with leaves, thinly sliced (leaves reserved)

1 tablespoon extra-virgin olive oil

3 thin slices pancetta, finely diced

2 tablespoons dry white wine

3 scallions, including tender green parts, cut into thin rounds

Handful of pine nuts, lightly toasted (see page 61)

Handful of dried currants soaked in 1/4 cup dry white wine

1 small head chicory or frisée lettuce, cut into bite-sized pieces

DRESSING

Grated zest and juice of 1 small lemon

Salt and freshly ground black pepper to taste

1 teaspoon Dijon mustard

1/4 cup extra-virgin olive oil

2 tablespoons reserved chicken poaching liquid

10 fresh basil leaves, cut into thin strips

Put the chicken breasts in a large Dutch oven or flameproof casserole with a lid. Pour on the chicken broth. Add enough cold water to just barely cover the chicken. Add the bay leaf and celery leaves. Bring it to a boil over medium heat. Turn the heat to low, cover, and simmer until the chicken is just tender, about 15 minutes. Using tongs, transfer the chicken to a cutting board and let cool to the touch. Remove and discard the skin and bones. Slice the breast meat into thick, neat slices and place them in a large, wide salad or serving bowl (the chicken should still be warm). Save the poaching liquid.

In a small skillet, heat the olive oil over medium heat. Add the pancetta and cook until crisp. Add the white wine and deglaze the skillet by stirring to scrape up the browned bits from the bottom of the pan. Pour the pancetta and skillet juices over the chicken slices. Add the scallions, chopped celery, pine nuts, lightly drained currants (you want a little of the raw wine taste), and chicory to the salad bowl. Season with a little salt and pepper.

To make the dressing: In a small bowl, combine the lemon zest and juice, salt, pepper, and mustard. Drizzle in the olive oil and about 2 tablespoons of the poaching liquid. Whisk well and taste for seasoning. Pour the dressing over the salad. Add the basil and toss gently. Serve right away.

NOTE   Strain and reserve the remaining chicken poaching liquid to use in soups or pasta sauces. Freeze it if you don't think you'll use it within 2 or 3 days.

SERVES FIVE. Wolfango Jezek is the creator of U Trappitu, one of my favorite Sicilian olive oils. The day I went to his farm outside Trapani to meet him, his wife, Irene, prepared an elaborate meal of Trapanese dishes. One was a braised lamb shoulder that I felt sure was flavored with a generous amount of cinnamon. When I asked her, she was perplexed. She hadn't added any cinnamon at all, just tomatoes and Marsala wine.

I never did get to the bottom of this. (I've also detected that cinnamon taste in some Sicilian bread, which also has no added cinnamon. Is it the water?) When I make my version of this dish I include a whole cinnamon stick, and it tastes exactly the way I remember it in Trapani.

Irene served this dish with *busiati,* a Sicilian pasta made by twisting semolina dough around a metal wire that looks something like a knitting needle. Originally, a thin reed was used. Making it by hand is a long, tedious process, and even in Sicily most people now buy *busiati* dried. I haven't found it in any store in America, but fusilli, fusilli lunghi, gemelli, or any other thin, twisted shape is a good substitute.

BRAISED LAMB SHOULDER WITH MARSALA AND CINNAMON

$^{1}\!/_{4}$ cup extra-virgin olive oil, plus more for drizzling

5 bone-in lamb shoulder chops (about 4 pounds total), about 1 inch thick, trimmed of excess fat

Salt and freshly ground black pepper to taste

Sprinkling of sugar

3 leeks (white part only), rinsed and chopped

1 carrot, peeled and finely diced

3 garlic cloves, lightly crushed

1 cup dry Marsala

1 bay leaf, preferably fresh

1 cinnamon stick

One 35-ounce can plus one 15-ounce can plum tomatoes, chopped, with juice

Generous handful of fresh basil leaves, chopped, plus a few sprigs for garnish

1 pound fusilli, fusilli lunghi, or gemelli pasta

1 cup grated pecorino cheese

In a large Dutch oven or flameproof casserole with a lid, heat the ¼ cup olive oil over medium heat. Pat the lamb chops dry and add them to the pan in batches, if necessary. Season with salt, pepper, and a little sugar (this will help them brown). Brown well on both sides, about 4 minutes on each side. Transfer the meat to a plate. Pour off all but about 2 tablespoons of fat from the pan. Add the leeks and carrot. Sauté over medium heat until softened, about 4 minutes. Add the garlic and sauté until fragrant, about 1 minute. Return all the lamb to the casserole and pour on the Marsala, letting it bubble for a few minutes. Add the bay leaf, cinnamon stick, and tomatoes. Bring to a boil. Reduce the heat, cover, and simmer until tender, 1½ to 2 hours. Skim the surface of fat once or twice while cooking. Taste for seasoning and add the chopped basil.

In a large pot of salted boiling water, cook the pasta until al dente. Drain and transfer to a large serving bowl. Add a drizzle of fresh olive oil and about 2 tablespoons of the grated pecorino. Toss.

Using a slotted spoon, transfer the meat to a serving platter. Spoon on some of the sauce. Pour the remaining sauce over the pasta and toss.

Serve the pasta first, with the remaining pecorino in a small bowl alongside. Serve the meat, garnished with basil sprigs, as a second course.

SERVING SUGGESTION   Serve the meat with a green salad dressed with extra-virgin olive oil, lemon juice, and a pinch of salt.

SERVES SIX AS A MAIN COURSE. Lamb is often flavored with fennel seeds or rosemary in Sicily and other parts of southern Italy. For this quick grill, however, for the main flavoring I've chosen mint, an herb used frequently in Sicilian cooking. The touch of honey not only adds sweetness but gives the meat a crisp crust. Black pepper is an important ingredient, because it balances the acidity of the tomatoes and the sweetness of the other ingredients.

GRILLED LEG OF LAMB WITH TOMATOES, MINT, AND HONEY

One 4-pound piece butterflied leg of lamb (see note)

4 garlic cloves, cut into thin slivers

$^1/_4$ teaspoon ground cinnamon

2 bay leaves, preferably fresh

Leaves from 5 or 6 large marjoram or oregano sprigs, chopped

Leaves from 5 or 6 large mint sprigs, chopped

2 tablespoons honey, preferably wildflower honey

$^1/_2$ cup dry Marsala

Extra-virgin olive oil for drizzling

Freshly ground black pepper to taste

Salt to taste

TOMATOES

4 cups cherry tomatoes, stemmed

3 scallions, including tender green parts, cut into thin rounds

Drizzle of honey

Leaves from 3 or 4 large mint sprigs, chopped

Leaves from 3 or 4 large marjoram or oregano sprigs, chopped

Salt and freshly ground black pepper to taste

Extra-virgin olive oil for drizzling

Put the lamb in a shallow dish. Make a few little cuts into the lamb in various places and insert the garlic slivers. Sprinkle the cinnamon over the lamb. Add the bay leaves, marjoram or oregano, and mint. Drizzle on the honey and pour Marsala over the meat. Drizzle on a little olive oil, grind on a generous amount of pepper, and turn the lamb over a few times in the marinade so all the flavors are well distributed. Let stand at room temperature for up to 2 hours, or cover and refrigerate overnight.

Light a fire in a charcoal grill or preheat a gas grill to a steady medium-high heat. Let the charcoal burn down to white coals (if the fire is too hot, you'll wind up burning the outside of the lamb while the inside remains raw). If the lamb has been refrigerated, remove it from the refrigerator 30 minutes before cooking. Remove the lamb from the marinade and season it well on both sides with salt. Grill the lamb, fat side down, about 5 inches from the heat, until well crusted, about 10 minutes. Turn and grill the other side, 8 to 10 minutes longer. If it begins to get too black, move it over to the side of the grill, where the heat is milder. Since boned leg of lamb is uneven in thickness, you will always wind up with some medium-rare and some medium meat (something for everyone), so aim for the thickest parts to be 130°F on a meat thermometer. Transfer the lamb to a carving board. Let it rest for about 10 minutes before carving.

While the lamb is resting, grill the tomatoes. Use a wire grill basket or poke a few holes in a piece of aluminum foil and pile them onto that. Put the tomatoes on the grill and cook, shaking them a bit, until they start to burst, 3 or 4 minutes. Transfer to a small bowl and add the scallions, honey, and half the mint and marjoram or oregano. Season with salt and pepper and drizzle with olive oil. Toss gently.

Carve the lamb into thin slices and arrange them on a serving platter in a circular pattern, leaving a space in the center. Pour the tomatoes into the center. Pour any lamb juices that have collected over the lamb. Give everything a fresh grinding of pepper, maybe a little salt, and a drizzle of fresh olive oil. Scatter on the remaining herbs and serve right away (this also tastes really good at room temperature).

SERVING SUGGESTIONS Leftover grilled lamb makes excellent sandwiches. Toast Italian bread, brush it with olive oil, and layer on the lamb and any remaining tomatoes. You could add crumbled ricotta salata or feta cheese as well.

NOTE My butcher almost always has boned leg of lamb ready to buy in large or smaller pieces. If yours doesn't, ask him to bone and butterfly one (butterflying flattens the meat out to a more or less even thickness, usually about 2 inches at its thickest, but it will always be a little uneven because that's the nature of the cut).

SERVES TWO AS A MAIN COURSE. The trick here is to sear the lamb chops quickly on high heat, leaving them very pink inside. Add the olives and let them warm, mellowing their flavor. The salad isn't absolutely necessary, but it's a nice way to extend the summer-herb theme.

LAMB CHOPS WITH THYME BLOSSOMS AND SAUTÉED OLIVES, WITH PARSLEY SALAD

4 loin lamb chops, about 2 inches thick

2 tablespoons extra-virgin olive oil

4 garlic cloves

Salt and freshly ground black pepper to taste

Large handful of Gaeta or niçoise olives

1 tablespoon brandy or Cognac

2 tablespoons dry red wine

1 tablespoon unsalted butter

Leaves from 4 or 5 large thyme sprigs with blossoms (if possible), chopped, plus a few sprigs for garnish

PARSLEY SALAD

1 large bunch flat-leaf parsley, stemmed (about 2 cups loosely packed leaves)

1 shallot, very thinly sliced

Extra-virgin olive oil for drizzling

Salt to taste

$^{1}/_{4}$ teaspoon red wine vinegar

Trim the chops of most excess fat, but don't remove all of it—it adds a lot of flavor to the meat and skillet sauce.

In a large skillet, heat the olive oil over medium-high heat. Add the garlic cloves and lamb chops at the same time, season with salt and pepper, and cook the chops, without moving them, until they are well browned on the bottom, about 5 minutes. Turn them over, season the other side with salt and pepper, and cook to medium-rare, about another 4 minutes. Put the garlic cloves on top of the chops while they finish cooking, so they don't get too dark. (If your chops are thinner than 2 inches, make sure to cut down the cooking time.) When you think they're almost done, test for doneness by inserting a thin, sharp knife into one of them along the bone; the meat should be pink.

Using tongs, transfer the chops to a serving platter. Pour off all but 1 tablespoon of the fat from the pan, but leave the garlic cloves. Add the olives and sauté for 2 minutes, shaking them around in the skillet (they will start to swell a bit). Add the brandy or Cognac and let it bubble for a few seconds. Add the red wine and let it bubble a few seconds longer. (It may seem fussy bothering with two types of alcohol for such a quick sauce, but the brandy adds depth and the red wine adds acidity, so it turns out to be a nice mix.) Turn off the heat and add the butter and chopped thyme. Stir until the butter is melted. Pour the sauce over the chops and garnish with the thyme sprigs.

TO MAKE THE SALAD: In a small salad bowl, combine the parsley leaves and shallot. Drizzle with olive oil, sprinkle with salt, and toss until the leaves are well coated. Add the vinegar and toss again. Serve alongside the chops on the plates.

TWO ITALIAN AMERICAN CLASSICS, REWORKED

Veal with peppers and pork chops with vinegar peppers were both extremely popular among Italian Americans in the sixties and seventies. They have their origins in the cooking of Campania and Calabria, but variations on them turn up in the mountainous Abruzzi as well. I like both dishes well enough, but I've never loved them as made by most Italian Americans. The problem is the peppers. People almost always make the pork chops with jarred pickled peppers, which are so acidic they make my eyes water. They overpower the pork, wine, and garlic, and absolutely smother any delicate fresh herbs like basil or parsley. And to make the dish even sharper, most cooks pour a healthy amount of the pickling liquid into the pan at the last minute. Those jarred peppers are properly served with rich, oily cured sausages like soppressata, where they taste delicious. Many traditional recipes call for gently pickling your own peppers, but even in Italy they use jarred peppers more often than not. I make a sautéed and gently vinegared pepper for my version of this classic.

Your choice of vinegar is very important for any dish that relies so heavily on vinegar for its flavoring. In the following recipe, I use Spanish sherry vinegar for its earthy, musty tone (most Italian Americans use white wine vinegar, which can be good if you choose a high-quality one). Also, I roast the peppers, which leaves them soft, sweet, and porous (better able to soak up seasonings).

Veal and peppers is traditionally made with green peppers with their skins left on. I've chosen sweeter roasted yellow peppers as a nice change for my recipe on page 240. They don't radically alter the character of the dish, but they do soften it.

SERVES TWO AS A MAIN COURSE. Manducatis is an old-fashioned southern Italian trattoria in Long Island City, New York, where they turn out refined versions of standbys such as *pasta e fagioli* and eggplant parmigiano, as well as cannelloni. They make a light and lively version of pork chops and peppers using red and green Italian frying peppers, the long skinny ones. I prefer the sweetness of red bell peppers, so they're what I've used here. Otherwise, the dish is similar in its subtle flavor.

Thick, pink pork chops look so beautiful raw that you just assume they will be juicy and wonderful when cooked, but I can't tell you how many times I've been disappointed by dry, tough ones, either when eating out or preparing them myself. Now, I've learned. Pork chops need to be cooked quickly, leaving them slightly pink, or else they will get tough. The best way I've found is to brown them on one side over high heat, turn them over, reduce the heat to medium-low, and finish cooking them gently and quickly until they are just tender and still fairly pink. The other method is long, slow braising. Anything in between will make them tough.

PORK CHOPS WITH GENTLE VINEGAR PEPPERS

3 tablespoons extra-virgin olive oil

2 fresh cherry peppers, halved and seeded

2 garlic cloves, very thinly sliced

1 small red onion, thinly sliced

2 red bell peppers, roasted, peeled, and cut into $1/2$-inch dice (see page 38)

2 oil packed anchovy fillets, chopped, or 1 salt-packed anchovy, filleted, soaked, drained, and chopped (see page 33)

Salt to taste

3 tablespoons Spanish sherry vinegar

2 large bone-in center-cut loin pork chops, about $1^{1}/_{2}$ inches thick

$1/4$ cup all-purpose flour

2 tablespoons dry white wine

Leaves from 2 large marjoram sprigs, chopped

5 or 6 fresh basil leaves, chopped

In a small skillet, heat 2 tablespoons of the olive oil over medium heat. Add the cherry peppers, garlic, and onion and sauté for 2 to 3 minutes to soften. Add the roasted peppers, anchovy, and salt and sauté for about 3 minutes, or until tender and fragrant. Pour on the vinegar and let it bubble until almost evaporated. Set aside.

In a heavy, medium skillet, heat the remaining 1 tablespoon olive oil over medium-high heat. Pat the pork chops dry, season them on both sides with salt, and coat them lightly with flour. When the pan is hot, add the chops and brown on one side, about 4 minutes. Turn the chops over, reduce the heat to medium-low, and cook until tender with a fair amount of pink at the bone, another 4 or 5 minutes, depending on the thickness. Add the white wine and let it bubble for a few seconds. Turn the heat to very low, cover the pan, and cook gently for about 1 minute, or until the chops have only a touch of pink to them.

If the peppers have cooled, reheat them gently. Add the marjoram and basil to the vine-gared peppers and stir.

Transfer the chops to a serving plate. If more than about 3 tablespoons of liquid is left in the pan, cook over high heat to reduce it and pour it over the chops; if it is already reduced to less, just go ahead and pour it over as is. Pour the peppers on top of the chops. Serve right away.

SERVING SUGGESTIONS   My mother always served this dish with chunks of oven-roasted potatoes seasoned with olive oil and pepper, and I still think they are the best accompaniment.

VARIATION   Another easy pork chop recipe I often make is seasoned with the typically Calabrian combination of hot chilies and fennel seeds: mince a fresh hot chili such as a long, skinny peperoncini (or use dried red pepper flakes) and mix with a palmful of fennel seeds and some coarse sea salt. Press this into the pork chops and sauté them in olive oil over medium heat until just tender (still a bit pink at the bone). Add a sliced garlic clove to the skillet in the last few moments of cooking (so it doesn't burn), then add a splash of white wine to deglaze the skillet and finish with a little chopped fresh flat-leaf parsley.

SERVES FOUR OR FIVE AS A MAIN COURSE. When I was a child, veal and peppers was a fast food available at virtually every pizza place in New York, usually spooned into a big hero sandwich. My father loved it, but he said it gave him *agita*, or indigestion (it was those pepper skins). My version is more of a brothy stew, with roasted and peeled yellow bell peppers. I like serving it with crunchy fried capers.

VEAL AND YELLOW PEPPERS WITH FRIED CAPERS

3 tablespoons extra-virgin olive oil

3 pounds veal shoulder, cut into 2-inch chunks

1/2 cup flour for dredging

Salt to taste

3 or 4 thin slices fatty prosciutto end, finely chopped

1 small onion, finely diced

2 garlic cloves, lightly crushed

1 whole allspice berry, ground

1/2 cup dry Marsala

1 1/2 cups homemade chicken broth (see page 315) or canned low-salt chicken broth

One 15-ounce can plum tomatoes, drained and well chopped

1 bay leaf, preferably fresh

3 yellow bell peppers, roasted, peeled, and cut into 1/2-inch dice (see page 38)

Palmful of salt-packed capers, soaked and drained (see page 29)

Grated zest and juice of 1/2 lemon

Large handful of fresh flat-leaf parsley leaves, chopped

In a large Dutch oven or flameproof casserole with a lid, heat 2 tablespoons of the olive oil over medium-high heat. Pat the veal chunks dry and toss them with the flour to coat. Add the veal to the pan and brown well all over (you may need to do this in batches). Veal can sometimes give off a foam as it begins to cook, and this can impede browning. Let the veal cook without moving it (which can cause it to give off more foam) until the foam evaporates and the meat starts to brown. Season the meat with a bit of salt. Add the chopped prosciutto and the onion and sauté until the onion softens, about 3 minutes. Add the garlic and allspice (I love this sweet spice with peppers). Sauté 1 minute just to release the flavors. Add the Marsala and let it bubble for about 2 minutes. Add the chicken broth, tomatoes, and bay leaf. Bring to a boil. Reduce the heat to low, cover, and simmer for about 1 hour.

Add the roasted peppers and simmer, uncovered, for about 30 minutes, or until the meat is very tender (uncovering the pot in the final stages of cooking will evaporate some liquid and help thicken the sauce). Skim the surface of excess fat and foam.

Pat the capers dry with paper towels. In a small sauté pan, heat the remaining 1 tablespoon olive oil over medium heat. Add the capers and sauté until they start to open up (looking like the little flowers that they in fact are) and become crisp, 2 to 3 minutes.

Add the lemon zest and juice and the parsley to the stew. Stir and taste for seasoning. Sprinkle with the capers.

SERVING SUGGESTIONS   Serve with polenta or rice, or just with good Italian bread.

SERVES FOUR OR FIVE AS A MAIN COURSE. Pork flavored with bay leaves is something I've been served in Basilicata, and it typifies the bold results that that region's cooks can attain using only a few ingredients. When I first thought to include fennel in this dish, I wondered if the intense flavor of the bay leaves would overpower it, but I was happy to find that the bay just adds depth and a sophisticated sweetness, and the flavor of the fennel shines through. To keep the boneless pork tender here, I brown the meat first on top of the stove, then roast it at a low temperature just long enough to cook it through.

PORK LOIN WITH BAY LEAVES AND CARAMELIZED FENNEL

3 tablespoons extra-virgin olive oil

6 or 7 fennel bulbs, trimmed, cored, and quartered (handful of feathery fronds reserved for garnish)

Generous pinch of sugar

Salt and freshly ground black pepper to taste

1 cup dry white wine

One 3-pound boneless center-cut pork loin, tied in 3 or 4 places

Palmful of fennel seeds, coarsely ground in a mortar

4 fresh bay leaves

5 garlic cloves

1 tablespoon Champagne vinegar

Preheat the oven to 350°F.

In a large skillet, heat 2 tablespoons of the olive oil over medium heat. Add the quartered fennel. Season with a pinch of sugar (to help it brown), salt, and pepper. Sauté the fennel until golden all over, about 10 minutes. Add one-fourth of the white wine and deglaze the skillet by stirring to scrape up any browned bits from the bottom of the pan.

Choose a large roasting pan that will hold the pork and fennel fairly snugly. Add the fennel to the pan, arranging it around the edges.

In the same skillet used to sauté the fennel, add the remaining 1 tablespoon olive oil over medium heat. When the skillet is hot, add the pork loin. Sprinkle on the ground fennel seeds and season it well with salt and pepper. Brown the pork well all over. Add the bay leaves and garlic cloves and sauté 2 or 3 minutes longer, just so they can release their flavors. Transfer the pork loin to the roasting pan, placing it in the middle of the fennel. Place the garlic cloves and bay leaves on the fennel. Add the remaining white wine to the skillet and deglaze the pan over high heat, stirring to scrape up any cooked-on pork juices. Pour this over the pork loin.

Roast the pork, uncovered, for about 30 minutes, or until faintly pink at the center. A meat thermometer inserted in the center should register about 145°F.

Transfer the pork to a carving board and let it rest for about 5 minutes. Carve the pork into thin slices and lay them out on a warmed serving platter. Using a slotted spoon, transfer the fennel to the platter and arrange around the pork (the fennel should be very tender and golden). Spoon off most of the fat from the pork cooking juices left in the roasting pan and add the vinegar to it (this will bring up all the flavors). Pour this thin sauce over the pork slices. Chop some of the fennel fronds and scatter them on top. Serve either hot or at room temperature.

VARIATION   When fresh figs are in season, add 3 or 4 halved green or purple ones to the roasting pan in the last few minutes of cooking the pork. This gives them time to heat through, but they'll keep their shape and stay juicy.

SERVES FOUR AS A MAIN COURSE. The aromas of parsley and an assertive grating cheese like provolone mingling together is a kitchen smell from my childhood that still plays an important role in some of my recipes. My mother always made *braciole* (stuffed meat rolls) with beef, but I prefer pork, because it seems to cook up juicier and retain more taste after long simmering (beef gives up a lot of its flavor to the sauce).

At Faicco's butcher shop on New York's Bleecker Street, where I buy all my pork products, they slice *braciole* from the shoulder cut. Usually the slices are about 5 by 6 inches and weigh about 8 ounces apiece, so I get four good-sized rolls. However, smaller slices work just as well for this recipe. If the slices are a little thick, thin them with a meat pounder. For easy rolling, you want them no thicker than about $1/8$ inch.

PORK BRACIOLE WITH PROVOLONE, PARSLEY, AND CAPERS

1 garlic clove

Large bunch of flat-leaf parsley, stemmed (about 1 cup packed leaves), plus a small handful of leaves for garnish

Large handful of salt-packed capers, soaked and drained (see page 29)

$3/4$ cup grated provolone cheese, preferably a southern Italian cheese, not a domestic brand, which can be salty and lacking in finesse

Salt to taste

3 pinches ground cayenne pepper

3 tablespoons extra-virgin olive oil

3 pounds pork shoulder, cut into $1/8$-inch-thick slices

3 medium shallots, finely diced

$1/8$ teaspoon ground cloves

1 bay leaf, preferably fresh

$1/2$ cup dry white wine

One 35-ounce can plum tomatoes, well chopped, with juice

In a food processor, combine the garlic, parsley, and capers, Pulse briefly to chop coarsely (you don't want a paste). Transfer to a small bowl and add the grated provolone, a pinch of salt (not much, because the cheese and capers will be slightly salty), and 2 pinches cayenne, and drizzle with 1 tablespoon olive oil. Mix everything together.

Lay the pork slices out on a work surface. Spoon 1 heaping tablespoon of filling onto each slice and spread it out, leaving a ¼-inch margin all around. Roll up lengthwise and tie in 3 or 4 places with kitchen twine. (It will look like a lot of meat, but it shrinks down considerably during cooking.)

Choose a large Dutch oven or a flameproof casserole with a lid. Heat 2 tablespoons of the olive oil over medium heat. Season the rolls with salt and the remaining cayenne and place them in the casserole. Brown them well all over (the browning will add great flavor to the sauce). Scatter on the shallots and season the meat with the ground cloves and bay leaf. Sauté 2 or 3 minutes longer, until the shallots have softened and given off flavor.

Add the white wine and let it boil for a couple of minutes, stirring to scrape up any cooked-on juices from the bottom of the pot. Add the tomatoes and a pinch of salt. The *braciole* should be almost completely covered by the liquid; if not, add a bit of warm water. Cover the casserole, lower the heat, and simmer, turning the *braciole* occasionally, until very tender, about 2 hours. Skim the surface of fat once or twice during cooking. Uncover the pot for the last 30 minutes of cooking so the sauce can reduce.

To serve the *braciole*, use a slotted spoon to transfer them to a cutting board. The sauce should be reduced to a medium thickness (it is not meant to be a dense tomato sauce). If it seems too thin, boil it over high heat for a few minutes. Skim the surface of fat. Taste and adjust the seasoning. Remove the strings from the *braciole* and cut the rolls into ¼-inch-thick slices on the diagonal. Place them on a warmed serving plate and spoon a little of the sauce over the top. Pour the remaining sauce into a small serving bowl and bring it to the table. Garnish the plate with the parsley leaves.

SERVING SUGGESTION It's customary to serve pasta dressed with the *braciole* sauce as a first course, then serve the meat separately. You can certainly do this if you like, but I prefer to forgo the pasta and instead offer a dish of roasted potatoes or rice, bringing the extra sauce to the table so guests can use it to pour on the rice or mop it up with bread.

SERVES FOUR OR FIVE AS A MAIN COURSE. Long, light green, slightly acidy peppers, known as Italian frying peppers, are what my mother always used to make this dish. My father grew them in his little garden and picked them when they were just starting to show specks of red. I don't see them around much anymore unless I go to Arthur Avenue in the Bronx, or another Italian neighborhood. The Spanish cubanelles that I often see here are slightly stubbier in shape but similar in flavor (see page 36 for more about sweet peppers). A farmer at my local greenmarket grows a pepper variety called corno di toro (horn of the bull). These look and taste similar to the ones my father grew, and I use these when I can get them during the summer months.

SAUSAGES AND ITALIAN FRYING PEPPERS WITH SAGE AND FENNEL SEED

3 tablespoons extra-virgin olive oil

1 large, sweet onion, such as a Vidalia, thinly sliced

1 large fennel bulb, trimmed, cored, and sliced

5 Italian frying peppers or cubanelle peppers, seeded and thinly sliced lengthwise (they're best when mostly green and just tinged with red)

3 garlic cloves, crushed

Small palmful of fennel seeds

Salt and freshly ground black pepper to taste

2 pounds sweet Italian pork sausages

¾ cup dry white wine

12 fresh sage leaves, lightly chopped

1 loaf crusty Italian bread for serving (optional)

In a large Dutch oven or flameproof casserole, heat 2 tablespoons of the olive oil over medium heat. Add the onion, fennel, and peppers and sauté for 2 or 3 minutes to start them softening. Add the garlic and fennel seeds and season lightly with salt (some sausages are very salty, so you don't want to add too much salt at the beginning). Add a little pepper and sauté until the vegetables are soft and have not taken on much color, about 10 minutes (if the peppers start to brown, turn down the heat).

While the peppers are cooking, place a large skillet over high heat and add the remaining 1 tablespoon olive oil. Prick the sausages in a few places (to prevent the skins from bursting) and sauté them on all sides until nice and brown on the outside but still slightly pink on the inside, about 8 minutes or so. If your sausages have given off a lot of fat, drain all but about 1 tablespoon off. Add the white wine and let it bubble for a few seconds, stirring to scrape up the cooked-on skillet juices (this adds a lot of flavor). Transfer the sausages and skillet juices to the peppers. Add the sage, cover the pot and cook just until the sausages are tender and all the flavors are nicely blended, about 5 minutes.

Serve in shallow bowls with the bread on the side to soak up all the juices, or split the bread and fill big hero sandwiches.

VARIATION   Sage and fennel is a wonderful flavor combination for pork dishes, and it's easy to prepare pork chops this way. To make them for 2, grind a palmful of fennel seeds to a powder and press the powder into 2 thick bone-in chops. Season with salt and pepper. Sauté in hot olive oil until browned on both sides. Add a splash of white wine, cover the skillet, turn the heat to low, and cook just until tender, about 5 minutes. Add about 6 chopped fresh sage leaves to the skillet and cook a few seconds longer. Serve with the skillet juices spooned over the top of the chops.

SERVES FOUR AS A MAIN COURSE. Living in Manhattan, I can't say I have an intimate involvement with any wine grape harvest, but when my travels have taken me to southern Italy during the *vendemmia* (the harvest, which usually occurs in October but can be earlier in Sicily), everyone seems so hopeful and full of great expectations, I naively feel I'm contributing to the good vibes just by standing there (of course, I'm merely gaping). Despite my lack of involvement in wine making, I feel compelled to celebrate the harvest with special dishes. Here's one I love.

BRAISED SAUSAGES WITH GREEN GRAPES, WINE, AND BAY LEAVES

1 tablespoon extra-virgin olive oil

2 pounds sweet Italian sausage, with fennel seeds, if possible

4 garlic cloves

2 bay leaves, preferably fresh

2 small rosemary sprigs

Small palmful of fennel seeds

Salt and freshly ground black pepper to taste

1/2 cup dry white wine

Large bunch of seedless green grapes, stemmed (about 1 1/2 cups grapes)

Handful of fresh flat-leaf parsley leaves, chopped

In a large skillet, heat the olive oil over medium heat. Pierce the sausages in a few places with a thin knife to make sure they don't burst. Add the sausages and the garlic to the skillet and brown the sausages on all sides. Pour off all but about 1 tablespoon of fat. Add the bay leaves, rosemary, fennel seeds, salt, and pepper and sauté for 1 or 2 minutes longer so all the flavors can be released. Add the wine, reduce the heat to low, and simmer until the sausages are tender, 4 or 5 minutes. Uncover the skillet and add the grapes. Cook for about 2 or 3 minutes until the grapes are soft and warm but not bursting. There should be some liquid in the skillet.

Put the sausages on a warmed large serving platter. Pour the grapes and all the skillet juices over the top and garnish with the parsley. Serve hot.

SERVING SUGGESTIONS   Accompany with hunks of Italian bread and a slightly bitter green salad (arugula is nice with sausages). Although it's not very Italian in spirit, I like this dish served with wild rice.

VARIATION   Pork sausages, with or without fennel seeds, sweet or spicy, play a big part in many recipes in southern Italy, and I can barely imagine making a dish like this with anything else. However, I recently made it with the excellent turkey sausages produced by Di Paola Turkey Farms, in Trenton, New Jersey, and it was delicious—different, but delicious. The common problem with many new-style sausages made with veal, chicken, or turkey is that they don't contain enough fat to add flavor, and their manufacturers try to make up for the lack of fat by adding weird seasonings. I recently had a chicken sausage from my supermarket that tasted like a pumpkin pie, and it was as dry as a bone. This is happily not the case with Di Paola, where they make the sausages in a more traditional southern Italian manner (see page 436 for their address and places that carry their products).

SERVES FOUR OR FIVE AS A MAIN COURSE. Sweet-and-sour flavoring, with its Arab and Spanish origins, is a strong theme in Sicilian cooking. This dish would more likely be made there with hare or rabbit than with chicken. The constant in *agrodolce* preparation is the cooking down of vinegar with sugar or honey until you have a pungent base in which to bathe meat, fish, or vegetables. To this, the cook may add almonds, pine nuts, raisins, capers, mint or basil, anchovies, or green olives—all signature flavors of Sicilian cooking.

CHICKEN AGRODOLCE

2 tablespoons extra-virgin olive oil

5 whole chicken legs, cut into thighs and drumsticks

Salt and freshly ground black pepper to taste

Flour for dredging

1 small onion, finely diced

1 celery stalk, finely diced, plus a handful of celery leaves, chopped

1 tablespoon sugar

2 tablespoons white wine vinegar

½ cup dry white wine

1 cup homemade chicken broth (see page 315) or canned low-salt chicken broth

1 bay leaf, preferably fresh

Pinch of ground cinnamon

Small handful of salt-packed Sicilian capers, soaked and drained (see page 29)

Handful of pine nuts, lightly toasted (see page 61)

Leaves from 3 or 4 large mint sprigs, chopped, plus a few sprigs for garnish

In a large skillet, heat the olive oil over medium-high heat. Season the chicken pieces with salt and pepper, then dredge them in flour, tapping off the excess. Sauté on one side until nicely browned, 4 or 5 minutes, then turn them and brown the other side, about 4 minutes. Pour off all but about 2 tablespoons of fat. Reduce the heat to medium, add the onion and diced celery stalks to the skillet, and sauté until soft, about 2 minutes. Add the sugar and the vinegar and simmer for about 1 minute. Add the white wine and let it bubble for 1 minute or two. Add the chicken broth, bay leaf, cinnamon, and a little more salt and pepper. Cover, reduce heat to low, and simmer until tender, about 35 minutes.

Add the capers and pine nuts. Simmer, uncovered, for a few minutes to blend all the flavors. You should have a nice moist glaze all over the chicken and a bit of liquid on the bottom of the skillet (if it seems too thin, just boil it down for a few minutes). Taste the sauce for a good balance of sweet to sour. You might want a tiny splash of extra vinegar.

Place the chicken pieces on a large serving dish. Scatter on the chopped mint and celery leaves and pour all the skillet juices over the top. Garnish with mint sprigs and serve hot.

SERVES FOUR AS A MAIN COURSE. Here's my take on a Neapolitan dish that became a staple of Italian American restaurants in the 1950s and '60s. When well prepared, it is light and sunny and shows off what southern Italian cooks do best: combining a few local flavors, in this case lemon and garlic, to produce a bold, enticing taste. As simple as this dish is, restaurants often spoil it with bitter, overcooked garlic— a good example of how brilliant southern Italian cooking can lose its finesse when transported.

I've refined the dish slightly, adding roasted lemon slices, with their skin's appealing bitterness, and a shot of Amalfi's limoncello liqueur, with its sweet, boozy edge.

CHICKEN WITH ROASTED LEMON AND GARLIC

2 small lemons, sliced into thin rounds

3 tablespoons extra-virgin olive oil

Sprinkling of sugar

Salt to taste

One 3^1/$_2$-pound free-range chicken, cut into 8 pieces, plus an extra drumstick and thigh (1 chicken doesn't quite serve 4)

1 slice fatty prosciutto end, chopped

5 garlic cloves, crushed

3 or 4 small rosemary sprigs

1 bay leaf, preferably fresh

Freshly ground black pepper to taste

^{1}/$_4$ cup limoncello liqueur

Juice of 2 lemons

Warm water, as needed

Leaves from 5 or 6 large flat-leaf parsley sprigs, chopped

Preheat the oven to 450°F.

Put the lemon slices on a baking sheet and toss them with 1 tablespoon of the olive oil. Lay the slices in one layer, sprinkle them very lightly with sugar, and roast until they start to brown at the edges, about 10 minutes. Take the pan from the oven, season the slices with a little salt, then set aside while you cook the chicken.

In a large skillet, heat the remaining 2 tablespoons olive oil over medium heat. Pat the chicken pieces dry and add them to the skillet. Sauté until well browned about 5 minutes. Add the prosciutto, garlic cloves, rosemary, and bay leaf and turn the chicken pieces over. Season with salt and pepper and brown the other side, about another 5 minutes. The garlic should turn lightly golden (if it starts to darken too much, place the cloves on top of the chicken pieces). Pour off all but about 2 tablespoons of fat from the skillet. Add the limoncello to the skillet and cook to reduce to about 1 tablespoon of liquid. Add the lemon juice and continue cooking the chicken, turning the pieces occasionally, until they are tender and opaque throughout, about 20 minutes. (You should ideally be able to do this without covering the skillet. A very thin coating of liquid should be on the chicken and in the skillet during cooking, but if it dries up too much, just add a splash of warm water from time to time.) When done, the chicken should have a nice, moist glaze, but with only a small amount of liquid left in the skillet. Remove the white meat from the skillet when it is just tender, and let the dark meat cook for about another 5 minutes.

Add the roasted lemon slices and the parsley to the skillet and give everything a gentle toss. Taste for seasoning. A little pinch of salt and a few fresh grindings of pepper will help pull the flavors together. Place the chicken and lemon slices on a large serving platter and pour all the skillet juices over the top. Serve hot.

SERVES FOUR OR FIVE AS A MAIN COURSE. *Alla cacciatora* means "in the style of the hunter's wife," and just about any Italian American can tell you that it also means with tomatoes, garlic, oregano, and red or green bell peppers. That is how my mother flavored chicken cacciatore, and it's how I was usually served it when as a kid I ordered it at New York Neapolitan restaurants or ate it at a friend's house. But the several times I've ordered something *alla cacciatora* in Naples or elsewhere in Campania, it has been flavored with tomatoes and rosemary, with no detectable bell pepper flavor. That version of the dish seems not to have survived the journey to America.

As much as I loved my mother's chicken cacciatore, here I've chosen to explore the rosemary-and-tomato angle, producing something simpler, with no peppers and no mushrooms or olives, just wine, herbs, and a light tomato base (I do add a hint of hot chili, which mingles with the rosemary in an unexpected but delicious way).

CHICKEN ALLA CACCIATORA WITH TOMATOES, WHITE WINE, AND ROSEMARY

12 free-range chicken thighs (thighs are juicy and hard to overcook)

Salt to taste

Flour for dredging

2 tablespoons extra-virgin olive oil

1 small chunk fatty prosciutto end, finely diced

2 shallots, finely diced

2 bay leaves, preferably fresh

Leaves from 3 or 4 large rosemary sprigs, finely chopped

Generous pinch of red pepper flakes

1/2 cup dry white wine

One 35-ounce can diced tomatoes, well drained, or canned whole tomatoes, chopped and drained

1/2 cup homemade chicken broth (see page 315) or canned low-salt chicken broth

1 tablespoon red wine vinegar

Pat the chicken thighs dry, season them with a little salt, and flour them lightly.

In a large skillet, heat the olive oil over medium heat. Add the chicken thighs, skin side down, and sauté until crisp and golden, 4 or 5 minutes. Turn them over and crisp the other side, about 4 minutes longer. Transfer the chicken to a plate. Pour off all but about 2 tablespoons of the fat in the pan. Over medium heat, add the prosciutto to the skillet and cook until crisp. Add the shallots and sauté until soft, about 1 minute. Return the chicken to the skillet, along with any juices it has given off, and stir the pieces to distribute the flavors. Add the bay leaves, rosemary, red pepper flakes, and a pinch of salt and sauté for 1 or 2 minutes to release their flavors. Add the white wine and let it bubble for about 1 minute. Add the tomatoes and the broth. (Draining the tomatoes and replacing their juice with chicken broth produces a lighter tomato presence. I like the sauce to be slightly brothy but studded with chunks of tomato, as opposed to a thick tomato sauce.) Partially cover and simmer until the chicken is tender, about 30 miinutes (partially covering the skillet will allow some evaporation, letting your sauce thicken, while still trapping enough steam and heat to cook the chicken evenly).

Add the vinegar to the skillet and mix it into the sauce (this will brighten all the flavors). Taste for seasoning. Transfer the chicken to a large serving platter. If the sauce seems too thin, boil it down over high heat for a few minutes (it should be somewhat liquid, but not soupy). Pour the sauce over the chicken and serve hot.

VARIATION   My father always ordered a dish called chicken *scarpiello* at Angelo's Restaurant, on Mulberry Street in New York's Little Italy, and you still see it on menus in old-fashioned Italian American restaurants. I've seen many things called *scarpiello*, which means "shoemaker style." Some have red and green peppers or vinegared peppers, others mushrooms and olives. The version I like best is with sausage, white wine, and rosemary. It is like my chicken *alla cacciatora*, but without the tomatoes and with chunks of sweet Italian sausage. I ordered it recently in a place in the Bronx called Enzo's, and it brought back a lot of memories. Here is how to make it: When browning the chicken thighs, add 2 sweet Italian sausages to the skillet. When the sausages have browned, take them out, chop them into thick chunks, and return them to the skillet. Omit the tomatoes and instead add a slightly more generous amount of white wine and chicken broth. Otherwise, proceed exactly as above. You'll end up with a fragrant, brothy sauce, and your chicken will be studded with juicy little chunks of sausage.

SERVES FOUR AS A MAIN COURSE. *Alla pizzaiola,* a staple style of southern Italian cooking, came to this country with Neapolitan immigrants. I have always wanted to love it, but after years of eating too many heavy versions at Italian American restaurants I've come to realize I don't (I've had both wonderful and terrible versions of it in Italy). In theory, it is a vibrant presentation of lightly braised meat, fragrant with the taste of tomatoes, olive oil, garlic, wine, and oregano—the signature flavors of the cooking of Campania. The flavor is meant to mimic that of Naples' cheeseless *pizza marinara* (*pizzaiolo* is Italian for "pizza maker"). It was developed to improve the tough beef that used to be the only kind available to most southern Italians, but the sauce is also used to enhance veal and pork (my mother used to make pork chops *pizzaiola* with thick slices of potato simmered in the sauce). Beef *pizzaiola* is still the most popular version, but I've found that rich and fatty duck breast marries very well with the lively sauce. I've omitted the traditional dried oregano favored by southern Italians and replaced it not with fresh oregano, which can be harsh, but with its cousin fresh marjoram, with its bold but sweet floral taste.

Traditional Italian American restaurant versions of the sauce were long-cooked with the addition of tomato paste, resulting in a dark, thick appearance and a bitter undertone. I prefer my lighter version, with its quickly cooked bright red sauce and direct flavors.

DUCK PIZZAIOLA WITH RED VERMOUTH

2 Moulard duck breasts, with skin (see note)

2 bay leaves, preferably fresh

Pinch of dried red pepper flakes

1/2 cup sweet red vermouth

Salt to taste

1 tablespoon extra-virgin olive oil

3 garlic cloves, thinly sliced

6 summer plum tomatoes, peeled and chopped (see page 26), or one 35-ounce can plum tomatoes, lightly drained and chopped

Leaves from 4 or 5 marjoram sprigs, chopped, plus a few sprigs for garnish

1/2 cup pitted black Gaeta or niçoise olives, halved

Using a sharp knife, score the duck breasts lightly through the skin in a crisscross pattern. Place them in a shallow bowl and add the bay leaves, pepper flakes, and sweet vermouth. Turn the duck breasts over in the marinade a few times to distribute the flavors. Let stand at room temperature, turning the duck once or twice, for about 30 minutes.

Remove the duck from the marinade and pat dry with paper towels. Reserve the marinade. Season the breasts liberally with salt.

In a large, heavy skillet, heat the olive oil over medium-high heat. Add the duck breasts, skin side down. Sear without moving them until they are nicely browned on the bottom, about 4 minutes. Reduce the heat to medium-low and cook until the skin is crisp and much of the fat has cooked out, about 5 minutes longer. Turn the breasts and brown the other side, 3 or 4 minutes for medium rare, or very pink at the center (duck breast becomes tough even if cooked to medium, so be careful not to overcook it). Using tongs, transfer the duck to a plate. Cover loosely with aluminum foil and let rest while you make the sauce.

Pour all but about 2 tablespoons of fat from the skillet. On medium-low heat, add the garlic to the skillet and sauté until it starts to turn very lightly golden, 1 or 2 minutes. Turn the heat to medium-high, add the marinade, and let it boil down to a few tablespoons, stirring to scrape up the browned bits from the bottom of the pan. Add the tomatoes, season with salt to taste, and cook to reduce for 3 or 4 minutes, or until the sauce thickens slightly. Add the chopped marjoram and olives, and simmer the sauce briefly just to let the flavors mingle and to reduce it lightly. Taste for seasoning.

Cut the duck into thin slices on the diagonal and arrange on a warmed serving platter. Pour on the sauce and garnish with the marjoram sprigs.

MOULARD DUCK   The Moulard duck is a European variety that has more flavor and much less fat than the Long Island (or Peking) kind. D'Artagnan raises and packages both whole and cut Moulard duck. The breasts I buy from them usually weigh about 1 pound apiece. Two breasts will easily serve 4. If you use Long Island duck breasts, which are generally much smaller, you will probably need 4 of them, and you'll also need to cut the cooking time.

SERVES FOUR AS A ONE-DISH DINNER. Here's an old family recipe that I love to make well into the fall. It's an excellent way to use up the last-of-the-season tomatoes and starchy green beans I find at my farmers' market in early October. Later on, you can use canned tomatoes. It comes from Castelfranco in Miscano. I remember my mother making it when I was very young, but then it was forgotten in my family for a quarter of a century, until my father fell ill and asked my mother to make it for him again. The version I've worked out is a bit different from the family original, containing a touch of cinnamon and currants in the meatballs.

CASTELFRANCO MEATBALLS WITH GREENBEANS AND POTATOES

MEATBALLS

12 ounces pork sausage meat

12 ounces ground beef

1/2 cup whole-milk ricotta cheese

1 large egg

1/2 cup grated aged pecorino cheese

1/4 cup homemade, dry bread crumbs (see page 308)

1 large shallot, minced

1 large garlic clove, minced

2 tablespoons dry white wine

Handful of pine nuts

1/3 cup dried currants

A pinch of ground cinnamon

A pinch of ground nutmeg

Salt and freshly ground black pepper to taste

Handful of fresh flat-leaf parsley leaves, chopped

1 tablespoon extra-virgin olive oil

1/2 cup extra-virgin olive oil for sautéing

3 slices pancetta, finely chopped

1 onion, finely diced

1 garlic clove, very thinly sliced

1/2 cup dry white wine

4 large, round tomatoes, peeled and chopped (see page 26), or one 35-ounce can plum tomatoes, chopped and lightly drained

1/2 cup low-salt canned chicken broth

A pinch of ground cinnamon

1 bay leaf, preferably fresh

Salt and freshly ground black pepper to taste

8 ounces green beans, trimmed and blanched until crisp-tender

2 boiling potatoes (not new potatoes), peeled, cut into large chunks, and cooked until just tender

Leaves from 3 or 4 marjoram sprigs, chopped

Handful of fresh flat-leaf parsley leaves, chopped

Italian bread for serving

Grated pecorino cheese for serving

In a large bowl, combine all the ingredients for the meatballs. Mix together briefly with your hands just until the ingredients are well distributed (working the mixture as little as possible will keep your meatballs light in texture). Form into small meatballs, about $^1/_2$ inch across.

In a large skillet, heat about $^1/_2$ inch olive oil over medium heat. Add the meatballs (you may need to add them in batches if the skillet is crowded) and brown them well all over. Transfer to paper towels to drain.

Pour all but about 2 tablespoons of fat from the skillet. Add the pancetta and sauté until crisp, about 5 minutes. Add the onion and sauté until soft, about another 4 minutes. Add the garlic and sauté until turning lightly golden, about 2 minutes. Add the white wine and cook to reduce by half. Add the tomatoes and chicken broth, cinnamon, bay leaf, salt, and pepper and simmer until slightly thickened, about 10 minutes (the sauce will still be quite brothy). Add the meatballs and blanched green beans and cooked potatoes, and simmer another 5 minutes to finish cooking the meatballs and bring all the flavors together. Add the marjoram and parsley and taste for seasoning.

Serve in large soup bowls, with plenty of good Italian bread and a bowl of grated pecorino brought to the table.

SERVES FIVE AS A MAIN COURSE. *Polpettone* is the Italian word for meat loaf (*polpettini* are meatballs), and it's actually a very southern Italian concept, growing, like so many fine dishes, out of both the South's poverty and its extravagance of spirit. My *polpettone* cooks up very tender, because in place of bread crumbs I use ricotta cheese. The meat is a little soft to work with, so I wrap it in prosciutto to hold it together (which also adds good flavor).

MEAT LOAF WITH RICOTTA AND PISTACHIOS, SICILIAN STYLE

1 pound ground pork

8 ounces ground beef, preferably chuck (this has more flavor than sirloin and a little more fat, so it won't cook up dry)

1 cup whole-milk ricotta, drained

2 large eggs

1 egg white

3 tablespoons extra-virgin olive oil

$^1/_2$ cup grated grana padano cheese

1 garlic clove, minced

Handful of pistachios

Generous handful of fresh flat-leaf parsley leaves, chopped

5 fresh sage leaves, chopped

3 or 4 scrapings freshly grated nutmeg

Salt and freshly ground black pepper to taste

4 ounces prosciutto di Parma, very thinly sliced

$^3/_4$ cup dry white wine

Preheat the oven to 400°F.

To make sure meat loaf is tender, it is best not to overmix the ingredients. Put all the ingredients, except for the prosciutto and wine, in the bowl at the same time and then quickly mix everything with your fingers. To make sure you've added enough salt or other seasonings since it is hard to re-season once it is in a loaf. While it's still in the bowl, pat the meat into a oval shape (the mixture will be very soft, but don't worry, it will come together as it cooks).

Choose a low-sided baking dish, about 10 by 12 inches, that will hold the meat loaf fairly snugly. Coat the bottom of the dish with olive oil and drape the prosciutto slices across the bottom of the dish crosswise, letting them hang over the side (resist the desire to trim the fat from the prosciutto—it will help it adhere to the meat loaf and keep it moist and flavorful). Tip the meat loaf out of the bowl onto the prosciutto and pat it into an oval. Pull the prosciutto around the meat loaf, then pat the pieces down against it. Drape a few more slices over the top to cover any empty parts and pat them down (you won't need string to hold them in place—the prosciutto will melt against the meat as it cooks, making a nice package).

Bake, uncovered, for about 15 minutes. Pour the wine around the meat loaf and continue baking for another 30 minutes, basting occasionally with the wine. When cooked, the meat loaf should feel firm but springy, and most of the pan juices will have been absorbed. Let the meat loaf rest at least 15 minutes so it can firm up for easier slicing.

VARIATION   I prefer meat loaf without any sauce, just sliced warm and served with a vegetable or a green salad, but a tomato sauce accompaniment is traditional. If you'd like to serve one, try Winter Tomato Sauce (see page 113).

SERVES FOUR AS A MAIN COURSE. Scaloppine—boneless veal cut from the upper hind leg section across the grain and then pounded tender—is a staple of fancy southern Italian kitchens. My mother made it often, but we just called it cutlets. Sometimes it would be *piccata* (with white wine and capers), but more often it got the parmigiana treatment (fried crisp, then covered with tomato sauce and mozzarella and melted in the oven for a few minutes). I've always preferred grabbing the cutlets when just fried, squeezing lemon juice on top, and eating them as is: oily, burning hot, and slightly puckery. And I love the mix of crisp, oily meat with a slightly astringent salad. That's what this recipe is all about.

VEAL SCALOPPINE WITH DANDELION AND SPRING ONION SALAD

FOR THE SALAD:

1 large bunch tender young dandelion greens, stemmed (about 2 loosely packed cups)

12 cherry tomatoes, stemmed and halved

1 small spring bulb onion, including tender green parts, very thinly sliced

Handful of pine nuts, lightly toasted (see page 61)

Small palmful of salt-packed capers, soaked and drained

DRESSING

2 tablespoons extra-virgin olive oil

Juice of $\frac{1}{2}$ large lemon

Salt and freshly ground black pepper to taste

$\frac{1}{2}$ cup finely ground, lightly toasted bread crumbs

$\frac{1}{2}$ cup finely ground pine nuts

Leaves from 3 or 4 thyme sprigs, chopped

Grated zest of 1 lemon

Salt to taste

Pinch of cayenne pepper

$\frac{1}{4}$ cup extra-virgin olive oil

1 large egg, lightly beaten

4 large, thin slices veal scaloppine (about 1$\frac{1}{2}$ pounds total)

In a large salad bowl, combine all the salad ingredients.

Put the bread crumbs and ground pine nuts in a large, shallow bowl. Add the thyme, lemon zest, salt, and cayenne and mix everything well.

In a large skillet, heat the olive oil over medium-high heat.

Pour the beaten egg in a large, shallow bowl and dip the scaloppine into it one at a time, coating well. Dredge the scaloppine in the bread-crumb mixture.

When the skillet is nice and hot, add the scaloppine and sauté, without moving them at all, until golden and crisp on the bottom, about 3 minutes. Turn over and brown on the other side, about 1 minute longer. Using a slotted metal spatula, transfer to paper towels to drain, then transfer to 4 dinner plates.

FOR THE DRESSING: Add the olive oil, lemon juice, salt, and pepper to the salad and toss gently. Divide the salad over the scaloppine. Serve right away.

SERVES FOUR AS A MAIN COURSE. Veal sweetbreads, as I've learned from years of experimenting, blend very well with sweet wine as long as you balance the flavors with a few herbal or even slightly bitter notes. Here, I've added artichokes, basil, and a shot of lemon.

What are sweetbreads? I try not to think about it too much, but they're the thymus gland of a calf. They have a delicate taste and are naturally very tender, like all veal cuts. They are covered with a thin membrane that needs to be removed before sautéing, so I always blanch them very briefly first. Then the membrane peels right off.

SWEETBREADS WITH ARTICHOKES AND MOSCATO WINE

2 to 2½ pounds veal sweetbreads

2 tablespoons white wine vinegar

4 tablespoons extra-virgin olive oil

3 garlic cloves, thinly sliced

2 dozen baby artichokes, trimmed (see page 85) and halved

Salt and freshly ground black pepper to taste

Leaves from 3 or 4 small thyme sprigs, chopped

Grated zest of 1 large lemon

¾ cup canned low-salt chicken broth, plus more as needed

Warm water as needed (optional)

½ cup flour for dredging

2 tablespoons unsalted butter

½ cup Moscato di Pantelleria or another sweet wine such as Baumes de Venise

Small handful of fresh basil leaves, chopped

Put the sweetbreads in a large pot and add cold water to cover by about 2 inches. Add the white wine vinegar and turn the heat to high. (This vinegar routine is something we did at a bistro I used to cook for. It seems to freshen the taste, but it evidently is not really necessary. None of the recipes I've ever seen for sweetbreads mentions this. You can skip the vinegar if you like, but to me, it adds a subtle uplifting flavor to the meat.) Bring the water to a full boil and turn off the heat. Let the sweetbreads sit in the water on the turned-off burner for 15 minutes.

Using a large skimmer, transfer the sweetbreads to a large pot of cold water (ideally, with a few ice cubes added). Let cool. Pull them from the water and pat them dry. You'll notice there's a thin whitish membrane covering the sweetbreads. Peel as much of this off as possible without breaking up the sweetbreads. You'll also notice that the sweetbreads have a natural dividing line down the middle and are held together there by more of the membrane. Separate them into 2 more or less equal pieces along this line, removing the membrane and any gristle that might be wedged in there (sometimes the sweetbreads break into a few smaller pieces, but that's fine). It is customary to weight the sweetbreads to flatten them; it gives them a uniform thickness, making them easier to sauté. To do this, place them on a large cutting board or a counter. Cover them with paper towels and place another cutting board or flat dish on top. Place some sort of weight on top (such as 2 or 3 large tomato cans). Let stand for about 1 hour.

In a large skillet, heat 2 tablespoons of the olive oil over medium heat. Add the garlic and sauté for 1 minute to release its flavor. Drain the artichokes and add them to the skillet. Season with salt, pepper, and thyme and sauté until lightly browned but still a little firm. Add half of the lemon zest and the ³/₄ cup chicken broth, and simmer at a lively bubble until they are fork-tender, 4 or 5 minutes. You should still have a fair amount of liquid in the skillet (if you don't, add a little more broth or some warm water).

Pour the flour onto a large plate and season with salt and pepper. Coat the sweetbreads in the flour, tapping off the excess. In another large skillet, melt the butter with the remaining 2 tablespoons olive oil over medium heat. Add the sweetbreads and sauté until well browned, 4 or 5 minutes. Flip them over and brown the other side, 3 or 4 minutes. (You want to use a medium, not high heat for this because the sweetbreads need some time to cook through. When tender, the flesh should pierce easily with a thin knife and be opaque, creamy white throughout.) Using a slotted metal spatula, transfer the sweetbreads to a warmed serving platter. Cover loosely with aluminum foil to keep warm.

Add the wine to the skillet you cooked the sweetbreads in and cook over medium heat, stirring to scrape up the browned bits from the bottom of the pan. Add the artichokes and their liquid, and simmer to heat them through and blend all the flavors. Add the remaining lemon zest and the basil and taste for seasoning. You should have a nice balance between the sweet wine and the slight bitterness of the artichokes. Pour the artichokes with all the skillet juices over the sweetbreads and serve right away.

SERVES FOUR AS A MAIN COURSE. My father had a nervous friend who periodically arrived at our house with a trunk full of porterhouse steaks. We eventually put a freezer in the basement to accommodate them all. His arrival always made my mother angry, but my sister and I couldn't understand why; we loved these steaks, and they seemed like a gift from heaven. Over the years, he arrived with carloads of other things (once about fifty identical teddy bears). Then he disappeared into Miami's seedier business community, and we didn't see him much anymore. I think about him occasionally and wish I had a friend who brought steaks to my house. Since I now have to actually buy them, I'm always on the lookout for good inexpensive cuts.

Skirt steak is an incredibly flavorful and nicely priced cut of beef. It is perfect for grilling but needs to be kept rare or medium-rare or it starts to become a little tough. Get your grill very hot and sear the steak quickly. You'll be rewarded with an elegant but quick and easy steak dinner.

Salmoriglio is an olive oil–based Sicilian sauce flavored, at its simplest, with lemon and oregano. Sometimes anchovies, garlic, capers, or mint is added. Traditionally, it's used to flavor fish, but I've found its pungency also marries well with grilled meats. The *sal* in the name refers to salt, which is an important flavoring, keeping the oil and herbs in balance. It should be sea salt.

Note: This is a semiemulsified sauce and will no doubt break as it sits, but that's the nature of the thing so don't worry if it starts to look a little weepy halfway through the dinner. Make it right before you start to grill the steak.

GRILLED SKIRT STEAK WITH SALMORIGLIO

SALMORIGLIO SAUCE

⅓ cup extra-virgin olive oil

Grated zest and juice of 1 large lemon

2 garlic cloves, minced

2 oil-packed anchovy fillets, minced, or 1 salt-packed anchovy, filleted, soaked, drained, and minced (see page 33)

Palmful of salt-packed capers, soaked and drained (see page 29)

Salt and freshly ground black pepper to taste

Leaves from 3 or 4 marjoram or oregano sprigs, chopped

2 pounds skirt steak

2 tablespoons extra-virgin olive oil

Salt and coarsely ground black pepper to taste

Leaves from 3 or 4 large flat-leaf parsley sprigs, chopped, plus a handful of parsley leaves for garnish

To make the sauce: In a small saucepan, combine the olive oil and lemon zest and juice. Add the garlic, anchovies, and capers and cook over low heat until it reaches a boil, about 5 minutes, whisking it frequently. Remove from the heat, season with salt and pepper, and add the marjoram or oregano. Give it a few more whisks before pouring it into a sauceboat.

Light a fire in a charcoal grill, preheat a gas grill to high, or heat a grill pan over high heat. Pat the steak dry and rub it with the olive oil. Season generously with salt and pepper.

Grill the steak, without moving it, until nice char marks appear on the bottom, about 4 minutes. Turn the steak and grill the other side for about another 4 minutes for rare, or about 1 minute longer for medium-rare, but try to resist letting it go any longer than that. (Remember, the steak will continue to cook a little after you take it off the heat, so it's better to pull it a bit less done than you like it.) Transfer the steak to a carving board and let it rest for a few minutes. Slice the steak thinly against the grain (this will make the slices tender) and place it on a serving platter. Pour on a little of the sauce and scatter on the parsley leaves. Bring the rest of the sauce to the table.

SERVES FOUR OR FIVE AS A MAIN COURSE. In most of southern Italy, a good-sized chunk of braising beef is inevitably slow-simmered in wine and aromatics, with maybe a touch of tomato. This dish is a southern Italian pot roast simmered in Primitivo di Manduria, a strong red wine from Puglia. The wine has a characteristic pruney flavor that works well with strongly flavored red meat. The orange zest and anchovy cook down, blending with the rich wine to add a subtle layer of flavor.

BRAISED BEEF WITH PRIMITIVO WINE

2 tablespoons extra-virgin olive oil

One 3½-4 pound boneless beef chuck shoulder roast (also called shoulder pot roast), tied in 3 or 4 places

½ cup all-purpose flour for dredging

Salt and freshly ground black pepper to taste

1 large onion, cut into large chunks

2 carrots, peeled and coarsely chopped

2 garlic cloves, lightly crushed

1 bay leaf, preferably fresh

3 or 4 marjoram sprigs

Pinch of ground cloves

2 long strips orange zest

2 oil-packed anchovy fillets, or 1 salt-packed anchovy, filleted, soaked, and drained (see page 33)

1 heaping tablespoon tomato paste

1 bottle Primitivo wine or another strong, dry red, like Cabernet

Handful of fresh flat-leaf parsley leaves, chopped

In a large Dutch oven or a flameproof casserole with a lid, heat the olive oil over medium-high heat. Coat the meat lightly in flour and add it to the pot. Season with salt and pepper and brown the meat on all sides. (Take your time doing this; the browning will add great flavor to the sauce.) Add the onion, carrots, and garlic and sauté for a few minutes so they can release their flavors. Add the bay leaf, marjoram, ground cloves, orange zest, anchovies, and tomato paste and sauté for 1 or 2 minutes. Pour in the wine and bring it to a boil. The meat should be just about covered with liquid (if not, add a little warm water). Reduce the heat to a simmer, cover, and cook slowly, turning the meat once or twice and basting it occasionally, until very tender, about 2½ hours. If the liquid gets too low, add warm water.

Transfer the meat to a carving board and cover it loosely with aluminum foil to keep it warm.

Skim the excess fat from the surface of the sauce. Pour the sauce through a fine-mesh sieve into a clean saucepan, pushing on the vegetables with the back of a large spoon so some of their juice can be incorporated into the sauce. Boil the sauce over high heat for a few minutes to concentrate its flavor (it should be just on the verge of looking syrupy). Slice the meat thickly (it will be very tender and start to fall apart a bit). Place the meat on a large serving platter. Scatter on the parsley and spoon on a few tablespoons of the sauce. Bring the remaining sauce to the table in a small sauceboat.

VARIATION To use leftover meat for a pasta sauce, shred the meat with your fingers (for 8 ounces of pasta—enough for 2 large servings—you'll need about 1 cup). Warm the shredded meat in all the leftover wine sauce in a small skillet. Add a handful of chopped fresh flat-leaf parsley and a drizzle of olive oil. Check the seasoning, adding a little fresh pepper to wake up the flavors. Cook 8 ounces of ziti or penne pasta al dente, drain it well, and add it to the skillet. Toss on medium heat for 1 minute or two, adding a handful of grated pecorino cheese. Serve hot.

Serves five as a main course. I love the rich taste and texture of tripe and enjoy cooking it on days when I have a few hours to leisurely spend in my kitchen. Calabria does a nice job with tripe, stewing it in the region's traditional flavors of tomato, red wine, and hot chilies. The version here leaves out the chilies and adds white wine and a last-minute flourish of fresh herbs that lightens up the whole dish.

I always buy tripe at Faicco's, on New York's Bleecker Street, where I know it will be extremely fresh. Tripe is the stomach lining of a cow, which sounds a lot less desirable than it turns out to be when well prepared. There are several cuts of tripe, but the most tender one is honeycomb (in Italy, tripe stews are often made with three different cuts, which does give you a more complex flavor, but some cuts are a little tough and gnarly). Any tripe you buy nowadays comes already partially cooked, which cuts the preparation time by several hours, although to become meltingly tender even precooked tripe needs at least 2 hours of simmering, soaking up all the wine and herb flavors to make a softened and nuanced dish.

BRAISED TRIPE WITH MINT AND PECORINO

2½ pounds honeycomb beef tripe

¼ cup white wine vinegar

Salt to taste

2 tablespoons unsalted butter

2 tablespoons extra-virgin olive oil, plus more for drizzling

3 or 4 thin slices fatty prosciutto end, chopped

4 shallots, finely diced

2 carrots, peeled and finely diced

1 celery stalk, finely diced

1 bay leaf, preferably fresh

⅛ teaspoon ground allspice

Freshly ground black pepper to taste

1½ cups dry white wine

One 35-ounce can plum tomatoes, well drained and chopped

1½ to 2 cups homemade mixed-meat broth (see page 328), homemade chicken broth (see page 315), or canned low-salt chicken broth

Leaves from 3 or 4 small mint sprigs, chopped

Generous handful of fresh basil leaves, chopped

6 Yukon Gold potatoes, peeled and halved

1 chunk mild pecorino cheese

Put the tripe in a large Dutch oven or a flameproof casserole with a lid. Add the vinegar and cold water to cover. Season with salt and bring to a boil over high heat. Turn off the heat and let the tripe sit in the pan for 15 minutes. Drain the tripe and rinse it under cold water. (This step refreshes the tripe and wakes up its flavor, and if any scum on the meat floats to the surface, it will rinse away.) Pat the tripe dry and slice it into thin strips.

In the same pot, melt the butter with the 2 tablespoons olive oil over medium heat. Add the prosciutto and sauté for about 1 minute, just to give off some of its fat. Add the tripe, shallots, carrots, celery, bay leaf, and ground allspice. Season with salt and pepper and sauté until the vegetables have softened, about 5 minutes. Add the wine and let it boil down by half. Add the tomatoes, $1\frac{1}{2}$ cups of the broth, and half the chopped herbs. Bring to a boil again, reduce the heat to very low, cover the pot, and cook at a gentle simmer until the tripe is very tender, about 3 hours (or bake in a preheated 325°F oven). If the liquid evaporates to uncover more than about one-fourth of the tripe, add a little more broth.

Taste the tripe for seasoning, adding more salt or pepper if needed. Add the rest of the chopped herbs and a drizzle of fresh olive oil. While the tripe is cooking, put the potatoes in a small saucepan of cold water, bring to a low boil, and cook until just tender, 6 to 8 minutes. Drain and dress with olive oil and salt to taste. Serve the tripe in deep pasta bowls or soup bowls, with a few potatoes alongside. Sprinkle with a generous amount of freshly grated cheese.

SERVES FOUR AS A MAIN COURSE. Here are *code di bue* (oxtails) simmered in the southern Italian triumvirate of tomatoes, white wine, and garlic. In Basilicata, you'll find recipes flavored with wild fennel, which I love, but this version combines the winey, tomatoey flavor with savory, rosemary and juniper berries, coaxing this dish into the direction of cold-weather fare.

OXTAIL STEW WITH TOMATO, WHITE WINE, AND GARLIC

2 tablespoons extra-virgin olive oil

4 pounds oxtails (try to get the wider, meatier middle cut, not the small tail ends)

Salt and freshly ground black pepper to taste

Flour for dredging

1 small chunk fatty prosciutto end

2 leeks, white part and tender green parts, cut into thin rounds

2 carrots, peeled and finely diced

3 garlic cloves

Leaves from 3 or 4 small winter savory sprigs, chopped, plus a few whole sprigs

3 or 4 small rosemary sprigs, plus leaves from 3 or 4 sprigs, chopped

3 juniper berries, lightly crushed

1½ cups dry white wine

One 35-ounce can plum tomatoes, drained and chopped

1½ cups homemade mixed-meat broth (page 328) or high quality purchased broth, preferably a mix of half chicken and half beef

Warm water, if needed

1 tablespoon balsamic vinegar

Leaves from 1 handful of flat-leaf parsley sprigs, chopped

Preheat the oven to 325°F.

In a large Dutch oven or a flameproof casserole with a lid, heat the olive oil over medium-high heat. Season the oxtails with salt and pepper and dredge them lightly in flour to coat. Put them in the pot (in batches if necessary) and brown them well on all sides. Add the prosciutto chunk, leeks, carrots, garlic, savory and rosemary sprigs, and juniper berries. Reduce the heat to medium. Sauté for 3 or 4 minutes to soften the vegetables and to release the essences from the herbs and spices. Add the white wine and cook at a lively bubble for about 5 minutes. Add the tomatoes and broth. The meat should be almost completely covered with liquid. If not, add more broth or water. Bring to a boil. Cover the pot and place it in the oven. Let the stew cook at a low simmer until very tender, 2½ to 3 hours (the meat should be falling off the bone).

Remove the pot from the oven and remove the meat with a slotted spoon. Skim most of the fat from the surface of the sauce. (Oxtails throw off a lot of fat. If you like, you can make the stew the day before serving, refrigerate it overnight, then skim the congealed fat from the surface before reheating.)

Add the balsamic vinegar to the sauce and give it a taste (this will heighten all the flavors). Season with salt or pepper if needed. If needed to intensify the flavors, boil the sauce down over high heat for a few minutes. Return the oxtails to the sauce and reheat briefly. Add the chopped herbs (this will give your dish two herb tastes: mellow and cooked, and bright and fresh).

SERVING SUGGESTIONS I like serving this accompanied with a bowl of small pasta, like cavatelli, tossed with olive oil and parsley, and maybe a little grated pecorino, but you can also just serve it with good Italian bread.

SAVORY TARTS

I get tremendous enjoyment from assembling and baking savory tarts, bringing them to the table, and slicing them up for a group. It's the only time I feel even remotely like a mom. It took me a while to get started, though. Since I never particularly enjoyed baking sweet things, I never considered myself a natural baker, and I always assumed anything with a crust and a filling would be fussy and irritating to put together. But after I made my first *pizza rustica*, for an Easter dinner years ago, I found that they actually are easy to make and don't have to look perfect. In fact I think they're much more appetizing when they have a slightly funky homemade finish. I also love how most crusts don't need to be prebaked, which would make me impatient.

My two favorite southern Italian tarts have always been *pizza rustica*, filled with salami, ham, and cheeses, and *pizza di scarola*, with escarole and strong flavors like anchovies, olives, and capers. Both are popular in Campania, but variations are made throughout the South. I offer slightly urbanized versions of both of these incredibly flavorful and very different tarts. A more recent discovery for me is a Sicilian tart filled with swordfish and encased in an orange-scented crust. The *impanata di pesce spada* that I make is fairly straightforward; the original is so whimsical and fantastic that it needs nobody's imaginative input. (I make another Sicilian fish tart, too, one with eels, that's quite a production and might make its way into another book if I get the nerve to include it.) Puglia is another good region for looking for these creations. A double-crusted onion and anchovy tart I sampled in Lecce was the inspiration for the more freewheeling open-faced version I offer here.

Savory tarts in southern Italy can be called *pizza, pisticcio, torta, impanata,* or various local names, but whether they're from Basilicata, Puglia, Sicily, or Campania, they all have one thing in common: They are inspirational and vary according to the temperament of the cook and the produce of the season. I often make my escarole tart with sweet additions like raisins and a splash of orange flower water instead of the more robust black olive and caciocavallo version I offer here (I've picked the latter because my friends all seem to like it best). Sometimes, I'll make the crust for the escarole tart and fill it with sautéed eggplant or broccoli rabe. *Caponatina* (page 122) or *peperonata* (page 127) both make good fillings for double-crusted tarts. I almost always include some type of soft or meltable cheese like mozzarella, caciocavallo, or ricotta, not only because it's delicious but also because it tends to prevent the filling from spilling out once you cut into the tart.

You can make the crust with a *pasta frolla* (a "short" pastry, using cold butter), or with an olive-oil pastry, which I particularly love (it's so easy; all you do is put everything together in a bowl, stir it, and roll it out, and it tastes delicious and rich with no butter). Traditionally, these crusts can include unexpected flavors like wine, orange zest, herbs, cinnamon, honey, or sugar. In fact, a sweet crust paired with a savory filling is one of the most alluring characteristics of some of the tarts from these regions.

Like many southern Italian savory dishes, these tarts taste even better at room temperature or only slightly warm rather than piping hot, and that's how they're usually served. This means you can make them ahead. They're also easier to slice that way.

SERVES SIX AS A FIRST COURSE OR AN APPETIZER. The crust for this improvised tart is fairly sweet, even by southern Italian standards, making for a nice play of
flavors with the acidity of the tomatoes. And to my palate, the flavor of fresh thyme is
heightened by a touch of sugar. You could almost serve this as a dessert, but I think it's
best when cut into thin wedges and offered as an antipasto, with a glass of fruity white
wine or Champagne.

RICOTTA AND CHERRY TOMATO TART
WITH THYME

CRUST

8 tablespoons unsalted butter

3 tablespoons sugar

Pinch of salt

2—3 tablespoons dry white wine

1½ cups all-purpose flour

½ cup grated pecorino cheese

RICOTTA CUSTARD

¼ cup whole-milk ricotta cheese,
drained if watery

½ cup heavy cream

1 large egg

3 or 4 scrapings freshly grated nutmeg

1 large garlic clove, minced

Pinch of salt

Freshly ground black pepper to taste

1 teaspoon flour

3 cups cherry tomatoes, stemmed and
halved

Salt and freshly ground pepper

Leaves from 5 or 6 large thyme sprigs,
chopped

Extra-virgin olive oil for drizzling

TO MAKE THE CRUST: Preheat the oven to 350°F. In a small saucepan, melt the butter over low heat; let it cool. With a pastry brush, use a little of the melted butter to
grease a 9—inch tart pan with removable bottom.

In a medium bowl, combine the remaining melted butter, the sugar, salt, and white wine.
Stir to blend. Add the flour and mix briefly to blend to a moist-looking, crumbly mixture. (Don't blend it so much that the dough forms into one big ball. If the dough seems
dry, add a little more water. This crust is more like a cookie than a traditional pastry
dough, so it cooks up crumbly, not flaky.) Empty the dough into the tart pan and pat it

down and out to the edges to form a more-or-less uniform thin crust building it up at the edge, a bit, to allow for shrinkage. Bake for about 15 minutes, or until set and slightly puffy. Remove the crust from the oven and sprinkle half the grated pecorino over it.

In a food processor, combine all the ricotta custard ingredients and blend until smooth.

Place the cherry tomatoes, cut side up, in the crust in a slightly overlapping circular pattern (they should fit snugly together). Season with salt and pepper and scatter on the thyme and the remaining pecorino.

Pour the custard evenly over the tomatoes, making sure you don't let any run over the edge of the crust. Drizzle lightly with olive oil and bake for about 1 hour, or until the top is golden brown and the custard is just set. Let cool on a wire rack for about 30 minutes before serving.

SERVES FOUR OR FIVE AS A LUNCH DISH, SIX OR SEVEN AS AN APPETIZER.

Pizza di scarola is the Neapolitan name for a double-crusted escarole-filled pie that is traditional on Christmas Eve. I used to see these pies in New York pizza shops, sold by the slice, when I was a child, a refreshing change from the pepperoni pizza I almost always went for. You don't see it around much nowadays, but you'll still find it in pizza shops in Naples. In addition to the escarole, so loved by Neapolitans (and by me), the pie is usually highly flavored with most of the classic southern Italian strong tastes, including anchovies, capers, olives. raisins, and pine nuts. My version concentrates on olives, using the Gaeta black olives famous in the region, and caciocavallo cheese, which melts beautifully.

The home versions of *pizza di scarola* that I've seen always seem to be made in a pie pan, but a round pizza pan or even a regular baking sheet works better, because the circulating air keeps the crust crisper.

PIZZA DI SCAROLA WITH GAETA OLIVES AND CACIOCAVALLO

DOUGH

2 cups all-purpose flour

Generous pinch of salt

1 large egg

1/4 cup dry white wine at room temperature

1/4 cup extra-virgin olive oil

FILLING

2 large heads escarole (about 2 pounds total), trimmed and chopped into bite-sized pieces (it looks like a lot, but it cooks down)

1 large garlic clove, minced

Salt and freshly ground black pepper to taste

3 or 4 scrapings freshly grated nutmeg

Extra-virgin olive oil for drizzling

Large handful of pine nuts, lightly toasted (see page 61)

3/4 cup grated caciocavallo cheese

1/2 cup black olives, preferably Gaetas, pitted and coarsely chopped

1 large egg

Extra-virgin olive oil for brushing

To make the dough: Put the flour in a shallow bowl. Add the salt and stir it in to distribute well. Put the egg, white wine, and olive oil in a small bowl and beat with a fork to blend everything. Pour this onto the flour and mix with your fork until you have a crumbly but rather moist mass. Knead briefly with your hands to form a smooth ball, about 3 or 4 minutes. Divide the dough into 2 pieces, making one section slightly larger than the other. Wrap both pieces in plastic wrap and let them rest at room temperature for about 1 hour (this will make it easier to roll out).

While the dough is resting, make the filling: Blanch the escarole in a large pot of boiling water for about 2 minutes. Drain it in a colander and run cold water over it to stop the cooking and to preserve its bright green color. When cold, squeeze all the water out of it with your hands (you want it really dry, so your tart doesn't cook up soggy). Put the escarole in a bowl and add all the remaining ingredients for the filling. Mix well until blended.

Preheat the oven to 375°F.

Sprinkle a little flour on a work surface and roll out the larger piece of dough until you have a more or less round shape about 12 inches across; trim the edges to make it even. Brush a pizza pan (or baking sheet) with olive oil and place the dough round on it. Roll out the other piece to an 11-inch diameter and trim. Pour the filling onto the large round and spread it out to about 1 inch from the edge. Place the smaller round on top. Brush the edges of the larger round with water and pull it up over the top, making little pleats all around, pressing to seal it while you do. Make a few small air vents in the top with a thin knife and brush the whole thing lightly with olive oil.

Bake until the tart is golden brown, about 35 minutes. Let it cool for about 20 minutes before serving (this will allow you to slice it more cleanly). To serve, cut into wedges.

SERVES SIX AS AN APPETIZER. I often make free-form tarts without a tart pan, rolling the dough into a large and more or less circular shape and placing it on a baking sheet. Then I reach into my bag of southern Italian flavors and improvise various toppings. I love slow-sautéed sweet onions seasoned with a touch of anchovy, which also makes a good pasta sauce.

SWEET ONION AND PROVOLONE TART

CRUST

1½ cups all-purpose flour

Generous pinch of salt

7 tablespoons cold unsalted butter, cut into small pieces

2 to 3 tablespoons cold dry white wine

TOPPING

2 tablespoons extra-virgin olive oil

2 sweet onions (Vidalias are a good choice), thinly sliced

2 oil-packed anchovy fillets, chopped, or 1 salt-packed anchovy, filleted,

soaked, drained, and chopped (see page 33)

Pinch of sugar

Salt and freshly ground black pepper to taste

½ cup grated provolone cheese, preferably an imported one (American versions tend to be very salty and lacking in flavor)

Leaves from 3 or 4 large oregano or marjoram sprigs, chopped

5 ripe plum tomatoes, thinly sliced

Handful of salt-packed capers, soaked and drained (see page 29)

TO MAKE THE CRUST: In a food processor, combine the flour and salt. Pulse just to blend the salt. Add the butter to the flour and pulse 2 or 3 times until the butter is the size of lentils. Add 2 tablespoons of the wine and pulse very briefly until you have a crumbly but slightly moist consistency (don't pulse until it forms a ball; the butter will be too puréed and you won't have a flaky crust). Pinch a section of the dough to see if it holds together. If not, add another tablespoon of wine and pulse once or twice. Turn the dough out onto a work surface and press it into a ball with your hands. Knead it once or twice just to make sure it holds together. Cover the dough with plastic wrap and let it rest in the refrigerator for about 30 minutes.

Preheat the oven to 375°F.

MEANWHILE, MAKE THE TOPPING: In a medium skillet, heat the olive oil over medium heat. Add the onions, anchovies, sugar, and salt and pepper. Sauté until the onions are very soft and lightly golden, about 10 minutes (if they start to brown too much, lower the heat).

On a floured work surface, roll the dough out into a large oval shape (about 12 inches long), building up the edges to form a little border. Transfer to a baking sheet. Spread the onions out on the dough. Scatter on the provolone. Sprinkle on the oregano or marjoram. Place the tomato slices on top in a circular pattern but not overlapping; they look nicer with a little space between them. Scatter on the capers and drizzle with olive oil, and grate pepper on top. Bake until nicely golden, about 35 minutes.

SERVES SIX OR SEVEN AS AN APPETIZER OR FIRST COURSE. *Impanata di pesce spada,* filled with swordfish, pine nuts, olive, raisins, capers, and caciocavallo, is a specialty from the Sicilian town of Messina. It seems so exotic and glorious, its existence has fascinated me. It's a good example of the southern Italian custom of combining cheese with seafood (never done with tossed pasta dishes, but common with baked pasta, stuffed fish, and elegant pies like this one). Orange is not always included in the crust, but one of the recipes I found included it, and it seemed so elegant I had to make my version that way.

Several pies go by the name of *impanata* in Sicily, and many historians believe the name derives from the Spanish *empanada* and is likely a legacy of Spanish rule.

SWORDFISH PIE WITH A SWEET ORANGE CRUST

DOUGH

2¹/₂ cups all-purpose flour

Grated zest of 1 large orange

Generous pinch of salt

2 tablespoons sugar

³/₄ cup (1¹/₂ sticks) cold unsalted butter, cut into small pieces

4 tablespoons cold dry white wine

FILLING

2 tablespoons extra-virgin olive oil

1 small onion, finely diced

1 celery stalk, finely diced

Large handful of pine nuts

One 15-ounce can plum tomatoes, chopped and very well drained

Salt and freshly ground black pepper to taste

Handful of golden raisins, soaked in ¹/₄ cup dry white wine

Handful of salt-packed capers, soaked and drained (see page 29)

1 pound swordfish, skinned and cut into ¹/₂-inch cubes

Handful of fresh flat-leaf parsley leaves, chopped

1 cup grated caciocavallo cheese

1 egg, lightly beaten

TO MAKE THE DOUGH: In a food processor, combine the flour, orange zest, salt, and sugar. Pulse briefly to blend. Add the butter and pulse once or twice until the butter is about the size of lentils. Add 3 tablespoons of the white wine and pulse once or twice more to a crumbly but slightly moist-looking texture (don't let it work itself into a ball).

Pinch a section of the dough to make sure it holds together. If it seems too dry, add the remaining 1 tablespoon wine and pulse once more. Dump the dough out onto a work surface and squeeze it into a ball. Knead briefly to make sure it holds together. Cut the dough into 2 pieces, one a little larger than the other, and wrap in plastic wrap. Refrigerate for about 30 minutes.

Heat the oven to 375°F.

TO START THE FILLING: In a medium skillet, heat the olive oil over medium heat. Add the onion and celery and sauté until soft and fragrant, about 5 minutes. Add the pine nuts and sauté for 1 or 2 minutes, or until lightly golden. Add the tomatoes, salt, and pepper and sauté for about 5 minutes. Add the raisins and white wine and let it bubble until evaporated. The sauce should be quite dry. Add the capers. Set aside.

On a floured work surface, roll out each ball of dough into a round, the larger piece about 12 inches in diameter, the smaller piece about 9 inches. Trim the edges of the dough to make them even. Fit the large round into the 9 inch pie pan, letting the edges hang over the rim. Spread the swordfish out on top of the dough. Scatter on the parsley and then the grated caciocavallo. Pour the tomato sauce on top, spreading it evenly. Place the small dough round on top and pull up the edges of the large dough round to form a border, folding and pinching the dough together all around. Make 2 slits in the top to let the air escape. Brush the top of the tart with the beaten egg.

Bake until nicely browned, about 50 minutes. Let stand for about 30 minutes before serving (this will make it easier to cut).

VARIATION   Another Sicilian fish pie, a specialty of Agrigento, contains the area's excellent preserved tuna. Preserved Sicilian Tuna (page 156) makes a great filling for this pie. You can substitute it for the swordfish in the recipe.

Serves six or seven as an appetizer or first course. This opulent pie can contain chunks of salami, prosciutto, mozzarella, and pecorino, all held together with ricotta and eggs. It's a celebration of the rich flavors of the southern Italian kitchen and is, to my mind, one of the genius dishes of Naples (spaghetti and clam sauce is another). We always bought these huge, thick pies from a baker in Glen Cove for Easter, but no one in my family ever made it at home, I suppose because it was so elaborate. When I started making it myself, I was actually surprised by how easy it is to put together. I have simplified the usually more complicated recipe, using an olive-oil dough instead of the richer *pasta frolla* (short pastry); it's the same dough I use for *pizza di scarola*, but with a little sugar and cinnamon added, which is customary. I've cut the ingredients into daintier bits, which makes it easier to slice.

Note: *Pizza rustica* is often baked in a high springform pan, but I prefer a 9-inch American pie pan, which gives it less height and makes more delicate slices.

MY PIZZA RUSTICA

CRUST

2 cups all-purpose flour
Generous pinch of salt
Generous pinch of sugar
Pinch of ground cinnamon
1 large egg
¼ cup dry white wine
¼ cup extra-virgin olive oil

FILLING

15 ounces whole-milk ricotta (sheep's milk is best), drained
2 large eggs, beaten

4 thin slices capocollo, cut into small squares
4 thin slices prosciutto di Parma, finely chopped
½ cup finely chopped caciocavallo cheese
Small handful of fresh flat-leaf parsley leaves, chopped
3 or 4 scrapings freshly grated nutmeg
Pinch of ground cloves
Salt and freshly ground black pepper to taste

1 egg, beaten

TO MAKE THE CRUST: Put the flour in a medium bowl and stir in the salt, sugar, and cinnamon. In a small bowl, beat the egg, white wine, and olive oil together. Pour this over the flour, mixing it in with a fork until uniformly moist. Place the dough on a floured work surface and knead it briefly, pressing it together with your hands to form a ball. Cut the dough into 2 pieces, one a little larger than the other. Wrap the pieces in plastic wrap and refrigerate for about 1 hour.

Preheat the oven to 350°F.

In a large bowl, mix together all the ingredients for the filling.

On a lightly floured work surface, roll out each dough ball, one into an 11-inch round, the other about 8 inches. Fit the larger round into the pie plate and trim the edges so you have an even 1-inch hang all around. Add the filling and distribute it evenly. Place the other round over the filling. Fold the overhang up over the top of the pie, making little pleats all around to seal it. Cut 4 short slashes into the top of the pie in a star pattern (you can just poke in some air vents, but the star pattern is traditional). Brush the top lightly with the beaten egg and bake for about 1 hour, or until golden and puffy (it will settle as it cools). Let cool to room temperature before cutting it into wedges.

VARIATION   Other cheeses, such as provolone, Parmigiano, or mozzarella, are sometimes added, either alone or in pairs. You can omit the prosciutto and add prosciutto cotto (cooked ham), or add chopped soppressata instead of the capocollo.

PIZZA NEAPOLITAN STYLE

I HAVE A RECURRING DREAM in which I'm somewhere in Manhattan looking for a very special pizza place. It's around a bend leading to a cove that doesn't exist in New York, but I go down through a subway tunnel and I know I've found it when at the end of the tunnel I see a spot of sunlight on very blue ocean water. I'm no longer at the tip of Manhattan but somewhere in southern Italy, probably around Amalfi. The restaurant is long and narrow, like a subway car, and they make pizza topped with ricotta, my favorite kind. When I try to order one, I'm told by the chef that I need to prove myself worthy of eating it. Before I can ask what my task is to be, I wake up. It's a kind of Wizard of Oz dream for the food obsessed.

In my waking hours, I know of several very good pizza restaurants in New York where, in true Neapolitan style, the crust is not cracker thin and the toppings are spare but flavorful, all quick cooked in a very hot wood-burning oven. It took me many years to realize that making pizzas at home could be worth the effort, and when I finally did try it, my attempts gave me more aggravation than pleasure until I figured out a few things.

First of all, having a pizza stone and a peel (a big wooden pizza paddle) really does help. The aim is to bake the dough quickly at high heat so the outside is crisp and the inside remains just slightly soft and pully, the texture of a good Neapolitan pizza. The pizza stone helps you achieve this by mimicking the floor heat of a wood-burning oven. The stone will not give you the smoky taste of the wood-burning oven, but it will give the crust a good crisp bottom, which is essential for the crust's texture. The first few times I used a stone and a peel I had a hard time getting the pizza off the peel and onto the stone without shooting half the topping onto the oven floor or folding the dough. But I've discovered that sprinkling polenta or any semicoarse cornmeal on the peel helps immensely, actually making the process just about effortless (and giving the crust a nice flavor, too). I used to use regular white flour for this, but it soaks up moisture very quickly, and unless you work speedily, the pizza starts to stick.

If there is one trick to producing a good pizza at home it is making sure you don't over-load the top, especially with wet ingredients like tomato sauce. Make sure your tomatoes are well drained. And once you have your pizza on the peel, work fairly fast to get the toppings on so the dough doesn't start to stick to the peel and get hard to slip off onto the stone (even with cornmeal, this can happen). Also, try not to get any of the ingredients too close to the edge of the dough; if they slip off onto the peel they can make sliding the pizza into the oven more difficult. If you have a pizza stone, you can roll your dough out very thin; if you don't use one and make your pizza on a baking sheet, it's better to roll your dough a little thicker. Otherwise, the slower cooking time will overbake the crust, turning it hard and crackerlike.

Southern Italians have this weird idea that beer is the perfect thing to drink with pizza. This is a custom that seems to be building momentum throughout Italy. To me, this starch-on-starch match is not appealing, and if you're the type of person (like I am) who gets full from one beer, don't even try going along with the crowd. I prefer a glass of wine. A slightly acidy red is wonderful with any pizza that's topped with salami or sausage (I love Nero d'Avolo wines from Sicily with rich, meaty pizzas). For a seafood-topped pie, in my opinion, nothing beats a dry rosé (try a bottle of Regaleali's rosato).

There are many classic Neapolitan pizza toppings, like the famous Margherita, with tomatoes, mozzarella, and basil, but the ones I've chosen are either unusual ones I've been served in southern Italy or, more often, my own southern Italian–style inventions.

MAKES ENOUGH FOR TWO TWELVE-INCH PIZZAS.

PIZZA DOUGH

1 cup warm water (110°F)	Generous pinch of salt
1 tablespoon extra-virgin olive oil	2$\frac{1}{2}$ cups all-purpose flour
1 package active dry yeast	

Pour the warm water and olive oil into a large bowl. Sprinkle the yeast and the salt over the water and give it a good stir. Let stand for about 5 minutes to give the yeast a chance to develop. Add 1 cup of the flour and stir well. Mix in 1 more cup of the flour to form a sticky ball.

Transfer the dough out to a well-floured surface, leaving behind any crumbly bits of flour that have not been incorporated. Knead the dough until smooth and elastic, about 5 minutes, adding 1 tablespoon more flour at a time if needed to keep the dough from sticking. The dough will be quite soft and tender. Transfer the dough to a lightly oiled bowl, turn to coat the dough, and cover the bowl with a damp kitchen towel. Let the dough rise in a warm place until doubled in size, about 1 hour.

Punch the dough down and divide it into 2 pieces. Form each into a ball. Transfer the dough to a floured work surface and let rise for about 15 minutes.

MAKES TWO 12-INCH PIZZAS. Bottarga, the pressed tuna roe of Sicily (or the Sardinian version made with gray-mullet roe), makes a nice change from the more usual anchovy-topped pizza. Bottarga's taste is a bit more complex than that of anchovies, and paired with the sweet tang of buffalo mozzarella it makes a simple but sophisticated pizza. I sometimes serve it cut into thin wedges as a stand-up antipasto offering.

I use an uncooked sauce made with drained canned tomatoes as a base for many of my pizza recipes. The sauce flash-cooks on the pizza and stays bright and fresh tasting.

PIZZA WITH BUFFALO MOZZARELLA, TOMATOES, AND BOTTARGA

RAW TOMATO SAUCE FOR PIZZA

One 35-ounce can Italian plum tomatoes, finely chopped and well drained

2 tablespoons extra-virgin olive oil

1 garlic clove, very thinly sliced

Salt and freshly ground black pepper to taste

Leaves from 3 or 4 large marjoram sprigs, chopped

1 recipe Pizza Dough (page 228)

1 pound buffalo mozzarella cheese, cut into thin slices

Freshly ground black pepper to taste

Extra-virgin olive oil for drizzling

About 20 scrapings of bottarga (see page 32)

Large handful of fresh flat-leaf parsley leaves

TO MAKE THE TOMATO SAUCE: Pour the drained, chopped tomatoes into a medium bowl; add the olive oil, garlic, salt, pepper, and marjoram. Stir to blend. You can make this 1 day ahead and refrigerate it, but let it return to room temperature before using.

Place the pizza stone in the oven on a middle rack and preheat the oven to 500°F. Let heat for at least 20 minutes.

On a floured work surface, roll out one of the dough balls to a 12-inch round. Sprinkle some cornmeal on your pizza peel or a baking sheet and slip the dough onto it.

Working rather quickly, ladle about half of the tomato sauce onto the dough to make a thin coating with a 1-inch border all around. Add about half of the mozzarella slices, season with pepper (no salt, since you'll be adding bottarga), and drizzle with olive oil. Slide the pizza onto the pizza stone and bake until the crust is browned and the cheese is bubbling, 10 to 14 minutes.

Slip the peel under the pizza and remove it from the oven. Cut about 10 shavings of bottarga onto the pizza with a sharp vegetable peeler. Scatter on the parsley leaves and serve right away. Make a second pizza using the remaining ingredients.

MAKES TWO 12-INCH PIZZAS. This is a pizza I sampled in a somewhat fancy outdoor restaurant in Palermo several years ago. I was famished when it arrived at my table, but even on a full stomach it would have been just about my all-time favorite pizza. The creaminess of the cheese, the sweetness of the zucchini blossoms, and the salty anchovies are my idea of a perfect blending of flavors. When zucchini blossoms are out of season, top it instead with little rounds of zucchini that have been sautéed in olive oil until tender.

PIZZA WITH MOZZARELLA, ZUCCHINI BLOSSOMS, AND ANCHOVIES

1 recipe Pizza Dough (page 288)
1 recipe Raw Tomato Sauce for Pizza (page 289)
1 red onion, very thinly sliced
1 pound mozzarella, cut into thin slices

About 16 zucchini blossoms, wiped cleaned, pistils removed (see page 93)
12 oil-packed anchovy fillets
Extra-virgin olive oil for drizzling
Freshly ground black pepper to taste

Place the pizza stone in the oven on a middle rack and preheat the oven to 500°F. Let it heat for at least 20 minutes.

On a floured surface, roll out one of the dough balls to a 12-inch round. Sprinkle some cornmeal on your pizza peel or a baking sheet and slip the dough onto it.

Working quickly, ladle on a thin layer of tomato sauce and scatter on half of the red onion. Place half of the mozzarella on top and then arrange half of the zucchini blossoms and the anchovies in a more or less even pattern around the pizza. Drizzle with olive oil and give it a few grindings of pepper. Slide the pizza onto the pizza stone and bake for 10 to 14 minutes. Make a second pizza using the remaining ingredients.

MAKES TWO 12-INCH PIZZAS. The marriage of ricotta and roasted peppers is a taste that goes back to my childhood. It is a perfect topping for pizza, with the sweetness and creaminess of the ricotta balancing out the sweetness and sharpness of the peppers. I love rosemary with roasted peppers, too. It seems to extend their smokiness.

PIZZA WITH RICOTTA, ROSEMARY, AND ROASTED PEPPERS

1 recipe Pizza Dough (page 288)

1 recipe Raw Tomato Sauce for Pizza (page 289)

2 garlic cloves, thinly sliced

3 red bell peppers, roasted, peeled, cut into thin strips (see page 38)

1 cup whole-milk ricotta, drained if watery

Leaves from 3 or 4 rosemary sprigs, chopped

$1/2$ cup grated caciocavallo cheese

Extra-virgin olive oil for drizzling

Salt and freshly ground black pepper to taste

Place the pizza stone in the oven on a middle rack and preheat the oven to 500°F. Let it heat for at least 20 minutes.

On a floured surface, roll out one of the dough balls to a 12-inch round. Sprinkle some cornmeal on your pizza peel or on a baking sheet and slip the dough onto it.

Ladle a thin layer of tomato sauce onto the dough. Scatter on half of the garlic and arrange half of the roasted peppers on top. Dot with dollops of half of the ricotta. Sprinkle with half of the rosemary and the caciocavallo. Drizzle with olive oil and season lightly with salt and more generously with pepper. Slide the pizza onto the pizza stone and bake for 10 to 14 minutes. Make a second pizza using the remaining ingredients.

Makes two 12-inch pizzas. A popular pizza topping throughout southern Italy blends escarole, olives, and capers. I've sampled variations on this in Calabria and in Naples. Here, I take inspiration from the topping, but I've softened the flavors by adding a few eggs that cook gently on top of the pizza in the final minutes.

PIZZA WITH ESCAROLE, FONTINA, AND BAKED EGGS

Leaves from 1 large head escarole, cut into bite-sized pieces

2 garlic cloves, thinly sliced

Extra-virgin olive oil for drizzling

Salt and freshly ground black pepper to taste

1 recipe Pizza Dough (page 288)

12 ounces fontina Valle d'Aosta, thinly sliced

Leaves from 3 or 4 marjoram sprigs, chopped

Handful of black olives, pitted and cut in half

6 large eggs

In a large pot of boiling water, blanch the escarole for about 4 minutes. Pour it into a colander and run cold water over it to preserve the green color. Drain very well, squeezing the excess water out with your hands. In a medium bowl, combine the escarole, garlic, a generous drizzle of olive oil, salt, and pepper. Mix well.

Place the pizza stone in the oven on a middle rack and preheat the oven to 500°F. Let it heat for at least 20 minutes.

On a floured surface, roll out one of the dough balls to a 12-inch round. Sprinkle some cornmeal on your pizza peel or on a baking sheet and slip the dough onto it.

Top the dough with a layer of half the fontina. Arrange half of the escarole on top. Scatter on half of the marjoram and black olives. Give it a drizzle of olive oil and slide the pizza onto a pizza stone. Bake for about 8 minutes. Slide out the oven rack and break 3 of the eggs more or less evenly spaced on top of the pizza. Put the pizza back in the oven and continue baking until the egg whites are firm but the yokes are still soft, 5 or 6 minutes. Make a second pizza with the remaining ingredients.

MAKES TWO 12-INCH PIZZAS. Ravello is a serene and beautiful town above the Amalfi Coast. When I arrived recently one night at 10:30 P.M., starving, I found nothing open until I noticed Netta Bottone's little restaurant Cumpa Cosimo just shutting the doors. I had eaten there years before, falling in love with her pesto and on another occasion her light-as-air ricotta-filled *crespelle*. When she noticed me standing around with a longing look, she cheerfully invited me in for something very quick, preferably a pizza. I ordered a pizza *frutta di mare*, not even asking what kind of seafood was on it (it was shrimp, calamari, and little shelled clams). When it came to the table, I noticed that she had cooked the pizza with tomato and herbs, then taken it from the oven and scattered on a cool, antipastolike seafood salad mixed with wild arugula—an excellent marriage of hot and cool, crisp and tender.

I don't often find spiky wild arugula in New York (occasionally at my greenmarket, but I can't count on it), but the big milder leaves we routinely find here are fine. This is an all-shrimp version of my Ravello pizza.

PIZZA WITH SHRIMP, ARUGULA, AND CAPERS

2 tablespoons extra-virgin olive oil, plus more for drizzling

1 pound of medium shrimp, shelled

1 garlic clove, thinly sliced

Salt and freshly ground black pepper to taste

1 tablespoon Pernod or another pastis

Handful of salt-packed capers, soaked and drained (see page 29)

1 recipe Pizza Dough (page 288)

1 recipe Raw Tomato Sauce for Pizza (page 289)

Handful of arugula leaves, stemmed and lightly chopped

In a large skillet, heat the olive oil over high heat. Add the shrimp and the garlic, season with salt and pepper, and sauté until the shrimp are evenly pink, 2 or 3 minutes. Add the Pernod or other pastis and let it boil away. Add the capers. Let this sit and come to room temperature while you continue with the pizza.

Place the pizza stone in the oven and preheat the oven to 500°F. Let it heat for at least 20 minutes.

On a floured surface, roll out one of the dough balls to a 12-inch round. Sprinkle some cornmeal on your pizza peel or a baking sheet and slip the dough onto it.

Top the dough with an even coating of tomato sauce, leaving a 1-inch border all around, and drizzle with olive oil. Slide the pizza onto the pizza stone and bake for 10 to 14 minutes.

Take the pizza from the oven and top it with half of the shrimp and then half of the arugula. Give it another drizzle of fresh olive oil and a pinch of salt and a few grindings of fresh black pepper. Make a second pizza using the remaining ingredients.

MAKES TWO 12-INCH PIZZAS. Here's a pizza with a fairly traditional taste that's a bit lighter in spirit due to the sliced tomatoes and touch of thyme, which goes extremely well with capocollo or other cured pork (you can use soppressata if it's very thinly sliced).

PIZZA WITH CAPOCOLLO, FRESH TOMATOES, AND THYME

1 recipe Pizza Dough (page 288)
1 pound mozarella, sliced
12 ripe plum tomatoes, thinly sliced
2 garlic cloves, very thinly sliced
Pinch of salt
4 ounces very thinly sliced capocollo, cut into thin strips

Leaves from 5 or 6 large thyme sprigs, chopped
Extra-virgin olive oil for drizzling
$\frac{1}{2}$ cup grated pecorino cheese
Freshly ground black pepper to taste

Place the pizza stone in the oven and preheat the oven to 500°F. Let it heat for at least 20 minutes.

On a floured surface, roll out one of the dough balls to a 12-inch round. Sprinkle some cornmeal on your pizza peel or a baking sheet and slip the dough onto it.

Make a layer of mozzarella on the dough, using half of it. Lay half of the sliced plum tomatoes out on top in a circular but not overlapping pattern. Scatter on half of the garlic and season the tomatoes with a little salt. Top with a layer of half the capocolla. Sprinkle with half the thyme and drizzle with olive oil. Sprinkle on half the pecorino and give it a few grindings of pepper. Slide the pizza onto the pizza stone and bake for 10 to 14 minutes. Make a second pizza using the remaining ingredients.

CALZONE

THE CALZONE, in Naples sometimes called *pizza ripiena* (stuffed pizza), is a pizza turned inside out, a sturdy shape that can hold ample luscious fillings. Its construction gives you leeway you don't have with pizzas. You can overload it, with no ill effects.

Yeast-dough-filled pockets are made in many regions of southern Italy. In Puglia, a calzone is fashioned like a double-crusted, filled round pizza. *Scaccia*, short for foccacia, is Sicily's version, stuffed, depending on the region, with pork sausage or lamb or a mix of cheese and anchovies or, on Christmas Eve, salt cod and olives—and many more local and personal renditions turn up all over the island. I've patterned my calzone recipes on the Neapolitan style, where you simply roll out pizza dough, fill it to your liking, and fold it over into a big half-moon shape. Since I have a pizza stone, I generally bake calzones on it to get a crisp crust, but it's not absolutely necessary. You can get good results by preheating your oven to its highest temperature and baking the calzone on a baking sheet.

The most well-known Neapolitan filling consists of *prosciutto cotto* (cooked ham) and ricotta, but endless variations are possible. My favorite calzones usually contain ricotta. I also love mozzarella in the filling, for its stringiness, and fresh goat cheese if I want a little tang. Cheese can be mixed with vegetables or meat to form a tasty filling. Tomatoes are usually not included in Neapolitan calzones, possibly because they don't have enough body to stay put. Sicilian calzones often include tomatoes, usually mixed in with meat or fish. I like some tomato in a calzone, but I try to make sure it's well enough drained not to make the dough soggy. The main thing when you're improvising a filling is to remember that it must have body. Anything too liquid will ooze out during cooking and also make the dough limp. So make sure your filling has some density.

Always taste the filling before putting it into the calzone. Anything encased in dough will be somewhat muffled by the breadiness, so give your filling a final check for salt and pepper, and if you've added a fresh herb, make sure you can taste it (you won't be able to tinker with the seasoning once the calzone is folded over and sealed).

Calzones are considered snack food in southern Italy, but for me they're a perfect full meal, maybe followed by a green salad. They're best served hot from the oven and cut with a serrated knife so you can divide them without squishing them too much.

For the following recipes, I suggest cutting the dough in half to make 2 large calzones, but you can make 4 smaller single-serving ones if you prefer.

MAKES TWO CALZONES. Eggplant and mozzarella is a great flavor combination that is used often to sauce pasta in Naples and in Sicily. The creamy, mild cheese mellows the eggplant's sharp edge, producing one of the classic tastes of the southern Italian kitchen. Walnuts, with their subtle bitterness, are a good complement to eggplant, and their crunch breaks up all the soft textures.

CALZONE WITH EGGPLANT, WALNUTS, AND MOZZARELLA

2 tablespoons extra-virgin olive oil, plus more for brushing

2 unpeeled eggplants, cut into $1/2$-inch dice

2 garlic cloves, thinly sliced

Salt and freshly ground black pepper to taste

4 plum tomatoes, seeded and diced

Handful of walnuts, lightly toasted (page 29) and chopped

3 or 4 small sprigs of marjoram, leaves chopped

1 recipe Pizza Dough (page 288)

1 pound fresh mozzarella, cut into $1/2$-inch dice

4 tablespoons grated pecorino cheese

Leaves from 3 or 4 large flat-leaf Italian parsley sprigs, chopped

Place a pizza stone in the oven, if you're using one. Preheat the oven to 500°F.

In a large skillet, heat the olive oil over medium heat. Add the eggplant and garlic, season with salt and pepper, and sauté until tender, 6 or 7 minutes. Add the tomatoes and cook for 3 minutes, or just until they soften. The mixture should be thick. If the tomatoes gave off a lot of juice, cook them a little longer to evaporate it (otherwise, it might run out of the calzones while they're baking). Add the walnuts and the marjoram and stir them in. Remove from the heat and let cool for a few minutes.

On a floured work surface, roll one of the dough balls out to an 11-inch round about $1/8$ inch thick.

Sprinkle a pizza peel or a baking sheet with cornmeal and slide the dough onto it. Scatter half of the mozzarella on one side of the round, leaving a 1-inch margin. Spoon on half of the eggplant. Sprinkle with half of the pecorino and half of the parsley.

Fold the dough over to form a half-moon shape and pinch the edges together, making little tucks to close it well. Poke a few tiny holes in the top to let out steam. Brush the top lightly with olive oil.

Slide the calzone onto the pizza stone and bake for about 18 minutes, or until golden. Serve hot. Make another calzone exactly the same way.

M**AKES TWO CALZONES**. Broccoli rabe flavored with olives, chilies, and anchovies is a traditional preparation in Puglia, and here I've taken those bold flavors to fill a calzone. It's a great choice for vegetarians who will tolerate a little anchovy (or, just don't tell them). I once brought a piece of a broccoli rabe calzone I had just made out to a knife sharpener who had stopped by in his truck and was working on my knives. He was from Mola di Bari in Puglia and had firm opinions about food. I had flavored this calzone with soppressata. He said it was good, but that a broccoli rabe calzone was not really right without anchovy. Just a touch, but it makes all the difference, he said. I realize now that he's absolutely correct. There's just something missing without it.

CALZONE WITH BROCCOLI RABE AND CHILIES

1 large bunch broccoli rabe, tough stems removed

2 tablespoons extra-virgin olive oil

3 garlic cloves, thinly sliced

½ of a fresh jalapeño chili, minced (using some or all of the seeds, depending on how much heat you like)

4 oil-packed anchovy fillets, chopped

1 tablespoon dry vermouth

Handful of black olives, pitted and roughly chopped

1 cup ricotta (whole milk is best), drained if watery

Pinch of salt, if needed

1 recipe Pizza Dough (page 288)

In a large pot of boiling water, blanch the broccoli rabe for about 4 minutes. Empty it into a colander and run cold water over it to bring up its green color. Squeeze as much water as you can from the broccoli rabe with your hands.

In a large skillet, heat the olive oil over medium heat. Add the broccoli rabe, garlic, chili, and anchovies at the same time. Sauté for 2 or 3 minutes to infuse the broccoli rabe with all the flavors. Add vermouth and let it boil away. Remove from the heat and let cool for about 5 minutes. Add the olives and ricotta to the broccoli rabe mixture and stir gently, adding the salt, if needed (if the anchovies are very salty, you probably won't).

Place a pizza stone in the oven, if you're using one. Preheat the oven to 500°F.

On a floured work surface, roll one of the dough balls out to an 11-inch round, making it a little thicker than for pizza dough.

Sprinkle a pizza peel or a baking sheet with cornmeal and slide the dough onto it. Spoon half of the broccoli rabe filling one side of the round. Fold the dough over to form a half-moon shape and pinch the edges together, making little tucks to close it well. Poke a few little holes in the top to let out steam. Brush the top lightly with olive oil.

Slide the calzone onto the pizza stone and bake for about 18 minutes, or until golden. Serve hot or warm. Make another calzone exactly the same way.

Makes two calzones. This recipe solves the problem of runny tomato fillings by roasting the tomatoes quickly in a hot oven, intensifying their flavor and concentrating some of their juices.

CALZONE WITH QUICK-ROASTED TOMATOES AND LAMB SAUSAGE

Two 35-ounce cans plum tomatoes, well drained

Extra-virgin olive oil for drizzling, plus 2 tablespoons

Salt and freshly ground black pepper to taste

2 garlic cloves, very thinly sliced

1 pound lamb sausage, preferably Merguez sausage

2 tablespoons dry red wine

1 recipe Pizza Dough (page 288)

1½ cups whole-milk ricotta, drained

½ cup grated caciocavallo cheese

Handful of fresh mint leaves, chopped

Preheat the oven to 450°F.

Cut the drained tomatoes in half lengthwise and lay them out on a baking sheet. Drizzle with olive oil and season with salt and pepper. Toss the tomatoes around with your hands until the seasonings are well distributed. Roast until they're just starting to brown at the edges, 20 to 30 minutes (depending on how much liquid they give off). In the last few minutes of roasting, scatter the sliced garlic over the tomatoes (if you add it earlier it might burn).

In a large skillet, heat the 2 tablespoons of olive oil over medium-high heat. Add the sausage and brown it well on all sides. Add the red wine, cover, reduce the heat to low, and cook for 1 or 2 minutes, just until the sausages are cooked through. Transfer the sausages to a cutting board and slice them into thin rounds.

Place a pizza stone in the oven, if you're using one. Preheat the oven to 500°F.

On a floured work surface, roll one of the dough balls out to an 11-inch round, making it a little thicker than for pizza dough.

Sprinkle a pizza peel or a baking sheet with cornmeal and slide the dough onto it. Spoon half of the roasted tomatoes on one half of the dough, leaving a 1-inch margin. Top with half of the sausage slices, half the ricotta, half the caciocavallo, and half the chopped mint.

Slide the calzone onto the pizza stone and bake for about 18 minutes, or until golden. Serve hot or warm. Make another calzone exactly the same way. Fold the dough over to form a half-moon shape and pinch edges together, making little tucks to close it well. Poke a few holes in the top to let out steam. Brush the top lightly with olive oil.

VARIATION   If you leave out the sausage and include a little extra ricotta, you've got a nicely flavored vegetarian calzone.

Makes two calzones. Prosciutto cotto (cooked ham) is used more than regular prosciutto in calzone fillings, because the latter can get rubbery when cooked. Ricotta and prosciutto cotto is a classic Neapolitan calzone filling. It's usually left quite simple, but I've elaborated on it by adding a generous amount of clove-scented sautéed leeks, whose sweetness blends nicely with the saltiness of the ham.

CALZONE WITH LEEKS AND PROSCIUTTO COTTO

2 tablespoons extra-virgin olive oil

5 leeks, including light green parts, rinsed and thinly sliced

Pinch of sugar

Pinch of ground cloves

1 bay leaf

Salt and freshly ground black pepper to taste

4 ounces prosciutto cotto, thinly sliced (cooked Parma ham is now available in this country and that would be my first choice for this, but any high-quality unsmoked cooked ham is fine)

2 cups whole-milk ricotta, drained for 15 minutes

1 tablespoon grated grana padano cheese

Handful of fresh flat-leaf parsley leaves, chopped

1 recipe Pizza Dough (page 288)

In a large skillet, heat the olive oil over medium heat. Add the leeks, sugar, cloves, bay leaf, salt, and pepper. Sauté until the leeks are just starting to turn very lightly golden, about 10 minutes. Remove from the heat and let cool for about 5 minutes.

In a medium bowl, combine the prosciutto cotto, ricotta, grana padano, and parsley. Season it with pepper to taste (due to the saltiness of the ham, you shouldn't need extra salt here).

Place a pizza stone in the oven, if you're using one. Preheat the oven to 500°F.

On a floured work surface, roll one of the dough balls out to an 11-inch round, making it a little thicker than for pizza dough.

Sprinkle a pizza peel or a baking sheet with cornmeal and slide the dough onto it. Spoon half of the ricotta mixture on one half of the dough, leaving a 1-inch margin. Top with half of the leeks. Fold the dough over to form a half-moon shape and pinch the edges together, making little tucks to close it well. Poke a few holes in the top to let out steam. Brush the top lightly with olive oil.

Slide the calzone onto the pizza stone and bake for about 18 minutes, or until golden. Serve hot or warm. Make another calzone exactly the same way.

BREAD AND BREAD CRUMBS IN THE SOUTHERN ITALIAN KITCHEN

I went through a period of manic bread baking when I was a teenager, and it left me not loving to bake bread, because, I think, the baking had been more driven than fun (driven toward what, I'm not sure). I am left with a slight fear that if I start baking bread again I may get carried away again. Luckily, living in New York, I've always been able to buy very good southern Italian–style bread. The bread I get at the ten-year-old Sullivan Street Bakery in SoHo, not too far from my home, is as good as, and in some cases better than, bread I've eaten in Campania or Sicily. It has a hard crust that flakes all over my dinner plate, and its yeasty interior is filled with little air holes that catch sauce. It tastes like the huge, round hard-crusted Italian bread of my childhood, full of air pockets, that was made on Arthur Avenue in the Bronx by Addeo Bakery (which is still in business, and still making the same bread).

I've eaten golden, crusty bread in a town world famous for it, Altamura, in Puglia. They make it with semolina, the same hard-wheat flour used to make orecchietti. It has a different taste from the Neapolitan-style Arthur Avenue bread I grew up with, which is made from soft-wheat flour. Most of the semolina bread I find here is too cakelike and is covered with sesame seeds, a Sicilian custom that is only appealing if the seeds are really fresh. Bread in New York labeled *pane pugliese* can be excellent (Sullivan Street Bakery makes one), but it's not quite like what I've had in Puglia. I wonder if this has something to do with the water. I've tried to make real Puglian bread from recipes in a few cookbooks I've brought back with me, and it hasn't been the same. The Puglian loaves are cooked in wood-burning ovens by people who do it for a living and presumably love what they do. The taste is hard to duplicate, even with imported semolina flour and the use of a pizza stone. Moreover, baking bread is one culinary pursuit that doesn't give immediate pleasure. You need the desire to repeat it over and over again until you've found your way.

The alternative, of course, is to search out good bread in America to go with home-made southern Italian food. The key is to look for a substantial, crisp, flaky crust, an airy, somewhat dry interior that can soak up sauce, and a deep, slightly yeasty bread smell. If you can't find that in an Italian bread, one labeled "French country loaf" or some such thing can be close in flavor, as long as it has a yeasty smell and a crisp crust. In my opinion, sour-dough bread, no matter how lovingly made, doesn't taste exactly right with southern Italian food. It doesn't blend naturally with tomato sauce and it clashes with olive oil, so save it for another cuisine. Also, try to avoid those long supermarket Italian loaves with the smooth, uniform crusts and cottony insides. I know that's not always possible. When I travel to upstate New York on vacation, they're all I can find. I believe they're the reason Italian Americans invented the klutzy, overloaded garlic bread offered at old-fashioned red-sauce restaurants: It was a desperate attempt to get some taste out of something bland. When I'm stuck with a boring supermarket loaf, I usually split it lengthwise and toast or grill it, then brush it lightly with good olive oil and give it a pinch of salt. It's not perfect, but it improves the texture and imparts a bit of flavor.

I tried mailing addeo bread to my father when he moved down to Florida and complained he couldn't find decent bread anywhere, but it arrived too hard. Good Italian bread should be purchased the day you'll eat it. My mother always freezes leftover bread; I was skeptical at first, but it does defrost with a decent texture. Zingerman's mail-order company carries a domestically made Sicilian-style semolina bread and a *pane pugliese* that are pretty good, and when I sent them, along with some pecorino, down to my father, they arrived fresh (check Sources for their address). But, I have to say, most bakers are not willing to mail order and I'm sure it's because they can't guarantee the freshness.

Friselle is another kind of bread baked in southern Italian kitchens, particularly in Puglia and Campania, but in Calabria and Basilicata too. It's hard through and crumbly, a twice-baked round that looks like a split, flattened bagel, sometimes made from whole wheat, sometimes from semolina flour. It's served drizzled with olive oil and water and topped with chopped tomatoes or olive oil–packed tuna, or sometimes cracked into pieces and tossed with tomatoes, onions, and olives in a summer bread salad. My grandmother used to drop a *friselle* into a soup bowl and pour the hot soup over it. I remember it being called *chianetta* at some bakeries in the Bronx, and to confuse matters, there was also a pillow-shaped hard biscuit made with lard and coarse black pepper that we also called *friselle*. My mother served that one as an accompaniment to *zuppa di pesce,* and often kept it in the kitchen for snacking. It left a a greasy slick on your tongue, which went very well with acidy white-wine-and-tomato-steeped seafood, but on its own it seemed kind of heavy. I can still find it at Addeo Bakery in the Bronx, but I don't think it fits in naturally with many of my updated southern Italian dishes, so I hardly ever buy it.

Taralli, stiff little mini-pretzel-size rings made with olive oil and wine, are my favorite hard bread. They were the first thing I was served when I went to lunch at my grandmother's cousin's house in Campolattaro, Campania. I was used to the packaged ones we'd had at home, but the ones he served were saltier, oilier, and had a more fragile, shattering quality. He told me he bought his from a woman in the neighborhood who made them with fennel seeds, white wine, and local olive oil. He served them to me with a bowl of green olives and a glass of sharp, very cloudy white wine that he had made himself (which actually tasted like watered-down nail polish remover). The *taralli* from my childhood were made on Arthur Avenue in the Bronx. They were okay, but not great. Luckily, imported *taralli* are now easy to find. I especially like the ones made by Ciro Federico in Puglia, which are available through esperya.com, an excellent Italian food website (see page 436 for their address). Some supermarkets sell a brand called Puglia Sapori, from Bari. They're also very good and are available in sun-dried tomato, rosemary, fennel seed, and chili varieties.

Dry bread crumbs, usually called *pangrattato* in Italy, are a very important ingredient in the southern Italian kitchen. They both impart texture and are used as a flavoring, sometimes sprinkled onto pasta dishes where cheese is considered inappropriate (mainly those using fish sauces and some sauces containing chilies).

Moist bread crumbs are called *mollica* in Italy. They're made with the white inside of fresher bread and added to meatballs and *involtini* fillings to stretch the meat, and to some sauces as a thickener. I don't use them as much as cooks in southern Italy do; they can sometimes impart a mushy texture. I find myself using dry bread crumbs more often, sometimes softened in a little water or wine.

MAKING DRY BREAD CRUMBS   Use day-old crusty Italian bread. If the inside is still moist, rip it into chunks and put them in a low oven until they're nice and dry. Pulse the chunks in a food processor to make not-too-fine dried crumbs. (The bread crumbs you buy in cans not only taste like cardboard but are too finely ground and can turn to mush. Stale bread makes stale-tasting bread crumbs, so never use bread that's more than a few days old. Ground *taralli*, by the way, make excellent dry bread crumbs. Just throw a few in the food processor and pulse them a few times until they're reduced to a not-too-fine crumb.)

MAKING SAUTÉED BREAD CRUMBS   Lightly sauté dried bread crumbs with olive oil in a skillet until they're crisp and flavorful for sprinkling over pastas, sometimes I add flavoring such as garlic or herbs or a pinch of chili, depending on the pasta dish. You can crisp up bread crumbs by toasting them briefly in a low oven, but I find that sautéing really brings out their flavor.

SOUPS

I love the big meal-in-a-bowl soups that are popular in Southern Italy for everyday eating. These thick vegetable *minestre* can include beans, greens, sausage, little tubes of pasta, potatoes, or wheat berries, among other things. *Zuppa* is another word for such a soup, one my family used when a big piece of toasted bread was placed in the middle of a bowl and a substantial soup was poured over it.

A *minestra* or *zuppa* can contain just about anything, but the southern Italian philosophy for choosing ingredients relies on a good marriage of flavors and steers away from clutter. A kitchen-sink approach is not part of the thinking. It's easy for soups always to taste pretty much the same (the way they often do at health-food restaurants), and I think that's because of people's tendency to throw in everything. I've learned to resist the temptation. Even minestrone, a slow-simmered soup containing a large assortment of vegetables, a pasta, and sometimes beans as well, should be prepared with rhyme and reason. I always try to use discretion and streamline my soup ingredients by highlighting one or two seasonal vegetables and including only one or two herbs, or, in the case of a minestrone, using vegetables that provide a good mix of textures, flavors, and even sometimes a color theme, just for visual pleasure. *Minestra maritata* is a classic southern Italian creation that my grandmother often made that marries several greens and is always flavored with a small amount of meat, usually pork. It doesn't contain any type of pasta, unlike most southern Italian "big soups." The greens, generally a mix of two or three, can be cabbage, escarole, dandelions, chicory, fennel greens, or an assortment of local or wild foraged greens (not so easy to come by here). My grandmother made her soup with dandelions (she picked them from local golf courses in Westchester), escarole, and sausage. The dandelion and baby meatball soup (see page 326), is inspired by the memory of this.

Big main-course soups traditionally tend to be water based; they get so much flavor from their myriad ingredients that they don't need meat broth, which was traditionally expensive for most southern Italians. Poverty aside, a meat or rich chicken broth can detract from a pure vegetable flavor, and you don't want to do that if you have seasonal produce to show off. You'll get a less complex but more direct taste with water. I have to admit I use broth more than tradition dictates in many of my big soups, but it's usually a very light broth, and I often dilute it with water (bouillon cubes are popular with home cooks throughout southern Italy, but I find their use to be a low point in the country's culinary thinking). Olive oil, on the other hand, plays a big part in flavoring southern Italian soups. I'll use a generous amount of estate oil to drizzle into a soup just before serving, not only because the oil adds flavor, but because it carries flavors, bringing herbs, a touch of garlic, or that little squeeze of lemon juice to the forefront. I always reseason all my soups with a pinch of fresh salt right before serving. It not only heightens the overall flavor but also makes individual flavors more distinct.

Delicate, brothy first-course soups that are often served on fancy occasions like weddings are the other side of soup making in southern Italy. Great care is taken to form the tiniest meatballs, finely chop spinach, make fresh egg pasta, julienne a frittata, or slice wild mushrooms and gently warm them in a homemade chicken or light meat broth. I really love this type of soup, but I must be a lightweight eater, for whenever I'm served soup as a first course, no matter how delicate, I can only pick at the main course that follows. This is a phenomenon my grandmother understood, but she insisted the fault lay in the American habit of eating hot brothy soups with cold beverages, like 7-Up or Coke. Cold drinks were banned from her table when she served a broth-based soup; she thought the hot and cold liquids would go into battle in your stomach, giving you painful cramps or, worse, preventing you from eating more. Thick meal-in-a-bowl soups were exempt from this rule, though, presumably because they were more like solid food. In fact, big soups like minestrone are often served at room temperature in southern Italy, although I don't remember ever eating them that way in my family.

Puréed soups don't have a long tradition in southern Italian home cooking. Before the invention of the food processor, they were a lot of work, and, like rich broths, more likely to be made only for very special occasions or at restaurants. *Crema* is the term used in Italy for this type of soup, but it refers to the smooth consistency of the thing, not the presence of cream. I love a soup with a thick, smooth texture but with a clear, distinct taste provided by one or two select vegetables and olive oil. One of the easiest ways to prepare a quick, great soup, and something I do year-round, is to choose one seasonal vegetable, asparagus for instance, and simmer it in water or a light broth with a chopped potato, onion or garlic, and a healthy dose of olive oil. When the vegetable is tender, purée it in a food processor, check for seasoning, then add a chopped fresh herb. No cream, no butter; the starch from the potato holds it all together. I offer several variations on this theme here, some a bit more involved, using classic southern Italian ingredients like zucchini, tomatoes, ricotta, basil, and arugula.

There is a fine line between soup and pasta in the southern Italian kitchen. Many soups contain some sort of pasta, and many pasta dishes, such as *pasta e fagioli* (pasta with beans), are often turned into a soup by just adding liquid. Soup and pasta can both be either a first course or the only course, but they are considered too similar ever to be served together in the same meal. A southern Italian will not, for instance, start a meal with a soup, no matter how light, and follow up with a pasta. And I think he or she is right in that.

SERVES SIX AS A FIRST COURSE. Zucchini is a mild vegetable whose taste can be overshadowed when it's mixed with other vegetables. I usually cook it alone, so I can really taste it. I suggest making this with small tender zucchini in the summer, when their flavor is at its best.

PURÉED ZUCCHINI SOUP WITH BASIL OIL AND RICOTTA

BASIL OIL

Large handful of fresh basil leaves

$\frac{1}{2}$ cup extra-virgin olive oil

SOUP

2 tablespoons extra-virgin olive oil

2 shallots, chopped

2 inner celery stalks, chopped

1 garlic clove, thinly sliced

$1\frac{1}{2}$ pounds small, tender zucchini, cut into $\frac{1}{2}$-inch dice

3 or 4 scrapings freshly grated nutmeg

Salt and freshly ground black pepper to taste

3 cups homemade chicken broth (see page 315) or canned low-salt chicken broth

Squeeze of lemon juice

1 cup whole-milk ricotta

About $\frac{1}{4}$ cup milk

To make the basil oil: Blanch the basil leaves in a small pot of boiling water for about 30 seconds. Using a slotted spoon, transfer them to a colander. Run cold water over the leaves to preserve the green color. Squeeze them dry in your palm and put them in a food processor. Add the olive oil and process until well puréed. Pour the oil into a little bowl. (The blanching will keep the basil green for a long time.)

In a large soup pot, heat the olive oil over medium heat. Add the shallots and celery and sauté until they start to soften and give off fragrance, 3 or 4 minutes. Add the garlic and zucchini. Season with nutmeg, salt, and pepper and sauté until the zucchini is just starting to become tender, about 3 or 4 minutes. (This sautéing step before you add the broth is important; it brings out the flavor of the zucchini.) Add the chicken broth, increase the heat to high, and bring it to a boil. Reduce the heat back to medium and cook at a medium boil until the vegetables are very tender, about another 10 minutes (cooking quickly will ensure that the soup keeps a nice green color). Purée in a food processor or with a hand blender in the soup pot. Return the soup to the pot and give it a squeeze of lemon juice. Taste and adjust the seasoning, adding few fresh grindings of pepper if needed.

In a small bowl, mix the ricotta with enough milk to thin it to the consistency of yogurt.

Reheat the soup if necessary and ladle it into soup bowls. Give each bowl a dollop of ricotta and drizzle the basil oil around it. Serve hot.

SERVES SIX AS A FIRST COURSE OR LUNCH. Like a traditional minestrone, this early-summer soup contains a good assortment of vegetables, but it's cooked quickly so that everything stays green and fresh and you can still taste and see all the individual vegetables. Most minestrones are slow-cooked, so the vegetable tastes combine, leaving one rich flavor. I like both approaches, but when I've got an abundance of seasonal summer vegetables, I prefer this one. I like serving this *minestra* at room temperature, as such soups are often offered during hot months in southern Italy. The vegetables are all cut about the same size so that everything cooks at about the same speed. Anellini, which means "little rings," is a popular Sicilian pasta shape and to my mind one of the most beautiful pastas for a soup. Setaro makes it (see Buon Italia on page 436), but if you can't find it, any small pasta will work fine.

A note on chicken broth: I now find fresh daily-made broths at several of my neighborhood markets. This is a tremendous luxury that allows me to make a good pot of soup on the spur of the moment. I realize you can't get them everywhere, and most people will need to make their own broth or use canned. I don't mind canned chicken broth (especially Swanson's), but I only use it when it's not essential to the flavor of the dish. For an easy homemade chicken broth, see below.

GREEN SUMMER MINESTRA WITH ANELLINI

¹⁄₄ cup extra-virgin olive oil, plus more for drizzling

2 young leeks, including light green parts, rinsed and chopped

1 summer onion, finely diced

3 inner celery stalks with leaves, stalks finely diced, leaves chopped

1 small fennel bulb, trimmed, cored, and diced

2 summer garlic cloves, thinly sliced

5 very small zucchini (about 4 inches long), finely diced

Salt and freshly ground black pepper to taste

5 cups homemade chicken broth (recipe follows)

³⁄₄ cup anellini pasta

4 or 5 Swiss chard leaves, chopped (middle rib removed if thick)

Handful of dandelion leaves, chopped

Squeeze of lemon juice

About 6 fresh basil leaves, chopped

Leaves from 3 or 4 tarragon sprigs, chopped

1 cup grated pecorino cheese for serving

In a large, wide soup pot (I like wide pots for green vegetable soups because the large surface allows you to bring the contents to a boil quickly so the vegetables will stay green and not get mushy), heat the $1/4$ cup olive oil over medium heat. Add the leeks, onion, celery and leaves, and fennel and sauté until the vegetables are just getting tender, about 4 minutes. Add the garlic and zucchini, season with salt and pepper, and sauté for another 3 minutes or so (this step is important; it prevents your soup from having a bland, boiled taste). Add the chicken broth and let it come to a boil. Adjust the heat so the soup cooks at a medium bubble.

While the soup is cooking, cook the pasta in a medium pot of salted boiling water until al dente. Drain the anellini and put it in a little bowl, tossing it with a good drizzle of olive oil so it won't stick together. Set it aside.

When the zucchini is just almost tender, about 10 minutes, add the Swiss chard and dandelion leaves to the pot. Cook until tender, about 5 minutes. Add the pasta and heat through for a minute. If the soup becomes too thick with the addition of the pasta, add a little hot water (I like my soups a little loose). Add a squeeze of lemon juice to sharpen flavors. Add the basil and tarragon. Taste for seasoning, adding more salt if needed. Add a few grindings of fresh pepper and a generous drizzle of fresh olive oil (I add a lot, probably about $1/4$ cup, because it adds so much flavor, but do what you're comfortable with). Serve the soup either hot or lukewarm, with grated pecorino alongside.

HOMEMADE CHICKEN BROTH   In a large saucepan, brown about 2 dozen chicken wings in a little olive oil, along with a chopped carrot, a piece of celery, a chopped small onion, and a bay leaf. Add about 8 cups of water and bring it to a boil. Reduce the heat and simmer, uncovered, for about $1^1/2$ hours. Strain, skim off the fat, and add salt. This will make about 5 cups. (If you come out with less, just add a little water to make the 5 cups you'll need for the recipe above.)

VARIATIONS   If you can't find all of the ingredients for the soup at the same time, that's fine. The idea is to make a seasonal soup with whatever beautiful green vegetables you can find. I often include escarole, arugula, or a handful of chicory leaves instead of Swiss chard.

SERVES FOUR AS A FIRST COURSE, LUNCH, OR LIGHT SUPPER. *Tenerumi* means "rags" in Italian, and most Sicilians understand it to refer to the runners, or viney stems, of the *cucuzza* squash, a type of zucchini also known as *zucca lunga*. This long, snaky, semi-hard-skinned squash is a Sicilian favorite whose runners, or tendrils, are prized for simmering in soups and stews. They cook up tender, almost creamy, with a taste of zucchini and a subtle lemony edge. I find *zucca lunga* and *tenerumi* at the Union Square Greenmarket in New York in late August and September. When I was a kid, Italian Americans grew it in their backyard gardens. Ask growers at your farmers' market about it. They just might be raising some, especially if they're themselves Italian American. *Zucca lunga* itself has a bland taste and a soft texture that reminds me more of cooked cucumber than of zucchini, but when I can find a big bunch of the lovely tendrils, I make a soup like this one.

TENERUMI SOUP WITH LEMON AND DITALI

1 large bunch *tenerumi* (about 2 pounds)

3 tablespoons extra-virgin olive oil, plus more for drizzling

1 onion, finely diced

2 inner celery stalks with leaves, stalks finely diced, leaves chopped

½ fresh jalapeño chili, minced (use seeds if you like a lot of heat)

2 garlic cloves, thinly sliced

1 small piece fatty prosciutto end, finely chopped

Salt to taste

2 large, round summer tomatoes, peeled, seeded, and finely diced (see page 26)

3 cups homemade chicken broth (see page 315) or canned low-salt chicken broth

1 cup ditali pasta

Grated zest of 1 lemon

Small handful of fresh basil leaves, chopped

1 chunk pecorino cheese for grating

Pick off all the nice-looking leaves, buds, and curly tendrils of the *tenerumi*, including the thin, tender stalks (don't use the thick stalks). Chop coarsely. In a large pot of salted boiling water, blanch the chopped *tenerumi* for about 3 minutes. Reserve 1 cup of the cooking water. Drain the *tenerumi* in a colander and run cold water over it until it is cool. (This step helps to preserve the green color and prevents bitterness.)

In a large, wide soup pot, heat the olive oil over medium heat. Add the onion, celery, and chili and sauté for 2 or 3 minutes to soften and release their flavors. Add the garlic and prosciutto and sauté a minute or so longer. Add the blanched *tenerumi* and season it with a little salt. Sauté until it is well coated with the flavorings, about 3 minutes. Add the tomatoes, chicken broth, and reserved *tenerumi* cooking liquid. Increase the heat and bring to a boil. Reduce the heat to medium and cook at a lively simmer until the vegetables are tender, about 10 minutes.

While the soup is simmering, cook the pasta in a medium pot of salted boiling water until al dente (leaving it a little firmer than usual). Drain it well and add it to the soup pot. Add the lemon zest and simmer for another 2 or 3 minutes to blend all the flavors. Taste for seasoning, adding a little more salt if you need to. Add a drizzle of fresh olive oil and the basil. Serve hot or at room temperature. Bring the pecorino to the table to grate over the soup.

ZUCCA LUNGA WITH TOMATOES   If you find yourself with an actual *zucca lunga* and would like to cook it, here's what to do: Cut the squash into sections and peel it with a sharp knife. Cut it into $1/2$-inch cubes. In a large skillet, heat about 3 tablespoons of good olive oil over medium heat. Add a few sliced garlic cloves and let them soften. Add the *zucca*, season with salt and a pinch of red pepper flakes, and sauté for about 5 minutes. Add about 1 cup chopped fresh or canned tomatoes, cover, and simmer until the *zucca* is tender but not falling apart, about 5 minutes. Add a little chopped fresh marjoram and flat-leaf parsley. Serve hot as a side dish, with grated pecorino cheese, if you like.

SERVES FOUR AS A FIRST COURSE OR LIGHT SUPPER. This soup is made like a gazpacho, but I've sweetened it with fruit, taken out the harsh raw green peppers, and added basil and parsley. I love the play of hot ingredients against cold ones, especially in the summer (hot pasta tossed with uncooked tomato sauce is in my opinion one of the brilliant inventions of the southern Italian table). I serve this soup very cold and sauté the shrimp at the last minute, plopping them on top. If you like, you can use small squid cut into rings instead of rock shrimp; both are good, being bite-sized and cooking in about 1 minute. You can serve it as a first course or, if you offer a few antipasto-type dishes first, a main dish.

COLD TOMATO AND GREEN GRAPE SOUP WITH ROCK SHRIMP

4 scallions, including tender green parts, trimmed and coarsely chopped

2 young summer garlic cloves, crushed

1 bunch seedless green grapes, stemmed

1 cucumber, peeled, seeded, and coarsely chopped

5 round ripe summer tomatoes, peeled, seeded, and coarsely chopped (see page 26), juice reserved

2 tablespoons estate-bottled extra-virgin olive oil

1 tablespoon Spanish sherry vinegar

Salt and freshly ground black pepper to taste

Leaves from 3 or 4 large flat-leaf parsley sprigs, chopped

12 fresh basil leaves, chopped

ROCK SHRIMP

1 tablespoon extra-virgin olive oil, plus more for drizzling

1 pound rock shrimp

1 summer garlic clove, thinly sliced

Salt to taste

Grated zest of $\frac{1}{2}$ lemon

$\frac{1}{2}$ cup blanched almonds, lightly toasted (see page 77) and coarsely chopped

Basil sprigs for garnish

In a food processor, combine the scallions and garlic. Pulse quickly to a coarse chop. Add the grapes and cucumber and process until fairly smooth. Add the tomatoes, olive oil, and Spanish sherry vinegar. Season with salt and pepper and process until smooth.

Transfer to a large bowl and add the fresh herbs. Refrigerate for several hours before serving. Taste the soup when it is cold and adjust the seasoning if needed; cold tends to dull flavor a bit.

When just about ready to serve, pour the soup into chilled bowls. Heat a large skillet over high heat for 1 minute and add the 1 tablespoon olive oil. Add the shrimp and garlic and sauté quickly, stirring once or twice so they cook evenly, just until pink and tender, about 1 minute. Season with salt and lemon zest. Scatter on the almonds and toss. Apportion the shrimp and place them in the soup bowls. Give each bowl a drizzle of fresh olive oil, and garnish with basil sprigs. Serve right away.

VARIATION This cold summer soup is just as nice without the shrimp. Garnish it with a dollop of basil pesto.

SERVES FOUR AS A FIRST COURSE OR A LIGHT SUPPER. Semolina, or ground durum wheat flour, is used to make several types of fresh pasta in Puglia, including their famous orecchiette, the little rounded ear shapes that I love. The flour is ground more coarsely than soft-wheat flour, giving pasta made from it a nice chewy texture. Eggs are usually not used in this type of pasta. Here, semolina is used to make quadrucci, little squares, a perfect shape for brothy soups like this one.

MINESTRA WITH WILD MUSHROOMS AND SEMOLINA QUADRUCCI

QUADRUCCI

1/2 cup all-purpose flour

1 cup semolina flour

Small handful of fresh flat-leaf parsley leaves, finely chopped

Leaves from 3 or 4 marjoram sprigs, chopped

Generous pinch of salt

1/2 cup warm water

SOUP

Handful of dried chanterelles or porcini mushrooms

2 tablespoons extra-virgin olive oil

2 large leeks, including tender green parts, rinsed and finely chopped

1 celery stalk, finely diced

1 small fennel bulb, trimmed, cored, and finely diced

1 pound mixed fresh wild and cultivated mushrooms, such as chanterelles, shiittakes (stemmed), cremini, and a few morels, if they're in season, sliced

Salt and freshly ground black pepper to taste

4 fresh or canned plum tomatoes, seeded and finely chopped

2 tablespoons sweet red vermouth

4 cups homemade chicken broth (see page 315)

1 chunk aged pecorino cheese

TO MAKE THE QUADRUCCI: Combine both flours in a medium bowl. Add the chopped herbs and salt. Stir to blend well. Gradually pour the warm water into the center of the flour, stirring it with your fingers until you have a big ball. Transfer the dough to a floured work surface and knead until smooth, 5 or 6 minutes. Cover the dough with plastic wrap and let it rest for about 30 minutes before rolling.

Put the dried mushrooms in a small cup of hot water so they can soften.

Cut the pasta dough in half and roll each section through a hand-cranked pasta machine, starting with the widest setting and working down to a middle setting, until you have two long, not-too-thin sheets of pasta. Place the sheets on a floured surface and cut them into approximately 1-inch squares with a sharp knife. Place the quadrucci on a floured baking sheet to dry while you make the soup.

In a large soup pot, heat the 2 tablespoons olive oil over medium heat. Add the leeks, celery, and fennel and sauté until soft, about 5 minutes. Using a slotted spoon, transfer the softened dried mushrooms to a cutting board and chop them lightly, reserving the water. Add the dried and fresh mushrooms to the pot, season with salt and pepper, and sauté until soft, 4 or 5 minutes. Add the chopped tomatoes and sauté for 1 minute. Add the vermouth and let it boil away. Strain the mushroom soaking liquid through a fine-mesh strainer into the pot (to remove any possible sand). Add the broth and bring it to a boil. Cook the soup at a lively bubble until the mushrooms are very tender and the soup is fragrant, about 10 minutes (this is a fast, fresh-tasting soup that should remain brothy). Skim the surface of the soup of any fat.

Meanwhile, cook the quadrucci in a medium pot of salted boiling water until they begin to float to the surface, about 2 minutes. (I like cooking the pasta in water instead of throwing it directly into the soup. This way any flour stuck to the quadrucci will be released into the water, not into the soup.) Drain the quadrucci and add them to the soup. Add a little hot water, or more broth if you have it, if the soup has become too thick (it should be somewhat brothy). Serve hot, with a little pecorino grated over each bowl.

SERVES FIVE AS A MAIN COURSE. The combination of beans and shellfish is high on my list of all-time favorite tastes, and you see it a lot in coastal Campania and Puglia and in Sicily. I love it with pasta, but with a cooked green it makes a soup with a very fresh taste and texture.

I chose cockles for this soup because their small shells look very pretty mingling with the beans, but small littleneck clams or other hard-shelled clams will do fine. Choose the smallest ones you can find.

CANNELLINI BEAN SOUP WITH COCKLES AND SWISS CHARD

2 cups dried cannellini or Great Northern beans, soaked overnight in cold water to cover by at least 4 inches

2 bay leaves, preferably fresh

Extra-virgin olive oil for drizzling, plus 2 tablespoons

Salt to taste

1 small chunk fatty prosciutto end, chopped

2 leeks, rinsed and finely diced

2 celery stalks, finely diced

2 garlic cloves

$^1/_2$ small fresh red peperoncini chili, seeded and minced (for just a hint of heat)

3 or 4 small rosemary sprigs

2 tomatoes, peeled, seeded, and chopped (see page 26) or one 15-ounce can diced tomatoes, drained

2 pounds cockles, scrubbed

$^3/_4$ cup dry white wine

1 bunch Swiss chard, thick center ribs removed, leaves coarsely chopped

Handful of fresh basil leaves, chopped

Hot water, if needed

Drain the beans and place them in a large pot. Add water to cover by about 4 inches. Add the bay leaves and turn the heat to high. When the water comes to a boil, reduce the heat to very low, partially cover the pot, and simmer without stirring the beans at all until they are tender, about 1½ hours (test them after 1 hour). Turn off the heat, uncover the pot, add a drizzle of olive oil, and season with salt (adding salt while they're cooking could toughen the skins). Let the beans sit on the turned-off burner for about 20 minutes (this further tenderizes the beans). Scoop out about one-fourth of the beans, along with 1 cup of the cooking water, and purée in a food processor until very smooth. Set aside.

In a large soup pot, heat the 2 tablespoons olive oil over medium heat. Add the prosciutto and cook until crisp. Add the leeks, celery, garlic cloves, chili, and rosemary and sauté until the vegetables are soft and fragrant, about 4 minutes. Add the tomatoes and sauté for 2 or 3 minutes longer. Add the bean purée and the remaining whole beans, along with all their cooking liquid. Season with a little salt and simmer over medium-low heat for about 10 minutes.

Meanwhile, put the cockles in a medium pot and add the white wine. Cook over high heat, uncovered, stirring frequently, until they've opened. Using a slotted spoon, transfer the cockles to the soup pot. Strain the cooking liquid through a fine-mesh strainer to remove any sand that they may have given off, and add the liquid to the soup pot along with the Swiss chard and basil. Turn off the heat and let the chard wilt for a few minutes. This soup should be of a medium thickness (not thick enough to stand a spoon in, but with a certain amount of body; if it seems too thick, add a little hot water). Check the seasoning, adding a bit more salt if needed. Serve hot.

VARIATION This soup is substantial enough to serve as is, but often I'll grill a few pieces of crusty Italian bread in a grill pan, rub them with garlic, and brush them with a little olive oil. This classic simple bruschetta goes very well with this soup.

Sᴇʀᴠᴇꜱ ꜰᴏᴜʀ ᴀꜱ ᴀ ᴍᴀɪɴ ᴄᴏᴜʀꜱᴇ ʟᴜɴᴄʜ ᴏʀ ꜱᴜᴘᴘᴇʀ ꜱᴏᴜᴘ. Here I've blended what for me are classic fall flavors—pumpkin, cooked greens, and, with their woodsy aromas, rosemary and Marsala wine—to create a southern Italian version of chicken soup.

Any small pasta can be used here, but I prefer very small ones such as orzo or acini. I've found a pasta called *grattoni,* made by Rustichella d'Abruzzi, an excellent artisanal pasta producer, that looks like little seed pearls and gives the soup an elegant appearance. Tubetti or anellini (little rings) are also good choices.

A word about the broth for this soup: Homemade chicken broth gives the best flavor for most soups where it's required, but I've found that for this recipe canned chicken broth works well, since the whole chicken adds so much of its own flavor.

CHICKEN SOUP WITH PUMPKIN, ESCAROLE, AND MARSALA

2 tablespoons extra-virgin olive oil, plus more for drizzling

1 slice fatty end-cut prosciutto or pancetta, finely chopped

1 large onion, finely diced

2 carrots, peeled and finely diced

One 3½-pound free-range chicken

Salt and freshly ground black pepper to taste

Leaves from 2 or 3 small rosemary sprigs, chopped

2 garlic cloves, lightly crushed

¾ cup dry Marsala

8 cups homemade chicken broth (see page 315) or canned low-salt chicken

Water, if needed

2 cups cubed pumpkin

½ cup small soup pasta (see headnote), cooked al dente, drained, and tossed with a drizzle of olive oil and a pinch of salt

Leaves from 1 head escarole, finely chopped

1 cup grated grana padano cheese

In a large Dutch oven or flameproof casserole with a lid, heat the 2 tablespoons olive oil over medium heat. Add the prosciutto or pancetta, onion, and carrots and sauté for 3 or 4 minutes to soften. Add the chicken, seasoning it with salt, pepper, and rosemary, and brown lightly all over, about 10 minutes. Add the garlic and sauté for 1 or 2 minutes to release its flavor. Add the Marsala and cook to reduce by half. Add the chicken broth and bring to a boil over high heat (the broth should just about cover the chicken; if more than an inch protrudes, add water). Reduce the heat to low, cover, and simmer, turning the chicken occasionally, until very tender, about 1 hour and 15 minutes.

Remove the chicken from the broth. Skim most of the fat from the surface of the broth. When the chicken is cool enough to handle, pull the meat off the bones and cut into little chunks. Discard the skin and bones. Return the broth to a boil. Add the pumpkin and cook, uncovered, until tender but not falling apart, about 10 minutes. Add the chicken, pasta, and escarole. Simmer on low heat for 2 or 3 minutes to blend the flavors and wilt the escarole. Taste for seasoning, adding a bit more salt, pepper, and fresh rosemary as needed to balance the flavors. Serve hot, topped with a sprinkling of grana padano.

SERVES FOUR AS A FIRST COURSE, OR A LIGHT LUNCH OR SUPPER. One of the constant torments of my mother's life is my hounding her about old family recipes that she insists she can't recall. I remembered a dandelion soup of my father's mother's in a vague way, probably because she made it only when I was extremely young (in my family, Italian dishes often gradually disappeared, to be seamlessly replaced by steaks, baked potatoes, boxed macaroni and cheese, and other things we grew to love, like Pop-Tarts and TV dinners). The resulting recipe is more of a composite sketch than actual fact. The baby meatballs were part of another family soup, chicken broth with little meatballs poached in it. I think the dandelion soup contained bits of sausage, but when I tried it this way I liked it so much I kept it as is. Now, I have a new family favorite.

DANDELION AND BABY MEATBALL SOUP

1 pound ground pork

1 garlic clove, minced

2 eggs, beaten

1/2 cup grated grana padano cheese, plus a handful of grana padano shavings

Handful of fresh flat-leaf parsley leaves, finely chopped

Leaves from 3 or 4 oregano or marjoram sprigs, chopped

Salt and freshly ground black pepper to taste

Extra-virgin olive oil for drizzling, plus 3 tablespoons

1 onion, finely diced

2 celery stalks with leaves, stalks finely diced, leaves chopped

5 cups homemade mixed-meat broth (recipe follows)

1 bunch tender dandelion greens, stemmed and finely chopped

1 handful of chicory leaves, stemmed and finely chopped

1 baguette, cut into thin rounds

Put the ground pork in a bowl. Add the garlic, eggs, grated grana padano, parsley, and oregano or marjoram. Season with salt and pepper and a drizzle of olive oil. Mix everything together with your hands. Roll the meat into tiny meatballs, as small as you can manage (marble size or a little bigger is perfect).

In a large soup pot, heat the 3 tablespoons olive oil over medium heat. Add the diced onion and celery, including the leaves, and sauté until soft and fragrant, about 4 minutes.

Add the mixed-meat broth and bring it to a boil. Reduce the heat to medium-low and drop in the meatballs, dandelions, and chicory. Let the meatballs gently cook through, about 4 minutes. By this time, the dandelion and chicory should also be tender.

Toast the baguette slices and place one in each soup bowl. Drizzle each one with a little olive oil and sprinkle on the shavings of grana padano. Ladle the hot soup over the toast. Serve hot.

EASY MIXED-MEAT BROTH

1 pound chicken wings, backs, and/or necks

3 or 4 veal bones

Extra-virgin olive oil for drizzling

$\frac{1}{2}$ onion

1 celery stalk, halved

1 small carrot

$\frac{1}{2}$ tomato

1 bay leaf, preferably fresh

3 or 4 fresh flat-leaf parsley sprigs

1 garlic clove, crushed

1 whole clove or allspice berry

3 or 4 black peppercorns

8 cups water

Salt to taste

Put the chicken parts and veal bones in a large soup pot. Turn the heat to medium and drizzle on a little olive oil. Turn the bones around in the olive oil and let them brown lightly for about 5 minutes. Add all the remaining ingredients except the water and salt and sauté 2 or 3 minutes longer. Add the water and bring to a slow boil. Reduce the heat to low and simmer for about 1$\frac{1}{2}$ hours. Pour the broth through a fine-mesh sieve into a container. Skim off the excess fat from the top and season with a little salt. You can make this up to 3 days ahead, if you like, and refrigerate it.

SERVES FOUR AS A LIGHT SUPPER OR LUNCH SOUP. The idea for this soup came from Kyle Phillips's website, italianfood.about.com, which is an excellent source for traditional regional recipes, especially some older forgotten ones. He calls such a Calabrian soup "distinctly non-French," I suppose because it has tomatoes and chilies, but I've Frenchified the idea somewhat by finishing it with a fontina-toast topping and running it under the broiler. Although the original *cucina povera* version is made with water, I've added a light broth to tame acidity from the tomatoes and onions and to add richness.

SPICY ONION SOUP CALABRIAN STYLE

1/4 cup extra-virgin olive oil

4 sweet onions (Vidalias are perfect)

Pinch of sugar

1 fresh red *peperoncini* chili, chopped (use at least some seeds)

Salt to taste

2 garlic cloves, thinly sliced

Pinch of ground cloves

1 long strip lemon zest

1/2 cup dry Marsala

One 15-ounce can plum tomatoes, chopped and drained

5 cups mixed-meat broth (see page 328) or high quality purchased broth, preferably a mix of 1/2 chicken and 1/2 beef

Handful of fresh flat-leaf parsley leaves, chopped

4 large pieces crusty Italian bread

8 ounces fontina cheese, cut into 4 slices about the same size as the bread

In a large soup pot, heat the olive oil over medium-low heat. Add the onions, sugar, *peperoncini,* and a pinch of salt. Cook, stirring occasionally, until the onions are very soft and lightly golden, about 30 minutes. Add the garlic, ground cloves, and lemon zest and cook for 1 minute to release their flavors. Add the Marsala and let it bubble and reduce by half. Add the tomatoes and broth. Increase the heat and bring to a boil. Reduce the heat, partially cover, and simmer for about 30 minutes. Skim the top of fat, if needed. The soup should be thin (like a traditional French onion soup). Taste to see if it needs a little more salt. Add the parsley.

To serve, toast the bread slices on one side. Turn them over and place the fontina on top. Run under the broiler until the cheese is melted and gooey. Ladle out the soup and place a cheese toast in each bowl. Serve hot.

SERVES SIX AS A FIRST COURSE. This is one of my favorite variations on a style of puréed soup I make all the time using a changing group of southern Italian flavors. The arugula taste comes through surprisingly clearly when the greens are puréed, and the soup ends up a lovely light green.

LEEK AND ARUGULA SOUP WITH GARLIC OLIVE OIL

½ cup plus 3 tablespoons extra-virgin olive oil, plus more for drizzling

3 young, firm garlic cloves, crushed

4 medium leeks, including light green parts, rinsed and chopped

2 large boiling potatoes, peeled and coarsely chopped

Freshly grated nutmeg to taste

Salt and freshly ground black pepper to taste

4 cups homemade chicken broth (see page 315) or canned low-salt chicken broth

2 bunches arugula, stemmed

Pour the ½ cup olive oil into a small saucepan. Add the garlic and turn the heat to low. Slowly simmer the garlic in the oil, turning the cloves over occasionally until they are the palest golden shade, 4 or 5 minutes. Remove from the heat and let the garlic cool in the oil. Remove the garlic and pour the oil into a small bowl.

In a large soup pot, heat the 3 tablespoons olive oil over medium-low heat. Add the leeks and sauté, without letting them brown, until soft, 5 or 6 minutes. Add the potatoes and season with nutmeg, salt, and pepper. Sauté 3 or 4 more minutes just to coat the potatoes with flavor. Add the chicken broth and increase the heat to high. Bring the soup to a boil, reduce the heat to medium, and cook at a lively bubble, uncovered, until the potatoes are tender, about 20 minutes. Add the arugula and let it wilt into the liquid for 2 or 3 minutes.

Purée the soup in a food processor and return it to the soup pot. Taste for a good balance of flavors. You should have a mellowness from the leeks and potato but a good bright jolt from the arugula. You might need to add a little more salt to bring up all the flavors. When you're ready to serve, reheat the soup gently over medium heat. Ladle the soup into soup bowls. Give each one a generous drizzle of garlic oil. Serve hot.

SERVES FOUR AS A LUNCH OR LIGHT SUPPER. I'm always surprised how often I see cabbage, a very northern-seeming vegetable, on southern Italian menus. In Basilicata, I've been served braised cabbage as part of an antipasto assortment (one time loaded with so much hot chili I could barely eat it). I think she learned it from my father's mother. Since the vegetable rarely inspires me, I force myself to buy and cook it, hoping something good will come of it. Here's that something good, a variation on a rice-and-cabbage soup I've been served in Campania, in a small restaurant near my grandmother's birthplace of Castelfranco in Miscano. I've substituted wheat berries for the rice, added sausage instead of pancetta, and played around with the flavorings.

MINESTRA OF CABBAGE, WHEAT BERRIES, AND SAUSAGE

3/4 cup hard-wheat berries (see page 96)

Extra-virgin olive oil for drizzling, plus 2 tablespoons

Salt to taste

3 Italian sweet pork sausages, removed from casings and crumbled

1/2 head green cabbage, cored and thinly sliced (about 2 cups)

1 onion, thinly sliced

2 garlic cloves, crushed

Freshly ground black pepper to taste

1/2 cup dry white wine

1 bay leaf, preferably fresh

Leaves from 4 or 5 thyme sprigs, chopped

3 or 4 fresh sage leaves, chopped, plus more as needed

4 cups homemade chicken broth (see page 315) or canned low-salt chicken broth

1 tablespoon Spanish sherry vinegar

1 baguette, cut into thin rounds

1 chunk pecorino cheese for grating

Put the wheat berries in a medium saucepan and add cold water to cover by about 4 inches. Place over high heat and bring to a boil. Reduce the heat to medium-low and simmer, uncovered, until the berries are tender to the bite, about 45 minutes. (They should taste pleasantly crunchy. Some of the berries will have burst, but that's normal.) If the water gets low at any point, add some hot water to the pot. When the berries are tender, drain and put them in a small bowl. Add a drizzle of olive oil and a generous pinch of salt and give them a toss.

In a large soup pot, heat the 2 tablespoons olive oil over high heat. Add the sausage, breaking it up into little bits with your spoon, and brown it well. Reduce the heat to medium and add the cabbage, onion, and garlic. Season with salt and pepper and sauté until the vegetables are soft, about 15 minutes (if they start to stick, add a little more olive oil). Add the white wine and let it bubble down to almost nothing. Add the bay leaf, thyme, sage, and broth. Bring to a boil and then reduce the heat down to medium and let the soup simmer, partially covered, for about 20 minutes (you want the cabbage very tender in southern Italian style, not at all crunchy). Depending on how fatty your sausages are, you might need to skim the soup once or twice.

Add the wheat berries, and let the soup simmer, uncovered, for about another 5 minutes to blend all the flavors. Add the Spanish sherry vinegar and taste for seasoning. The vinegar will sharpen the flavors, but you might need a little extra salt or pepper, or a few more sage leaves to add freshness.

To serve the soup, toast the baguette slices on both sides and drop one or two into each soup bowl. While still hot, grate pecorino over the toast and into the bowl. Pour the hot soup into the bowl and serve right away.

VARIATION Farro, a grain similar to spelt that is used in Umbrian cooking, is a good substitute for wheat berries. You can cook it the same way as the wheat, but it doesn't take as much time (check the package for cooking time).

PASTA

There is a pasta dish I loved so much as a child that it still remains my favorite: You make a quick-cooked tomato sauce, flavored maybe with a little garlic and herbs (my family used dried oregano in winter and basil in the summer). You toss it with penne, rigatoni, or ziti pasta (something substantial), then plop a large dollop of ricotta on top and mix it in. A variation is to first toss the hot pasta with ricotta and then mix in the tomato sauce. The ricotta is creamier and more luxurious that way, but both ways have their charm. When I make this pasta for friends, we invariably become gluttons. Occasionally, I add little bits of soppressata to the tomato sauce, but that's as complicated as I'll get with it. And I've never met a child who didn't like it.

Dried durum-wheat pasta is the soul of the southern table. Dried pasta like spaghetti, ziti, and rigatoni were invented in southern Italy and are preferred over fresh egg pasta for many pasta creations. When you think of the southern Italian flavor palate, this certainly makes sense. Olive oil is dried pasta's perfect flavor match. Tomatoes, garlic, cooked greens, clams, and chunky ragùs made without cream or butter all come alive when tossed with a wheaty al dente pasta.

As I've discovered over the years, Italian dried pasta is not all of the same quality. Some is far superior in both taste and texture. The best dried pasta is made by small artisanal producers, most of them in southern and central Italy. These companies turn out much less pasta than the big producers. It is pushed through brass dies and extruded slowly to produce a rough texture and an almost matte finish that allows sauce to cling to the surface much more efficiently than on the slickly textured commercial brands. Slow air-drying gives the pasta a deep, nutty taste.

Large companies mass-produce pasta with new steel machinery and heat-dry it quickly so it doesn't develop this more complex flavor and rough texture. Artisanal pastas also cook up firmer than the other brands; in fact, they're hard to overcook. Setaro, an old company in Campania, remains my favorite. It turns out a huge assortment of traditional shapes, from tiny anellini to use in soups to huge shells called lumaconi, perfect for stuffing. I like how it's packaged in two-pound bags; I suppose the people at Setaro would never consider that anyone could want to cook less than that. Latini, a new company in central Italy, follows traditional artisanal methods in forming and drying its pasta and puts great effort into growing and harvesting the very best durum wheat. Martelli, in Tuscany, and Rustichella di Abruzzi, from the central mountain region, are also excellent artisanal brands. Benedetto Cavalieri, an eighty-year-old company based near Lecce in southern Puglia, turns out pasta with an especially appealing wheaty taste and perfect texture, and I'm always very happy with the way it cooks up. Pasta di Gragnano is another old artisanal pasta company in the Naples area, whose products I've just started finding in this country (check the source list on page 436 for places that carry these fine pastas). Of the big commercial producers, Barilla and DeCecco make decent pastas, and when I can't find the brands I really want I'll buy either one of those.

Fresh pasta made with soft-wheat flour and eggs is considered fancy fare in southern Italy (anything made with eggs is above the everyday). It's reserved for special occasions, when it's used for ravioli, celebratory lasagne, tagliatelle, and cannelloni. But everyday fresh pasta also exists, usually fashioned from sturdy semolina flour made from durum wheat (the same flour used for dried pasta) and without eggs. Orecchiette, the little ear-shaped pasta of Puglia (my alltime favorite pasta shape); *lagane,* short chewy strips used in *pasta e fagioli* in Basilicata and neighboring regions; and *troccoli,* a squared-off spaghetti made around Foggia in northern Puglia, not far from where my grandmother was born, are some of the pastas routinely made fresh for everyday eating and sauced simply with vegetables, chickpeas, and a good dose of olive oil.

I've made my own orecchiette. It's not particularly difficult, but dragging the little pasta rounds over a wood surface to produce the proper ruffed-up texture and hollowed-out shape that makes this pasta hold sauce so beautifully requires practice. And you have to make a lot of orecchiette even to feed just two. I have to admit I don't have much patience with repetitive pasta making, and evidently most of the women of Puglia don't either nowadays. A dwindling number of them are interested in turning out this regional specialty. Packaged orecchiette is available here, but many brands are too slick-looking (if dried pasta looks shiny, that's a bad sign). Sapori di Puglia (Il Trullo) makes one with a rough, homemade texture that cooks up firm and wheaty; I always look for that brand. But the truth is that semolina flour, even though it is a little coarser than soft-wheat flour, is fairly easy to work with and makes smooth easy-rolling pasta with a nice chewy texture and warm yellow hue. If you want to try your hand at a really easy one, see the recipe for Minestra with Wild Mushrooms and Semolina Quadrucci on page 320.

SAUCE FOR PASTA

THE NOTION OF PASTA SAUCE existing separately from the pasta itself is I believe more American than Italian in concept. A big bowl of pasta topped with a thick sauce is not really how pasta was designed to be eaten. Pasta sauces are oftentimes not fully finished and poured on top of cooked pasta, but finished with the pasta in a skillet. If, for instance, I want to make a dish of penne with wild mushrooms, I'll drop the penne in the water. Then I'll heat a few tablespoons of olive oil in a large skillet, and add to this some sliced garlic and a large handful of sliced wild mushrooms. When the pasta is al dente, I'll drain it and add it to the skillet along with the mushrooms, tossing and adding fresh herbs, a handful of arugula, or possibly a few diced tomatoes, maybe a handful of grated pecorino, more olive oil, some pasta cooking water to loosen the texture, more salt, and possibly a grating of nutmeg, tossing everything briefly to blend all the flavors. The famous *aglio e olio* (garlic and oil) sauce from the Naples area is made exactly this way.

In Italy, the term *condimento* is often used to describe a savory coating for a pasta, where pasta and sauce join and become one. With this technique, every piece of pasta is coated with flavor and there is less chance of oversaucing (when you wind up with a big puddle of sauce in your bowl after finishing most of the pasta). Even a fully finished ragù makes a better marriage of flavors if it is allowed to mingle in a skillet with the pasta for a minute before serving, instead of being poured into a big pasta bowl. If you've ever been to an Italian restaurant with an open kitchen you'll have seen cooks tossing pasta in skillets in this fashion. It's easy to do. Yet I don't always do it this way. Usually my decision has to do mainly with whether all the ingredients will fit into my skillet; spaghetti with a huge amount of shellfish takes up so much room, I doubt any home cook would have a skillet large enough to accommodate it. And if I'm making pasta for a huge group, a pound and a half or more, it's just not really practical. What I do instead is toss the pasta and sauce in a big warmed serving bowl, fine-tuning it as I toss by adding more olive oil, herbs, pasta cooking water, possibly some grated cheese, or maybe a squeeze of lemon. It works perfectly well.

HOW TO COOK THE BEST PASTA

THE MOST IMPORTANT THING to remember when you're cooking any type of pasta is to bring a very large pot of water to a hard boil before dropping in the pasta. For 1 pound of pasta, a 6- to 8-quart pot is not too big. You want the water to return quickly to a boil after you drop in the pasta; this will happen quicker if you start out with a lot of water. Pasta needs to cook quickly so it stays firm and flavorful. If your pasta lies around in barely boiling water, it will be mushy through and through by the time it's cooked enough to eat. The second most important thing is to add a lot of salt to the boiling water. I'll add a heaping tablespoon for a pound of pasta. If the water doesn't taste lightly salty, you haven't added enough, and your pasta will taste flat. It's strangely hard to make up for a lack of initial salting by adding more salt to the sauce. Somehow the balance of flavor is never quite right.

Once you add your pasta to the boiling water, give it a brief stir to make sure it isn't sticking together. If you use enough water, it should return to a boil quickly. Resist covering the pot. You want the pasta to boil freely, not steam. Fresh pasta can cook in a minute or even less (when it starts to float to the surface it's done, generally speaking). Dried pasta takes longer. Check how long the instructions on the package say and start checking several minutes before that. I like my dried pasta quite al dente. For me, and for most southern Italian cooks, it's done when it's tender with no unpleasant hardness, but has an obvious bite to it. After cooking several packages, you start to recognize this state. You'll notice in my recipes I don't give exact times for cooking dried pasta, just suggesting al dente, a term which only applies to dried durum wheat pasta, not fresh egg pasta, which is fairly soft before and after cooking. Cooking times vary according to brand, even for the same shape, so taste testing a few minutes before the package says it will be ready is the best method.

Once you've drained your pasta, add it to your skillet or put sauce on it right away or it will, I guarantee, stick together within seconds. Sometimes I'll drain the pasta and toss it with a little olive oil just to prevent sticking. This helps to give you a little more time to finish the sauce.

SERVES SIX AS A FIRST COURSE. FOUR AS A MAIN COURSE. Here is my interpretation of a traditional Puglian pasta I've eaten several times in the Bari area of southern Puglia, always made a little differently. It translates very well using our young summer zucchini and waxy little Yukon Gold potatoes.

Cavatelli (also spelled *cavateddi*), one of my favorite pasta shapes, is found throughout southern Italy. It looks like little curled lozenges. I like serving it with a puréed sauce like a pesto or a sauce that contains tiny chunks of vegetables, which look pretty mingling with the pasta.

CAVATELLI WITH ZUCCHINI. POTATOES. AND RICOTTA SALATA

4 Yukon Gold potatoes, peeled and cut into ½-inch dice

1 pound cavatelli or penne pasta

3 tablespoons extra-virgin olive oil, plus more for drizzling

About 8 scallions, including tender green parts, cut into thin rounds

8 or 9 young zucchini (about 4 inches long, or smallest ones you can find), cut into ½-inch dice

Leaves from 3 or 4 thyme sprigs, chopped

Salt and coarsely ground black pepper to taste

2 tablespoons dry white wine

½ cup grated ricotta salata, plus more for serving

Generous handful of fresh basil leaves, chopped

In a large pot of salted boiling water, cook the potatoes until they're just tender and still holding their shape, about 4 minutes. Using a skimmer, transfer the potatoes to a colander and drain. Return the water to a boil, drop in the pasta, and cook until al dente.

Meanwhile, in a large skillet, heat the 3 tablespoons olive oil over medium heat. Add the scallions and zucchini. Season with the thyme, salt, and pepper and sauté until the zucchini is tender but still firm enough to keep its shape, 3 to 4 minutes. Add the potatoes to the skillet and sauté for 1 or 2 minutes longer to coat them with flavor.

Add the white wine and stir to scrape up all the skillet juices so they can be incorporated into your sauce (this adds a lot of flavor to the dish).

In a warmed large serving bowl, combine the grated ricotta salata and basil. Season with fresh pepper and a drizzle of olive oil.

Drain the pasta, reserving about $1/2$ cup of the cooking water, and add it to the serving bowl. Toss briefly to coat the pasta. The heat of the pasta will allow the basil to release its aroma. Add the zucchini sauce to the bowl and toss gently, adding a little of the pasta cooking water if you need it to loosen the sauce. Serve hot. Serve more grated ricotta salata at the table.

SERVES SIX AS A FIRST COURSE, FOUR AS A MAIN COURSE. This is a reworking of a pasta dish I had for lunch at a small trattoria in Trapani, on Sicily's western coast, which used dried favas that had been cooked down to a rough purée. Dried favas are popular in Puglia and in Sicily for making a delicious ancient puréed dish called *macco*, but I don't like the gray-green look of the purée when it's mixed with pasta, so I've substituted fresh favas, with their beautiful bright green color so dear to my American heart (most southern Italian home cooks always go for flavor above presentation).

Freshly dug spring onions start showing up at my greenmarket around the end of May. They are relatively small, shiny-skinned, and juicy (because they haven't wintered over). They are often sold with their green stems still intact, which are sweet and edible once you pull off the outer layer. I always try to use a little in a dish.

DITALI WITH FAVA BEANS, PEAS, SPRING ONIONS, AND MINT

3 tablespoons extra-virgin olive oil, plus more for drizzling

2 thin slices pancetta, finely chopped

2 spring onions, including tender green parts, thinly sliced

1 pound ditali pasta

1½ pounds fava beans, shelled and peeled (see page 76)

Salt and freshly ground black pepper to taste

2 tablespoons dry white wine

1 cup homemade chicken broth (page 315) or canned low-salt chicken broth

¾ cup fresh or thawed frozen peas

Squeeze of fresh lemon juice

1 cup grated aged pecorino cheese

Small handful of fresh mint leaves, chopped

In a large skillet, heat the 3 tablespoons olive oil over medium heat. Add the pancetta and sauté until it just starts to turn crisp, about 4 minutes. Add the onions and sauté until soft, fragrant, and just starting to turn golden, about another 4 minutes.

In a large pot of salted boiling water, cook the pasta until al dente.

Meanwhile, add the peeled fava beans to the skillet. Season with salt and pepper and sauté over medium-low heat for about 2 minutes to coat the beans with flavor and soften them slightly. Add the white wine and let it boil away. Add the chicken broth and peas and simmer for about 5 minutes to finish cooking all the vegetables and blend the flavors (the sauce will thicken a bit, but I like keeping this pasta a little brothy, so make sure you still have about $1/2$ inch of liquid in the skillet).

Drain the ditali and add it to the skillet. Toss briefly over low heat until the pasta is coated with flavor. Pour the pasta into a warmed large serving bowl. Add the lemon juice, 2 tablespoons of the grated pecorino, the chopped mint, a few gratings of pepper, and a healthy drizzle of fresh olive oil. Give the whole thing a toss and bring it to the table, along with the remaining pecorino, for those who would like a little extra cheese.

SERVES SIX AS A FIRST COURSE, FOUR AS A MAIN COURSE. *Pasta con lentic-chie* is popular in the area where my grandmother was born, near the border of Puglia and Campania, and versions of it are made in many places in southern Italy. It is often made with broken spaghetti, but I'm not crazy about the messy look of that, so I usually make it with vermicelli, which has a sleek, delicate texture.

This is a *cucina povera* dish that tastes really wonderful but can have a murky appearance if you make it with our brown lentils, which cook up mushy. Tiny Castelluccio and Colfiorito lentils from Umbria and green Le Puy lentils from France are all available here; they stay firm and elegant, so I always go out of my way to use one of them for this dish (see page 436 for sources).

VERMICELLI WITH LENTILS, PANCETTA, AND ROSEMARY

1 cup Castelluccio or Colfiorito lentils or French green lentils

1 bay leaf, preferably fresh

Salt to taste

Extra-virgin olive oil for drizzling, plus 3 tablespoons

3 thin slices of pancetta, finely diced

1 red onion, finely diced

1 small carrot, peeled and finely diced

2 garlic cloves, thinly sliced

Leaves from 3 or 4 rosemary sprigs, chopped

Red pepper flakes to taste, plus a small bowl of them to bring to the table

1 pound vermicelli pasta

2 tablespoons dry white wine

Small handful of fresh flat-leaf parsley leaves, chopped

In a medium saucepan, combine the lentils and bay leaf. Add cold water to cover by at least 4 inches. Place the pan over high heat and bring it to a boil. Reduce the heat to low and simmer, uncovered, until the lentils are tender but firm, about 20 minutes. In the last 5 minutes of cooking, season the water with salt and add a generous drizzle of olive oil. Drain the lentils, reserving their cooking liquid.

In a large skillet, heat the 3 tablespoons olive oil over medium heat. Add the pancetta and saute until crisp, but not too brown. Add the onion and carrot and sauté until soft,

3 or 4 minutes. Add the garlic, rosemary, and pepper flakes, season with salt, and sauté a minute or two longer so they can release their flavors.

Meanwhile, add the vermicelli to a large pot of salted boiling water and stir to ensure that it doesn't stick together. Cook until al dente.

Add the lentils to the skillet and sauté for 1 minute to blend all the flavors. Add the white wine and let it boil away. Add enough of the reserved lentil cooking liquid to create a moist but not soupy texture (about 1/2 cup). Simmer while the pasta is cooking.

Drain the vermicelli and add it to the skillet, cooking for about 1 minute to blend all the flavors. Taste for seasoning and add the parsley and a generous drizzle of fresh olive oil. The texture should be moist, but not brothy like a soup. Add a bit more lentil cooking liquid if it is too dry. Transfer to a warmed large serving bowl and serve right away.

VARIATIONS   My father always added quite a bit of dried red pepper flakes to this dish. Bring a small bowl of it to the table if you like heat. *Olio santo* is also customary (see page 38). Grated cheese is not often used on this dish, and I agree with tradition here, feeling that cheese ruins the slightly slippery texture of the lentils.

PASTA E FAGIOLI

There are so many variations on pasta with beans across the South that I would almost call it the regional dish. My mother made several versions, one with cannellini beans and ditali pasta, and she almost always cooked a few pork chops in the sauce for flavor (the tender pork chops were then served as a side dish). The family across the street, who were from Sorrento, in Campania, made *pasta e fagioli* with short strips of fresh pasta they called *lagane*. In Puglia, they often use chickpeas. Borlotti (cranberry beans) also make a great dish. Since this is a starch-on-starch combination, you want to add as much savor to the dish as you can, avoiding blandness. A little pork fat always helps, and I've used pancetta here for a lentil version; if you want to forgo that, make sure to sauté a flavorful *soffritto* (see page 69 for more on this essential flavor base). For my *soffritto*, I blend red onion, garlic, rosemary, and a pinch of red pepper flakes. Fresh leafy herbs added at the end of cooking are another uplifting touch. I use flat-leaf parsley; basil and mint are other options. For another version of *pasta e fagioli*, see Lasagnette with Chickpeas and Mussels, page 370.

SERVES SIX AS A FIRST COURSE. FOUR AS A MAIN COURSE. *Spaghetti del padrino* is the name for this electric pink spaghetti on the menu at Gigino Trattoria, on Greenwich Street in TriBeCa in Manhattan. It's my favorite dish on the menu. I spent some time playing around with these ingredients at home until I came up with a version that tastes pretty much like Gigino's inspired creation.

SPAGHETTI WITH ROASTED BEETS, ESCAROLE, AND ANCHOVIES, GIGINO STYLE

3 beets, greens trimmed to 1 inch (greens reserved for another use), beets scrubbed

⅓ cup plus ¼ cup extra-virgin olive oil

Sea salt and freshly ground black pepper to taste

Leaves from 1 large head escarole, chopped

1 pound spaghetti pasta

3 garlic cloves, very thinly sliced

3 salt-packed anchovies, filleted, soaked, and drained (see page 33)

2 tablespoons dry white wine

Small handful of salt-packed capers, soaked and drained (see page 29)

Handful of fresh flat-leaf parsley leaves, chopped

Preheat the oven to 400°F. Wrap the beets in aluminum foil and roast them until tender, about 1-1½ hours depending on their size. Remove the foil and run the beets very briefly under cold water, cooling them slightly, and slip off their skins.

Trim and slice the beets into thin rounds, then slice the rounds into strips. Place the strips (they should still be quite warm) in a warmed pasta serving bowl. Drizzle on the ⅓ cup olive oil. Season with salt and pepper and give the mixture a gentle toss.

In a large pot of salted boiling water, blanch the escarole for 1 minute. Using a skimmer, transfer it to a colander. Run cold water over it to preserve its color. Squeeze it dry with your hands.

Bring the water back to a hard boil and drop in the spaghetti. Cook until al dente.

Meanwhile, in a large skillet, heat the ¼ cup olive oil over medium heat. Add the garlic and sauté until fragrant and very lightly colored, about 1 minute. Chop the anchovies and add them and the escarole to the skillet. Sauté for about 1 minute longer. Add the white wine and let it bubble for a few seconds.

Drain the spaghetti, reserving about $1/2$ cup of the cooking water. Add the spaghetti to the serving bowl and toss. The beets will turn it bright pink. Add the escarole and any skillet juices, the capers, and parsley and toss to blend well. Season with pepper and a bit of salt if needed (you may not need any if the anchovies and capers are sufficiently salty). Add a little pasta water to loosen the sauce if needed. This pasta is good served hot, but since it contains no cheese or butter, the texture stays loose even as it cools off, making it appealing at room temperature as well.

SERVES SIX AS A FIRST COURSE, FOUR AS A MAIN COURSE. Here's an improvised pasta I made for my husband and myself after finding a bunch of really nice-looking zucchini blossoms at the greenmarket one summer day. Unfortunately, they're often not as fresh here as in Italian markets, so when I see really open, bright yellow ones I grab them and then figure out what to do with them. The fresh ones respond well to quick cooking, as in this five-minute recipe that combines the two favorite flavors of Campania, tomatoes and mozzarella.

ZITI WITH TOMATOES, ZUCCHINI BLOSSOMS, AND MOZZARELLA

2 tablespoons extra-virgin olive oil, plus more for drizzling

1 large onion, thinly sliced

1 pound ziti pasta

4 oil-packed anchovy fillets, coarsely chopped, or 2 salt-packed anchovies, filleted, soaked, drained, and coarsely chopped (see page 33)

4 cups cherry tomatoes, stemmed, halved

12 zucchini blossoms, wiped clean, pistils removed (see page 93)

Salt and freshly ground black pepper to taste

3 or 4 scrapings of freshly grated nutmeg

2 tablespoons dry white wine

8 ounces mozzarella cheese, cut into 1/2-inch dice

In a large skillet, heat the 2 tablespoons olive oil over medium heat. Add the onion and sauté until soft and fragrant, 6 or 7 minutes. Meanwhile, cook the ziti in a large pot of salted boiling water until al dente.

Add the anchovies and let them melt into the onion for a minute or so. Add the cherry tomatoes and sauté just until they start to give off some juice, 3 or 4 minutes. Add the zucchini blossoms, season with salt, pepper, and nutmeg, and let the blossoms soften in the sauce for a minute or so. Add the white wine and let it bubble for a few seconds.

Drain the ziti well and add it to the skillet. Toss on medium heat for about 1 minute to blend all the flavors. Transfer the ziti and all the skillet juices to a warmed large serving bowl. Add the mozzarella, a drizzle of fresh olive oil, and a few gratings of pepper and toss gently. Serve right away.

VARIATION If you don't have zucchini blossoms, the pasta is almost as good without them. You can, if you like, add a handful of chopped arugula instead (add it when you add the mozzarella, so it can melt with the heat of the pasta).

SERVES SIX AS A FIRST COURSE. My friend John Colapinto's grandfather came from a town in Basilicata called Pisticci, and I promised John I would try to go there if I ever traveled nearby. It just so happened that I did on my last trip. It is a town surrounded by deep, dry gullies and rebuilt after earthquakes in that shoebox-cluster style that southern Italians have taken to, but it's full of young people (unlike many towns in the deep South, where there's been a mass exodus), with a vibrant Sunday *passeggiata* and a sophisticated market.

The version of *bucatini di fuoco*, pasta flavored with hot chilies, that I ate in a trattoria in Pisticci, was made with the addition of a skinny, dark green wild chicory that we don't have here. Our frilly-edged chicory, which I love raw in salads, takes on a harsh taste when cooked, so I've substituted dandelion greens, which have a sweet and pleasantly bitter edge when cooked.

The dish in Pisticci was seasoned with a chili sauce so spicy it made my ears ring, but it had a smoky, toasted edge that gave depth to the sauce under all the heat. The chef showed me the chilies he had sun-dried himself and ground up with olive oil and garlic. I tried drying fresh chilies in my oven the way I do tomatoes, but my cats and husband started choking from the fumes, so I've made my version of this sauce with purchased dried chilies that I briefly sauté in a pan to add a little toastiness.

BUCATINI WITH DANDELIONS, TOMATOES, AND BASILICATA CHILI SAUCE

CHILI SAUCE
4 small dried red chilies
2 garlic cloves
5 tablespoons extra-virgin olive oil

PASTA
1 tablespoon extra-virgin olive oil
Three ⅛-inch-thick slices pancetta, finely diced
4 scallions, including tender green parts, cut into thin rounds

Small palmful of fennel seeds, ground in a mortar
2 tablespoons dry white wine
One 35-ounce can diced plum tomatoes with juice
Salt to taste
1 pound bucatini pasta
1 bunch young dandelion greens, stemmed, and chopped

To make the chili sauce: Put the chilies and garlic in a mortar and grind them to a paste with a pestle, adding 1 tablespoon of the olive oil. Place this paste in a small saucepan, add the remaining 4 tablespoons of olive oil, and cook over very low heat until warm, about 1 minute. The sauce should be rather dense. Transfer the sauce to a small serving bowl.

In a large skillet, heat the 1 tablespoon olive oil over medium heat. Add the pancetta and sauté until crisp. Add the scallions and ground fennel seeds and sauté until fragrant, about 1 minute. Add the white wine and let it bubble while you stir to scrape up all the cooked-on skillet juices. Add the tomatoes and a generous pinch of salt, and cook, uncovered, at a low bubble for about 10 minutes.

Meanwhile, cook the bucatini in a large pot of salted boiling water until al dente.

Add about 1 tablespoon of the chili sauce to the skillet and taste the sauce. It should be quite spicy, but the amount of chili you add is up to you. Add the dandelion greens to the skillet, turn off the heat, and let them wilt with the heat of the sauce.

Drain the bucatini, reserving about $1/2$ cup of the cooking water, and add it to the skillet. Toss over medium heat very briefly just to blend everything, adding a splash or so of cooking water to loosen the sauce, if needed. Transfer to a serving bowl and bring it to the table, along with the remaining hot sauce. It is customary to serve pasta containing hot chilies without grated cheese in southern Italy.

SERVES SIX AS A FIRST COURSE. I try not to add olives to dishes haphazardly. When I do add them, they serve as an important highlight or play a major supporting role. Here, tart green olives are sautéed with garlic and vermouth to add another layer of depth to their already striking flavor. The idea for this pasta came from one cooked by Rosalba Ciannamea, the owner and chef at Il Frantoio, in Ostuni, Puglia, a working olive-oil farm and tranquil inn. She seasoned the dish with her fragrant home-dried oregano. I haven't found anything here, even imported Sicilian oregano still on the branch, to be as fragrant and surpassingly gentle as hers, and I use fresh marjoram instead. The sautéing is my idea. My favorite olives for this pasta are not Italian ones but green picholines from France. They remind me of the sweet green olives I ate in Puglia, which I can't seem to find here.

FUSILLI WITH SAUTÉED GREEN OLIVES AND BREAD CRUMBS

7 tablespoons extra-virgin olive oil, plus more for drizzling

1/2 cup homemade dry bread crumbs (page 308)

Salt to taste

Pinch of sugar

4 garlic cloves, very thinly sliced

4 oil-packed anchovy fillets, coarsely chopped, or 2 salt-packed anchovies, filleted, soaked, drained, and coarsely chopped (see page 33)

1/2 fresh red peperoncino chili, minced (including seeds if you like a lot of heat)

One 35-ounce can plum tomatoes, finely chopped, with juice

Leaves from 3 or 4 marjoram sprigs, chopped, plus more sprigs if needed

Large handful of fresh flat-leaf parsley leaves, chopped

1 pound fusilli pasta

1 cup unpitted green picholine olives, or other sweet and not too salty green olives (see headnote)

2 tablespoons dry vermouth

In a small skillet, heat 2 tablespoons of the olive oil over medium heat. Let the skillet heat a few seconds, then add the bread crumbs. Season with salt and sugar and sauté until they are crisp and lightly golden. (Be careful not to let them burn, which can happen before you know it. It's best to watch them and turn the heat down if you think this is likely.) Remove from the heat and let cool for a few minutes in the skillet. Transfer to a small serving bowl.

In a large skillet, heat 3 tablespoons of the olive oil over medium heat. Add the garlic, anchovies, and chili (this is the flavor base for your sauce). Sauté for 1 or 2 minutes until the garlic releases its flavor and the anchovies melt. Add the tomatoes with their juice, season with salt, and cook at a lively simmer, uncovered, for about 5 minutes, until the sauce thickens lightly but still has a nice bright color. Turn off the heat and add all the herbs, letting their flavors open up in the warm sauce.

Meanwhile, add the pasta to a large pot of salted boiling water, giving it a stir to make sure it isn't sticking. Cook until al dente.

In a medium skillet, heat the remaining 2 tablespoons olive oil over medium-high heat. Add the olives, shaking them around until hot and lightly puffed up, about 2 minutes. Add the vermouth and let it bubble for a few seconds. Add the olives with all the skillet juices to the tomato sauce and stir them in.

Drain the fusilli and add it to the skillet. Sauté over medium heat to blend everything well for about 1 minute. Taste for seasoning, adding extra salt or a few sprigs of marjoram if desired. Add a drizzle of fresh olive oil and pour the pasta into a warmed serving bowl. To serve, sprinkle each serving with a generous amount of the sautéed bread crumbs.

NOTE   Tomatoes can take a lot of olive oil. The oil carries and disperses flavors, such as garlic, throughout the sauce, and it also has a mellowing effect on the tomato's acidity, making the sauce sweet, without long cooking. I always add several tablespoons of oil at the start and then complete the sauce, after cooking, with a generous drizzle of fresh oil for a fruity finish.

   I love the way unpitted olives look in a sauce, and I like their warm juiciness when you bite into them. If you prefer, you can pit the olives, but I would leave them in large pieces for texture.

SOUTHERN ITALIAN WAYS WITH WINTER SQUASH

I look to southern Italian pasta cooking for inspiration when I'm trying to figure out what to do with a big American pumpkin. Pasta with pumpkin is a common fall dish throughout southern Italy. The combination may not sound exciting, but it makes for a beautiful, gentle dish, especially when delicately seasoned with fresh black pepper, pecorino, and just a touch of garlic or onion. Hard squashes marry extremely well with most Italian grating cheeses like Parmigiano-Reggiano, grana padano, and pecorino, where the salty sweetness serves to elevate the squash's neutrality. Prosciutto and salami also go well with winter squash, and you can often find little flecks of these meats flavoring a squash-and-pasta dish (see Chicken Soup with Pumpkin, Escarole, and Marsala, page 324, for ideas about blending these flavors). A variety of herbs marry extremely well with winter squashes, assertive ones like rosemary or sage deepening the squash's savory tones, and basil or parsley flowing naturally with its sweetness. Winter squashes also make rich, warming risottos.

In America, we enjoy a much wider variety of winter squashes than southern Italians do. There I've noticed only a few varieties of pumpkin and an oblong green squash. In the late fall and through the winter at the Union Square Greenmarket in Manhattan, I've counted about fifteen varieties of winter squash, in shades of yellow, green, orange, and even blue and pink, including calabaza, Delicata, Hubbard, kabocha, and Buttercup. I've seen but haven't yet actually purchased something called a Pink Banana, which is bright pink and about three feet long. Maybe one of the farmers will sell me a chunk. Cheese pumpkin, the squat, beige variety that is the choice for pumpkin pie, is sweet and delicate cooked in a risotto or a pasta dish; butternut has good flavor and is easy to find. Getting to know these gorgeous vegetables is a matter of taking them home and cooking them, acquainting yourself with their various textures.

As you may already know, winter squash can be a real drag to peel. Make sure you have a sharp, sturdy chef's knife. To prevent the squash from slipping out from under you, first cut a slice from the bottom, so it will sit flat. Then cut a slice from the top, to make it easy to get your knife into the skin. Now, slice off the skin in downward motions, in long strips.

SERVES SIX AS A FIRST COURSE. I would never have thought to pair pumpkin with tomatoes before I ordered a pasta containing both in a restaurant in Campania. The acid of the tomatoes lifted the blandness of the pumpkin, mingling natural sugars to create a unique sweetness. Roasting is a great cooking method for winter squashes, because it concentrates their flavor and browns their surfaces to increase sweetness.

This is a good dish to make in early fall, when pumpkins are just starting to come into season and tomatoes and basil are making their farewell.

Lasagnette is a dried ruffle-edged pasta about one-fourth the width of dried lasagne sheets. It's served tossed with a sauce, as opposed to lasagne sheets, which are baked.

LASAGNETTE WITH PUMPKIN, TOMATOES, AND BASIL

^{1}/$_2$ cheese pumpkin, peeled, seeded, and cut into ^{1}/$_2$-inch dice (about 2^1/$_2$ cups)

12 ripe plum tomatoes, quartered

3 shallots, thinly sliced

3 garlic cloves, very thinly sliced

Extra-virgin olive oil for drizzling

Salt and freshly ground black pepper to taste

Pinch of ground cloves

Pinch of sugar

1 pound lasagnette pasta

1 cup grated pecorino cheese

Large handful of fresh basil leaves, chopped

Preheat the oven to 425°F.

Place the pumpkin on a baking sheet. Place the tomatoes on another baking sheet. Scatter the shallots over the pumpkin and the garlic over the tomatoes. Drizzle both vegetables with a generous amount of olive oil and season with salt and pepper. Sprinkle the cloves and sugar over the squash. Mix the vegetables on both sheet pans well with your hands and spread them out in a single layer. Bake until tender and just browning at the edges, 15 to 20 minutes for the tomatoes and about 25 minutes for the pumpkin.

In a large pot of salted boiling water, cook the pasta until al dente. Drain, reserving about $\frac{1}{2}$ cup of the cooking water. Transfer to a warmed large serving bowl. Drizzle with a generous amount of olive oil (enough to coat the pasta) and toss briefly. Add the pumpkin, tomatoes, and any juices from the baking sheets. Add 2 tablespoons pecorino, the basil, a few grindings of pepper, a pinch of salt, and a little of the reserved cooking water to loosen the sauce if necessary (depending on how much juice your tomatoes give off). Toss gently, trying not to break up the squash pieces. Serve hot, serving the remaining pecorino alongside.

SERVES SIX AS A FIRST COURSE, FOUR AS A MAIN COURSE. *Pasta cacio e uova* (pasta with cheese and eggs) is a simple dish from Campania. It's somewhat like pasta carbonara, from Abruzzi, but usually without the pancetta or guanciale (cured pork cheek). I like the concept of it, but sometimes I find it a little bland, so I'm always trying subtle variations. In the spring, I often add asparagus. In summer, I add a large handful of mixed herbs like parsley, basil, tarragon, and maybe some chives. This recipe includes the long, skinny light-green frying peppers that were so popular in Italian American households when I was a kid. They have a much softer, sweeter flavor than green bell peppers, so they don't throw this delicate dish off balance.

BUCATINI WITH EGGS, PECORINO, AND GREEN FRYING PEPPERS

2 tablespoons extra-virgin olive oil

3 green frying peppers, seeded and sliced into thin strips

Pinch of sugar

Salt and freshly ground black pepper to taste

2 garlic cloves, thinly sliced

½ cup dry white wine

3 large eggs at room temperature

1 cup grated grana padano cheese

Handful of fresh flat-leaf parsley leaves, chopped

1 pound of bucatini pasta

In a large skillet, heat the olive oil over medium-low heat. Add the pepper strips, sugar, salt, and pepper and sauté until the peppers are soft, about 8 minutes. Add the garlic and sauté for 1 or 2 minutes longer so it can release its flavor. Add the white wine and cook to reduce it by half (you should still have some liquid left in the pan).

In a large serving bowl, crack in the eggs and add about half of the grana padano. Season with a pinch of salt and more generously with pepper. Add the parsley and mix well.

Meanwhile, cook the pasta in a large pot of salted boiling water until al dente. Drain the bucatini, leaving a little water clinging to it, and add it to the serving bowl. Toss quickly to blend well (the heat from the pasta will gently cook the eggs, making a creamy sauce). Add the peppers and all the skillet juices and toss again. Serve right away, with the remaining grana padano brought to the table.

SERVES FOUR AS A LIGHT LUNCH DISH OR AN ANTIPASTO OFFERING.
Here's a dish my mother often used to make with leftover tomato-sauced spaghetti, but I like a purer, whiter version, flavored only with pecorino, herbs, and a hint of nutmeg. I often include a handful of celery leaves, which gives this hearty frittata a fresh, delicate taste.

SPAGHETTI FRITTATA

4 ounces spaghetti pasta

Extra-virgin olive oil for drizzling, plus 2 tablespoons

5 large eggs

1/2 cup grated mild pecorino or grana padano cheese

Handful of fresh flat-leaf parsley leaves,

chopped (about 1/4 cup)

Leaves from 5 celery stalks, chopped

Freshly grated nutmeg to taste

1 small garlic clove, minced

Salt and freshly ground pepper to taste

In a large pot of salted boiling water, cook the spaghetti until al dente. Drain in a colander and run cold water over it to stop the cooking. Drain well. Transfer the spaghetti to a medium bowl and add a generous drizzle of olive oil, stirring it around to coat all the strands so they won't stick together.

In another medium bowl, combine the eggs, pecorino or grana padano, parsley, celery leaves, nutmeg, and minced garlic. Season well with salt and pepper and whisk to blend. Add the spaghetti and stir until well blended.

Pour the 2 tablespoons of olive oil into a 10-inch skillet, spreading the oil to cover the entire skillet bottom. Turn the heat to medium-low and let the oil heat for about 30 seconds. Add the spaghetti mixture and flatten it a bit with a spatula so it's evenly distributed. Cook without disturbing for about 4-5 minutes. Now, shake the skillet. If the frittata moves easily in the skillet and the edges have started to turn a deep golden, it's done on the bottom. If not, let it cook for another minute or so.

Since this is such a thick frittata, I don't flip it; instead, I run it under a broiler to finish its cooking. Preheat the broiler. Place the frittata under the broiler about 6 inches from the heat source until the top is lightly golden, 2 or 3 minutes. Press with your fingers to see if it's firm. If not, broil for a few seconds longer. Remove from the broiler and let rest in the skillet for about 5 minutes (this will allow it to firm up a bit more). Place a large flat plate over the skillet and turn the frittata out onto it, skillet-browned side up. Serve warm or at room temperature, cut into wedges.

SERVES FOUR OR FIVE AS A MAIN COURSE. Here is my take on the baked ziti so common throughout southern Italy. Most Italian Americans are familiar with the tomato, ricotta, and mozzarella version, which is simple and delicious. I've had many varieties of it in restaurants in Campania, served in individual ramekins, and with sausage, bits of salami, or baby meatballs often added. Sometimes it's moist and flavorful, sometimes dry with overcooked pasta, but however it comes to the table, it's invariably described as the specialty of the house.

In southern Italy, roasted peppers are more likely to be paired with strong southern Italian flavors like capers, olives, or anchovies, but sometimes I like to take an opposite approach, joining their sweetness with other sweet tastes, like the mozzarella and a hint of orange in this variation on a classic southern-style baked ziti.

BAKED ZITI WITH ROASTED RED PEPPERS, ORANGE ZEST AND MOZZARELLA

1 pound ziti pasta

3 tablespoons extra-virgin olive oil, plus more for drizzling

3 shallots, thinly sliced

2 garlic cloves, thinly sliced

3 large red bell peppers, roasted, peeled, and cut into thick strips (see page 38)

Leaves from 5 or 6 thyme sprigs, chopped

Salt and freshly ground black pepper to taste

One 28-ounce can diced tomatoes with juice, plus a 15-ounce can, drained

Grated zest and juice of 1 large orange

Large handful of fresh basil leaves, chopped

1 pound mozzarella, cut into 1/2-inch dice

3 heaping tablespoons grated Parmigiano-Reggiano cheese

1/2 cup lightly sautéed homemade bread crumbs (page 308)

Preheat the oven to 425°F.

In a large pot of salted boiling water, cook the pasta until almost al dente (about a minute less than usual since you'll be baking it.)

Meanwhile, in a large skillet, heat the 3 tablespoons olive oil over medium heat. Add the shallots and sauté until soft, about 3 minutes. Add the garlic, the roasted pepper strips, and thyme. Season with salt and pepper. Sauté until the peppers are fragrant and tender, about 5 minutes. Add the tomatoes and orange zest and juice. Simmer, uncovered, at a lively bubble for about 8 minutes. Check for seasoning, adding more salt if needed.

Drain the pasta well and add it to the skillet, tossing it with the sauce.

Pour the pasta and sauce into a 9-by-13-inch baking dish. (I always go for wide and shallow as opposed to deep for baked pasta dishes. You get more surface for a crisp top and you don't have to heat it so long that it becomes mushy). Add the basil, mozzarella, and 1 heaping tablespoon grated Parmigiano, and toss gently to mix. Add the remaining 2 tablespoons Parmigiano to the bread crumbs. Mix them together and sprinkle evenly over the top of the pasta. Drizzle with a generous amount of olive oil and bake, uncovered, until bubbling and lightly browned on top, not more than 20 minutes so it stays moist. Serve hot.

NOTE   Most recipes for baked pasta ask you to let them sit for about 15 minutes before serving. I don't do this, preferring the texture to be gooey and luscious, not firm.

SERVES SIX AS A FIRST COURSE, FOUR AS A MAIN COURSE. Orecchiette with *cima di rape* (broccoli rabe) may be the most popular pasta dish in Puglia. I've had it many times in Puglian towns, always without meat but often with a touch of anchovy and a little hot chili. The Italian American version almost always contains sausage. I find that a little heavy, but I like it with pork, so I've included a bit of chopped prosciutto in this one.

Orecchiette is a Puglian pasta, made with water and semolina, and shaped like little hollow half circles (the name actually means "little ears," and they do look a little like that). Orecchiette is still made by hand by some patient Puglian women, but you can buy good commercial brands here. Look for one by Sapore di Puglia. It has a desirable roughed-up matte texture and cooks up properly chewy.

ORECCHIETTE WITH BROCCOLI RABE, PROSCIUTTO, AND WHITE WINE

2 bunches broccoli rabe, well trimmed of tough stems and lightly chopped

1 pound orecchiette pasta

1/4 cup extra-virgin olive oil, plus more for drizzling

5 thin slices prosciutto di Parma, excess fat removed, chopped, and reserved, prosciutto cut into thin strips

4 garlic cloves, thinly sliced

Salt and freshly ground black pepper to taste

1/2 cup dry white wine

8-ounce chunk grana padano cheese

In a large pot of salted boiling water, blanch the broccoli rabe for 2 minutes. Using a large skimmer, transfer the broccoli rabe to a colander. Reserve the pot of water. Run cold water over the broccoli rabe to stop the cooking and preserve its bright green color. Squeeze out the excess water with your hands.

Bring the water to a boil again, add the pasta, and stir to keep it from sticking. Cook until al dente.

In a large skillet, heat the ¹/₄ cup olive oil over medium heat. Add the chopped prosciutto fat and the garlic and sauté until the garlic is barely golden and the fat has melted. Add the broccoli rabe, season with salt and pepper, and sauté until well coated with oil, about 3 minutes. Add the wine and let it boil for a minute, leaving some liquid in the skillet.

Drain the orecchiette, leaving a little water clinging to it, and add it to the skillet. Add prosciutto strips. Grate on 1 or 2 tablespoons of grana padano. Add a drizzle of olive oil, and toss gently for a minute to blend all the flavors. Transfer to a large serving bowl. Bring the remaining chunk of grana padano to the table for those who might like extra.

VARIATION   If you want to make the more traditional Puglian nonmeat version, add about 4 anchovy fillets and 1 small dried red chili, crumbled, when you add the garlic in the recipe. Leave out the prosciutto and prosciutto fat.

SERVES FOUR AS A FIRST COURSE. My mother's father was Sicilian, but since both her parents died very young, talking about old family recipes still seems to upset her at times. She'll remember pieces of dishes in a vague way and then not want to discuss it further when I ask for details. Here's one she remembers more vividly, evidently because many of the Italian women in her neighborhood thought the seasoning was unusual and used to gossip about it. This was a dish of big ravioli filled with a slightly sweet cinnamon-scented ricotta (the other women used nutmeg and no sugar). I re-created them from her memory and she says the taste is pretty much on target. My mother says these were usually dressed with the homemade tomato paste her grandmother dried on boards in her Connecticut backyard, maybe thinned with a little water. She says the paste was so concentrated it was almost black. That's not to my taste, so I've come up with a lighter sauce.

THE RUSSO FAMILY'S CINNAMON RAVIOLONI WITH TOMATO AND SHALLOT SAUCE

PASTA

3½ cups all-purpose flour

4 large eggs

Pinch of salt

1 tablespoon extra-virgin olive oil

FILLING

1½ cups whole-milk ricotta, drained for 15 minutes

1 large egg

Pinch of ground cinnamon

½ teaspoon sugar

2 tablespoons grated grano padano cheese

Salt and freshly ground black pepper to taste

SAUCE

2 tablespoons extra-virgin olive oil

2 shallots, thinly sliced

One 35-ounce can plum tomatoes, chopped, with juice

Salt and freshly ground black pepper to taste

3 or 4 large sprigs of flat-leaf parsley, coarsely chopped

Extra-virgin olive oil for drizzling

Chunk of grana padano cheese for grating

TO MAKE THE PASTA: Since this is a old family recipe, I like making the pasta using the traditional well method rather than in a food processor (see page 368 for this method). Mound the flour on a work surface and make a well in the center. Crack the eggs into the well and add the salt and olive oil. Start mixing the flour into the eggs with a fork, pulling in the flour from the sides. When you have a mass of sticky dough balls, start working them together with your hands until you have a nice big ball, continuing to pull in flour as you do. Flour another work area and transfer the dough ball to it, leaving behind any little bits of dough and flour that have not been incorporated. Knead the dough until smooth and satiny, 5 or 6 minutes. Cover the dough with plastic wrap and let it rest unrefrigerated for about 30 minutes.

While the dough is resting, mix all the ingredients for the filling together in a bowl. The filling should be very slightly sweet with a subtle cinnamon edge, but it will also have a salty note due to the pecorino. Put the bowl in the refrigerator while you roll out the pasta (this will firm it up a bit, making it easier to fill the *ravioloni*).

Divide the dough in quarters, keeping the pieces you're not working on covered with plastic wrap so they don't dry out. Run a piece of the dough through the widest setting of a hand-cranked pasta machine 2 times. Start running it through thinner and thinner settings until you get to the next-to-last setting and the pasta is very thin and smooth. Lay the pasta sheet on a floured surface. Roll out another piece of dough in the same way and lay it alongside the other one. Drop heaping tablespoons of the ricotta filling at 2½-inch intervals on one of the pasta sheets. Place the other pasta sheet on top and press around the filling to get rid of any air pockets. Cut the pasta into 2½- or 3-inch squares and seal the edges all around with the tines of a fork, making a little ridged pattern. (I frequently use a 3-inch ravioli cutter, which is very convenient, but it makes them all uniform. When I want a real old-fashioned look, I do them by hand.) You should have 16 to 18 *ravioloni*. Lay the *ravioloni* out on a well-floured baking sheet. Roll out the remaining dough and fill the *ravioloni* in the same fashion. Cover them loosely with a towel to keep them moist. Turn them over once if they sit for more than 1 hour (they can sometimes get soggy and stuck to the sheet pan). If they need to sit for longer than 2 hours, refrigerate them, loosely covered.

To make the sauce: In a large skillet, heat the olive oil over medium heat. Add the shallots and sauté until soft, 3 or 4 minutes. Add the tomatoes, season with salt and pepper, and simmer, stirring frequently, for about 15 minutes. Add the parsley. Set aside and keep warm.

To serve the *ravioloni*, cook them in a large pot of salted boiling water until they float to the surface, 3 or 4 minutes. Using a large skimmer and letting them drain well, transfer to a warmed large platter. (Pouring them into a colander might break them apart. This method is much gentler.) Pour the sauce over and drizzle everything with fresh olive oil. Serve right away, bringing the chunk of grana padano to the table for grating.

SERVES SIX AS A FIRST COURSE, FOUR AS A MAIN COURSE. Pasta with eggplant is almost the national dish of Sicily. Here, I've included almonds, an important Sicilian crop, and a touch of cinnamon, which adds great warmth to the eggplant, soothing its slight bitterness. The use of spice and nuts in a pasta dish is typically Sicilian and would be considered very foreign in the north.

CAVATELLI WITH EGGPLANT AND ALMONDS

1/4 cup extra-virgin olive oil, plus more for drizzling

2 unpeeled eggplants (I like the long, violet ones, which have fewer seeds than the dark purple variety), cut into 1/2-inch dice

4 scallions, including tender green parts, chopped

2 garlic cloves, very thinly sliced

Scant 1/8 teaspoon ground cinnamon

3 or 4 scrapings freshly grated nutmeg

Salt and freshly ground black pepper to taste

2 tablespoons dry Marsala

One 35-ounce can plum tomatoes, finely chopped, with juice

1 pound cavatelli pasta

Leaves from 4 or 5 large mint sprigs, chopped, plus a few sprigs for garnish

1/2 cup whole blanched almonds, lightly toasted (see page 77)

1 large chunk ricotta salata cheese for grating

In a large skillet, heat the 1/4 cup olive oil over medium heat. Add the eggplant and sauté until soft and lightly browned, about 8 minutes. About halfway through the sautéing, add the scallions and garlic (if you add them first, they might burn). If the eggplant starts to stick to the skillet, add a little more olive oil. Season the eggplant with the cinnamon, nutmeg, salt, and pepper and sauté 1 minute longer to release these flavors. Add the Marsala and let it bubble for about 1 minute. Add the tomatoes and simmer, uncovered, until the sauce is lightly thickened, about 8 minutes.

Meanwhile, in a large pot of salted boiling water, cook the pasta until al dente. Drain, reserving 1/2 cup of the pasta water. Transfer the cavatelli to a warmed large serving bowl. Add a generous drizzle of fresh olive oil and the chopped mint and toss. (This allows the oil from the mint to open up with the heat of the pasta. I love this smell.) Add the almonds to the eggplant sauce. Pour the sauce over the pasta and toss again. Add a little pasta water if needed to loosen the sauce. Grate on some ricotta salata and garnish with the mint sprigs. Serve right away, with the remaining ricotta salata brought to the table.

SERVES FIVE AS A FIRST COURSE. Slightly sweetened bread crumbs are sometimes used to top *pasta con le sarde* (pasta with sardines) in Sicily, and I love their sweetness with the oily fish, so I pair them here with anchovies, another rich, pungent fish. Try to find salt-packed anchovies. Their flavor is superior to that of oil-preserved variety, especially when heated.

LINGUINE WITH ANCHOVIES, PARSLEY, AND SWEET BREAD CRUMBS

BREAD CRUMBS

2 tablespoons extra-virgin olive oil

1 cup homemade dry bread crumbs (page 308)

1/4 pinch sugar

Salt to taste

PASTA

1 pound dried linguine pasta

1/2 cup extra-virgin olive oil, plus more for drizzling

5 garlic cloves, very thinly sliced

8 salt-packed anchovies, filleted, soaked, and drained (see page 33) and roughly chopped

1 jalapeño chili, minced, using the seeds if you like some heat

2 tablespoons dry white wine

Large handful of fresh flat-leaf parsley leaves, chopped (about 1/2 cup)

Grated zest of 1 lemon

In a small skillet, heat the olive oil over medium heat. Add the bread crumbs, sugar, and salt, and sauté until crisp and just starting to turn light golden. Transfer to a small serving bowl. Add the linguine to a large pot of salted boiling water, giving it a stir to make sure it doesn't stick together. Cook until al dente.

Meanwhile, in a large skillet, heat the 1/2 cup olive oil over medium-low heat. Add the garlic, anchovies, and chili and sauté until the garlic is fragrant and lightly golden and the anchovies have dissolved, 2 or 3 minutes. Add the white wine and let it bubble for a few seconds, leaving a little liquid in the skillet.

Drain the linguine, leaving a bit of water clinging to it, and add it to the skillet. Add the parsley, lemon zest, and a drizzle of fresh olive oil and toss well over medium heat for about 1 minute. Pour into pasta bowls and top each one with a generous sprinkling of the bread crumbs. Bring the remaining bread crumbs to the table.

SERVES FOUR AS A MAIN COURSE. Here's another of those minimal-effort summer dishes that have incredibly bright, clear flavors and take maybe 10 minutes to put
together. It has all my favorite tastes—tomatoes, garlic, fresh herbs, seafood, and lots of
olive oil. Think of it as a blueprint to alter to your liking. Grilled shrimp, scallops, chunks
of swordfish, tuna, or any other firm fish that stands up well to grilling can take the
place of the squid.

PENNE WITH GRILLED CALAMARI, TOMATO, AND HERB SALAD

4 large summer tomatoes, peeled, seeded, and cut into ¹/₂-inch dice (see page 26)

Salt to taste

¹/₃ cup extra-virgin olive oil, plus more for drizzling

¹/₂ small fresh red peperoncino chili, minced

1 tablespoon balsamic vinegar

2 garlic cloves, thinly sliced

Leaves from 3 or 4 thyme sprigs, chopped

Handful of fresh flat-leaf parsley leaves, chopped

Palmful of salt-packed capers, soaked and drained (see page 29)

1 pound penne pasta

1¹/₂ pounds small squid, cleaned (see page 195 to clean your own)

2 red onions, thinly sliced

Put the tomatoes in a colander in a sink. Sprinkle a little salt over them and let them
drain for about 30 minutes (fresh tomatoes can be very juicy and give off too much liquid, making pasta watery). Pour the tomatoes into a large serving bowl. Add the ¹/₃ cup
olive oil, the chili, balsamic vinegar, garlic, herbs, and capers. Mix well and let stand at
room temperature while you cook the pasta.

In a large pot of salted boiling water, cook the penne until al dente. Drain well and add
to the serving bowl. Toss and set aside while you grill the squid. (The pasta will be just
warm or even almost room temperature by the time you serve it. With the just-grilled
hot squid, it's a great contrast.)

Light a fire in a charcoal grill, preheat a gas grill to high, or heat a grill pan over high heat. Put the squid and red onions in a bowl. Drizzle on good amount of olive oil and season with salt. Toss to coat. Grill the squid and onions in a grill basket or on a wire-mesh grill rack until both show good grill marks, about 2 minutes. Turn and grill the other side about 1 minute, or until the squid are opaque (don't cook them any longer than this or they will be tough). Transfer the squid to a cutting board and cut the bodies into thick rings. Add the rings, tentacles, and any cooking juices, along with the onions, to the pasta bowl. Toss gently and taste for seasoning. Serve right away.

SERVES FOUR AS A MAIN COURSE. *Scialatielli* is a thick, ribbon like homemade pasta from the Amalfi region that has recently become popular throughout Campania and also in New York restaurants. It's flavored with basil or parsley, pecorino, and milk and has a soft but slightly chewy texture that I love. You'll most likely find it accompanied with a seafood sauce of some kind. I asked a restaurant chef in my neighborhood how he makes it, and what he told me sounded too Americanized, so I've patterned the recipe here after one I found in Arthur Schwartz's excellent book *Naples at Table*. The sauce is flavored with a broth made from shrimp shells and sweet white wine. The sauce also includes the shrimp itself and ripe summer tomatoes. The dish has a main-course kind of feel, and I suggest serving it that way.

SCIALATIELLI WITH SWEET SHRIMP BROTH

SCIALATIELLI

3½ cups all-purpose flour

Handful of fresh flat-leaf parsley leaves, chopped

2 tablespoons grated aged pecorino cheese

Generous pinch of salt

3 large eggs

½ cup whole milk, or as needed

2 tablespoons extra-virgin olive oil

SAUCE

4 tablespoons extra-virgin olive oil

1½ pounds large shrimp, shelled (shells reserved for broth)

½ cup sweet white wine, such as Moscato or Malvasia

1 cup warm water

Salt to taste

3 garlic cloves, thinly sliced

Freshly ground black pepper to taste

8 summer plum tomatoes, peeled, seeded, chopped, and drained in a colander for 15 minutes if watery

Grated zest of 1 lemon

Handful of fresh flat-leaf parsley leaves, chopped

Extra-virgin olive oil for drizzling

TO MAKE THE *SCIALATIELLI:* In a large, wide bowl, combine the flour, parsley, pecorino, and salt. Mix until well blended.

Crack the eggs into a small bowl. Add the milk and olive oil and beat with a fork until blended. Make a well in the middle of the flour mixture and slowly pour the egg mixture into it, mixing in the flour with your fingers. Keep mixing until you have a messy-looking ball. Knead the dough a few times in the bowl to make a more uniform-looking ball. Transfer the dough to a floured surface, leaving behind any little bits of dough that haven't been incorporated. Knead the dough until smooth and silky, adding a little more flour if it seems sticky, about 5 or 6 minutes. Cover the dough with plastic wrap and let it rest for about 30 minutes unrefrigerated before rolling it out.

Cut the dough into 4 equal pieces. Working with one piece at a time (keep the rest wrapped in plastic so it doesn't dry out), run it through a hand-cranked pasta machine 2 or 3 times at the widest setting, then move on to thinner and thinner settings until you've come to the third-from-the-last setting. This will give you a slightly thick texture (as I remember this pasta when I had it in Amalfi recently). Lay the pasta sheets on a floured surface and cut them into $1/4$-inch-wide strips. The strips should be about 4 or 5 inches long, so if you have really long sheets of pasta, cut them in half. Lay the strips out on floured baking sheets (it's best if they're not touching too much because they can stick). If you're not cooking the pasta within 1 hour, cover it with kitchen towels so it doesn't dry (you can refrigerate it if you have room).

TO MAKE THE SAUCE: In a medium saucepan, heat 2 tablespoons of the olive oil over medium heat. Add the reserved shrimp shells and sauté until they turn pink, 2 or 3 minutes. Add the sweet wine and let it bubble for about 1 minute. Add about $1/2$ cup of water and cook at a lively bubble for about 10 minutes, or until the broth is reduced to about $1/2$ to $3/4$ cup and has a nice, sweet, shrimpy taste. Add a pinch of salt and strain the broth into a small bowl.

In a large skillet, heat the remaining 2 tablespoons olive oil over high heat. Add the shrimp and garlic at the same time (since the heat is high, you might burn the garlic if you add it first). Spread the shrimp out in a more or less single layer, season them with salt and pepper, and sauté quickly, turning them on only once. When they're nice and pink on both sides, after about 2 minutes, add the tomatoes and shrimp broth and heat through for about 1 minute (try not to let it go any longer or the shrimp might overcook). Remove from heat and set aside until the pasta is cooked.

Meanwhile, in a large pot of salted boiling water, cook the pasta just until it comes to the surface, about 2 minutes. Gently drain it into a colander and pour it into a warmed large serving bowl. Pour on the shrimp sauce and add the lemon zest, parsley, and a drizzle of fresh olive oil. Season with a pinch of salt and a few more grindings of pepper. Toss gently and serve right away.

SERVES **FOUR AS A FIRST COURSE**. My husband and I always go out to dinner for our wedding anniversary, but if we had to stay in, here's what I'd cook for him. Bottarga, the pressed tuna or red mullet roe famous in Sicily and Sardinia, is shown off to its greatest advantage when tossed with pasta. The white wine in the tagliatelle gives it a sleek texture and imparts a subtle acidity that works well with the saltiness of the fish roe. This is a rich first-course pasta to serve before a simple roasted fish.

WHITE WINE TAGLIATELLE WITH BOTTARGA AND BURST CHERRY TOMATOES

TAGLIATELLE

3 cups unbleached all-purpose flour

4 large eggs

Pinch of salt

2 to 3 tablespoons dry white wine

1 teaspoon extra-virgin olive oil

SAUCE

3 tablespoons extra-virgin olive oil

3 garlic cloves, very thinly sliced

4 cups sweet cherry tomatoes, stemmed

1/2 cup dry white wine

Pinch of salt

Freshly ground black pepper to taste

About 15 scrapings of bottarga (preferably Sardinian gray-mullet roe; see page 32)

Large handful of fresh basil leaves, chopped

TO MAKE THE PASTA: Put the flour in a food processor. Add the eggs, salt, 2 tablespoons of the wine, and olive oil. Pulse until a loose ball forms. If it is still dry and crumbly, add 1 tablespoon white wine and pulse a few more times. Transfer the somewhat messy dough ball to a floured surface and knead it, adding more flour, 1 tablespoon at a time, to prevent it from sticking, until smooth and satiny, about 5 minutes. Wrap the dough in plastic wrap and let it rest unrefrigerated for about 30 minutes.

Cut the dough into 4 pieces. Run 1 piece of dough through a hand-cranked pasta machine 2 times at the widest setting. Keep running it through progressively thinner settings until you get to the next-to-last setting. Lay the pasta sheet out on a floured surface uncovered. Repeat with the remaining dough. Letting the sheets dry briefly makes them easier to cut. Starting with the first sheet, use a sharp knife to cut the pasta sheets into $1/4$-inch-wide ribbons. (If the sheets are very long, you might want to cut them in half crosswise first.) Lay the tagliatelle out on floured baking sheet, trying not to overlap them. If not cooking the pasta within an hour or so, refrigerate it, covered with a kitchen towel, to keep it moist.

TO MAKE THE SAUCE: In a large skillet, heat the olive oil over high heat. Add the garlic and tomatoes at the same time and sauté, shaking the skillet a few times, until the tomatoes start to burst, 4 or 5 minutes. Add the white wine and cook to reduce by about half. Season the tomatoes with a tiny pinch of salt (you'll be adding salty bottarga in a minute) and more generously with pepper.

Meanwhile, cook the pasta in a large pot of salted boiling water until it comes to the surface, 3 minutes. Drain well and transfer to a large serving bowl. Add the tomatoes and all the skillet juices and a drizzle of fresh olive oil. Toss gently. With a sharp vegetable peeler, shave the bottarga into the bowl. Add the basil and give the pasta another gentle toss. Serve right away.

VARIATION   Pasta with red pepper flakes, garlic, olive oil, and bottarga is a dish I had several times in Sicily. It goes better with a firm spaghetti than with the delicate fresh pasta above. To make it for 2: Heat $1/2$ cup good olive oil over medium heat. Add 4 sliced garlic cloves and a generous pinch of red pepper flakes. Sauté until the garlic starts to turn golden. Add 8 ounces of spaghetti, cooked al dente, and toss over low heat until it's well coated with oil. Shave on about 10 scrapings of bottarga and add a handful of fresh flat-leaf chopped parsley leaves. Toss again gently and divide between 2 serving plates.

SERVES SIX AS A FIRST COURSE, FOUR AS A MAIN COURSE. This is my version of a pasta I had at Zaccaria, a seafood trattoria in Atrani, on the Amalfi Coast. Just about everything, except the pasta, is thrown on an open grill, and the grill cook eats oranges and apples and throws the peels into the fire. All the fish and the restaurant itself have a smoky, fruity aroma.

All Zaccaria's mussel dishes are made with briny and sweet local black Mediterranean mussels, some no bigger than half an inch long. I usually buy blue Long Island mussels from a greenmarket fish seller, and they're excellent, but occasionally I find the Mediterranean variety in a fish shop, and I use it for a special treat (see page 438 for a source for black mussels in this country). Cultivated mussels are also fine, and they tend to be much cleaner than wild ones.

I've substituted chickpeas for the cannellini beans in the original. I've also added a little orange zest to the sauce just to echo the aroma of the restaurant. The trio of orange, basil, and hot chilies that I've used to season this pasta excels for many seafood dishes, and it's worth remembering when you have an improvisational confrontation with a bag of clams or a salmon fillet.

LASAGNETTE WITH CHICKPEAS AND MUSSELS

1 cup dried chickpeas, soaked overnight in cold water to cover

Salt to taste

1 bay leaf, preferably fresh

Extra-virgin olive oil for drizzling, plus ¼ cup

2 pounds small mussels, scrubbed and debearded, if necessary

½ cup dry white wine

3 leeks, including light green parts, rinsed and chopped

2 celery stalks, thinly sliced

½ small fresh red peperoncino chili, minced (using some or all of the seeds, depending on how much heat you like)

4 short strips orange zest

Leaves from 4 or 5 thyme sprigs, chopped

1 pound lasagnette pasta

Handful of fresh basil leaves, chopped

Drain the chickpeas and transfer to a large pot. Add cold water to cover. Bring to a boil. Reduce the heat to a gentle simmer and partially cover the pot (this allows some steam to escape but keeps enough in the pot to speed the cooking along). Salt can toughen the skin of dried peas or beans, so don't add any until the final minutes of cooking. The cooking time for chickpeas can vary, depending on how old the peas are, but figure on at least 1½ hours. When the chickpeas are tender to the bite, turn off the heat but leave the pot on the burner. Add a generous amount of salt, the bay leaf, and a drizzle of olive oil to the pot. Let stand for about 20 minutes (this further tenderizes and flavors the chickpeas). Drain the chickpeas, reserving about 1 cup of the cooking liquid.

Put the mussels in a large pot and pour the white wine over them. Turn the heat to medium and cook, stirring frequently, until they open, 4 or 5 minutes. Using a large skimmer, transfer the mussels to a bowl. Strain the mussel cooking juice through a fine-mesh sieve into a small bowl, just to make sure there isn't any sand.

In a large skillet, heat the ¼ cup olive oil over medium heat. Add the leeks, celery, chili, orange zest, and thyme. Season with a little salt and sauté until the vegetables are soft and fragrant, about 5 minutes. Add the chickpeas and reserved mussel cooking liquid and simmer on low heat until the sauce is lightly thickened, about 4 minutes. Add the mussels to the skillet and stir to mix them in. Turn off the heat and let stand on the burner.

Meanwhile, cook the pasta in a large pot of salted boiling water until al dente. Drain and pour into a warmed large serving bowl. Add the chickpeas and mussels with all the skillet juices to the bowl. Add the basil and a little of the chickpea cooking liquid if needed to loosen the sauce (the texture should be slightly liquid, not dry). Serve right away.

VARIATION   Often on summer vacations, if I'm near the ocean, I find myself making spaghetti with mussels, a simpler version of this recipe. The classic white wine, garlic, and parsley version is still my favorite. It typifies easy, dramatic summer cooking at its best. To make it for 2 people, start cooking about 8 ounces spaghetti. In a large, deep pot, heat ½ cup olive oil over medium heat. Add 4 thinly sliced garlic cloves and 1 chopped red peperoncino chili. Sauté for 1 minute, then add about 1½ pounds well-cleaned small mussels and ½ cup dry white wine. Cook, stirring the mussels frequently, until they open, about 4 minutes. Drain the spaghetti and add it to the pot, along with a squeeze of lemon juice and a generous handful of chopped fresh flat-leaf parsley. Toss for a few moments over medium heat, adding a little salt if needed, and pour into a serving bowl.

SERVES SIX AS A FIRST COURSE, FOUR AS A MAIN COURSE. Pasta with clams has fascinated me since I was a child. I love any dish where olive oil makes up much of the sauce, and that plus briny clam juices, garlic, lemon, and white wine produces a taste that was etched in my mind at a young age. I always ordered it when my father took us out for dinner, and my mother often made some version of it on Christmas Eve. Many of my friends ask me to make it for them, saying it's a favorite of theirs as well. And it happens to be one of the most popular pasta dishes in Naples, where it originated. There are many variations, but they all fall into two basic categories: with tomatoes and without tomatoes. I find the "white" versions to be closest to people's hearts. I used cockles here because I like the way their little shells look tangled up with the spaghetti (very much like the mini clams I've been served around Naples and Capri). Manila or littleneck clams do fine, though I'd try to find the smallest, tenderest ones I could.

SPAGHETTI WITH COCKLES, PANCETTA, AND PARSLEY

3 pounds cockles (from New Zealand or Rhode Island), scrubbed

³/₄ cup dry white wine

1 pound spaghetti pasta

¹/₃ cup extra-virgin olive oil, plus more for drizzling

2 thin slices pancetta, finely chopped

5 fresh, moist garlic cloves, very thinly sliced

Grated zest and juice of 1 large lemon

Coarsely ground black pepper to taste

Very large handful of fresh flat-leaf parsley leaves (about 1 cup), coarsely chopped

---

Put the cockles in a large pot and pour on ³/₄ cup white wine. Turn the heat to medium and cover the pot. After a minute or so, uncover the pot and stir the cockles a bit. They should start opening in a minute or so. (A nice thing about cockles is that they all pretty much open at the same time, unlike clams. They also are usually fairly sand free, so you don't need to strain the clam cooking broth before adding it to the sauce.)

Meanwhile, in a large pot of salted boiling water, cook the spaghetti until al dente.

In a large skillet, heat the $1/3$ cup olive oil over medium-low heat. Add the pancetta and sauté until crisp (this tiny bit of pancetta is not traditional, but I like the way it emphasizes the brininess of the cockles). Add the garlic and sauté until just faintly golden, about 2 minutes. Pour about half of the cockle cooking liquid into the skillet, Add the lemon zest and juice and let the sauce bubble for a minute or so (this will intensify its flavor). Add the cockles with all the remaining liquid to the skillet. Heat through for about 30 seconds to warm the cockles (you don't want to overcook them). Taste the sauce to see if it needs salt (it may or may not, depending on the saltiness of your cockles), but grind on a generous amount of coarse pepper (this blends so well with cockles and clams).

Drain the spaghetti and put it on the serving platter. Give it a generous drizzle of fresh olive oil and add all the parsley (the heat from the pasta will release the flavor of the parsley into the oil, intensifying it). Toss well. Pour on the cockle sauce and toss again gently. Serve right away.

VARIATION   To make a classic red sauce version, leave out the pancetta and add 3 round tomatoes that have been peeled, seeded, and chopped (see page 26) to the skillet after you sauté the garlic. Reduce the amount of lemon juice to about 1 teaspoon and omit the zest.

SERVES FOUR AS A MAIN COURSE. When I was a teenager, I had little salt-cod balls in tomato sauce at the Brooklyn home of a friend whose family was from Sorrento. He hated the dish and was even embarrassed by the smell of it in the house; I found it wonderful. I've patterned these fresh tuna *polpettini* after what I remember from that experience.

Bucatini is a long, spaghettilike pasta, but with a hole through the middle. It's also called perciatelli, which in Southern dialect means pierced through.

BUCATINI WITH TUNA POLPETTINI AND TOMATOES

1 pound tuna steak, skinned and cut into large chunks

1 garlic clove, minced

$\frac{1}{2}$ cup homemade dry bread crumbs (see page 308)

2 tablespoons grated pecorino cheese

1 large egg

Small handful of fresh mint leaves, chopped

Small handful of capers

Salt and freshly ground black pepper to taste

Generous squeeze of lemon juice

Extra-virgin olive oil for drizzling

SAUCE

2 tablespoons extra-virgin olive oil

About 6 scallions, including tender green parts, cut into thin rounds

2 garlic cloves, thinly sliced

2 oil-packed anchovy fillets, chopped, or 1 salt-packed anchovy, filleted, soaked, drained, and chopped (see page 33)

1 tablespoon dry white wine

One 28-ounce can plum tomatoes, finely chopped, with juice, plus one 15-ounce can, chopped and drained

Salt and freshly ground black pepper to taste

1 pound bucatini pasta

3 tablespoons extra-virgin olive oil, plus more for drizzling

Small handful of fresh mint leaves, chopped

12 fresh basil leaves, chopped, plus a few sprigs for garnish

In a food processor, pulse the tuna chunks 2 or 3 times until well chopped but not puréed. Transfer the tuna to a large bowl. Add the garlic, bread crumbs, pecorino, egg, mint, and capers. Mix gently with your hands. Season with salt, pepper, lemon juice, and a drizzle of olive oil. Mix again and taste for seasoning. Roll the tuna into ½-inch-diameter balls and set them aside while you make the sauce.

TO MAKE THE SAUCE: In a large skillet, heat the 2 tablespoons olive oil over medium heat. Add the scallions, garlic, and anchovies and sauté until fragrant, 3 or 4 minutes. Add the white wine and let it boil away. Add the tomatoes and increase the heat to high. Cook at a lively bubble, stirring frequently, until the sauce has thickened, about 10 minutes. Season with salt and pepper.

In a large pot of salted boiling water, cook the bucatini until al dente.

While the pasta is cooking, set up another large skillet over medium-high heat and add the 3 tablespoons olive oil. Add the tuna balls and brown them, turning once or twice, 3 or 4 minutes. (You want to keep them moist and slightly pink in the centers.) Add the tuna balls to the tomato sauce and, over low heat, stir them in the sauce for a minute.

Drain the bucatini and place it in a large serving bowl. Add the basil, mint, and a generous drizzle of olive oil. Toss (the heat of the pasta will release all the herbs' flavors). Put the tuna balls in a serving bowl, top with a spoonful of the sauce, and garnish with basil sprigs. Use the remaining sauce to dress the bucatini. Serve everyone a bowl of pasta with a few of the tuna balls on top.

SERVES FOUR AS A MAIN COURSE. There's an old-fashioned southern Italian restaurant on the West Side of Manhattan called Ralph's that I go to for the one dish on the menu that intrigues me. I always order the ziti with chicken livers, which has a nice depth of flavor from tomatoes and herbs. I love it on a really cold night with a glass of the acidic house red wine. My version includes brandy, and I've replaced Ralph's dried oregano with saffron and bay leaf.

CAVATELLI WITH CHICKEN LIVERS, TOMATO, AND SAFFRON

1 pound chicken livers

3 tablespoons unsalted butter

2 tablespoons extra-virgin olive oil, plus more for drizzling

2 thin slices pancetta, chopped

1 large onion, finely diced

2 bay leaves, preferably fresh

Salt and freshly ground black pepper to taste

1 garlic clove, thinly sliced

$^1/_4$ cup brandy

One 35-ounce can chopped tomatoes, drained

$^3/_4$ cup canned low-salt chicken broth

Large pinch of saffron threads, dried and ground (see page 42)

1 pound cavatelli pasta

Handful of fresh flat-leaf parsley leaves, chopped

1 good-sized chunk pecorino cheese

Trim all the stringy connecting tissue from the chicken livers and separate them into lobes. Cut the larger lobes in half to make $^1/_2$-inch pieces. Pat the chicken livers dry with paper towels (so they will brown more easily).

In a large skillet, melt 1 tablespoon of the butter with the 2 tablespoons olive oil over medium heat. Add the pancetta and sauté until just starting to crisp. Add the onion, bay leaves, salt, and pepper. Sauté until the onion is soft, about 4 minutes. Add the garlic and sauté for 1 minute. Add half the brandy and let it boil away. Add the tomatoes and cook at a lively bubble for about 4 minutes (you want them to cook quickly so they don't break down into a purée). Add $^1/_2$ cup of the chicken broth to loosen the sauce. Add the ground saffron and simmer for 1 minute so its flavor can open up, then turn off the heat.

Meanwhile, cook the pasta in a large pot of salted boiling water until al dente.

In another large skillet, melt the remaining 2 tablespoons of butter over high heat. When the butter foam begins to subside, add the chicken livers, season them with salt and pepper, and brown them quickly on all sides, leaving them slightly pink in the center, 2 or 3 minutes (I cook the chicken livers in a separate skillet so they will brown well over high heat without burning other ingredients). Add the remaining brandy to the skillet and let it bubble a few seconds. If the skillet flares up (which often happens when you add alcohol over high heat), pull it off the heat for a second. Add the remaining chicken broth and stir to scrape up all the cooked-on skillet juices so they can be incorporated into the sauce. Add the chicken livers and skillet juices to the tomato sauce and stir to blend. Taste for seasoning, adding more salt if needed and a few grindings of pepper.

Drain the cavatelli and pour it into a warmed large serving bowl. Add a generous drizzle of olive oil and the parsley and toss. Add the chicken liver sauce and toss again, gently. Serve, bringing the chunk of pecorino to the table for grating.

VARIATIONS   This sauce is also good without the chicken livers (the pancetta adds good flavor). You can substitute 1 pound of sliced wild mushrooms for the livers, sautéing them with the onion.

SERVES SIX AS A FIRST COURSE, FOUR AS A MAIN COURSE. A *timballo*, a pasta baked inside a pastry cylinder (*timballo* means "drum" in Italian), is one of the show-off glories of the aristocratic Neapolitan and Sicilian kitchens, elaborately filled with meat, ragù, eggs, chicken livers, or vegetables. *Timballi* are a lot of work and nowadays aren't often made by home cooks; they're more often ordered from a caterer for a special occasion. I'm always looking for ways to get that *timballo* taste without all the work, and here I've made a baked pasta in the same spirit but much easer to put together. I've omitted the crust but kept the rich interior with duck ragù, duck liver, and a luxurious béchamel. I've chosen an egg pasta for it. In southern Italy that signals a fancy occasion, and I'd serve this for a special dinner or as a buffet dish at a party.

Béchamel (*besciamella* in Italian), the flour-thickened, milk-based white sauce, shows up in Neapolitan and Sicilian dishes descended from lavish court cooking. It appears in celebratory baked pastas such as cannelloni and lasagne, but also as a filling for Sicilian *arancini* (fried rice balls) and Neapolitan *crocche di besciamella,* which are simply deep-fried balls of béchamel. In Sicily they are called *croquettes di latte* and are frequently served as part of a fritto misto (a mix of deep-fried vegetables and meats).

BAKED TAGLIATELLE WITH BRAISED DUCK, BLACK OLIVES, AND BÉCHAMEL

RAGÙ

1 tablespoon extra-virgin olive oil

3 whole duck legs, plus 1 duck liver that has been trimmed and cut into small pieces

Salt and freshly ground black pepper to taste

2 or 3 thin slices fatty prosciutto end, finely diced

1 large onion, finely diced

2 small carrots, peeled and finely diced

1 garlic clove, crushed

Pinch of ground cloves

1 cup dry red wine, such as Sicilian Nero d'Avola or Chianti

One 35-ounce can plum tomatoes, chopped, with juice

1 teaspoon imported tomato paste

1/2 cup canned low-salt chicken broth, plus more as needed

1 bay leaf, preferably fresh

Leaves from 3 or 4 large marjoram sprigs, chopped

Handful of black olives (Gaetas are a good choice), pitted

BÉCHAMEL SAUCE

2 tablespoons unsalted butter

2 tablespoons all-purpose flour

1 1/2 cups whole milk

Pinch of ground cloves

Freshly grated nutmeg to taste

Pinch of cayenne pepper

Generous pinch of salt

1 pound tagliatelle pasta

1 chunk young pecorino cheese for grating

TO MAKE THE RAGÙ: In a large Dutch oven or a flameproof casserole with a lid, heat the olive oil over medium heat. Add the duck legs, seasoning them with salt and pepper, and brown them well on both sides, letting much of the fat melt away. Drain off all but about 2 tablespoons of the duck fat. Add the prosciutto, onion, and carrots and sauté until the prosciutto is crisp and the vegetables have softened, about 4 minutes. Add the garlic and ground cloves and sauté a minute or so longer to release their flavors. Add the red wine and let it bubble for a few minutes. Add the tomatoes, tomato paste, the 1/2 cup chicken broth, the bay leaf, and marjoram. Bring to a boil. Reduce the heat to very low, cover, and simmer until the duck is very tender, about 2 hours. In the last 15 minutes of cooking, add the chopped duck liver.

MEANWHILE, MAKE THE BÉCHAMEL: In a saucepan, melt the butter over medium heat. Add the flour and whisk to blend them together, then cook, stirring, about 1 minute to cook off the raw flour taste. Add the milk and whisk well. Let this come to a low boil, whisking constantly, until the sauce starts to thicken. Reduce the heat to low and simmer for 2 or 3 minutes, whisking, until the sauce is smooth and thick. Stir in the ground cloves, nutmeg, cayenne, and salt. Set aside.

Preheat the oven to 425°F.

Remove the duck from the casserole and let cool to the touch. Remove the duck meat from the bones, discard the skin, and chop the meat into little pieces. Skim the fat from the surface of the sauce and return the duck to the pot. Add the olives and taste for seasoning. The sauce should have body but not be so thick that it will make the dish dry. If it seems too thick, add a little more chicken broth.

In a large pot of salted boiling water, cook the tagliatelle until tender, 1 or 2 minutes for fresh egg pasta. Drain well and add it to the casserole with the sauce. Toss gently and pour into a baking dish about 9 by 13 inches. Smooth the top and grate a thin layer of pecorino over the pasta.

Reheat the béchamel gently to make it pourable and pour it more or less evenly over the top of the pasta. (It doesn't have to cover every inch of pasta. I usually drizzle it over in a lazy ribbon pattern.) Sprinkle on a little more pecorino and bake, uncovered, until bubbling hot and very lightly browned, 15 to 20 minutes. Serve right away (I like serving it hot and loose, so I don't let it rest the way many recipes suggest).

SERVES SIX AS A FIRST COURSE, FOUR AS A MAIN COURSE. In keeping with the ways of southern Italy, I use very little capocollo here, just enough to give the pasta and tomato a little flavor. Try to find round, not teardrop-shaped, cherry tomatoes for this sauce, as they give off more juice to coat the pasta.

Paccheri is a very large tube pasta from Naples. Setaro makes an excellent one. If you can't find it, any large tube-shaped pasta, such as rigatoni or ziti, will work fine.

PACCHERI WITH CHERRY TOMATOES, CAPOCOLLO, AND ARUGULA

1 pound *paccheri* or other large tube pasta

2 tablespoons extra-virgin olive oil, plus more for drizzling

About 6 very thin slices capocollo, cut into matchsticks

2 garlic cloves, very thinly sliced

4 cups cherry tomatoes, stemmed

Salt to taste

2 tablespoons dry red wine

1 large bunch arugula, stemmed

6 fresh basil leaves, coarsely chopped

One 8-ounce chunk provolone cheese for grating

Add the pasta to a large pot of salted boiling water and give it a good stir to prevent sticking. Cook until al dente.

Meanwhile, heat a large skillet over high heat. Add 2 tablespoons olive oil. When the oil is shimmering, add the capocollo, garlic, and cherry tomatoes all at once. Let everything sit for a few moments without moving, and when the tomatoes start hissing and popping, give the skillet a few good shakes so everything cooks evenly. After 1 or 2 minutes, the tomatoes should start bursting and the garlic should be very lightly colored (the juices from the tomatoes will prevent it from getting too dark). When most of the tomatoes have burst, add a little salt and the red wine, shaking the skillet for a few seconds to loosen all the cooked-on juices and help the alcohol burn off.

Drain the pasta, leaving a little water clinging to it, and place it in a warmed serving bowl. Pour on the tomatoes and all the skillet juices. Add the arugula, basil, and a generous drizzle of fresh olive oil. Grate on a small amount of provolone (about 5 quick gratings) and give everything a good toss. The heat from the pasta will wilt the arugula slightly. Serve hot, passing the remaining chunk of provolone for grating at the table.

SERVES FOUR AS A MAIN COURSE. They like to blend pork, fennel, and hot chilies in Basilicata, and I've borrowed the combination to fashion a simple ragù with bold flavors. Aglianico del Vulture is Basilicata's most famous red wine. It is dry, intense, and spicy, and one of my favorites from anywhere in the South. Use a big glass of it to give this ragù an authentic southern flavor, and drink the rest with the dinner.

RIGATONI WITH SPICY PORK AND FENNEL RAGÙ

2 tablespoons extra-virgin olive oil

2 thin slices pancetta, finely diced

1 pound boneless pork shoulder, cut into 1-inch cubes

2 sweet Italian pork sausages, removed from casings and crumbled

Pinch of sugar

1 large onion, finely diced

1 fennel bulb, trimmed, cored, and finely diced (fronds reserved and chopped)

2 garlic cloves, thinly sliced

2 bay leaves, preferably fresh

Small palmful of fennel seeds

Salt to taste

2 small dried red chilies, broken in half

1 cup dry red wine, Aglianico del Vulture if available, otherwise another strong, dry red

One 35-ounce can plum tomatoes, finely chopped, with juice

Handful of fresh basil leaves, chopped

1 tablespoon balsamic vinegar

1 pound rigatoni pasta

1 chunk aged pecorino cheese for grating

In a large Dutch oven or flameproof casserole with a lid, heat the olive oil over medium heat. Add the pancetta, pork shoulder, sausage, and sugar (to help the meat brown). Sauté until the meat is lightly browned all over, at least 10 minutes (this is important for adding flavor to ragù, so try not to skimp on this step). Add the onion, fennel and fronds, garlic, bay leaves, fennel seeds, a pinch of salt, and the chilies. Sauté until the vegetables start to soften, about another 5 minutes. Reduce the heat at any time if the skillet bottom gets too dark. Add the red wine and let it bubble for a few minutes. Add the tomatoes and bring everything to a boil. Reduce the heat to low, cover the pot, and simmer for about 2 hours, or until the ragù has good body and the meat is starting to shred. You might need to skim the surface once or twice during cooking, depending on the fattiness of your meat. Add the basil and a splash of balsamic vinegar (this will sharpen all the flavors). Taste for seasoning, adding more salt, if needed. Set aside and keep warm.

In a large pot of salted boiling water, cook the rigatoni until al dente. Drain, reserving about $\frac{1}{2}$ cup of the cooking water. Transfer the pasta to a warmed large serving bowl. Pour on the ragù and toss, adding a little pasta cooking water, if needed, to loosen the texture. Serve hot, bringing the chunk of pecorino to the table for grating.

SERVES SIX AS A MAIN COURSE. Lamb and sweet peppers are a beautiful flavor pairing that I turn to often when making stews and pasta dishes. This ragù is based on one from my grandmother's town of Castelfranco in Miscano, in northern Campania, but there it would be served tossed with cavatelli. Ground cloves occasionally show up in ragù in various southern regions; I've detected this spice in dishes I've been served in inland towns in Campania and Basilicata. I like the subtle way it deepens the sauce's flavor.

Mixing fresh goat cheese into a traditional ricotta-based filling gives this lasagna an unexpected tang. I'm always looking for ways to add freshness to meat lasagne, which can be very rich. Abundant fresh herbs, such as the basil used here, can really do the trick.

LASAGNA WITH LAMB AND RED PEPPER RAGÙ AND CAPRINO

RAGÙ

2 tablespoons extra-virgin olive oil

2 pounds ground lamb

5 or 6 thin rounds of caciatorini or soppressata, finely chopped

2 garlic cloves, thinly sliced

Pinch of ground cloves

Salt and freshly ground black pepper to taste

2 bay leaves, preferably fresh

Leaves from 3 or 4 oregano sprigs, chopped

1 cup dry red wine

Two 35-ounce cans plum tomatoes, chopped, with juice

2 red bell peppers, roasted, peeled, seeded, and finely diced (see page 38)

PASTA

3 cups all-purpose flour

Generous pinch of salt

4 large eggs

2 or 3 tablespoons dry Marsala

1 tablespoon extra-virgin olive oil

RICOTTA FILLING

2½ cups whole-milk ricotta

1 small log fresh goat cheese (about 6 ounces) at room temperature

3 or 4 scrapings freshly grated nutmeg

Salt and freshly ground black pepper to taste

Large handful of fresh basil leaves, chopped

1 cup grated pecorino cheese

Extra-virgin olive oil for drizzling

TO MAKE THE RAGÙ: In a large Dutch oven or flameproof casserole with a lid, heat the olive oil over medium heat. Add the ground lamb, caciatorini or soppressata, and garlic. Season with the ground cloves, salt, and pepper and sauté, stirring occasionally, until lightly browned. Add the bay leaves and oregano and sauté a few moments longer until they release their fragrances. Add the red wine and let it bubble for a few minutes. Add the tomatoes and bring to a boil. Reduce the heat to low, cover, and simmer until the meat is very tender and the sauce has thickened, about 2 hours (if after about 1½ hours of cooking it still looks very thin, cook it for the remaining time uncovered). Add the roasted red peppers and taste for seasoning. Remove and discard the bay leaves. You can make the ragù the day before, if you like; just make sure it's not icy cold when you layer it into the lasagne or it won't cook quickly.

WHILE THE RAGÙ IS SIMMERING, MAKE THE PASTA: To save time, start the pasta in the food processor. You'll need about ½ cup less flour than with the traditional well method (page 361), since the food processor incorporates more flour than the well method does.

Put the 3 cups flour in a food processor. Add a generous pinch of salt and pulse to blend it in. In a small bowl, beat the eggs, 2 tablespoons of the Marsala, and the olive oil together with a fork. Pour this over the flour and pulse several times until a ball starts to form. If the mixture remains dry and crumbly, add another tablespoon of Marsala and pulse once or twice more. Transfer the still-somewhat-loose ball of dough to a floured surface. Knead the dough for about 5 minutes, adding more flour to the work surface if it sticks. The dough should be smooth and silky. Wrap it in plastic and let rest for about 30 minutes.

Divide the dough into 4 sections (keeping the ones you're not immediately working with covered in plastic so they don't dry out). Run the dough through the widest setting on a hand-cranked pasta machine. Do this several times. Keep rolling it through thinner and thinner settings until you've made the pasta as thin as it can be (to keep the lasagne's texture light, the pasta should be very thin and delicate). Cut the pasta sheets into sections about the length of your baking dish (a 9-by-13-inch dish or equivalent is a good size) and lay them out on floured baking sheets.

TO MAKE THE FILLING: In a small bowl, combine the ricotta and goat cheese. Season with nutmeg, salt, and pepper. Add the basil and mix well.

In a large pot of salted boiling water, cook the pasta sheets a few at a time. They're cooked when they float to the surface, probably a minute or less. Using a large skimmer, transfer the pasta to a colander. Run cold water over the pasta until cooled and lay the sheet out on kitchen towels. Repeat with all the pasta sheets.

Preheat the oven to 425°F.

Coat the baking dish lightly with olive oil and put in a layer of pasta. Ladle out a thin layer of ragù. Put down another layer of pasta and top this with a thin layer of the ricotta mixture. Sprinkle on a thin coating of grated pecorino. Repeat until you've almost reached the top of the baking dish, about 6 layers of pasta, ending with a thin layer of ragù, the remaining pecorino, and a generous drizzle of olive oil.

Bake, uncovered, until bubbling and lightly browned, about 20 minutes. (Cooking lasagne quickly, uncovered, on a relatively high heat, helps it stays moist and fresh and crisp on the top.) Let rest for about 10 minutes before cutting.

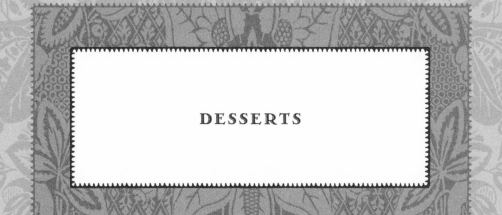

DESSERTS

The dessert I recall most vividly from my childhood is something my father always made in the summer, usually to bring out at the end of an outdoor barbecue: a big bowl of peaches, sliced but not peeled, sprinkled with a tiny amount of sugar, and doused with a sharp red Italian wine. The peaches took on a purplish tint and had an alluring sweet-and-sour taste. I think this memory set my taste for desserts at that point (and my healthy interest in wine, too). Not that our household wasn't filled with packaged cakes, candy, and cookies, but this dessert especially appealed to me, and it did so at an early age, at least partly because it was made by my father (come to think of it, my father prepared many fruit desserts, not only big bowls of fruit salad but also strawberries with balsamic vinegar, a newly trendy dish that he started making in the 1970s).

When you think of a southern Italian dessert, you may think not of fresh fruit but of rich, elaborately decorated baked desserts, mainly Sicilian and Neapolitan. The oldest of these, made with nuts and honey, have Arab and Greek roots; others, which incorporate pastry cream and chocolate, came later and were influenced by French cooking. Cannoli with ricotta, jasmine, and chocolate is one of my favorites. Another is cassata, a layered sponge cake flavored with maraschino liqueur and rose water and covered with candied citron and orange. Sicilian pastry shops are filled with marzipan shaped and colored to look like figs dripping with dew, Easter lambs, or bunches of grapes. Many of those sweets were first made in convents during the Middle Ages and began to be sold commercially in the nineteenth century, mainly to make money to keep the convents open. Saint Agatha's nipples (known in Sicily, where they were created, as *minni di virgini*—"virgins' breasts") are beautiful little white mounds with cherries in the middle, and they still make them at DiRoberti's pastry shop on Second Avenue in New York City's East Village (the marzipan filling has somehow morphed into electric green over the years). I sometimes go to the shop just to stare at them, they're so beautifully perverse. I occasionally get a craving for a St. Agatha's nipple or a slice of cassata, but my aversion to cooking with exact measurements has steered me away from complicated baking, so when I want such a treat, I do what most southern Italians do: I buy it.

But when I'm having people over, I serve what Italians usually serve after a big dinner: fruit or cheese. This is an entirely separate category of southern Italian desserts, and it's what I seek out recipes for when I travel. Some of the ones I offer in this book are traditional; others I've invented, using the cheeses, fruits, nuts, and wine of the southern Italian kitchen. I particularly like using Marsala fortified wine, from Sicily. Its rich flavor is wonderful just poured over fruit (see the recipe for cantaloupe with Marsala on page 407), and it adds richness to crusts for fruit tarts (I use it in the crust for fig *crostata* with honey and mint, page 402). I always keep a few types of honey on hand too, usually both a mild wildflower variety and a stronger chestnut honey, which I like to drizzle over salty cheeses like caciocavallo. Big bags of really fresh shelled pistachios and almonds, which I find imported vacuum-packed from Sicily at Buon Italia, a local Italian shop, are the freshest I have ever bought in this country (they also mail order; see page 436 for their address). A bottle of limoncello is a great thing to have on hand for flavoring fruit salads (I like a little sprinkled over fresh figs). Sweet dessert wines, especially Moscato and Malavasia from the Sicilian islands of Pantelleria and Lipari, aren't hard to find in America, and they're wonderful for poaching fresh pears or apricots or dried fruit, or just poured over sliced fruit garnished with a few mint or basil sprigs (for more about sweet wines, see page 64). I use fresh herbs with fruit more than southern Italians traditionally do. It became a kind of a fad at Mediterranean-style restaurants in New York several years ago, and I've tasted some creations that were terrible (I recall a very bitter rosemary ice cream at a restaurant that will remain nameless), but the pairing of certain herbs with sweetness has real merit and possibilities. You just have to experiment and use the herbs in small doses. I'm particularly happy with the peach and basil pizza on page 410, because there, I think, the pairing tastes entirely natural.

The Puglians have a custom of serving raw vegetables after dinner, and my family always did the same thing on holidays. Raw fennel, celery, and sometimes radishes came out after a huge Thanksgiving feast. At first, I took it to be some sort of mental lapse on my family's part and was slightly embarrassed if I had friends over to witness it, but gradually I came to appreciate the raw fennel as a digestive and looked forward to it no matter how stuffed with turkey or lasagne I was. A bowl of nuts always emerged after big holiday dinners as well, to the dismay of us kids. Whole walnuts in their shells, Brazil nuts, a big nutcracker—it all made a mess on the table, the shells getting into everybody's Sambuca and Amaretto. In retrospect, I learned to love this custom too. Now, when I bring out a bowl of nuts for guests they seem intrigued, and it's a good way to get people to linger at the table (if they're people you want to linger).

Not only is unadorned fruit a popular final sit-down course in southern Italy, but they even make it into a formal production. Often after dinner at restaurants and at private homes in Italy, a bowl of whole fruit floating in ice water will arrive at the table. You choose a pear, for instance, and daintily peel and slice it with a knife and a fork, never touching it with your fingers. It took me years to learn how to cut a whole apple on my plate without having it shoot across the room. At restaurants in Sicily, you'll often be presented with a plate of whole *fichi di India*—prickly pears—especially after a fish meal. They come in the most gorgeous colors, ranging from light yellow to orange and pink. They're filled with large pitch-black seeds that Sicilians swallow whole. If you ever travel to Sicily and notice *fichi di India* hanging from trees, don't pick them. As I learned the hard way, they're covered with very fine, very sharp needles that take forever to work out of your skin (they're removed from fruit before it is sold, so you don't have to worry about them at a restaurant). I sometimes find prickly pears in markets here, imported I believe from Central America, but they're never as juicy and brilliantly colored as the ones I've had in Sicily. I've also been served fresh citron, sprinkled with sugar, in Puglia, and citron is another rarity here. The Sweet Orange Salad with Pomegranate Seeds and Orange Liqueur (page 404) is an easy alternative.

I'm thrilled when somebody serves me cheese for dessert, but some people are disappointed by it, and you really have to gauge your guests if you plan to offer it instead of something sweet. A good way to please everyone is to serve a cheese course and include something sweet with it. *Cotognata,* a thick quince paste, is a southern Italian specialty that I find here in the cheese department at my supermarket. It's very nice with a young pecorino. In Lecce, Puglia, I've been served *cotognata* with slightly warm sheep's milk ricotta, and I now serve this at home and everybody loves it. Honey is fabulous drizzled over southern Italian cheeses, especially sharper ones, even provolone. I have had exquisite fruit jams in Puglia and Sicily, and some of them make wonderful accompaniments to cheese (see Southern Italian Cheese Plate with Pear Marmalade, page 393).

If you love ice cream, I suggest you purchase a small electric ice cream maker. Making gelato and *sorbetto* at home is incredibly easy, and you can go wild blending flavors and creating just about anything your heart desires. Sicily is where ice cream was born, the idea of frozen flavored water arriving there with the Arabs. I have eaten the best ice cream in my life in Sicily, and I came back wanting to taste those flavors again. I've discovered to my amazement that I can come fairly close to duplicating these flavors at home: gelato and *sorbetto* made from jasmine, orange, and rose-blossom essence, almond milk, pistachios, tangerine and lemon, ricotta scented with Marsala, figs, and wild strawberry, all with concentrated flavor that relies on the finest local ingredients, not on the richness of excessive cream and eggs. I've re-created several of my favorite Sicilian recipes here and added a few of my own invention.

SERVES **SIX**. The combination of sugar, chilies, and rosemary seemed odd but somehow promising when I first thought of it to flavor almonds, and to my delight the mix of sweet, spicy, and herby worked nicely. I sometimes serve these as a starter, with drinks, but they're also good included on an after-dinner cheese plate.

BAKED SWEET ALMONDS

1 pound whole blanched almonds
1 teaspoon sugar
Generous pinch of sea salt

Leaves from 3 rosemary sprigs, finely chopped
1 small dried red chili, minced
1 teaspoon extra-virgin olive oil

Preheat the oven to 350°F.

In a large bowl, mix the almonds with the sugar, salt, rosemary, and chili. Add the olive oil (just enough to allow the flavorings to adhere to the almonds, not to make them oily). Toss with your fingers until the almonds are well coated. Pour the almonds onto a baking sheet and spread them out in one layer. Bake until fragrant and very lightly golden, about 15 minutes. Let the almonds cool on the pan and then transfer them to a serving bowl.

NOTE   For another version of spiced nuts, see my Spinach Salad with Pears, Spiced Walnuts, and Ricotta Salata (page 139).

SERVES SIX. *Croccante di mandorle* (almond brittle) is very popular in southern Italy. Most of the recipes include a little honey, so it's not as tooth-crackingly hard as American versions (which are usually made with peanuts). In Sicily, I've had it chopped into little chunks and scattered over ice cream. Almond is the most popular brittle, but I've seen versions made with walnuts, hazelnuts, and pine nuts, and my all-time favorite is pistachio, since the nuts are bright green, rich, and slightly soft.

PISTACHIO BRITTLE

Almond oil for coating
2 tablespoons wildflower honey
1 cup sugar
Juice of 1 large orange

Juice of $1/2$ lemon
$1^1/2$ cups unsalted pistachios
Generous pinch of salt

Spread a thin coat of almond oil over a marble or ceramic surface (I use a wide, shallow ceramic gratin dish). Oil the blade of a large rubber spatula.

In a medium saucepan, combine the honey, sugar, and orange and lemon juice. Cook over medium heat without stirring until it starts to turn golden. Add the pistachio nuts and a pinch of salt, stirring them into the syrup, and continue to cook until the syrup is a rich medium brown. Pour onto the oiled surface and smooth with the spatula. Let cool for about 30 minutes. It should now be very hard. Wedge it off the surface with the spatula and break it up into ragged 2-inch pieces.

SERVING SUGGESTION To serve over ice cream, place a few of the pieces of *croccante* under a kitchen towel and give it a few good whacks with a hammer until you have a rubble of uneven little bits. Scatter over Ricotta Gelato (page 424).

SERVES SIX. I was served *a marmellata di pere* as part of a breakfast offering at Il Frantoio, a working olive-oil estate and serene place to stay in Puglia, a little south of Bari. The sweet preserve appeared again one night at dinner, as a *condimento* for a little molded cheese flan. It stayed in my thoughts, and I've devised my own version of its very good flavor combination. I've added Poire William (pear eau-de-vie) and lemon zest to cut the sweetness and add a touch of complexity to the marmalade.

A selection of three cheeses is ideal for this—for instance, 4 ounces each of an imported caciocavallo, a young pecorino such as a primo sale, and an aged pecorino such as a pepato. Look through the cheese section on page 49 for specific high-quality regional cheeses that are available here. Soft cheeses such as fresh mozzarella and burrata are not generally eaten after dinner in southern Italy. You're more likely to find them on antipasto tables or as a first course.

SOUTHERN ITALIAN CHEESE PLATE WITH PEAR MARMALADE

PEAR MARMALADE

5 ripe, firm pears, such as Bartlets, peeled, cored, and finely diced

1/2 cup sugar

1/4 cup Poire William or grappa

Grated zest of 1 lemon

1/4 cup hot water

4 ounces *each* of 3 southern Italian cheeses (see headnote)

1 handful *each* of dried figs and dates

TO MAKE THE MARMALADE: In a large saucepan, combine all the ingredients for the marmalade. Cook over medium-low heat, stirring frequently, until thick and smooth, about 30 minutes. If it starts to brown, reduce the heat to very low and cover. Pour the marmalade into a big bowl or jar and let cool. Use now or cover and refrigerate for up to 1 week.

Put the pear marmalade in a small serving bowl. Arrange the cheeses on a cheese board with the marmalade in the center. Garnish with the dried figs and dates.

NOTE   Marmalades made from orange, lemon, citron, and quince are very popular in southern Italy. Some of the best I've had were made by Maria Grammatico in her now-famous pastry shop in Erice, Sicily. I've brought jars from her shop back home with me and cherished them. Some of her marmalades and pastries are now exported and available here (see the source list on page 436).

SERVES FOUR. I bought a jar of rosemary-flavored honey in the town of Lecce on my last trip to Puglia, and I was surprised by its beautiful aroma and taste, having expected that the herb flavor might make it harsh. When I finished the jar, it occurred to me that I could easily make my own rosemary honey, and now I do. It's a perfect match for a soft but somewhat assertive cheese like caciocavallo.

CACIOCAVALLO WITH ROSEMARY HONEY AND PINE NUTS

1 cup acacia or orange flower honey

3 small rosemary sprigs

One 8-ounce chunk caciocavallo at room temperature

Freshly ground black pepper to taste

Handful of pine nuts, lightly toasted (see page 61)

Pour the honey into a small saucepan and drop in the rosemary sprigs. Set over low heat just long enough to make the honey liquid and warm to the touch, about 4 minutes. Turn off the heat and let the pan sit on the turned-off burner for about 15 minutes (this will allow the oil from the rosemary to be released). Remove the rosemary sprigs if you like, but I usually leave them in for a slightly rustic look.

To serve, cut the caciocavallo into ¼-inch-thick slices and place a few on each serving plate. Grate on a little pepper, drizzle with the honey (which should still be slightly warm; you can reheat it gently if it isn't), and garnish each serving with pine nuts.

SERVES SIX. I like to serve a selection of a few goat cheeses, some fresh, some aged, accompanied with a plate of these warm *crostini*. I don't often find southern Italian goat cheeses in this country, but caprino from northern Italy, or chèvre from France, or a good America brand like Coach Farms are all fine substitutes.

FIG PESTO CROSTINI WITH CAPRINO

PESTO

4 dried figs, preferably Calimyrna figs, stemmed and coarsely chopped

Handful of pine nuts

Leaves from 3 or 4 thyme sprigs

2 oil-packed anchovy fillets

½ small garlic clove

1 tablespoon extra-virgin olive oil

1 tablespoon grappa or brandy

Freshly ground black pepper to taste

2 or 3 goat cheeses (a mix of fresh and aged cheeses is best), about 4 ounces each

1 baguette, cut into thin rounds

Extra-virgin olive oil for brushing

Large mint sprigs for garnish

TO MAKE THE PESTO: In a food processor, combine all the ingredients and process to a fairly smooth paste.

Arrange the goat cheeses on a large cheese board. Toast the baguette slices on both sides and brush them lightly with olive oil. Spoon a little of the fig pesto on each toast and arrange them around the cheese. Garnish with the mint sprigs.

SERVES FIVE OR SIX AS A DESSERT. *Ricotta al forno*, baked ricotta, is popular in many parts of southern Italy. I've seen it most often in Sicily, where it's baked until firm and dark brown on top. Lately, I've been finding baked lemon ricotta imported from Bari, Puglia, at my Italian food market. It's quite lemony and only slightly sweet, lovely tasting but a little dry. I thought I'd try making my own. I added eggs, so the texture is more like a ricotta cheesecake, but without a crust and much simpler to prepare.

BAKED LEMON RICOTTA WITH RASPBERRY SAUCE

BAKED LEMON RICOTTA

1¹/₂ pounds whole-milk ricotta, sheep's milk if available, drained for about 30 minutes

3 large eggs

1 egg yolk

¹/₂ teaspoon vanilla extract

Grated zest of 2 lemons

Juice of 1 lemon

¹/₂ cup confectioners' sugar

1 tablespoon unsalted butter, softened, for greasing the mold

RASPBERRY SAUCE

3 tablespoons granulated sugar

1 tablespoon grappa or brandy

2 tablespoons water

Squeeze of lemon juice

4 cups raspberries

Preheat the oven to 325°F.

TO MAKE THE BAKED RICOTTA: In a food processor, combine all the ricotta ingredients and pulse until smooth (if you do this by hand, it will have a grainy texture, which is actually more traditional, but I like the way the food processor smooths the lumps out of the ricotta, making it silky).

Butter a 4-cup springform mold and pour in the ricotta mixture.

Put the mold in a large baking dish and add warm water to the baking dish to come halfway up the sides of the mold. (The water bath helps to make the ricotta creamy like a custard, not dry and crumbly.) Bake for about 1 hour and 10 minutes, or until lightly browned on top, firm at the sides, and slightly jiggly at the center. Let cool completely before removing it from the mold (this will firm it up further). Remove the springform sides but leave the base, since the ricotta tends to be somewhat delicate in texture.

TO MAKE THE SAUCE: In a medium saucepan, combine the sugar, grappa or brandy, and water over high heat. Bring to a boil over high heat and cook just until it thickens and large bubbles start to form on the surface, about 5 minutes (it shouldn't go so long that it starts to caramelize). Turn off the heat and add the lemon juice and raspberries, stirring them in the syrup for a minute. Let raspberries cool, then pour into a bowl. You will have lightly warmed raspberries (still relatively whole) bathed in a bright red syrup.

TO SERVE, cut the baked ricotta into thick wedges and serve it topped with the warm raspberry sauce.

VARIATION Baked ricotta is also fine with no sauce at all, and more often than not that's how I eat it.

SERVES FOUR. I've often been served fresh figs for dessert in Southern Italy, always in a simple presentation. When I visited Gangivecchio, the old Sicilian family estate of Wanda and Giovanna Tornabene, their family fig tree was loaded with the biggest green figs I'd ever seen (check the bibliography for a Sicilian cookbook by Wanda Tornabene). We had them every night, unadorned, peeled at the table with a knife. My fig recipe would probably seem ridiculous to most Sicilians, with its pairing of strong cheese with honey and almonds, but to my Italian American sense of indulgence, it's perfect.

ROASTED FRESH FIGS WITH GORGONZOLA

12 fresh green or purple skinned figs

4 ounces Gorgonzola dolce (the softer, less aged Gorgonzola)

Handful of whole blanched almonds, coarsely chopped

A drizzle of acacia or mixed wildflower honey

Freshly ground black pepper to taste

Extra-virgin olive oil for drizzling

Preheat the oven to 400°F.

Lightly oil a 10- or 11-inch round baking dish. Cut a cross into the top of each fig, so you can open it up like a flower (about ½ inch deep). Stuff a little piece of Gorgonzola into each opening and place the figs standing upright in the baking dish. Scatter the almonds over the figs and drizzle on the honey. Top with a few grindings of fresh pepper and a drizzle of olive oil. Bake until the figs are warm and puffy and the cheese has melted, about 12 minutes. Serve warm.

VARIATIONS I often serve these as a dessert, but they're also nice plopped on top of a lightly dressed frisée or arugula salad as a first course (one night I served them before a pork roast, and the flavor combination was perfect).

For an uncooked version of this dish, simply arrange halved figs on a serving plate. Drizzle them with honey and give them a few grindings of black pepper. Present them alongside a nice piece of Gorgonzola dolce. A young pecorino is also lovely with fresh figs.

Serves six. Alle Due Corti, a restaurant in the baroque city of Lecce in southern Puglia, is passionate about presenting classic Puglian dishes with simplicity and charm, and they offer these almond and chocolate figs at the end of a meal. Variations on these figs in Calabria and Basilicata can include fennel seeds, orange or candied lemon, or bay leaf. Sometimes they taste like a Christmas fruitcake; other times they're baked with *vincotto*, boiled-down grape must (see page 413). But I like the chocolate-dipped ones from Due Corti the best.

I always wanted to make my own, but feared the job would be fussier and more time-consuming than my usual culinary projects, so I put it off for years. When I finally got around to it, I discovered to my pleasure that they were quick to make and tasted much the way I remembered them.

DRIED FIGS WITH ALMONDS AND CHOCOLATE

1 pound soft dried Calimyrna figs

Handful of whole blanched almonds, lightly toasted (see page 77)

Tiny pinch of ground cinnamon

4 bay leaves, preferably fresh

2 tablespoons sweet Marsala

1 cup semisweet chocolate chips

2 tablespoons nonultrapasterized heavy cream

Preheat the oven to 350°F.

With a thin knife, make a hole in the base of each fig and insert an almond. Place the figs in a baking dish, leaving a little space between them. Sprinkle the figs very lightly with cinnamon and insert the bay leaves in among the figs. Drizzle on a little Marsala and bake the figs until they're lightly browned and slightly puffy, about 30 minutes.

In a double boiler over simmering water, melt the chocolate chips with the cream, stirring to blend. Drizzle the chocolate mixture over the figs. Serve warm (traditionally, the chocolate is allowed to harden and the figs are served at room temperature, but I like them warm and slightly sticky).

NOTE   To order these already made, go to www.organicalia.com, the website of a Calabrian food company that carries other Calabrian specialties as well.

Some southern Italian desserts are beyond my grasp, because my love for them doesn't match the effort required to reproduce them with feeling, but I've always loved *pasta di mandorle*, the southern Italian almond paste that in Sicily is called *pasta reale* and is formed into fruit and animal shapes or used to fill and glaze elaborate cakes like cassata. I had always bought it, but recently I learned that it's surprisingly easy to make. I followed the technique in the book *Bitter Almonds*, about the Sicilian pastry chef Maria Grammatico, written by her and Mary Taylor Simeti. Ms. Grammatico spent her younger years in a convent and learned to make pastries and sweets there. She emerged to open one of the best pastry shops on the island—which is saying a lot, since sweets are a Sicilian obsession. I've visited her store, in the mountaintop town of Erice, where she and her brother, who helps out in the kitchen, don't mind inviting you to watch them work and let you take lots of photos.

One of the problems with making this paste here is that our almonds are not as oily and flavorful as the Sicilian ones. Ms. Grammatico suggests adding almond extract, but I find that phony tasting, so I prefer to use a splash of *orzata*, almond syrup and a drizzle of almond oil, instead. The lemon zest is my own addition, to break through the pure sugar-on-sugar taste. If you can find imported Italian almonds that are really fresh, by all means use them. (Buon Italia imports airtight bags of Italian nuts into this country; see page 436.)

DATES FILLED WITH ALMOND PASTE AND LEMON

PASTA DI MANDORLE

1 cup whole blanched almonds, preferably very fresh ones

1 teaspoon almond oil

3/4 cup granulated sugar

2 tablespoons water, plus more as needed

1/4 teaspoon vanilla extract

1 tablespoon *orzata* syrup

Confectioners' sugar for kneading

About 30 moist dried dates

1 tablespoon limoncello liqueur or fresh lemon juice

Grated zest of 1 large lemon

To make the pasta di mandople: In a food processor, combine the almonds, almond oil, and granulated sugar. Process until finely ground, almost powdery. Add the 2 tablespoons water, vanilla, and *orzata* and process until it forms a sticky ball. If it stays crumbly, add a little more water.

Sprinkle a little confectioners' sugar on a work surface and transfer the almond paste ball to it. Knead briefly, about 1 minute, then wrap it in plastic wrap. Use now, or refrigerate for up to 2 weeks.

Make a lengthwise slit in the dates and pull out the pits. Drizzle the dates very lightly with the limoncello or lemon juice, getting a few drops into the slits. Fill each date with a little slab of almond paste and press the sides together gently so the almond paste is sticking out a bit. Sprinkle each date with lemon zest. Serve now or cover and refrigerate for up to 2 weeks; return to room temperature before serving.

SERVING SUGGESTION   Since these are almost achingly sweet (but in a good way), any after-dinner drink as sweet as amaretto or Sambuca or limoncello itself is likely to seem too much with them. I like them best with espresso, or grappa.

VARIATION   If the almond paste seems too sweet for you, you can instead fill the dates with soft goat cheese, Gorgonzola, or ricotta.

SERVES SIX. Nobody in New York has much luck growing figs, even the old Italian guys in Brooklyn who wrap their little fig trees in burlap for the winter usually only produce a handful, but in midsummer and again in the fall dark purple Mission figs and my favorite green-skinned varieties show up in the markets, usually from California. When I can get my hands on a good bunch of them, I always make a variation on this tart. Fresh figs go very well with basil, thyme, or the mint I've chosen for this dessert tart.

GREEN FIG CROSTATA WITH HONEY AND MINT

CRUST

½ cup (1 stick) unsalted butter

4 tablespoons granulated sugar

Pinch of salt

2-3 tablespoons sweet Marsala

1½ cups all-purpose flour

¼ cup whole, unsalted pistachios, coarsely ground in a food processor

CUSTARD

¾ cup nonultrapasterized heavy cream

1 large egg

2 tablespoons wildflower honey

½ teaspoon vanilla extract

1 teaspoon all-purpose flour

5 or fresh 6 mint leaves, finely chopped, plus about 6 whole sprigs for garnish

15 fresh green figs, halved lengthwise

Grated zest of 1 small lemon

Confectioners' sugar for dusting

TO MAKE THE CRUST: Preheat the oven to 375°F.

In a small saucepan, melt the butter and let it cool completely (if you use hot melted butter, the crust will come out as hard as a rock). With a pastry brush, use about 1 tablespoon of the melted butter to grease the tart pan.

In a medium bowl, combine the remaining melted butter, 3 tablespoons of the granulated sugar, the salt, and Marsala. Stir to blend well. Add the flour and mix briefly until you have a mass of moist, crumbly dough (don't blend it so much that it forms a big ball). If it seems dry, add a little more marsala. Tilt the dough into the tart pan and pat it down and out to the edges and all the way up the sides to form a thin crust. Bake for about 15 minutes, until lightly colored and slightly puffy. Remove the crust from the oven. Sprinkle the inside with the chopped pistachios and the remaining 1 tablespoon sugar.

TO MAKE THE CUSTARD: In a small bowl, combine all the ingredients and whisk until well blended.

Scatter the chopped mint in the crust. Place the figs, cut side up, in the crust in a slightly overlapping circular pattern. Sprinkle with the lemon zest. Pour the custard evenly over the figs. Bake until the crust is golden and the custard is set, about 45 minutes. Let cool on a wire rack for about 30 minutes before serving. Dust the top with confectioners' sugar. Garnish slices with mint sprigs.

SERVES FOUR OR FIVE. Here's a sweet version of the orange salads that are popular throughout Sicily. They're more often assembled with savory additions such as olives, onions, olive oil, anchovies, and/or black pepper. This one can serve as a segue between main course and dessert or as a dessert in its own right. Use raisins if pomegranates are out of season or hard to find.

SWEET ORANGE SALAD WITH POMEGRANATE SEEDS AND ORANGE LIQUEUR

7 oranges, peeled and cut into thin rounds (a mix of blood oranges and regular ones looks lovely)

Handful of whole blanched almonds, toasted and coarsely chopped (see page 77)

Seeds from ½ pomegranate

Generous splash of Grand Marnier or other orange liqueur

Pinch of salt

Pinch of ground cinnamon

Handful of fresh fresh mint leaves

Confectioners' sugar for dusting

About 30 minutes before serving, arrange the orange slices on a nice-looking serving dish. Scatter on the almonds and pomegranate seeds. Drizzle on the orange liqueur. Let sit, unrefrigerated, to develop flavor. Right before serving, season the oranges with the salt and cinnamon, scatter on the mint leaves, and dust with confectioners' sugar.

MAKES TWO CUPS: SERVES FIVE OR SIX. Here's something nice to do with summer cherries if you ever tire of eating them straight. I've steeped them in white wine, a touch of almond-flavored liqueur, and lemon zest. The cherry juice produces a gorgeous shocking-pink syrup that's not too sweet.

AMARETTO CHERRIES

$1/2$ cup dry white wine
$1/2$ cup amaretto liqueur
3 strips lemon zest

$1/2$ cup sugar
$1^1/2$ pounds fresh sweet cherries, with stems if possible

In a large, wide saucepan (wide and shallow is better than very deep so the cherries can spread out and won't require excessive liquid to cover them), combine the wine, amaretto, lemon zest, and sugar. Bring to a boil over medium heat and cook for about 5 minutes, or until the sugar has dissolved and some of the alcohol has burned off. Add the cherries and cook at a low boil for about 5 minutes, just until the cherries are tender and give up some of their color, creating a pink syrup. Turn off the heat and let the cherries cool in the liquid. Refrigerate overnight (this deepens their flavor) but return to room temperature to serve. These cherries will keep about 5 days in the refrigerator.

SERVING SUGGESTIONS   Serve over vanilla or chocolate ice cream, or with ricotta cream (page 414). I also like them poured over a simple chocolate cake so the juice soaks the cake.

MAKES ABOUT TWENTY-FOUR STRAWBERRIES. My father always kept a bottle of Strega liqueur in his well-stocked bar, and it was the first alcoholic drink my friends and I experimented with, because the bottle jumped out at us with its golden-sunburst design. My friends and I drank a lot of this very strong liqueur one afternoon, and it was an experience I will never forget. My sister said the taste reminded her of Frank's Shoe Repair shop, in Glen Cove, New York.

Strega is a golden, bittersweet liqueur from Benevento, a city in inland Campania, a place purported to be infested with witches (*strega* is Italian for "witch"). In the early 1990s, I decided to spend a night in Benevento after visiting my grandmother's birth town nearby. I can't say it was the coziest southern Italian spot. I found the people inhospitable, and suspicious when I asked questions about their food, and their fancy businessman's hotel had hot water that came and went for a few hours and then no water at all. The taste of Strega always startles me and reminds me of that ancient city. It is said to contain seventy herbs, including saffron. A Strega-flavored chocolate bar I bought in Benevento inspired this recipe.

STREGA- AND CHOCOLATE-DIPPED STRAWBERRIES

3/4 cup semisweet chocolate chips
(I like Ghirardelli brand)
3 tablespoons nonultrapasteurized heavy
cream

1 tablespoon Strega liqueur
2 dozen unhulled large ripe fresh
strawberries

In a double boiler over simmering water, melt the chocolate with the cream. Remove from the heat, add the Strega, and whisk briefly until smooth. Dip each strawberry in the chocolate and lay them out on parchment paper or waxed paper to dry for about 20 minutes.

SERVES FOUR. When I first smelled these two fragrant ingredients together, I knew how good this was going to taste. This classic Sicilian pairing of flavors works best with a really ripe summer cantaloupe and a high-quality Marsala like Florio.

Note: I usually don't get fussy about using kitchen gadgets in my recipes, but I have to say that using a melon baller makes a big difference in the presentation of this dessert.

CANTALOUPE WITH MARSALA

1 large, ripe cantaloupe, halved and seeded

$^3/_4$ cup sweet Marsala

Drizzle of honey

3 or 4 short strips lemon zest

Pinch of salt

4 mint sprigs for garnish

Scoop out the melon flesh with a melon baller and put the melon balls in a pretty serving bowl. Pour on the Marsala and add the honey, lemon zest, and salt (the salt heightens the flavor of the melon in a subtle but worthwhile way). Stir, cover, and refrigerate until chilled, about 2 hours, stirring occasionally. Serve cool, garnished with the mint sprigs.

NOTE   If you have only dry Marsala, add 1 tablespoon sugar to the bowl.

SERVES FOUR. Even though zabaglione is traditionally made with Marsala, the Sicilian fortified wine, it is as far as I can determine not a Sicilian invention but a northern fancy-restaurant concoction. Nonetheless, it is served in many Sicilian restaurants, often poured over strawberries. Upstate New York blueberries show up midsummer at my local farmers' market. In a good year they're sweet and luscious, but they always have a slight sourness, I think it complements the rich sweetness of zabaglione even better than strawberries do.

BLUEBERRY GRATIN WITH ZABAGLIONE

4 cups ripe summer blueberries, stemmed if necessary

Grated zest of 1 lemon

4 egg yolks

1/4 cup granulated sugar

1/4 cup dry Marsala

1/4 cup packed brown sugar

Divide the blueberries among 4 shallow ovenproof ramekins (the kind used for crème brûlée). Sprinkle the lemon zest over them.

Have ready a shallow pan filled with ice to cool the zabaglione. Preheat the broiler.

Place a stainless-steel or copper bowl over a saucepan filled with an inch or 2 of simmering water (the bowl should not touch the water). Add the egg yolks and granulated sugar and whisk for several minutes until the mixture has begun to warm and is frothy. Add the Marsala and continue whisking until the mixture holds soft peaks and has doubled in volume. This will take about 5 minutes of constant whisking. Keep the heat at a steady low temperature; if it gets too hot, the eggs might scramble. If you feel the bowl starting to get too hot, turn down the heat. You can also pull the bowl off the saucepan to let it cool for a few moments. Transfer the bowl to the ice bath and whisk until cool, about 4 minutes. Pour the zabaglione evenly over the berries. Put the brown sugar in a small sieve and use a spoon to push it through to make a thin layer over each ramekin. Place the ramekins under the broiler about 2 inches from the heat source, and broil until lightly browned, about 1 minute. Serve right away.

VARIATION   For a simpler version of this, put the blueberries in wineglasses, make the zabaglione, and pour it warm over the berries.

SERVES FOUR TO SIX. Peaches in red or white wine was something my father always put together for backyard barbecues—something refreshing after the meat medley we usually worked our way through (my father didn't think it was a real barbecue unless he offered sausages, chicken, ribs, and steak). The caramel is my addition. I love the smell of caramel as it cooks, and I even like the gasoline smell of burnt caramel, though of course I try not to burn it.

PEACHES IN WHITE WINE AND CARAMEL

10 unpeeled ripe peaches, cut into thick slices

1/2 cup sugar

1/2 cup water

1 cup or more dry white wine, something light and unoaked like a Frascati

2 or 3 strips lemon zest

3 allspice berries

4 or 5 black peppercorns

4 or 5 fresh lemon verbena leaves or mint leaves

Put the peach slices in a wide serving bowl. You can just pile them in or, for a more pulled-together look, place them in a slightly overlapping circular pattern.

In a small saucepan, combine the sugar and water and cook over medium heat until it turns a nice dark caramel, swirling the pan a few times so it cooks evenly (watch it intently when it first starts turning golden, as it can go from golden to black and smoking before you know it). Pour the caramel evenly over the peach slices. Pour on enough white wine to just cover the peaches, and add the lemon zest, allspice, and peppercorns. Let stand at room temperature for about 1 hour before serving. The wine will dissolve the caramel, creating a sweet, dark liqueur. You can easily double or triple the recipe to feed a crowd. Garnish with lemon verbena or mint leaves just before serving.

NOTE   I think this tastes good either at room temperature or chilled, but eat it the same day you make it; otherwise the peaches will start to become mushy.

SERVES SIX. Flavoring peaches with basil is an idea I got from my grandmother's cousin Tony when I went to visit him in Campolattaro, a small town in Campania to which he moved in the 1980s, having spent most of his adult life in Westchester. His cellar, filled with an amazing assortment of preserved fruits and vegetables, contained jars of peaches with a few basil leaves stuck into each one. I had thought basil leaves were used to flavor only preserved tomatoes, and I didn't ask him about it at the time. However, though I never sampled those peaches, I thought about them from time to time over the years, wondering how they would taste. I finally put the two together and realized he had been on to something.

Several things go by the name *pizza* in southern Italy, including open-faced sweet tarts, like this one. A *pizza dolce* like this usually includes fresh or candied fruit and nuts.

PEACH AND BASIL PIZZA

CRUST

1½ cups all-purpose flour

Generous pinch of salt

1 tablespoon sugar

Grated zest of ½ lemon

1 large egg

2 or 3 tablespoons cold dry white wine

½ cup (1 stick) cold unsalted butter, cut into small pieces

5 unpeeled ripe peaches, cut into thin slices

¼ cup granulated sugar

Grated zest of 1 lemon

1 tablespoon amaretto liqueur

Handful of whole blanched almonds, lightly toasted (see page 77) and coarsely ground in a food processor

Small handful of fresh basil leaves, chopped

Confectioners' sugar for dusting (optional)

TO MAKE THE CRUST: In a food processor, combine the flour, salt, sugar, and lemon zest and pulse once or twice to blend. In a small bowl, whisk the egg with the white wine. Add the butter to the food processor and pulse 2 or 3 times until the butter is broken up into pea-sized bits. Pour the egg mixture over the dough and pulse once or twice more to blend until the dough starts to come together and is crumbly and moist, adding a little wine if it seems dry. Turn the dough out onto a floured work surface and press into a ball. Give it a few brief kneads just to make sure it holds together. Wrap in plastic wrap and refrigerate for about 30 minutes.

Preheat the oven to 400°F.

Put the peaches in a bowl and toss with the granulated sugar, lemon zest, and amaretto.

Remove the dough from the refrigerator and transfer to a floured work surface. Roll the dough out into a large round, about 12 inches. Trim the edges to make it more even. Sprinkle the ground almonds over the surface, leaving a 3-inch border. Scatter on the basil. Pile the peaches into the center of the circle and let them spread out in a natural way, leaving a 3-inch border all around. (If they have given off a lot of juice, leave some of it in the bowl; it might make the crust soggy.) Fold the edge up and around the fruit, pleating as you go, creating a ruffly edge. You should have a large opening in the middle where the peaches stick out.

Bake until the crust is a deep golden brown, 35 to 40 minutes.

Transfer to a wire rack and let cool for about 30 minutes. Dust with confectioners' sugar to serve, if you like.

SERVES FOUR OR FIVE. I sometimes find cultivated versions of little wild straw-berries at the Union Square Greenmarket in May. They're incredibly sweet, much like the *fragoline di bosco* I've been served in restaurants in Italy in the spring. I like this dessert best with them, though it works well with any type of strawberries, as long as they're sweet.

STRAWBERRIES WITH RED WINE AND VANILLA SYRUP

3 tablespoons sugar
$\frac{1}{2}$ Madagascar vanilla bean, split lengthwise
2 short strips orange zest

$1\frac{1}{2}$ cups dry red wine
4 cups fresh sweet strawberries, hulled and halved (if using wild ones, leave them whole)

In a small nonreactive saucepan, combine the sugar, vanilla bean, orange zest, and wine. Boil over medium-high heat until reduced by about three-fourths. Let cool to room temperature.

Put the strawberries in a large serving bowl and pour the wine reduction over them, stir-ring a few times. Let stand, stirring once or twice, for about 1 hour before serving.

SERVES SIX. *Vincotto* is a spicy, sweet syrup made by boiling down grape must. It is an ancient form of sweetening still made in southern Italy during the grape harvest. I've come across it mostly in Sicily and in Puglia. I bought a bottle of *vincotto* in a fancy gourmet shop in Lecce, Puglia, and I suppose because of my poor Italian the woman standing next to me asked me dubiously what I planned to do with it. I said I wasn't sure; I just wanted it, and she told me she drizzled it over cantaloupe. That sounded promising. When I got home I tried the cantaloupe dish and loved it. I was inspired to create this dish by the popular dessert strawberries with balsamic vinegar, which is similar in spirit but a little less pungent. I also like *vincotto* drizzled over Parmigiano-Reggiano, and you can also add a splash to brighten up the sauce for a roast pork dish or a stew.

The best *vincotto* available in this country is made in Puglia by Gianni Calogiuri, from the cooked must of Negroamaro and Malvasia grapes (see Sources, page 436). It comes in all sorts of funky flavors like fig and hot chili; the plain one is the most versatile.

STRAWBERRIES WITH VINCOTTO

4 cups fresh ripe strawberries, hulled but left whole (if huge, halve them lengthwise)

2 tablespoons *vincotto*

1 tablespoon honey at room temperature

Grinding of black pepper

Leaves from 3 or 4 mint sprigs, chopped

Vanilla ice cream for serving (optional)

Put the strawberries in a large bowl. Pour on the *vincotto* and honey. Grind on a little pepper (just a touch, to heighten the flavor of the strawberries). Toss gently and let stand at room temperature for about 30 minutes. By this time, the strawberries will have given off some juice and blended with the *vincotto*. Add the chopped mint and gently toss. Serve as is, or over vanilla ice cream, if you prefer.

SERVES SIX. My mother's father worked simultaneously as a bookie, a tap dancer, and a pastry cook. He died before I knew him, but I'm told he was an excellent cassata baker, turning out the elaborate Sicilian cakes for my mother's birthday (something that embarrassed her in front of her little friends, who had store-bought American cakes on their birthdays). I didn't inherit his passion for baking, but I love sweetened ricotta cream, which makes up some of the layers of cassata. Here, it's an accompaniment to sweet spiced pears. I also like to eat it as is.

Malvasia is an ancient grape that produces a sweet wine on the Sicilian island of Lipari (and several other places as well). The wine has a golden color and a honey aroma. Hauner is a good brand that's imported to this country. Baumes de Venise from France, which is easier to find, can be used instead.

PEARS POACHED IN MALVASIA AND STAR ANISE, SERVED WITH RICOTTA CREAM

6 fairly firm pears, such as Bosc, peeled, stems left on

1 cup Malvasia or other sweet wine

2 cups dry white wine

$^1/_2$ cup sugar

2 star anise pods

1 vanilla bean, split lengthwise

2 long strips lemon zest

RICOTTA CREAM

$1^1/_2$ cups whole-milk ricotta, preferably sheep's milk

Generous pinch of salt

2 teaspoons confectioners' sugar

1 teaspoon high-quality vanilla extract, such as Madagascar

Freshly grated nutmeg to taste

Tiny pinch of ground cinnamon

1 tablespoon hot water, or as needed

Cut a slice off the bottom of each pear so it can sit upright. In a large, wide pot, combine the Malvasia, white wine, granulated sugar, star anise, vanilla bean, and lemon zest. Bring to a boil and cook for 3 or 4 minutes. Add the pears and enough water to just cover them. Bring to a boil again. Reduce the heat to low, partially cover, and simmer until the pears are just tender, about 20 minutes; they may take longer, depending on how hard they were to begin with.

MEANWHILE, MAKE THE RICOTTA CREAM: In a food processor, combine all the ricotta cream ingredients except the hot water and pulse a few times until smooth. Add the 1 tablespoon hot water and pulse again. This should loosen it up to the texture of thick cream, which is what you want. If it's still very stiff and thick, add a little more water and pulse again. Pour into a small bowl and set aside. (It's best never refrigerated, but if you have to, make sure to return it to room temperature before serving, working in a little hot water if it has become too thick.)

Test one of the pears with a thin knife. If it goes in easily, they're ready. Using a slotted spoon, transfer the pears to a shallow serving bowl. Increase the heat to high and boil the liquid down to a syrup. When large bubbles appear on the surface, it will have reduced enough. Let the syrup cool to room temperature and then pour it over the pears (if you pour it on hot, it will just turn liquidy again). I leave all the star anise pods and vanilla bean in because I like the way it looks, but if you prefer a more formal presentation, remove them.

Serve the pears in small bowls with plenty of syrup poured over them. Give each serving a large dollop of ricotta cream.

VARIATION   Try the ricotta cream spooned over fresh strawberries or sliced peaches.

MAKES TWO EIGHT-INCH FRITTATAS, ENOUGH FOR FOUR TO SIX AS AN
ANTIPASTO OR TWO AS A BRUNCH OR LUNCH DISH. This is a good dessert for
a formal dinner and also a pleasant brunch dish. Or, serve wedges of it as an antipasto,
with prosecco or Champagne.

FRITTATA WITH STRAWBERRIES AND RICOTTA

4 large eggs

About 12 fresh wild strawberries or
6 regular-sized ones, hulled (larger
ones sliced)

1 tablespoon sugar

2 tablespoons ricotta cheese

Freshly grated nutmeg to taste

1 tablespoon Parmigiano-Reggiano
cheese

Pinch of salt

Freshly ground black pepper to taste

2 tablespoons extra-virgin olive oil

Mint or basil sprigs for garnish

Put the eggs in a small bowl and whisk lightly to blend. Stir in all the remaining ingredients except the olive oil and garnish.

Heat an 8-inch skillet over medium heat. Add 1 tablespoon of the olive oil and heat. Add half of the egg mixture, shaking the pan to let it spread out to cover the skillet bottom. Let it cook undisturbed until you can see it has started to brown at the edges, about 1 minute. Shake the skillet to see if the frittata moves easily; if not, let it cook a few seconds longer. Invert the frittata onto a plate and then slide it, cooked side up, back onto the skillet. Cook on the second side until it is lightly browned, about 1 minute or so longer.

When the frittata is cooked, slide it out onto an individual serving plate. Make a second frittata, adding the remaining 1 tablespoon olive oil to the skillet. Garnish with mint or basil sprigs. Serve warm or at room temperature.

SERVES FIVE. Early September brings a variety of plums to my greenmarket, and I especially like the pointy Italian ones, with their dusty blue matte finish. They're less juicy for eating, but that's exactly what makes them great for cooking: They don't bake into a big mush.

I realize that not everyone will have a bottle of herby Galliano liqueur at home, but it goes well with fruit. Any type of sweet liqueur or a fruit brandy can be used instead.

ITALIAN PLUM CRISP

1½ pounds fresh purple Italian plums, halved and pitted

1 tablespoon sugar

1 tablespoon Galliano liqueur (see headnote)

½ cup all-purpose flour

½ cup whole blanched almonds

½ cup packed light brown sugar

7 tablespoons cold unsalted butter, cut into little pieces

Pinch of salt

Preheat the oven to 400°F.

Toss the plums in the sugar and Galliano. Butter a baking dish (I use a 10-inch round ceramic tart pan). Place the plums in the dish, cut side up. In a food processor, combine the flour, almonds, brown sugar, butter, and salt. Pulse 3 or 4 times until the mixture is coarse and crumbly.

Sprinkle the flour mixture over the plums. Bake until the top is lightly browned and the dish is bubbling at the edges, about 20 minutes. Let stand for about 10 minutes before serving (this gives the top a chance to crisp).

SERVING SUGGESTION   Serve with ricotta or a drizzle of heavy cream, if you like.

SERVES SIX. If you travel to southern Italy in the winter, you'll be find baked apples on the dessert wagons, especially in Campagna. Apples are so much a part of my New York upbringing that I was amazed to learn that it was even possible to grow them in the Mezzogiorno. I've never seen this exact recipe anywhere, but it makes so much sense to me to combine these ingredients that I can't believe some cook, somewhere in southern Italy, hasn't come up with it as well. I like eating these for lunch. I used a Fiano di Avellino wine from Campania because of its slight honey flavor.

BAKED APPLES WITH PINE NUTS, RAISINS, AND WHITE WINE

6 firm apples, such as Cortland, Jonathan, Rome, or Granny Smith

3 tablespoons unsalted butter at room temperature

4 or 5 scrapings freshly grated nutmeg

Drizzle of extra-virgin olive oil

2 tablespoons wildflower honey

2 tablespoons sugar

³/₄ cup Fiano di Avellino or other dry, fruity white wine, such as an unoaked Chardonnay

Handful of raisins

Handful of pine nuts, lightly toasted (see page 61)

Preheat the oven to 350°F.

Core the apples and cut away a round strip of skin from the top of each one. Slice a thin layer off the bottom of each apple so it will stand upright. Coat an 8-by-11-inch baking dish with about 1 tablespoon of the butter. Put the apples in the dish and dot the remaining 2 tablespoons butter over and inside them. Sprinkle on the nutmeg and drizzle with olive oil. Drizzle on the honey and sprinkle with sugar. Pour wine around the apples to a depth of about 1 inch. Bake, uncovered, until tender, 50 minutes to 1 hour, depending on the variety you use. Baste the apples occasionally while cooking to keep them moist.

Transfer the apples to a serving platter. Strain the cooking liquid through a fine-mesh sieve into a small saucepan. Add the raisins, bring to a boil, and cook until syrupy and reduced to about ¹/₂ cup. Pour over the apples and scatter on the pine nuts. Serve warm.

Makes about one quart. In Sicily, I've been served watermelon desserts of surpassing beauty and formality. In Trapani, I enjoyed a watermelon gelatin garnished with jasmine flowers, and at a restaurant in Palerno I ordered watermelon pudding, which was presented in a pastry shell and topped with shaved chocolate and almonds. Watermelon *sorbetto* is a Sicilian favorite too, flavored with Arabian flavors such as pistachios, cinnamon, jasmine flower water, and candied fruit. I love all these, but watermelon *sorbetto* dotted with chocolate is my favorite.

WATERMELON SORBETTO WITH BITTERSWEET CHOCOLATE

$1/2$ cup sugar, plus more to taste

$1/2$ cup water

One 5-pound piece ripe watermelon, peeled and cut into chunks

1 teaspoon vanilla extract

Tiny pinch of ground cinnamon

Grated zest of $1/2$ lemon

1 egg white, whisked until foamy

Large handful of unsalted pistachios

$1/2$ cup bittersweet chocolate chips

Mint sprigs for garnish

In a small saucepan, combine the $1/2$ cup sugar and the water. Bring it to a boil and let it bubble for about 2 minutes, stirring to dissolve the sugar. Let this cool completely.

Add the watermelon chunks to a food processor a few at a time, processing to a fairly smooth purée (don't worry about the seeds). Strain through a fine-mesh sieve into a large bowl (help it along by whisking it). Continue until you've used up all the watermelon. You should have about $4^{1}/_2$ cups of juice. Add the sugar syrup, vanilla, cinnamon, lemon zest, and egg white, mixing well. Taste for sweetness, adding a little sugar if needed (a very tiny amount of undissolved sugar won't affect the texture of the *sorbetto*). Chill the watermelon mixture for several hours, or until very cold.

Pour into an ice-cream maker and process according to the manufacturers' instructions until halfway frozen. Add the pistachios and chocolate chips and continue freezing. Garnish with mint sprigs to serve.

SERVES FIVE OR SIX. If you've never tasted homemade fruit gelatin, its clear fruit taste will surprise you. Fruit *gelatina* is very popular in Sicily. In the spring, you might be served one made with wild berries; in the summer, watermelon gelatin is a classic, usually elaborately decorated with cinnamon or chocolate shavings, pistachios, fresh jasmine flowers, candied pumpkin, or citron. What sets southern Italian gelatins apart from American gelatin molds is, more than anything else, the purity of the fruit flavor. No matter how baroquely decorated, underneath it all is the taste of unadulterated seasonal fruit.

Honeybells are in season in Florida in January. When my parents wintered there, they sent me a case every year. The fruit is a hybrid of the Dancy variety of tangerine and a Duncan grapefruit, and it tastes like the sweetest, juiciest orange of your dreams.

Mascarpone is a very soft, fresh cow's milk cheese available in large supermarkets or Italian specialty stores. Lillet is a French aperitif that tastes like an orange-flavored vermouth. It comes in white and red; I use the white for this.

HONEYBELL-AND-LILLET GELATINA WITH SWEET MASCARPONE

1 tablespoon grapeseed or canola oil

3½ cups fresh Honeybell or other sweet orange juice (about 16 oranges), strained through a fine-mesh sieve (for a really clear *gelatina,* line sieve with cheesecloth)

½ cup white Lillet wine

½ cup sugar

2 envelopes unflavored gelatin

MASCARPONE

1 cup mascarpone cheese at room temperature

3 tablespoons confectioners' sugar

2 egg whites

GARNISH

Orange segments

Mint sprigs

Unsprayed fresh edible flowers (optional)

Coat a 4-cup mold lightly with the oil.

In a medium saucepan, combine half of the orange juice with the Lillet and sugar. Place over medium heat until almost boiling, stirring once or twice to dissolve the sugar.

Pour the remaining orange juice into a large bowl and sprinkle on the gelatin, giving it a good stir. Let stand until completely dissolved, about 3 minutes. Stir again, then add the hot orange juice mixture. Stir well and pour into the prepared mold. Refrigerate overnight.

To make the mascarpone: Combine the mascarpone and confectioners' sugar in a large bowl. In a separate bowl, beat the egg whites with a whisk or electric mixer until stiff peaks form. Pour the egg whites on top of the mascarpone and fold them in until blended (this will lighten the mascarpone).

Turn the *gelatina* out onto a large, flat platter (if you give it a gentle shake, it should just plop right out). Garnish the *gelatina* with orange segments, mint sprigs, and flowers, placing some in the center and some around the base of the mold.

Serve in thick slices, with a dollop of the mascarpone.

VARIATION This is also beautiful made with blood orange juice, but you might need a little extra sugar.

MAKES ABOUT ONE QUART. I make a variation on this *sorbetto* every year with the sweet, dark Concord grapes that come into season in the late summer on the East Coast. In fact, the *sorbetto*'s flavor reminds me of the slightly sweet red wine certain family members used to make in the 1960s with their backyard Westchester Concords (the wine tasted like a blend of Manischewitz and Chianti).

CONCORD GRAPE AND RED WINE SORBETTO

½ cup sugar

1 cup dry but fruity red wine, such as a Sicilian Cerasuolo di Vittoria

2 pounds purple Concord grapes, stemmed

Juice of ½ lemon

½ egg white

1 tablespoon mascarpone cheese or crème fraîche

In a small saucepan, combine the sugar and wine. Bring to a boil and cook until the sugar has dissolved and the wine is slightly reduced, 4 or 5 minutes.

In a food processor, pulse the grapes until as smooth as possible. (The seeds will break up a bit, but they don't impart any bitterness to the juice.) Do this in batches, if you need to. Pour the grape juice through a fine-mesh sieve and press on the skins with the back of a large spoon to extract as much juice as possible.

Pour the grape juice back into the food processor, and add the warm wine syrup, lemon juice, egg white, and mascarpone or crème fraîche. (The heat from the wine will open up the flavor of the grapes, making the mixture very aromatic.) Pulse a few times to blend well. (Taste and notice how the lemon heightened the grape flavor, making it pop out.) The amount of sugar you'll need will vary with the sweetness of your grapes. If you need a little extra, sprinkle some in. Refrigerate the mixture for at least 2 hours. Pour into an ice cream maker and freeze according to the manufacturers' instructions.

MAKES ABOUT ONE QUART OF GELATO. I first tasted ice cream flavored with orange flower water in the baroque town of Noto, Sicily, and its perfume stayed on my tongue long after I finished eating it. I thought about the flavor for about a year until I finally got around to making this ice cream myself. The taste came out pretty much how I remember it.

Traditionally, gelato isn't as high in fat as French or American ice creams; the emphasis is more on the flavoring. In fact, some gelato is made only with milk, sugar, and flavoring. I've added some cream and egg here, but at a minimum.

ORANGE FLOWER GELATO

1½ cups nonultrapasterized heavy cream
1½ cups whole milk
1 teaspoon vanilla extract

½ teaspoon orange flower water
Grated zest of 2 large oranges
3 large egg yolks
½ cup sugar

In a medium saucepan, combine the cream, milk, vanilla, orange flower water, and orange zest. Heat over medium heat until bubbles form around the edges of the pan.

In a large bowl, whisk the egg yolks with the sugar until light and foamy. Gradually add the milk mixture, whisking constantly. Pour the mixture back into the saucepan and cook over medium-low heat, stirring constantly with a wooden spoon, until thickened enough to coat the spoon, about 5 minutes. Refrigerate until well chilled, at least 2 hours. Pour into an ice cream maker and freeze according to the manufacturers' instructions.

NOTE   Orange flower water is a very strong floral essence and a little goes a long way, so don't add more than I've suggested or the gelato may become too perfumey.

SERVING SUGGESTION   *Gelato affogato* refers to ice cream that has been drowned in liqueur or sometimes hot espresso. I like this particular ice cream with a cordial glass of orange liqueur poured over the top.

MAKES ABOUT ONE QUART. The Sicilian restaurant Bussola in the East Village in Manhattan is known for its gelato, in particular its ricotta gelato. I've eaten it many times over the years. I love it for its slightly gritty texture and its ricotta-cheesecakelike taste. I never asked for the recipe, but over the years I've ruminated and maybe fantasized about it, and I've devised my own version, which includes a pinch of cinnamon, honey, Marsala wine, and rum.

RICOTTA GELATO WITH MARSALA AND RUM

2 cups nonultrapasteurized heavy cream

Pinch of ground cinnamon

1 teaspoon vanilla extract (Madagascar vanilla if you can find it)

1 tablespoon dry Marsala

1 teaspoon rum

1 tablespoon wildflower honey

3 large egg yolks

$1/2$ cup sugar

$1^1/2$ cups whole-milk ricotta

Warm water, if needed

Pour the cream into a medium saucepan. Add the cinnamon, vanilla, Marsala, and rum. Cook over medium heat until bubbles form around the edges of the pan.

In a large bowl, whisk the honey, egg yolks, and sugar together until light and fluffy. Add the cream mixture and whisk until blended. Return to the saucepan and cook over medium-low heat, stirring constantly, until thickened enough to coat the spoon, 4 or 5 minutes. Purée the ricotta in a food processor until it is smooth (if it is very thick, add a little warm water to make it easier to purée). Add the ricotta to the cream mixture and stir well to blend. Refrigerate the ricotta custard mixture for at least 2 hours.

Pour into an ice cream freezer and freeze according to the manufacturers' instructions.

MENUS

L arge, extended families in southern Italy still sit down to an early Sunday dinner the way Italian Americans used to do here (some no doubt still do). We did to some extent, maybe not with a large group, but with my immediate family and often a close friend who was treated like family. My definition of family has changed quite a bit since I've come to adulthood. I have no children and neither do my siblings. As a result, friends are more entwined in my life than they were for my parents. Cooking southern Italian food for my friends, maybe introducing them to flavors they didn't grow up with, is an ongoing joy to me.

The southern Italian love of celebrating with food and wine is something I share, but my celebrations are earthbound, honoring birthdays, big winter storms, or a book getting written more often than saints' days, communions, and christenings. One thing southern Italians celebrate more than we do is the harvest and food production. In my grandmother's town of Castelfranco in Miscano, there's a caciocavallo festival every September. Basilicata has a hot chili festival, and the Gargano region of Puglia celebrates the new olive-oil crop in November. I love attending these kinds of festivities when I'm in Italy, but it's even more wonderful to find them at home. I have found pockets of food celebration around New York. Every September, for example, there's a garlic festival in upstate New York where dozens of regional growers display their garlic varieties and you can sample garlic ice cream and garlic fried chicken wings. I plan entire meals around spring asparagus, summer garlic, or tomatoes. It makes a city girl feel connected to the harvest.

Most southern Italians have stricter ideas about the flow of a meal than I do. If you order at a restaurant in Sicily or Campania, you're pretty much expected to select some type of antipasto, not a green salad, as a starter. At a proper lunch or dinner, a pasta or soup should be served next, followed by a fish or meat dish, with a vegetable on the side, or sometimes brought after. Green salads can also come with a meat course or sometimes after (and occasionally do a starter in fancier restaurants). Then you get hard cheeses, then fruit or dessert and an after-dinner drink if you want it, after which the waiter will bring your espresso. When I eat out in New York, I often make dinners of two first courses, and at home my entire evening meal might be a big bowl of pasta. But when I'm having people over, I tend to be more traditional.

It's extremely important for me to be able to talk to my guests when I have them over for dinner, so I've designed all the following menus with this in mind. You can make some dishes ahead and serve them at room temperature; some are last minute but quick to get on the table; and some use store-bought foods. These are just suggestions for meals, mixing flavors and textures that I feel harmonize well together.

VEGETABLE ANTIPASTO BUFFET

I like to offer an assortment of small vegetable dishes when I have friends over for informal cocktail parties. I try to pick dishes with contrasting qualities: spicy and mellow, hot and cold, acidy tomatoes, salty olives, mild ricotta, crunchy raw fennel. The whole point of this kind of sampling is for everyone to experience a variety of flavors and textures.

Zucchini Parmigiano with Scamorza and Basil (page 94), served at room temperature and cut into little squares

A big bowl of sheep's-milk ricotta drizzled with extra-virgin olive oil

Braised Baby Artichokes with Mint, White Wine, and Olive Oil (page 90)

Tomato Pesto (page 112)

Crusty Italian bread

Oven-Roasted Gaeta Olives with Rosemary, Garlic, and Orange (page 20)

A big bowl of assorted raw vegetables, such as fennel, radishes, celery, endive

Locorotondo white wine from Puglia

PUGLIAN ANTIPASTO WITH SALAMI, CHEESE, AND A TASTE OF THE SEA

An antipasto selection I was served at Ai Portici in the beautiful town of Martina Franca in Puglia was made up of the town's excellent capocollo, local green olives, burrata (the cream-filled mozzarella that is famous in the area), a dish of spicy octopus salad, a bowl of *taralli*, and a pitcher of Martina Franca white wine, which is light and fruity. It made a big impression on me.

A few big bowls of green olives, such as the mild Cerignolo and a cracked Sicilian-style olive

A bowl of toasted whole almonds

A plate of cured meats with soppressata, capocollo, and prosciutto

A platter of sliced burrata or mozzarella cheese

Octopus and Potato Salad (page 162)

Baked Mussels Filled with Sicilian Pesto (page 164)

A big green salad made with some bitter greens like arugula

A few bags of *taralli*, fennel and pepper flavored

Salice Salentino red wine from Puglia

A CELEBRATION OF SPRING ASPARAGUS

Asparagus and salmon is my idea of a spring feast. This is a simple but richly flavored dinner, after which the light freshness of strawberries with *vincotto* makes the perfect dessert.

Asparagus, Fennel, and Spring Onion Salad (page 83)

Baked Salmon with Gremolata Crust (page 204)

Roasted Asparagus with Orange Zest and Parmigiano (page 82)

Crusty Italian bread

Strawberries with *Vincotto* (page 413)

Regaleali Rosato wine from Sicily

A LUNCH TO IMPROVE YOUR MOOD

I sometimes get a little anxious on weekend afternoons when I don't have anything set to do. This is an unfortunate American trait that I'm working to overcome. Taking the time to slow down and cook a civilized lunch for myself and a few friends puts things in perspective.

White wine with Campari (page 7)

A platter of sliced mozzarella sprinkled with herbs and
drizzled with good olive oil

Crusty Italian bread

Veal Scaloppine with Dandelion and Spring Onion Salad (page 262)

Amaretto Cherries (page 405), served with Ricotta Cream (page 414)

Etna white wine from Sicily (the first glass mixed with Campari)

SUMMER GARLIC FEAST

The arrival of juicy first-of-the-season garlic at my farmers' market every year excites me but also agitates me, because I want to cook with it at its peak before it turns dry. Planning a few celebratory meals each summer like this one settles me down.

A plate of sliced summer tomatoes, sprinkled with a little minced summer garlic, sea salt, chopped basil, and good olive oil

Spaghetti Aglio e Olio (page 23)

Lamb Chops with Thyme Blossoms, Sautéed Olives, and Parsley Salad (page 236)

Broccoli with White Wine and Summer Garlic (page 115), served at room temperature

A bowl of summer berries

Aglianico del Vulture red wine from Basilicata

A PASTA DINNER WITH SUMMER FLAVORS

Pasta and salad is my idea of a perfect dinner. This is the kind of meal I bring to the table when I invite people over during the middle of the week. You can cook the peppers and the calamari on an outside grill and eat al fresco, if you like.

Peperonata with Almonds, Basilicata Style (page 129)

Penne with Grilled Calamari, Tomato, and Herb Salad (page 364)

A green salad made with dandelion and a mix of mild lettuces

A few soft goat cheeses

A bowl of fresh cherries

Cirò red wine from Calabria

STEAK AND POTATOES, SOUTHERN ITALIAN STYLE

Steak-and-potato dinners come in many forms. I love bistro-style steak frites, or a more serious sirloin with red wine sauce and potato gratin. This rendition with southern Italian flavors is, for steak and potatoes, light in spirit, herby and olivey, and very quick to prepare.

Tomato and Cantaloupe Salad with Moscato Vinaigrette (page 110)

Grilled Skirt Steak with Salmoriglio (page 267)

Warm Fingerling Potato Salad with White Wine and Parsley (page 106)

Sliced peaches soaked in red wine

Nero d'Avola red wine from Sicily

ITALIAN AMERICAN SUNDAY DINNER, UPDATED

Braciole stuffed with pecorino and parsley, hunks of pork, and sausages all floating together for hours in a big pot of burnished red sauce is a taste and aroma memory of my childhood I will never forget. I occasionally make a traditional Sunday sauce like that myself, but it's designed for a large group. When you're going to serve only four, here's a great dinner to make instead. The aroma of the slow-simmered beef, with its red wine, tomato paste, and garlic, is just as enticing as the big Sunday sauce, but a lot less work for the cook.

Bruschetta with Artichoke Pesto (page 86)

Braised Beef with Primitivo Wine (page 268)

Carrots with Sicilian Capers (page 99)

A big bowl of penne pasta tossed with olive oil, grated pecorino cheese, and a ladle of the beef cooking broth

An arugula and watercress salad tossed with good olive oil, sea salt, and a few drops of lemon juice

Italian bread

Caciocavallo with Rosemary Honey and Pine Nuts (page 394)

A big bowl of green and purple grapes

Store-bought biscotti served with little glasses of Sambuca

Espresso

Primitivo di Manduria red wine from Puglia

A PASTA DINNER WITH FALL FLAVORS

Here's another of my favorite pasta-and-salad duos. You can serve the salad before or after the pasta.

A platter of sliced soppressata, a bowl of Gaeta olives, and a bowl of *taralli*

Lasagnette with Pumpkin, Tomatoes, and Basil (page 351)

Spinach Salad with Pears, Spiced Walnuts, and Ricotta Salad (page 139)

Salice Salentino red wine from Puglia

A BIRTHDAY DINNER FOR MYSELF

If I want a homemade birthday dinner I have to cook it myself, which I don't mind, since I cook with all the flavors I love best, always including anchovies, cheese, and a luscious red wine to drink, all luckily available in early December.

Linguine with Anchovies, Parsley, and Sweet Bread Crumbs (page 363)

Swordfish Involtini with Bay Leaves and Lemon (page 196)

Plum Tomatoes Baked with Caprino, Rosemary, and Black Olives
(page 111)

A green salad served with pecorino and caciocavallo cheeses

Store-bought cannoli

Strega- and Chocolate-Dipped Strawberries (page 406)

Cerasuola di Vittoria red wine from Sicily (I love red wine with swordfish)

CHRISTMAS EVE

This menu is typical of the relatively simple fish dinners I make every Christmas Eve. Anything with more than two dishes is still a fair amount of work, so I make the anchovies, gelato, and figs the day before.

Marinated Anchovies (page 154), served without the mozzarella

Arugula Salad with Almonds, Pomegranate Seeds,
and Mozzarella (page 77)

Fusilli with Sautéed Green Olives and Bread Crumbs (page 346)

Roasted Whole Sea Bass with Rosemary Oil (page 210)

Blood Orange Salad with Fennel (from page 136),
made without the anchovies

Ricotta Gelato with Marsala and Rum (page 424)

Dried Figs with Almonds and Chocolate (page 399)

Fiano di Avellino white wine from Campania

SWEETS AND WINE FOR LUNCH

At a family funeral a few years back, I had a chat with my father's two aunts, Lucy and Filomena, both in their nineties (neither ever married and both still wore high heels and short skirts), and I noticed they were holding tumblers of red wine and had plates piled high with pastries and cookies. Assuming they had already eaten a good lunch, I asked about the large amount of sweets, and Lucy told me, "We only eat dessert now. We don't eat regular food anymore." Maybe I have to wait fifty years until my taste buds are shot, but for now I usually want something savory for lunch. I do, however, occasionally get in the mood for a fruit tart and wine. It's less renegade than what my great aunts went in for, but still sweet and special.

Baked Lemon Ricotta with Raspberry Sauce (page 396)

Peach and Basil Pizza (page 410)

Baked Sweet Almonds (page 391)

Moscato di Pantelleria sweet wine from Sicily

Espresso

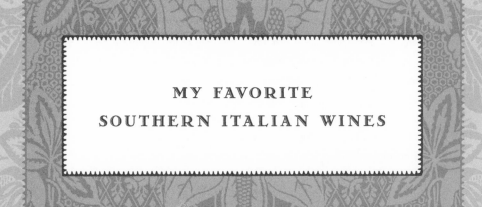

MY FAVORITE
SOUTHERN ITALIAN WINES

The wine business in southern Italy has changed dramatically in the last fifteen years or so. Previously, many producers, especially in Puglia and Sicily, went for quantity over quality. Now, you find wine makers experimenting with international grape varieties and turning out Sicilian Merlot and Campanian Chardonnay. But when I go searching for real southern Italian flavor, I look to the indigenous grapes of the regions that produce the best and most unusual wines. These are the wines that make southern Italian dishes sing with originality.

Here are my choices of some of the best southern Italian wines, made from local grape varieties, that you can buy in America. I also mention my favorite producers. This is just a sampling of what you might find in your local wine shop or on the Internet. With new wines from the south coming into this country all the time, you really never know what great bottles a wine shop might carry, so the best thing to do is simply to ask. If, for instance, you pick up a bottle of the Nero d'Avola wine from Sicily I mention here and like it, chances are you'll be able to find other Nero d'Avola wines in your area, maybe from a producer I never knew existed. I find that if I go into a wine shop and ask about a particular southern Italian grape variety, they may very well have something I didn't know was available. Just asking what they have from, say, Puglia or Basilicata is also a good starting point.

One of the best sources for southern Italian wines in this country is Vino, a shop in Manhattan. It also has a website, www.vinosite.com, that lists all its wines by region, so you can easily check for specific bottles (and they do mail order, too). The shop is run by Charles Scicolone, a Sicilian American who holds southern Italian wines dear to his heart. He also gives fun, unintimidating classes on wines from all the regions of southern Italy.

WINES AND GOOD PRODUCERS
TO LOOK FOR

The smell of red wine made from the Nero d'Avolo grape is, to me, the smell of Sicily. I guess it is what you would call full bodied, but when I discovered this taste on my first trip to the island I ordered it with everything from grilled swordfish to asparagus to lamb stew, until it filled my head with its rich bouquet. I suppose, strictly speaking, it's a red-meat kind of wine. Morgante makes an excellent Nero d'Avola I buy here. Cerasuolo di Vittoria, made primarily from the Frappato grape, is another rich red, with a sour cherry taste and a very fruity aroma. Its acidity makes it a perfect match for a tomato sauce. Val dell'Acate is the one I most often buy. Whites from Mount Etna are dry and slighty acidic, perfect for herby fish dishes smothered in olive oil. Bianco d'Alcamo is another dry, light white to look for. Regaleali is an old, established producer whose fine wines are quite easy to find here. I love their rosato with a mozzarella and tomato salad.

Planeta is a young company that produces wines from indigenous grapes sometimes blended with international varieties like Merlot and Syrah with unique results. Their 100% Nero d'Avola is called Santa Cecilia and it is excellent.

Campania produces two of my favorite southern Italian white wines, Fiano di Avellino and Greco di Tufo. Both are dry but have a haunting honey scent that seems to echo their ancient heritage. The Fiano di Avellino has become my family's Christmas Eve wine, since it goes so perfectly with all the rich, garlicky, and tomato-soaked fish dishes I love to serve. Falanghina, a lighter white from Campania, is something I first began noticing at Roman wine bars, served by the glass. It's a good choice for linguine with clam sauce. Taurasi, made from Aglianico grapes, is my all-time favorite red, deep and rich. I save it for special occasions when I serve a big, impressive roast. Mastroberardino is a first-rate producer. Piedirossi and Falerno are two other good reds you should look for. In addition to the wines from the Mastroberardino estate, I'm also very fond of all the wines I've tasted from Feudi di San Gregorio. Terredora and I Normanni are also very good producers who ship their wines to America. Pallagrello and Casavecchia are two other old, indigenous grape varieties that are making a comeback in Campania. Vestini is the producer to look for.

Cirò is the famous wine of Calabria. It's a strong, tart red made from the Gaglioppo grape, and it's my choice for spaghetti with meatballs or for veal and peppers. I also love it with sharp, salty cheeses such as provolone or an aged pecorino. Librandi is a very good producer whose Cirò Riserva is worth seeking out.

Neigboring Basilicata also has one standout red wine, Aglianico del Vulture, which is dry and perfumey. I recently served it with a grilled leg of lamb with great success, but I'd also drink it with a spicy pizza. D'Angelo is the brand I most often find in this country; Paternoster is another good producer.

Southern Puglia is home to Primitivo di Manduria, a very rich, intense red with a slight pruney taste that is at its best with rich foods, especially meats seasoned with garlic, strong herbs like rosemary or oregano, and lots of olive oil (the oil seems to soften its taste). Vinicola Savese makes the best one I've tasted in this country. Salice Salentino and Copertino are two attractively bitter reds made in southern Puglia from the Negroamaro grape; they're perfect with a plate of salami or a pasta tossed with Puttanesca sauce. Some of these wines also taste a bit pruney to me, but they're lighter bodied than Primitivo. Copertino rosato (rosé) is also available. I've tried several Salice Salentino wines in this country, and my favorite is the one made by Agricole Valone. When I want to escape the Puglian prune, I go for a bottle of Castel del Monte Il Falcone from north in the region. It's a smooth, sophisticated red that's great with a steak. Rivera makes the Il Falcone I buy in New York. Locorotondo makes a famous white wine, very light and refreshing for a summer barbecue of grilled sardines, and I've also tasted a good rosato from Locorotondo, but I haven't been able to find it in the United States. The nearby area of Martina Franca also makes excellent whites, which I sampled while in Puglia. I've yet to see them here, but it's probably only a matter of time, so I periodically ask my shops about them. Conti Zecca and Taurino are two other excellent producers of Puglian wine.

SOURCES

THE INTERNET IS INVALUABLE for hard-to-find Italian food products. It has enabled me to get hold of Sicilian and Puglia olive oils I tasted in Italy, artisanal pastas, obscure southern Italian cheeses, bottarga, olives, *vincotto*, and all sorts of other great things. I'm constantly searching the Internet for new sources. Here are my favorite sources for first-rate southern Italian products. Some of the places have retail shops that are worth visiting if you're in the area, and most will fill mail orders by phone. Some have a website through which you can order, and some are websites only. These places will provide all the ingredients I've mentioned throughout the book.

BECK GROVE
Fallbrook, CA
(760) 723-9997
www.lavignefruits.com

A grower of Moro and Torocco blood oranges. You can order the fruit directly or ask them for the name of a retailer in your area.

BUON ITALIA
75 Ninth Avenue
New York, NY 10011
(212) 633-9090
www.buonitalia.com

An Italian food wholesaler with a well-stocked retail shop in the Chelsea Market in Manhattan and a good website. They carry a large selection of Setaro pasta from Campania, buffalo mozzarella, southern Italian olive oil, bottarga, Flott-brand salt-packed anchovies and tuna, capers from Sicily, Gianni Calogurii's *vincotto* imported from Puglia, and Agrimontana Italian honey and jams, plus a very unusual assortment of other Italian food products.

DI PAOLA TURKEY FARMS
883 Edinburg Road
Hamilton, NJ 08693
(609) 587-9311

They make excellent turkey sausages with real Italian flavor. They also raise and sell organic turkeys. They sell to various NYC green markets and some stores on the East Coast. Call for their list of retailers. Due to the freshness of their products, they don't handle any mail order.

DIPALO FINE FOODS
200 Grand Street
New York, NY 10013
(212) 226-1033

An old New York store, the last top-notch food shop left in Little Italy. They pride themselves on their large assortment of imported cheeses and carry many southern Italian ones, including caciocavallo basilicata; caciocavallo ragusana from Sicily; the pecorino basket cheeses from Puglia and Sicily called incanastrata; scamorza; sheep's milk ricotta, their own ricotta and mozzarella; imported buffalo milk cheeses; and burrata from Puglia. Also a large assortment of southern Italian products.

ESPERYA.COM

A source for U Trappitu Sicilian olive oil and other southern Italian estate olive oils such as the lovely Ciro Federico oil from Puglia, plus capers from the Sicilian island of Pantelleria, the highest-quality buffalo mozzarella from Campania, Sapori del Salento products from Puglia (including *lampascioni*—wild onions), sun-dried tomatoes, tomato sauces, and lemon and quince jelly. Also Latini pasta, pasta di Nola from Campania, and Martelli fine artisanal pastas.

FAICCO PORK STORE

260 Bleecker Street
New York, NY 10014
(212) 243-1974

Great homemade soppressata and cacciatorini, excellent fresh pork products, tripe, and a good selection of Italian products such as cheeses, pastas, and olive oil.

WWW.FARAWAYFOODS.COM

They stock Olio Verde Sicilian olive oil, Ittica d'Or Sicilian sea salt, Rustichella d'Abruzzo artisanal pasta, and a large selection of Italian condiments.

A. G. FERRARI FOODS

3490 Catalina Street
San Leandro, CA 94577
(510) 346-2100
www.agferrari.com

For pasta di Gragnano from Naples, Sicilian capers, Calabrian peppers, Cerignolo olives, Sicilian wildflower honey, Sicilian fruit marmalades, and olive oils from Basilicata and Puglia.

FORMAGGIO KITCHEN

244 Huron Avenue
Cambridge, MA 02138
(888) 212-3224
www.formaggiokitchen.com

They stock Ravida Sicilian olive oil, caciocavallo Podolico riserva, Sicilian *ricotta al forno* (baked ricotta), and other hard-to-locate southern Italian cheeses.

KALUSTYAN'S

123 Lexington Avenue
New York, NY 10016
(212) 685-3451
www.kalustyans.com

Middle Eastern foods. A source for Turkish and Chinese pine nuts and Spanish saffron.

MANICARETTI ITALIAN FOOD IMPORTS

(800) 799-9830
www.manicaretti.com

They carry Olio Verde Sicilian olive oil (made by Gianfranco Becchina), Ascolane olives from Ascoli Picena in the Marche, Caravaglio capers and caper berries from the Sicilian island of Salina, Italian honey, and Maria Grammatico's marzipan and marmalades from her shop in Erice, Sicily. Check the website for a list of stores and other websites that carry their products.

MARKET HALL FOODS

5655 College Avenue
Oakland, CA 94618
(888) 952-4005
www.rockridgemarkethall.com

Antonio Caravaglio's capers from Salina. A source for all Manicaretti imports (see above).

MUSTARD SEED GOURMET FOODS

113-B David Green Road
Pelham, AL 35124
(800) 630-0684
www.mustardseedfoods.com

Another source for U Trappitu Sicilian olive oil. They also carry Flott Sicilian tuna packed in olive oil.

NIMAN RANCH

www.nimanranch.com

Italian-style *lardo* and sausages. Excellent source for organic beef, pork, and lamb products. Check the website for a list of stores that carry their products.

OLD CHATHAM SHEEPHERDING COMPANY

155 Shaker Museum Road
Old Chatham, NY 12136
(888) 734-3760
www.blacksheepcheese.com

Fresh sheep's milk ricotta and other sheep's milk cheeses. They sell to many retail food stores, so call them for a place near you that carries their products.

WWW.ORGANICALIA.COM

A Calabrian food company that carries dried figs, hot chilis, and many other Calabrian specialties.

PHIPPS COUNTRY STORE AND FARM

2700 Pescadero Road
Pescadero, CA 94060
www.phippscountry.com

A bean farm that grows a huge assortment of beans, including many Italian and Mediterranean varieties such as the best gigante beans I know of, cannellini, borlotti, favas, chickpeas, and many others, all dried from recent harvests.

SEEDS FROM ITALY

P.O. Box 149
Winchester, MA 01890
(781) 721-5904
www.growitalian.com

A large variety of imported Italian vegetable seeds, including wild arugula, *cima di rape*, chicory varieties, Sicilian purple cauliflower and eggplant varieties, San Marzano tomatoes, and a ton of others.

TAYLOR SHELLFISH FARMS

130 S.E. Lynch Road
Shelton, WA 98584
(360) 426-6178
www.taylorshellfish.com

Black Mediterranean mussels year-round. Order directly through them or call to ask about where they distribute near you. They also grow clams and oysters.

TODARO BROTHERS

555 Second Avenue
New York, NY 10016
(877) 472-1022
www.todarobros.com

Flott Sicilian salt-packed anchovies, olive oils, and a huge stock of other Italian products.

VINO E OLIO

1021 Ives Dairy Road #113
Miami, FL 33179
(877) 846-6365
www.vinoeolio.com

Tonno Rosso Sicilian tuna, many types of southern Italian olive oil, artisanal pasta, pesto, olive pastes, and olives from Campania and Sicily.

VINO ITALIAN WINES AND SPIRITS

121 East 27th Street
New York, NY 10016
(212) 725-6516
www.vinosite.com

The best source in America for southern Italian wines.

WILD EDIBLES

318 Grand Central Terminal
New York, NY 10017
(212) 687-4255
www.grandcentralterminal.com/wild-edibles.htm

Black Mediterranean mussels and other Mediterranean fish like branzino, orata, sardines, and red mullet.

ZINGERMAN'S DELI

422 Detroit Street
Ann Arbor, MI 48104
(888) 636-8162
www.zingermans.com

Ravida olive oil and sea salt from Sicily, and La Spineta, Caricato, and Petraia olive oils from Puglia, plus a great assortment of other first-rate Italian products.

BIBLIOGRAPHY

Bettoja, Jo. *Southern Italian Cooking*. New York: Bantam Books, 1991.

Bianchi, Anne. *Italian Festival Food*. New York: Macmillan, 1999.

Brennan, Georgeann. *Olives, Anchovies, and Capers*. San Francisco: Chronicle Books, 2001.

Bugialli, Giuliano. *Foods of Sicily and Sardinia*. New York: Rizzoli, 1996.

Colonna, Giovanni. *La Cucina Pugliese*. Lecce: Capone Editore, 1999.

Correnti, Pino. *Il libro d'oro della cucina e dei vini di Sicilia*. Milan: Mursia, 1976.

Creti, Giorgio. *Cucina del Salento*. Lecce: Capone Editore, 2002.

de Blasi, Marlena. *Regional Foods of Southern Italy*. New York: Viking, 1999.

Dolamore, Anne. *A Buyer's Guide to Olive Oil*. London: Grub Street, 2000.

Grammatico, Maria, and Mary Taylor Simeti. *Bitter Almonds: Recollections and Recipes from a Sicilian Girlhood*. New York: William Morrow & Company, 1994.

Gray, Patience. *Honey from a Weed*. New York: Harper & Row, 1986.

Italian Cheese. Bra: Slow Food Arcigola Editore, 1999.

Jenkins, Nancy Harmon. *Flavors of Puglia*. New York: Broadway Books, 1997.

Johnson, Hugh, and Jancis Robinson. *The World Atlas of Wine*. 5th ed. London: Mitchell Beazley, 2001.

Lanza, Anna Tasca. *The Flavors of Sicily*. New York: Clarkson Potter, 1996.

Middione, Carlo. *The Food of Southern Italy*. New York: William Morrow & Company, 1987.

Palmer, Mary Amabile. *Cucina di Calabria*. New York: Faber and Faber, 1997.

Penta de Peppo, Marinella. *L'arte della cucina, secondo la tradizione napoletana*. Milan: Arnoldo Mondadori Editore, 1994.

Pupella, Eufemia Azzonlina. *Sicilian Cooking*. Florence: Casa Editrice Bonechi, 1996.

Sada, Luigi. *La Cucina Pugliese*. Rome: Newton Compton Editori, 1994.

Schwartz, Arthur. *Naples at Table*. New York: HarperCollins, 1998.

Simeti, Mary Taylor. *Pomp and Sustenance*. New York: Alfred A. Knopf, 1989.

Tornabene, Wanda, and Giovanna Tornabene. *La cucina siciliana di Gangivecchio*. New York: Alfred A. Knopf, 1996.

INDEX

ABA 7392

TOWNSHIP OF UNION
FREE PUBLIC LIBRARY

FREE PUBLIC LIBRARY UNION, NEW JERSEY

3 9549 00332 5827